The Divided Home/Land

The Divided Home/Land

Contemporary German Women's Plays

Edited by Sue-Ellen Case

Ann Arbor

THE UNIVERSITY OF MICHIGAN PRESS

PT
1258
.D58
1992
160967
Feb.1994

Library of Congress Cataloging-in-Publication Data

The Divided home/land : contemporary German women's plays / edited by
Sue-Ellen Case.
    p. cm.
    Includes bibliographical references.
    ISBN 0-472-09406-8 (alk. paper). — ISBN 0-472-06406-1 (pbk. :
alk. paper)
    1. German drama—20th century—Translations into English.
    2. German drama—Women authors—Translations into English.
    3. English drama—Translations from German. I. Case, Sue-Ellen.
II. Title : Divided homeland.
PT1258.D58   1992
832'.9140809287—dc20   92-11470
                                                                     CIP

Acknowledgments

First, I would like to acknowledge the talent, expertise, and labor of these translators, who made this project possible. Many other people have provided assistance. Katrin Sieg was my research assistant at the University of Washington for this project. Her labor went far beyond her assignment. Her work with the German presses, her expert translations, and her knowledge of the authors' work and context was of immeasurable help—here and in Germany. LeAnn Fields at the University of Michigan Press gave continued support and encouragement. She was wonderfully flexible in times of trouble and responsive to the varied and complex needs of the project. Ursula Ahrens provided me with plays and contacts in the contemporary scene, as did Renate Klett. Susan Cocalis guided the selection of texts. The DAAD (German Academic Exchange Service) provided grant assistance for the necessary time with the authors in Germany. Ginka Tscholakowa made it possible for me to stay in Berlin. Ursula Niedenzu at the German Consulate in Seattle provided me with documents on the conditions of women in Germany. The Goethe Institute and the Consulate in Seattle have provided me with time in Germany and the necessary contacts to continue the work in this field. And the friendship of Gerlind Reinshagen helped me to imagine such a project.

Das Glühend Männla (The Little Red-Hot Man) © Verlag der Autoren, D-Frankfurt am Main 1990.

Ichundlch (IandI) © Kösel Verlag, Munich.

Klavierspiele (Piano Plays) © Verlag der Autoren, D-Frankfurt am Main 1984.

Grateful acknowledgment is also given to the following: Ursula Ahrens for permission to publish the translation of "FIT: Women in Theater"; *Modern Drama* for permission to reprint "The Politics of Brutality: Toward a Definition of the Critical Volksstück" by Susan L. Cocalis. *Modern Drama* 24, no. 3; Gerlind Reinshagen and Renate Klett for permission to publish the translation of "An Interview with Gerlind Reinshagen"; Heidi von Plato for permission to publish the translation of "Worlds of Images: The First Women's Theater Troupe, ANNA KONDA"; Gerlind Reinshagen and Anke Roeder for permission to publish the translation of "Theater as Counter-Concept: An Interview with Gerlind Reinshagen"; Friederike Roth and Elisabeth Henrichs for permission to publish a translation of "Building Sentences, Ripping Out Hearts, Knocking Off Heads: An Interview with Friederike Roth" by Elisabeth Henrichs. First published in *Theater Heute* (March 1991); and Katrin Sieg for permission to publish her translations of "The Emigrants' Chorus," "Lucky Hans," "The Witch," and "The Cold" by Erika Mann.

Contents

Sue-Ellen Case

Introduction

This is the first anthology of contemporary German women playwrights to be published in English. Until now, those scholars interested in German theater in English translation have had access only to plays written by men, and those interested in feminism and theater have had to focus primarily on plays written in English in the United States and Britain. For both the general theater critic and the feminist scholar, this limitation has most certainly influenced the notions we have derived from such texts regarding historical periods and critical and dramatic strategies. The imperial role English plays in the international scene today and the consequent imbalance in the translation trade have produced a social and theatrical hegemony for Anglo-American texts, including the feminist critique and its dramaturgical interests. While German feminist histories and theories are often written within a model comparing them to the Anglo-American tradition, feminism in the United States and Britain rarely encompasses differing critiques from outside their national boundaries.[1] Two exceptions to this general isolationist practice do occur: the attention to the issues of so-called Third World women, and the rather intense reception, in the late 1970s and 1980s, of French feminist theory and plays. Translations of Wittig, Cixous, Irigaray, Duras, and Benmussa radically altered our notions of how women may intervene in the system of representation, given their different history and ideological base. The French example may encourage a more intense pursuit, on our part, of further translations. Moreover, there is a growing willingness to pose international feminist issues, and even a growing international forum for women and theater, as evidenced by the first two International Women Playwrights' Festivals in Buffalo and Toronto.

It is within these kinds of considerations that I am pleased to introduce these German women playwrights, along with a sample of interviews and other materials pertinent to their plays, in order to present their vital historical context and theatrical inventions to the reader of English and the theater worker. I am certain that the reception of these German works, like the French texts, will alter the future of our work. While the French broke open the debate about feminist uses of psychoanalytic and semiotic methodologies, the Germans offer new strategies of representing historical materials, and a critique of fascism, congruent with gender politics. They also offer their unique version of the postmodern text, derived from the dialogue between the French critique and the German materialist tradition.

In the short introductions to the individual plays, I have suggested some ways in which these playwrights' achievements have altered traditional assumptions about the history and practice of German theater, political theater, and the feminist reception and use of theater. Here, I would like to treat more general critical topics, to offer a partial social history of women in Germany in the past two decades, and to contextualize the selection of plays I have made from the larger universe of playwrights and texts. Yet I must offer a few cautionary remarks to the reader. While this anthology is offered as an introduction to these texts, it cannot hope to provide a general introduction to German theater or German history. A basic knowledge of German historical periods and theatrical traditions must be assumed. Such terms as *epic theater*, the *social gest*, and the *Weimar era* are fully considered elsewhere in books on Bertolt Brecht and in general histories of German theater. Likewise, general feminist critical terms are employed. I have footnoted a few helpful texts but assume a basic acquaintance with feminist critical terminology.

Dividing Home from Land

This book comes at a particularly profound moment in German history (though there have been several in the twentieth century): during the process of the reunification of East and West Germany. Ironically, the book bears the title of "Divided Home/Land," just when it would seem that that particular division is being healed. Yet, for the women writers in this book, the title captures multiple divisions in their plays and in their biographies—divisions that continue to tear open the divide as well as to begin to heal it.

Dividing the home from the homeland has long been an earmark of the patriarchy as it has set apart domestic (private) life from the public arena. That division has always been gender marked: women were confined to the home, while men maintained sole access to the public forum. Women are, in that sense, not a part of "history" as it is written in national narratives of public life. By the same token, the nation and history are not traditionally perceived to operate in the home, nor in the broader category regarded as private life. As playwrights, the women represented in this volume directly confront the inheritance of that public/private schism in their attempt to dramatize the lives of women and in their drive to be produced within the public, collective artform of the theater.

This schism cuts even deeper for women in Germany because of the institution of federally supported theater—a stage controlled by official governmental monies and agencies. At first glance, it would seem that state-supported theater (in both Germanies) has been enabling to the theater artist by providing secure working conditions, sufficient production funds, and the creation of stable ensembles. This commitment to theater may be felt not only in the opulence of production elements, the houses themselves, the long rehearsal periods, and the depth and breadth of projects, but also in the public visibility of theater in many of the cities throughout Germany—the sense that it is an important artform, that it is still a popular one, and that it has a critical role to play in the history of the city/state itself.

Unfortunately, all of this "richness" has served to shut out the woman playwright. The male ownership of the public realm in the theater, linked directly to primarily male governmental agencies, has created in that public and state-supported stage a male preserve that was, until the 1980s, almost completely closed to women. The woman playwright in the United States has a more difficult time finding a theater that can afford to develop a new play, but the proliferation of poor theaters along the fringe, set apart from political appointments and the other restrictions of large state subsidies, has allowed her to sneak backstage and eventually to make an appearance (even in spite of recent decisions by the National Endowment for the Arts). In Germany, the central role state-subsidized theater plays in the society blocks such marginal successes. The powerful role of the *Intendant* (artistic director), appointed through the bureaucracy, has been filled almost exclusively by men who, in turn, have hired male directors, who have selected plays by male playwrights. Women have been consigned to the role of dramaturge—not even to the role of chief dramaturge, but to the role of assistant.

Moreover, the partnership between the state and these theaters makes their stages seem "representative," or "official." Their seasons, their styles, and even their experiments seem to define German theater. Journals like *Theater Heute,* placed in libraries around the world by quasi-governmental agencies such as the Goethe Institute or *Inter Nationes,* concentrate almost solely on the work in these state houses—their directors, actors, and playwrights. The fringe theaters that do exist around this fixed center seem doubly disenfranchised. This secures the invisibility of the woman playwright, since she is absent from the state theaters, and, even if she does find a venue in an experimental house, she remains critically unattended. Theater festivals operate similarly. The annual *Theatertreffen* in Berlin, which purports to represent the critics' choice of the best plays of the season, once, and only once (1984), included, in a tent behind one of the major state theaters, a festival of women's plays and performances.

This divide between public and private, and between state and alternative theaters, manifests itself in various ways in the texts and lives of these playwrights. In the earlier part of the century, the oppressive effect of this schism is evident in the biography of Marieluise Fleißer, who managed to get her work on stage in the Weimar period (1919–33), but was driven off the stage by critics who found her work unsuitable for a woman playwright, as well as by leftist male directors such as Brecht, who wanted to re-form her gender politics. Her subsequent flight out of theater and back into marriage and the role of housewife illustrates the internalized pressure for women to abandon the public voice for domestic silence. The effect on her was to produce a nervous breakdown—a crisis in self-confidence and in her ability to write.

The critical reception of Fleißer and more recently for authors such as Gerlind Reinshagen further illustrates this public / private schism by marking texts based on women's experience as "too subjective" and "emotional" rather than as social or political. The *Neue Sachlichkeit,* or New Objectivism in the 1920s, that spawned Brecht and, later, the post-Brechtian tradition of the history play or the socially-committed text inscribes public issues and rhetorical devices derived from mass movements into the structure and address of the "political" theater. This tradition shuts out the women's plays that, located in the private sphere and written in the discourse of desire and intimacy, continue to give voice to sexual and emotional oppression. Because these playwrights write about women's domestic and personal experiences, they do not write the "history" play as it has been traditionally defined, nor what has been considered the "socially engaged" text within the German tradition. Yet, from a feminist perspective, Fleißer

and Reinshagen have invented new forms of the history play and representations of social engagement that, in their radical alterity to the canon, are
visible only through the perspective of gender politics.

As late as the 1980s, this kind of critical and historical blindness to
women's experiments continued to collude with the patriarchal structures
of authority in theater practice. The interview in this volume with Friederike
Roth, author of one of the only woman's texts on gendered relationships
to be produced in the early 1980s, records the way that the anger and
violence of the male actors and director during the production process of
the play continued to legitimate male authority. Roth's experience illustrates
how, without the support of women directors, chief dramaturges, and *In-
tendants,* the isolated woman's text becomes subject to contrary and even
hostile interpretations and productions. On the other hand, when a few
women practitioners do make their way into the state system, they often
become alienated from the women's community. When I attended the
discussions of the Women in Theater (Frauen im Theater [FIT]) section of
the Berlin Theater Festival in 1984, I was struck by the split between the
few women who had managed to enter these bastions of culture and the
women who had participated in the alternative, or autonomous, women's
movement and critique.[2] The professional women felt that the autonomous
movement did not understand their struggle to survive in such theaters
and, further, that because of the struggle they could not afford any connection with the feminist movement. When an anthology was proposed on
the topic of women in theater, most felt that they could not afford to appear
in it. In contrast, the women in the autonomous movement felt that there
was nothing in the state theaters for them; they were not part of what was
officially constituted there as the "German audience."

In addition to an oppressively patriarchal production process in the theater,
the history of the German stage suppresses what contributions women have
managed to create. Even though the first recorded woman playwright,
Hrotsvit von Gandersheim, was German, and the first German director,
Caroline Neuber, was a woman, women are almost completely absent from
the official histories, even up to the present. The books published in English
by Michael Patterson, Christopher Innes, and Denis Calandra, with titles
such as *New German Dramatists* and *Modern German Drama,* include no
women. Likewise, theater festivals in this country and the repertories of
regional theaters interested in contemporary German theater include Franz
Xavier Kroetz and Heiner Müller, but no women. More than a decade ago,

I approached two journals and one book publisher with the idea of a project on German women playwrights and was turned down because they thought they had done too much about Germans lately (specifically Kroetz and Müller); my protestation that none were women was received as beside the point. One publisher, herself a woman, told me that the German women playwrights were inferior writers. I think that this anthology will correct that misperception.

The situation is no better in Germany. Only one anthology of women's plays has appeared in the past few decades: *Spectaculum: Theaterstücke von Frauen.*[3] Interestingly, the selection of plays is similar to this volume's, illustrating that the notion of women in theater and an area of interest in German women playwrights is still in an introductory stage in Germany as well. A volume of interviews and short essays on the topic was published by a women's press, though it is difficult to obtain: *Fürs Theater Schreiben: Über zeitgenössische deutschsprachige Theaterautorinnen* (To Write for Theater: On Contemporary German-Language Women Authors). More recently, Anke Roeder's book of interviews with these women playwrights, *Autorinnen: Herausforderungen an das Theater* (Women Authors: Challenges to Theater), has appeared, along with one feminist critical anthology on Ginka Steinwachs, and a book on Gerlind Reinshagen.[4] All of these volumes have appeared only in the late 1980s and are not particularly well known.

Consequently, the periods and types of drama constituted through the omission of these plays organize only partial, and in that sense unworkable, critical and historical categories: from the Expressionists, through Brecht and Erwin Piscator, Docudrama, and hyperrealism (Kroetz), to Müller. The plays in this volume offer different treatments of documentary evidence, of distancing devices or what might, in reverse, be called proximity devices, and fragmentary, open texts that prompt an alteration of traditional terms and eras.

In addition to the fragmentary partiality of the histories, the plays in the canon abound with the operations of misogyny and violence toward women, creating theatrical periods and styles that equate versions of the dramatic with cruelty toward women. If one were to reconstitute the existing terminology from the perspective of gender, Expressionism, for example, would register a confluence of the metaphoric inscription of male subjectivity with aggressive, paranoid fantasies that represent sexual women as a threat to a coherent consciousness. This treatment of women is especially painful in the works of those male playwrights who sought some kind of social reform, or even attempted to represent women's plight. Women as sexual objects, proximate to violence, appear over and over again—in Frank Wedekind's portrayal of Lulu, Oskar Kokoschka's *Murderer the Women's Hope,* Brecht's *Baal,* Peter Weiss's *Marat/Sade,* Kroetz's *Farmyard,* and Müller's *The Task.* Changes of style, eras, and political agendas do not seem to alter the dramatic treatment of female characters.

In the women's plays collected here, such images, when they do appear, are dramatically interrogated for their patriarchal function. In place of the generalized sexist portrayals of women that endure throughout various historical periods, these authors examine the uses of sexism for specific historical projects (as in *IandI*) and its effect on women's participation in cultural production (as in *Piano Plays*). Before considering the achievements of these playwrights, it seems important to return to the proliferation of divisions suggested by the title of this book, to construct a social base for the revision of German theatrical history.

The title *The Divided Home/Land* may be read as a patriarchal division, but it also stands for other ideological divisions of the German home and land in this century. During World War II, the division of home from land became excruciating in the lives of the exiles. Most painful were the lives of exiled Jews, represented here by Else Lasker-Schüler. The isolation she endured in Switzerland and Jerusalem, along with her ensuing poverty, register in the title *IandI*: the division cutting into the very center of identity. Erika Mann's antifascist cabaret was also forced into exile during World War II, playing outside of Germany while focusing on the Nazi regime. Yet, while Mann and Lasker-Schüler were both authors in exile, their class and "racial" (the fiction of the Jewish "race," as the Nazis called it) differences provided them with contrasting material circumstances. Whatever psychological damage Erika Mann may have suffered, while in exile in Switzerland as secretary to her father, Thomas Mann, she lived in opulence, while Lasker-Schüler lived in imminent danger of death.

Yet these playwrights do not represent all German women as victims of the Nazi regime. Gerlind Reinshagen's play *Sunday's Children* actually forges the relation of home to land by dramatizing the role of women in support of fascism. Reinshagen portrays the domestic realm, which, although divided from the public one, became a personal arena for authoritarian practices that reinforce state ideology. In the case of fascist women, there was no divide between home and land. Yet, in Reinshagen's *Ironheart,* Billerbeck displays the painful contradictions that can occur in a character who has both embraced an authoritarian persona and is herself a victim of gender oppression.

Women in the Divided Germany

After World War II, ideological and metaphorical divisions between home
and land became geographically concrete in the creation of the two Germanies. In 1949, Germany was divided into two states: one designated as
"communist," or "state socialist" (the German Democratic Republic, or
GDR), against the other, "capitalist" or "capitalist with strong socialist
agencies" (the Federal Republic of Germany, or FRG). The Cold War forced
a contrast between the different economic organizations of the states, playing
them off one another as if they were oppositional. The two Germanies
became cast in protagonist/antagonist roles in the NATO melodrama of
capitalism versus communism. This combative ideological game determined
an exhibitionism and an intransigence in the cultural and political production of both. The comparative, agonistic relationship of the two states
seeped into other areas of concern that do not seem to be directly related.

For example, although there is not a GDR playwright in this volume,
the model of the GDR and the condition of women there haunt some of
the texts. The national divide has been compelling for German women,
who have been affected by the different policies those systems established
for women in the workplace. Yet, in spite of those differences, the stability
of the patriarchy manifested itself, rendering gender a visible site of oppression within contrasting economic and state structures. The legal, political, domestic, and cultural position of women in the two Germanies
illustrates the peculiar way in which patriarchal structures intertwine with
state ideology—even in seemingly contrasting systems. *The Little Red-Hot
Man* is situated in the border zone between the two Germanies, where
women look out of their windows, in the shadow of the divide, remembering
village people who emigrated to the GDR or considering their own lives in
comparison to the different employment opportunities there. The divided
Germany is in the location and in the storytelling in this play. In the play
George Sand, the title character is a woman living through a revolutionary
process, which divides her motives surrounding her artistic production. She
confronts contradictory economic choices, informing and informed by her
gender and sexuality. In one scene, Sand is stretched over a gorge—per-
sonifying divided conditions.

Beyond literal mention in the texts, the contrasting economic conditions
in the GDR offer a backdrop against which the conditions in the West
appear more vividly. Women's labor conditions, as portrayed in Reinshagen's
Ironheart, are foregrounded by the office next door: the constant comparative

frame in the *mise-en-scène*. While it is not literally the East that is pictured there, the window onto neighboring labor conditions that underscore those in the foreground registers as a structural allusion to the divided home/land. This may be particularly evident in works by women like Reinshagen, who work in Berlin, where until recently the division was always visible. The looking across, the mirror image that does and does not reflect, may be read as a dramatic displacement of Berlin's divided topography.

This indirect dynamic can be made more specific through a cursory consideration of state practices concerning women in the two Germanies.[5] Whether or not these conditions come to play in the reading of specific texts, they do organize a specifically German historical/critical context within which issues of gender and sexuality are represented. I realize that in narrativizing this history, I may be mystifying more than clarifying. However, the intense media coverage of recent events in Germany, such as "the fall of the wall," with all its "fall of Rome" resonances has redefined German identity, both within Germany and on the international scene. Hence, any reading or production of a German play at this point in history will bring into play, either wittingly or unwittingly, this new sense of what it means to be German.

After World War II, the Soviet Military Administration (SMAD) in the GDR immediately set up a policy of equal pay for equal work, based on models developed by earlier socialist feminists such as Clara Zetkin and Rosa Luxemburg. By state policy, the workplace was restructured to provide women full participation in the work force. This initiative was successful and, by 1970, 80 percent of all women belonged to the work force. Economically, this provided a new sense of how gender literally works in a society.

The Federal Republic of Germany also suspended all discriminatory labor laws—at least it appeared so in the state rhetoric.[6] At the same time, however, it instituted a practice of governmental noninterference—an important posture after the Nazi regime, but one that, in fact, worked against women; a return to so-called normalcy after the war for many meant a return to the traditional family unit, which reduced women's power. Since industry was not forced to change, it did not. By the 1970s, 48 percent of women were in the work force—many fewer than in the GDR, but more than in earlier regimes. In other words, more women remained in the traditional role of housewife in the FRG than in the GDR.

Perhaps an even more dramatic difference between the two Germanies was in the state support systems that allowed women to work. The GDR provided state-funded child care. By the mid-1970s, 92 percent of the nation's children were in child care. Moreover, child-care units were often conveniently located within apartment complexes. Six months maternity leave with full pay for each pregnancy was also part of the labor code, with no discrimination between wed and unwed mothers.[7] In the FRG, these costs and conveniences remained a private responsibility.

In the area of reproductive rights, the GDR legalized abortion in 1972, while the issue remained problematic in the FRG. During reunification, abortion became the single issue concerning women to come to the fore. While the loss of state-supported child care went relatively unnoticed with the end of the GDR, the debate over abortion rights emerged as the isolated women's issue. Its isolation as an issue signals the way in which gender politics and patriarchal structures have been separated from what has traditionally been called "politics." Abortion rights have been an issue in Germany since the Weimar era. Fleißer dramatized the problem in *Purgatory* in 1924, and the problem still remains.

On another sexual front, lesbians were able to be more "out" in the FRG than in the GDR, with large grass-roots communities in the major cities such as Berlin and Hamburg. Lesbian presses, coffeehouses, and demonstrations, existing in Germany since the turn of the century, proliferated in the 1970s as part of the feminist political movement. Since the 1920s, Berlin had gay and lesbian bars, films, and plays.[8] In the GDR, it was dangerous to be lesbian-identified. The organizations and clubs that did exist were closeted. Unfortunately, the sexual revolution was abandoned in the socialist experiment.

In spite of the above differences, what the two Germanies had in common was a rapidly growing divorce rate, creating the financial and social problems of single-mother families as well as the lowest birthrate in their respective blocs. Somehow, the family unit was dissolving in both Germanies, reflecting the existence of gender problems in the personal realm in both, in spite of competing ideological and economic systems.

Nevertheless, in governmental representation in both countries, the patriarchy remained intact. Neither system provided women with leadership roles in the government. Although a large percentage of women enjoyed the training of higher education in the GDR, their work was still concentrated in the lower-paying sectors—likewise in the FRG. One can see this phenomenon dramatized in Reinshagen's *Ironheart*. The presence of a young, upwardly mobile man in an office of women, who are condemned to remain in their positions regardless of talent or energy, causes tension and collapse. Gendered inequality in professional advancement is even more glaring in the university systems in both countries. Most academic women work on renewable contracts, even though their degrees and initial publications are commensurate with men's. Only 7 percent of full professors in the FRG and 7.4 percent in the GDR are women. The absence of women in academia helps account for the fewer numbers of critical articles on women playwrights and the attendant paucity of critical strategies for dealing with their unique forms. The fact that a number of women were already employed in English departments in the United States helped to prepare the way for work on women authors, the organization of women's studies programs, and the rise of feminist theory. Moreover, there is an obvious relationship in the United States between the rise of women's studies and feminist theory in the universities and the growing popularity of women's texts in theaters and in the general readership.

The persistence of the patriarchy prompted an unofficial but powerful feminist resistance in the FRG, which was not possible in the GDR. In part, this was a result of the more democratic system, which enforced less state control of public spaces. In part, feminism was imported from the FRG's "big sister," the United States, along with other cultural and social U.S. imports into this NATO-allied nation. Origins aside, the 1970s brought a widespread autonomous feminist movement in the FRG that saw a pro-liferation of women's journals, book publishers, bookstores, coffeehouses, battered women's shelters, and rape crisis centers, as well as organizations for women in the trades, collective living experiments, and opportunities for women filmmakers. The feminist journals *Emma, Die Schwarze Botin* (The Black Messenger), and *Courage* all began in the 1970s. *Frauen und Film,* a feminist film quarterly, began in 1974. Women's archives were founded. The first was *Frauenforschungs- Bildungs- und Informations-Zentrum* (FFBIZ) in Berlin, and others followed, such as the *Feministisches Archiv und Dokumentationszentrum* (FAD) in Frankfurt.[9] Exhibitions such as *Kein Ort. Nirgends* (after the title of the novel by Christa Wolf, translated as *No Place On Earth*) were organized. This 1987 Berlin exhibition recorded and displayed two hundred years of women's lives and the women's move-ment in Berlin. It resulted in the publication of a complete catalog entitled *Fundorte* (Places of Discovery), which contains previously unpublished doc-uments and photographs of women. All these journals and archives made historical documents of women's lives available to women in the grass roots community and to scholars, as well as providing interpretations of women's experience and their art.

Organizations like FIT, reviewed here by Ursula Ahrens, and the first women's theater group, Anna Kondo, came along later. Although the movement has barely begun to infiltrate national theaters, it has provided an atmosphere in which reception of women playwrights is possible. The publication in 1989 of Anke Roeder's book of interviews with women playwrights, *Autorinnen,* by the major press Suhrkamp testifies to the awakening of the dominant culture to women in theater. Further, the three-part series on German women in theater produced by Goethe House in New York in 1991–92 exhibits a growing cultural awareness that German women playwrights deserve international visibility.

In the GDR, certain authors came to represent women's issues. Christa Wolf, a central figure for women in both Germanies, worked in East Berlin. Her novels and essays set gender in the context of socialist development, as well as within the production modes of classical traditions. Wolf pioneered the articulation of female subjectivity within socialist systems. Maxie Wander's book *Guten Morgen, du Schöne*[10] provided interviews with women in the GDR, who talked about their lives in terms of gender concerns. This book became a major source of information among women about their own strategies and needs. Christa Wolf wrote the introduction to Wander's book, outlining the import of such interviews in the GDR and, more broadly, locating political activism for GDR women vis-à-vis feminist organizing in Western capitalist countries: "These women don't see themselves as adversaries of men—unlike certain groups in capitalist countries . . . [where] in the absence of a strong labor movement women are driven into sect-like alliances against men." Wolf concludes with a question that necessarily links women's issues with other movements for social change: "How can women be 'liberated' as long as all people are not?"[11] In other words, within the socialist context, women's organizing around issues of gender oppression could in no way be separatist but must be linked with other socialist projects that include political alliances with men. In part, it was this kind of official state position on women's rights that prevented anything like a feminist movement as we know it from developing in the GDR.

Reunification brought a new visibility of women's issues in the erstwhile GDR. As early as November 1989, the UFV (Unabhängiger Frauen Verband [Independent Women's Association]), an unaffiliated coalition of women in the East, was seated at the Roundtable, the group of East political parties, to work out future considerations for women in the GDR. Historical conditions changed the course of those deliberations when the Roundtable was dissolved by the quickening pace of reunification. Still, the impulse toward organizing women around their own issues was immediately evident during the transition. Since that initial organization, there has been a series of events that illustrates the interests, needs, and issues of women in the former "East." For example, in June 1991 there was a sit-in for abortion rights at Humboldt University (the first time a women's issue occupied that university), and later a women's demonstration took place in Alexanderplatz during the Gulf War. Other similar social interventions have followed.

Außerhalb von Mitten Drin (literally, outside of being in the exact middle [similar to the feminist sense of being on the margins]), a major art, music, and performance festival for women artists from the GDR, took place in Berlin in May–June 1991. These events, along with a three-volume publication on the participating artists, mapped out possible new directions, styles, and themes of GDR women in cultural production.[12] The performances suggested that a new form may emerge from such work. While there has not been a tradition of underground, avant-garde work by women in the GDR, there has been rigorous classical training in the arts. One new form that seemed to be emerging is the avant-garde uses of that classical training. Bringing gender politics and a sense of contemporary performance to classical training provides a form that constructs/deconstructs simultaneously. Although we might recognize this form in the West as well, here the deconstruction is often impelled by elements of popular culture. The experiments I witnessed lacked the mediation of the popular. For example, a performance by Annette Jahns, a singer from the Dresden Opera, consisted, in part, of a professionally executed set of Schumann's *Lieder.* Performed with movement, the effect was to undo the Romantic tradition by performing it in a way that revealed what it did to its female object. Now it may seem that in the West, for example, Elfriede Jelinek creates a similar form in her play *Clara S.,* which undoes Robert Schumann through the character of Clara. The difference is that Jelinek has written a text that intercedes—she has created a language that cuts into the Romantic. In the performances I saw by GDR women, the only vocabulary was the classical one. Simply through costume and movement, and the way the forms were situated, the performance of the classical was simultaneously the undoing of it. By singing or dancing cramped into a corner, or crawling into a classical column, creating the image of the woman's body swallowed up by the column, Jahns critiqued the classical tradition in which she was trained.

Another form emerging from the cultural situation of women in the erstwhile GDR is a collage of texts. In a transitional culture, in which there are still relatively few plays by women and even fewer feminist texts, certain combinations of extant texts can provide a new and useful signification. Angelika Waller, a prominent GDR actor from the Berliner Ensemble, created such a collage for the *Außerhalb von Mitten Drin* performance series. Waller incorporated interviews with GDR women about Western terrorists from the 1970s whom the GDR had protected and then later turned over to Western courts during reunification. These interviews primarily concerned the way GDR women regarded the women terrorists, such as Inge Vieth. Waller combined these documentary materials with the Medea monologue from Heiner Müller's *Despoiled Shore*. In combination with other texts and in her style of presentation, Waller made Müller's Medea signify the feminized GDR, with Jason as the citizen who would desert her to marry the rich and politically powerful woman of the West.

The full spectrum of issues for women in performance in the erstwhile GDR is only beginning to emerge. One actor from the Volksbühne (East) related to me her confusion when, after reunification began, some women were pleased to finally be performing a text by Marguerite Duras, which highlighted sexual and domestic issues. At the time of the opening the Persian Gulf War broke out, and male colleagues accused their production of bourgeois irrelevancy. Once again, the pendulum of political activism, as demonstrated in the Brecht-Fleißer exchange, between gender and ungendered national politics, swings to thwart the representation of women's issues on the stage.

Other issues for GDR women in theater arising from reunification focus on the problem of performing for a new audience with different dramaturgical requirements and tastes. One actor described her anxiety about the Western taste for opulence and luster on the stage, in contrast to her training in ensemble playing, where characterizations were encouraged that emphasized a collective identity over individual brilliance.[13]

Reunification has also brought with it the publication of new plays by women from both the erstwhile East and West, which dramatize the issues of the divide and the reunion. Irina Liebmann from the GDR has a new anthology entitled *Quatschfresser* in which the play *Was Singt der Mond?* (What does the Moon Sing?), written in lyric form, focuses on two characters—West Mask and East Mask. From West Germany, Elfriede Müller's play *goldener Oktober* is explicitly about the reunification process. The play contains several subplots and a multitude of characters, including a manure manager from the West whose job is to dump it in the East (based on the historical fact that West Berlin dumped its garbage in the GDR). Elfriede Müller's play addresses the way in which the media represented reunification as a kind of heterosexual family reunion. She, however, represents this union as an abusive one. Perhaps the most compelling subplot concerns an East Berlin woman who, because of unemployment, is forced to turn to prostitution. She is romantically pursued by a department store detective from KdW (Kaufhaus des Westens—one of the chic department stores in West Berlin). He woos her with capitalist goods both to win her over and to reanimate the value of the merchandise. Like Waller's Medea, the East is feminized and bought.

I hope this short section on the past few decades of shifting social identities and textual / performance strategies for women in Germany provides a background for the plays in this volume that may help to mitigate a totally Anglo-American reception of them. Certainly, the issues, as well as the representational and economic strategies, are only briefly outlined here. Yet they may guide the reader to further research, through some of the works cited here, or serve simply to develop some general sense of the social fabric within which these plays were written.

Playwrights beyond This Book

The authors in this volume represent only a few German women playwrights. The page limitation of this volume, along with the exigencies of rights, the availability of translators, and the requirements of my own taste, make it impossible to represent all of the important trends, styles, and authors in this area. I was unable to locate, for example, a GDR author whose plays focused on the lives of women; likewise, the collection includes no plays by a Turkish "guest-worker" playwright—two realms of experience important to the configuration of the contemporary German cultural and material landscape. Yet, although I cannot include all of the plays and authors that seem integral, brief descriptions of other projects may help situate the plays in this volume within their broader context of German women authors. First I describe two playwrights from earlier decades who represent topics and styles that could not be included in this volume. Then I briefly survey the contemporary scene.

Christa Winsloe (1888–1944) appears to be the only lesbian playwright whose dramatization of a lesbian encounter has reached the mainstream. *Gestern und Heute* (Yesterday and Today), which became the movie *Mädchen in Uniform* (1931) raises the issue of lesbian representation in the context of authoritarian education. Both Ruby Rich and Richard Dyer have discussed the film in terms of Weimar politics and lesbian identity.[14] Outside of treatments of the film, very little is known about Winsloe, this play, or her other works. The play was first titled *Ritter Nerestan* (Knight Nerestan) and opened in Leipzig in 1930, then as *Gestern und Heute* in 1930 in Berlin. There is one extant English translation / adaptation, published in 1939 and entitled *Girls in Uniform*. The play is set in a girls' school and explores the contradiction between the authoritarian structures of the institution and the taboo lesbian attraction between teacher and student.

Winsloe wrote four plays in all, each about lesbian experience. While in exile, she wrote *Aiono* (1943) about a girl who lives her life in drag. An out lesbian, Winsloe emigrated to the United States in 1934. She was unable to get a visa to remain in the United States and moved into exile in Southern France. In 1944, she was shot and killed while illegally trying to cross the border back into Germany. The events of her death remain mysterious.

It would seem, although the documentation is not complete, that the tradition of women playwrights in Germany enjoyed some growth from the Weimar era through World War II and then suffered a period of inactivity for two decades. The only play by a woman produced in the 1960s appears to have been Ulrike Marie Meinhof's *Bambule*. Although the play does not appear in this volume, it is important in providing a sense of what women's contribution to Docudrama might be. Written as a documentary piece for TV in 1969, produced for TV in 1970, and performed in the theater in 1979, *Bambule* is about the Eichenhof welfare home for adolescent girls in West Berlin—an institution for orphans as well as juvenile delinquents. Meinhof exposes how authoritarian structures are imposed on the daily life of these young women through such means as institutional rules on eating and the forming of friendships. She dramatizes institutional controls and punishments as merely the extreme forms of dominant social structures. The play suggests that the most damaging form of punishment is isolation.

Meinhof worked in such an institution in 1968, the same year as the terrorist torching of a department store in Frankfurt by some of her political allies and the subsequent trial of some of those involved—Andreas Baader among them. At the time her play was to be aired on TV, Meinhof aided Baader in his escape, and they went underground, becoming what is referred to as the Baader-Meinhof Group. Shortly after, the Red Army Faction (RAF), the major international terrorist group of the 1970s, was formed. Central to this period in Germany, Meinhof's play focuses on the effects of punitive institutionalization and its violence on the sense of being human. Her life, unfortunately, was a testament to these issues: Meinhof was arrested in 1972, incarcerated in a prison built especially for isolating terrorists, and found dead in her cell in 1976. It has since been debated whether she committed suicide, as the authorities insist, or was murdered, as the Left asserts. Her prison experience helped to focus the attention of the Left on the conditions of incarceration of political prisoners—particularly those in solitary detention, which the Left interpreted as a form of state torture and terrorism.

Franca Rame wrote a play about Meinhof in her cell entitled *I, Ulrike Cry*. It is a monologue by Meinhof as she waits for her jailer to kill her. Meinhof's play, and her own life, inspired debate in the 1970s about the authoritarian measures employed by institutions that pose as humanitarian, or as agencies of democratic states. In Meinhof's play, one of the girls incites a riot. In her own life, Meinhof practiced terrorism. Meinhof raised the issue of what forms of resistance were effective against state institutionalized violence.

From the mid-1980s on, women playwrights have begun to flourish on the German scene. Although I cannot list them all, a few projects and people will serve to indicate the direction of new women's plays. Gisela von Wysocki has written two influential plays: the first, published in 1987, is *Abendlandleben oder Apollinaires Gedächtnis. Spiele aus Neu Glück* (Occidental Life, or Appolinaire's Memory: Plays from New Luck). This is a brilliant, complex, postmodern text of fragments and stage pictures, similar in compositional style to that of Steinwachs's *George Sand*. The situation of the play is a brain operation for Apollinaire, who has been wounded by a grenade in World War I. A mirror is placed onstage enabling the audience to see down into Apollinaire's brain, from whence come images suggestive of Western culture, including Lenin and Sigmund Freud's patient Anna O. Wysocki's second play, *Schauspieler, Tänzer, Sängerin* (Actor, Dancer, Singer), which was published in *Theater Heute* in 1989, explores the representational character of those roles. Wysocki, who holds a Ph.D. in philosophy and music theory, wrote her dissertation on "The Potentials of Subjectivity in Irrationalist Throught." She is also an important feminist literary critic who has published on Fleißer, Virginia Woolf, Sylvia Plath, Marguerite Duras, and Greta Garbo. In the future, I hope to see translations of her plays as well as of her critical writings.

Elfriede Müller's *Die Bergarbeiterinnen* (The Women Miners) (1988) has received a modicum of critical attention. In the play, an actor, Kali, returns to the mining region that was her home to attend local festivities. Her discussions with the people from her region are socially critical, highlighting themes of gender and cultural and material production. Ria Endres, who wrote her dissertation on Thomas Bernhard and has published studies of Samuel Beckett and Elfriede Jelinek, has written a play about the patriarchy entitled *Acht Weltmeister* (Eight World Champions) (1987). Heidi von Plato, who in this volume describes her feminist theater troupe, has recently begun to publish her plays. *Hasenjagd* (Rabbit Hunt) (1989) is a biting critique of fascism using scenes of childhood sexuality and parent-child relations.

Perhaps the most influential contemporary writer missing from this volume is Elfriede Jelinek. An Austrian, her work has nevertheless been important to the German stage. Her first play, *Was geschah nachdem Nora ihren Mann verlassen hatte oder Stützen der Gesellschaft* (What Happened after Nora Left Her Husband, or Pillars of Society) (1984) is a witty socialist-feminist emendation of the Ibsen play. Nora goes to work in a factory and is confronted with the material contradictions facing women in the workplace and in the home. The play *Krankheit oder Moderne Frauen* (Illness, or Modern Women) (1987) is a biting, witty postmodern condemnation of patriarchy and dominant heterosexuality. Undercutting the Romantic tradition, the play presents Emily Brontë as a nurse / vampire and Heathcliff as a gynecologist / dentist / yuppie. Through monologues composed of clichés, advertising slogans, and classical references—in other words, the already constructed language of dominant ideology—the characters deconstruct their own subject position, social standing, historical moment, gender identification, and desire as they speak.

Although I do not want to attempt any overview of German women playwrights in the twentieth century, I would like to make a few general observations based on the works of the playwrights discussed above and of those in this book. Many of these playwrights have written across genres, publishing novels, producing radio plays, and writing dissertations and literary criticism. It seems this practice is less common in the United States. Perhaps the cross-genre writer appears more frequently in Europe because of the way in which advanced education and the arts in general are less specialized there than they are here in the United States. These writers still participate to some extent in the older humanist tradition of an intellectual life that is neither exclusively academic nor narrowly professional.

Along with the breadth of their published works, several of these playwrights hold doctoral degrees. Some have majored in philosophy, others in literary theory—training that their plays may reflect in their use of abstract forms and ruminative investigations of social and personal experience. In fact, like much of German literature, the plays seem more interested in articulation, in ideas, than in "action" in the most denotative sense of the word. Some of the plays move at a slower tempo than the action-packed variety (a good example here would be *Ironheart*, in which the playwright carefully notes the slow tempo in her stage directions) and incline more toward monologue than fast-paced dialogue (the way the grandmother's scenes fit into the short, episodic form of *The Little Red-Hot Man*, for instance). Literary allusions are scattered across characters' names and throughout the dialogue. Steinwachs's and Lasker-Schüler's texts are a pastiche of allusions and quotations, but even Billerbeck in *Ironheart* speaks with rich literary resonances. These plays operate intertextually as part of the way in which they mean. They contextualize themselves as they go.

Yet these texts are eminently playable on the stage. They have a unique, exciting sense of *mise-en-scène*, derived from their metaphoric resonances and allusions. The focus on language often creates wonderfully nuanced female characters who can articulate what has long gone unsaid on the stage. I hope the readers of this volume will go on to develop productions of these plays as well as historical / critical studies of them that will secure their rightful place on the international stage for German women playwrights.

Brecht and Women

Finally, I would like to turn to a critical topic that surfaces in any overview of German and even international political theater in the twentieth century: the conception of Brechtian influence. The absence of German women's plays from Anglo-American feminist scholarship has had several critical consequences, but one notable example is the way in which the Brechtian influence upon feminist theater has been worked out vis-à-vis British texts rather than the German ones that spring directly from his theatrical tradition and practice.[15] While the British feminist adaptations of Brechtian techniques, such as those by Caryl Churchill, are generally illuminating, they do abstract those techniques from their historical and material conditions, importing strategies specific to the German context into the British one. In one sense, this importation cuts away the very historical-material base upon which Brecht insisted.

This international trade in Brechtian strategies has encouraged the impression that Brecht had a *theory* of the stage rather than assorted *techniques* for intervening in a particular stage practice. For example, the notion of the gest (*gestus*), so central to Brechtian practice, is an intervention into a specifically German method of actors' training, tradition of blocking, and use of physical properties and sets, as well as the role the German director plays in the rehearsal process. Brecht's political revision of the gest is a critique of the way in which all of these stage practices had evolved within his own specific tradition. The Cold War relation of Western capitalist states to the GDR, where Brechtian practice was housed, made the abstraction of these methods a necessary historical one—an abstraction not shared by actors in the GDR.[16] Thus, abstracting Brecht's interventions into general principles, such as the way many have written about and practiced the Alienation effect, has participated in the Cold War practice of suppressing the history of East bloc countries, while assimilating their cultural/political productions into the Western Left.[17]

Likewise, the politics of Brecht's stage practice were historically, economically, and nationally specific. The crisis around the practice of Epic techniques in the early years of the GDR illustrated the way in which such strategies, devised within a historical capitalist period, did not necessarily serve the later socialist experiment. After all, what would Alienation mean within a collective model of state socialism? By the same standard, how does it collude with, rather than critique, high capitalism? Alienation, gest, and other Brechtian dramaturgical devices are inscribed with the political and economic system they address, or within which they were devised in their structural elements. When such strategies begin to take on transcendent stable meanings which can then be situated within other political, cultural context, on the one hand they abandon the Marxist historical construction of practice, while on the other they carry historical traces that may not apply to the current political situation. The dark, angry irony of Heiner Müller's later formal experiments resounds with his critical reaction to such practices of importation and adaptation. Ultimately, Müller opts for a stage practice in which the text runs independently from its productions, underscoring its elements agonistic to contemporary political practices and national locations.

While these considerations interrogate the importation of Brecht into other national literatures and historical periods, another factor in his practice threatens the specifically feminist uses of his methods. Brecht's Epic stage is based on his scientism, his belief in the efficacy of the documentary, and the power of the empirical. This stable critique distances, where proximity may better serve, for it is in the structures of intimacy and in the intimate sphere of the domestic that the social system oppresses women. The oppressive system of internal, psychological, patriarchal policing under which women suffer may be more like Brecht's own stable system than like a feminist deconstruction of it. In other words, the objectivity and alienation in his approach become parts of the epistemological problem when brought to bear upon an understanding of sexual oppression. Not only did Brecht himself police Fleißer's text for a political dramaturgy that better fitted that traditional sense of public history and economy and his legacy continue to problematize a politics of the personal in both the GDR and the FRG, but, theoretically, his strategies themselves are unfit to reveal the metonymic slippage of desire and its itineration through oppressive and liberatory mechanisms.

Heiner Müller once described it as the failure of Brecht's macro-net to capture the fine mesh of social realities. But more, it is the appeal in these strategies to a public foundation of fact—a stable system of values that threatens the representation of sexual politics. In Fleißer, the social realm breaks down subjective realities, like the crowds who deny the empirical reality of Roelle's angels. This is not to say that there is not a public, institutional policing of desire. More important, however, in these plays with women characters at their center, is the portrayal of the "something else" that exists alongside, in spite of, beyond, under, or in the interstices of those institutions. Thus, the Brechtian theatrical practice breaks down in representation, where empirical, documentary evidence borders the personal in women's social experience.

Perhaps something like the proximity effect, in contrast to the distancing effect, would better inform the feminist stage. This notion of a proximity effect might help to clarify Brecht's constant revisions of the Fleißer text or lead to a new reading of Lasker-Schüler's contiguous, disorderly, accelerated scenarios. Fleißer and Lakser-Schüler offer the close-up, the in-the-midst-of dramaturgy that is unstable in its referents and narrative and therefore well suited to the operations of desire and its oppression.

The translation of these plays by German women thus opens up a new, feminist analysis of Brecht that could accommodate how, within roughly the same historical period and stage tradition, his sense of the political was both assimilated and contradicted by playwrights who would portray gender / sexual oppression and invent its dramaturgy. The later playwrights, such as Gerlind Reinshagen, both continue within his tradition and contradict it with their reliance upon the lyric. Reinshagen, Steinwachs, and Roth all employ the lyric in their texts to open up the portrayal of the woman subject and her possible alternative space. In contrast, say, to Brecht's great empirical Galileo, the women characters in their plays portray the power of the personal, private metaphor. Even when there is something like the social gest, it operates without the stability that Brecht's use of the strategy implies.

Consider, if you will, in *Ironheart,* Ada's display of her sadomasochistic bruises in the workplace as a social gest. Yet beyond what her sexual practice means and what it means to display it in the workplace, there is the doubt that it even occurs. It is not certain how she really got the bruises—where her fantasy begins and ends. If anything, Ada destabilizes such knowing about people in her place in the narrative. The feminist critic of these texts, then, is challenged to go beyond Brecht, or against him, to describe a new kind of political theater. Employing the social fabric of women's lives in Germany, both within national narratives of identity and beyond them, both split by the divide of home / land and healing with it, both after the wall and living on with the internalized wall, the feminist reader of these texts may explore these new interventions into the system of representation of women.

1991

NOTES

1. For a further discussion of German / American feminisms and their national alliances, see my essay "Writing Feminism: The Misfortunes of a German / American Comparison," in *Rethinking Germanistik,* ed. R. Bledsoe, B. Estabrook, J. C. Federle, K. Henschel, W. Miller, and A. Polster (New York: Peter Lang, 1991), 193–99.

2. For a lengthier discussion of this meeting, see my report on this conference written with Ellen Donkin, "FIT: Germany's First Conference for Women in Theatre," *Women and Performance,* Fall 1985, 65–73.

3. *Spectaculum: Theaterstücke von Frauen* (Frankfurt am Main: Suhrkamp Verlag, 1987).

4. *Autorinnen: Herausforderungen an das Theater,* ed. Anke Roeder (Frankfurt am Main: Suhrkamp, 1988). *Fürs Theater Schreiben: Über zeitgenössische deutschsprachige Theaterautorinnen,* a special edition of *Schreiben* 9, nos. 29–30, published by Zeichen + Spuren Frauenliteraturverlag, 1986. Anthology on Ginka Steinwachs: *ein mund von welt: ginka steinwachs,* ed. Sonia Nowoselsky-Müller (Bremen: Zeichen + Spuren, 1989). On Reinshagen: Jutta E. Kiencke-Wagner, *Das Werk von Gerlind Reinshagen: Gesellschaftskritik und utopisches Denken* (Bern: Peter Lang, 1989).

5. The following factual information was culled from two articles that appeared in the DAAD special issue 1990 of *German Studies Review:* Christian Lemke, "Beyond the Ideological Stalemate: Women and Politics in the FRG and the GDR in Comparison"; and Marilyn Rueschemeyer and Hanna Schissler, "Women in the Two Germanies."

6. For a critique of the federal laws concerning this issue, see Ulrike Marie Meinhof, "Falsches Bewußtein," in her *Die Würde des Menschen ist antastbar* (Berlin: Verlag Klaus Wagenback, 1988), 125–33.

7. For a detailed description of women's legal rights in the GDR, see Patricia Herminghouse, "Legal Equality and Women's Reality in the German Democratic Republic," in *German Feminism: Readings in Politics and Literature,* ed. E. H. Altbach, J. Clausen, D. Schultz, and N. Stephan (New York: State University of New York Press, 1984), 41–46.

8. For literature and information on earlier lesbian issues in Germany, see *Lesbians in Germany: 1890's–1920's,* ed. Lillian Faderman and Brigitte Eriksson (Tallahassee: Naiad Press, 1990).

9. This information is taken from the research of Karen Jankowsky in the German Department at the University of Wisconsin, Madison.

10. Maxie Wander, *Guten Morgen, du Schöne* (Darmstadt and Neuwied: Hermann Luchterhand Verlag, 1979).

11. Christa Wolf, translated as "In Touch," in *German Feminism,* 167–68.

12. The three publications all bear the title *Außerhalb von Mitten Drin* and are divided according to genre: theater / music, literature / film, and the plastic arts. They were published by the Neue Gesellschaft für bildende Kunst, Berlin.

13. Some of this information is culled from a report by Renate Ullrich, from the Institute for the Analysis of Social Data in Berlin. She delivered the report at the International Symposium on Women and Theatrical Language, Berlin, June 1991. Materials from interviews with East German women in theater have recently appeared in Renate Ullrich's *Mein Kapital Bin Ich Selber,* 1991.

14. See Ruby B. Rich, "*Mädchen in Uniform:* From Repressive Tolerance to Erotic Liberation," in *Re-Vision,* ed. Mary Ann Doane, Patricia Mellencamp, and Linda Williams (Los Angeles: American Film Institute, 1984), 100–130; and Richard Dyer, *Now You See It: Studies in Lesbian and Gay Film* (London and New York: Routledge, 1990), 27–43.

15. See, for example, Janelle Reinelt, "Beyond Brecht: Britain's New Feminist Drama," in *Performing Feminisms: Feminist Critical Theory and Theatre,* ed. Sue-Ellen Case (Baltimore: Johns Hopkins University Press, 1990), 150–59; and Elin Diamond, "Brechtian Theory / Feminist Theory: Toward a Gestic Feminist Criticism," *Drama Review* 32, no. 1 (Spring 1988): 82–94.

16. See Jurgen Holtz, "Self-Portrait of an East German Actor," *Performing Arts Journal / 13* 5, no. 1: 27–28.

17. For a discussion of Brecht within the German tradition see John Rouse, *Brecht and the West German Theatre: The Practice and Politics of Interpretation* (Ann Arbor: UMI Press, 1989).

Marieluise Fleißer

BORN IN 1901 in Ingolstadt, Bavaria, Marieluise Fleißer began her study of theater in Munich. She wrote *Purgatory in Ingolstadt* in 1924, and it opened in Berlin in 1926. She wrote her second play, *Pioneers in Ingolstadt,* in 1927. *Pioneers* (a term for soldiers) became a controversial play that gained notoriety in the press for its sexual material. Its reception raises several issues that illuminate the historical and critical position of *Purgatory* as well. *Pioneers* was first performed in Dresden in 1928 and then brought to Berlin by Bertolt Brecht, who actively encouraged Fleißer to make major changes in the text according to his own understanding of how "political" theater should be done. Brecht's 1929 production of *Pioneers* caused a critical scandal concerning the representation of sexuality in the play, recalling the age-old German notion of "the stage as moral institution." As Susan Cocalis notes, however, in her groundbreaking article on Fleißer, the scandal surrounding this representation rested specifically on the fact that such scenes about sexuality had been written by a woman author.[1] This contention may remind the feminist critic of the way in which Aphra Behn was also reproached for such writing in her era in London. In both contexts, the accusation is gender specific, since Behn's male contemporaries in seventeenth-century England made their success on bawdy texts, and in Germany a number of plays on the theme of sexual practice were already well known by Fleißer's time—particularly those by Frank Wedekind.

Fleißer was also reproached by the city fathers of Ingolstadt, who accused her of besmirching the name of her hometown through her critical portrayal of that city's social life. After such notoriety and public attack, and the painful process of rewriting her play (insisted upon by Brecht), Fleißer retired from the stage. She withdrew from Berlin and from writing, became a housewife, and eventually moved back to Ingolstadt. She suffered a nervous breakdown and a definite crisis in self-confidence as a writer. Then, in 1935, her work was forbidden by the Nazis. After the war, she wrote another, more surrealistic play about her experience of Berlin life (including a portrayal of Brecht) entitled *Tiefseefisch* (Deepseafish). In the 1970s, her work once again gained currency in the theater through the influence of Rainer Fassbinder and Franz Kroetz, who claimed her creation of the *Volksstück* (Folk Play) as their model. Her plays were then produced by some of the foremost directors in Germany, and, in 1972, her collected works were published by the prestigious Suhrkamp Verlag. She died in 1974. In the late 1970s, her work began to be embraced by feminist critics.

Purgatory in Ingolstadt

Susan L. Cocalis defines Fleißer's "purgatory" as the place where the gender battle is played out most fiercely—without the possibility of resolution. Fleißer critically represents gendered oppression as lodged in heterosexual practices and in the social structures that surround the emotion of "being in love." Cocalis contends that in most representations, when a woman breaks with a traditional relationship with a man, she is represented as a bad woman—the Lilith. But, in Fleißer's work, this break with the repression lodged in the traditional sexual and emotional role is dramatized without the binary of the bad. Since the woman is already trapped in the position of a sex object, it is no surprise that she plays out that object role inhumanely, for alienation is inherent in the role itself. In other words, if the woman acts as if she were cold or punishing, it is not from her own agency but merely a consequence of her already alienated position. Fleißer does not portray the untraditional woman as mythically bad but as necessarily alienated within patriarchal constructions of sexuality.[2]

Fleißer's plays are thus critical and "distanced," but not in the Brechtian sense. Whereas Brecht's distancing is mediated through an empirical presentation of material conditions, Fleißer's works through a critical representation of emotional relationships between men and women. This difference between Brecht's scientistic discourse and Fleißer's emotional one caused the agonizing process of revisions when he staged *Pioneers*. Historically, Brecht's notion has also won out. Brecht's sense of what constitutes political theater has become the rule and Fleißer's the exception. Moreover, against the historical backdrop of her time as it has been perceived through this Brechtian lens, Fleißer's discourse seems to align itself with that of the

Expressionist playwrights, who also wrote plays of the emotions and desire. Their subsequent devaluation by Piscator and Brecht as mystifications has likewise devaluated Fleißer. Only by working through feminist critical strategies of the personal as political can one begin to recover the politics of Fleißer's style.

Purgatory in Ingolstadt opens in the midst of family squabbling: central to the play is the absence of the mother and the presence of the father— the traditional (in the Lacanian sense) presence/absence dyad around which gender/labor/love issues arise. Beyond, and twining within, that family structure, the issue of "illicit" sex and the question of abortion (a political issue at the time, as now) are dramatized through the narrative of the pregnant Olga, who is rejected by the man she desires but desired by another—the social outcast. In this gender hell, Olga is cast as "damaged goods," not worthy of legitimate desire. She is the devalued feminine. Only the outcast Roelle desires her, and he is unable, socially, to "be a man."

While Olga's mother is absent, Roelle's is ever-present and nurturing, creating the social portrait of the effeminized "Mama's boy." At the intersection of his masculine performance anxiety and his sexual desire, Roelle claims a kind of sham phallus: He promises that angels will appear to him in front of witnesses. In other words, although he cannot ante up in the gender economy of his society, he has the "potency" to penetrate the real world with emissaries from the "above." Ironically, this claim to the penetration of the social by the metaphysical puts Roelle in the context of the Catholic church, the social agency that controls angel value. When the angels do not show up, Roelle's potency is deemed unauthorized, and thus his promise of angel power becomes a site of even deeper gender humiliation. Within this dramatic treatment of angels and the Church, Fleißer reveals the Church to be a social institution aligned with the patriarchy. Through its authorizing powers, the Church measures manhood, and through its perspective on pregnancy and ban on abortion, it also regulates and authorizes womanhood. In Fleißer, the Catholic church is characterized not as sacral but, rather, as a definitive player in the organization of the gender system and in the sexual commerce between genders.

In the same scene in which Roelle fails, Fleißer brings the pregnant Olga onstage, still drenched from an attempted suicide by drowning. Here, Fleißer plays on the traditional heroine's narrative in the German theater of the nineteenth century. Friedrich Hebbel's play, *Maria Magdalena,* for example, ends sadly and beautifully with the drowning of the sexually shamed title character, the Magdalene. In Fleißer's play, however, Olga survives the drowning only to suffer further public debasement. Like Roelle, Olga has no way out of her social purgatory. Neither does the dramatic narrative, as Fleißer constructs it: She refuses the socially restorative death of the woman as a solution. In Fleißer's *Purgatory,* the failed man without his angels and the failed woman, still wet from the river, meet to further torture one another with unappeased desire and rejection: the Janus face of gendered, heterosexist oppression.

It would seem, then, that Fleißer's work simply kills all hope for women as that of the male playwrights had already done. Yet there is another way such a narrative may be read that brings out its political effect. As one critic put it in a study of Fleißer's short stories:

> Since her suffering and limitations are not prettified, the text negates the legitimacy of such self-enclosed patterns of individual female existence. And the power of that negation derives directly from the way in which the reader brings together the empathetic and the critical perspective in the act of reading and understanding. . . . The narrative rhythm draws the reader so thoroughly into both her fiction-making and her determinist melancholy that he [*sic*] can only respond by asking the largest possible questions about the historical and ongoing damage to women.[3]

In other words, without the closure that the beautiful, sad drowning of Olga would provide for the play (the kind afforded Ophelia or Maria Magdalena), one cannot, through aesthetic closure and sentimental release, countenance the humiliation of the woman within such a social system. Instead, the continuing suffering of both women and men causes the reader to recoil in horror and to interrogate the patriarchal prejudice that causes it.

Thus, Fleißer has invented her own sense of Epic form—far different from Brecht's but more suitable to the representation of women's experience. Fleißer's Epic distances the narrative, not of labor relations, but of sexual ones. The phrase "falling in love" is acted out in *Purgatory.* The mystification of power relations between men and women through love and sex is revealed to be a dynamic in which women are relegated to men's ownership of desire. This means that, for women, desire does not legitimate; in fact, it might produce illegitimate children and thus cause women to become social outcasts. Men, within the patriarchy, retain the right of legitimate desire if they opt to "own" up to their sexual behavior. This rightful ownership of emotions and sexual activity, however, is only available to men who measure up to the standards of social potency organized by their society.

Where Brecht staged class, Fleißer staged gender, and where he demystified labor relations, she demystified emotional/sexual ones. Fleißer rendered visible and specific the material operations of emotional and sexual experiences, thus opening them to change. This kind of drama is what Cocalis labels the critical *Volksstück*. In its domestic operations and its sense of the personal, this form of the drama is particularly suited to feminist politics of the stage. To emphasize that Fleißer's use of this form is not peculiar to her but is, rather, a tradition of women's writing in Germany, this volume also includes the most recent example of the form: *The Little Red-Hot Man* by Kerstin Specht.

NOTES

1. See Susan Cocalis, "Weib ist Weib: Mimetische Darstellung contra emanzipatorische Tendenz in den Dramen Marieluise Fleißers" ("Woman Is Woman: Mimetic Representation versus the Emancipatory Trend in the Dramas of Marieluise Fleißer"), in *Die Frau als Heldin und Autorin: Neue kritische Ansätze zur deutschen Literatur,* ed. Wolfgang Paulson (Munich: Francke Verlag, 1979), 201–10.

2. Cocalis, "Woman Is Woman," 206.

3. Donna Hoffmeister, "Growing Up Female in the Weimar Republic: Young Women in Seven Stories by Marieluise Fleißer," *German Quarterly* 56, no. 3 (May 1983): 396–407.

Marieluise Fleißer

Purgatory in Ingolstadt

Translated by Gitta Honegger

Characters

BEROTTER		CRUSIUS
OLGA		PEPS
CLEMENTINE	HIS CHILDREN	GERVASIUS
CHRISTIAN		PROTASIUS
ROELLE		1. ALTAR BOY
ROELLE'S MOTHER		2. ALTAR BOY
HERMIONE SEITZ		STUDENTS

SCENE I

Living room of the BEROTTERS. BEROTTER, OLGA, CLEMENTINE. CLEMENTINE *calls in from backstage.*

CLEMENTINE: Where's that key to the linen closet? Everything always gets misplaced around here.

BEROTTER (*to* OLGA): Can't you tell her?

CLEMENTINE: I have to get these beds made.

BEROTTER (*to* OLGA): You want Hermione Seitz to lie in an unmade bed?

OLGA: On top of the bureau.

BEROTTER: Did you take something without asking again? How often do I have to tell you that's not permitted around here?

OLGA: Clementine never gets me things.

CLEMENTINE (*enters*): I always have to yell first. Olga, your blouse is dirty again.

OLGA: You never get me anything new.

CLEMENTINE: What's Hermione going to think?

OLGA: If it were up to me, she doesn't have to come at all.

BEROTTER: Mrs. Seitz is in the hospital. Where is she supposed to go?

OLGA: You don't know Hermione.

BEROTTER: In the convent she was your friend.

CLEMENTINE: She always ate your rice soup which you didn't like.

OLGA: Mother wouldn't have liked to see her coming to our house.

CLEMENTINE: Look who's talking about Mother!

BEROTTER: I can't do that to Mrs. Seitz.

OLGA: And you like seeing Mrs. Seitz.

BEROTTER: I am not going to argue with you. What a blessing you are to your father. (*to* CLEMENTINE, *about* OLGA) She knows Latin. She wants to impress me.

CLEMENTINE (*about* OLGA): She didn't even cry at the funeral.

BEROTTER: Wants to have a say around here.

CLEMENTINE: And she didn't go to church today either.

BEROTTER: You didn't go to church? You're setting a nice example. Some older sister!

OLGA: In church the evil enemy circles around the confessional.

CLEMENTINE: That's your bad conscience.

BEROTTER: I never know if I should make you go. I don't want to hear about your mortifications. You always exaggerate.

CLEMENTINE: If only we didn't have you!

OLGA: That's what you tell me every day.

BEROTTER: I'd like to know why you're coming home at all after school. (*to* CLEMENTINE, *about* OLGA) She never goes near the kitchen.

OLGA: And you never take me to a restaurant.

BEROTTER: You don't know how to talk.

OLGA: That has something to do with you. You wouldn't let me grow up like a human being.

BEROTTER: I never favored one child over another.

OLGA: You didn't like my face—a child notices that kind of thing. You always told me I hold my head all twisted.

BEROTTER: You didn't get your meanness from your mother.

CHRISTIAN (*enters*): Hello.

BEROTTER: You don't throw your school bag like that. Pick it up and put it down properly.

CHRISTIAN: Don't worry, the writing tablet's not in there.

BEROTTER: Are you getting fresh with me?

CLEMENTINE: He got that from Olga.

CHRISTIAN: Roelle really can annoy me.

OLGA: What about Roelle?

CHRISTIAN: Is there something between you and Roelle?

OLGA: That was a long time ago.

CHRISTIAN: I always say you can make that up about any girl. I know my Olga.

OLGA: He stinks. He is afraid of water.

CHRISTIAN: He says he knows something about you, and, if he wants to, he'll report you to the police.

OLGA: Boys always think they can force you.

CHRISTIAN: He wants to come here when he has the time.

OLGA: All talk!

CLEMENTINE: Olga interrupted me. Now your collar's not ready.

CHRISTIAN: Convent dummy!

CLEMENTINE: Listen to that. He would never insult his Olga.

CHRISTIAN: Your Roelle keeps telling everyone how Hermione Seitz lost her petticoat in the middle of Regent's Square.

CLEMENTINE: My Roelle doesn't say that.

BEROTTER: Olga, you shouldn't treat young Roelle like that. —You passed him as if he were air, although he said hello to you.

OLGA: He has a neck like a worm.

CLEMENTINE: Well, he wears such tight collars.

BEROTTER: Poor thing. His face was flaming red. Now if I know someone takes an interest in me. You'll suffer someday, you are harsh.

OLGA: When we were children, he wanted something dirty.

CLEMENTINE: He never wanted anything dirty from you. Olga always claims everybody for herself.

BEROTTER: He's human, after all. The nuns must have taught you to be so well mannered. You aren't that dainty otherwise.

CLEMENTINE: Our Olga is too good for us.

CHRISTIAN: You shouldn't scold her because of Roelle. Roelle is a coward. No one likes to be around him. He doesn't want to smoke with all the others so he won't get sick. He doesn't dare go in the water.

CLEMENTINE: Of course, you have to help your Olga. Now I want to say something: What about that dog?

CHRISTIAN: It wasn't her fault.

CLEMENTINE: Someone put pins in his eyes.

OLGA: Not me.

CLEMENTINE: He kept tripping from one side to the other. And you watched.

BEROTTER: What kind of person are you?

OLGA: They chased him in front of my window. That's no way to act. It made them feel so strong.

BEROTTER: Who did the chasing?

OLGA: Let me go.

CLEMENTINE: He might haunt you someday.

OLGA: It was the little brown one, with the soft ears. (*to* CLEMENTINE) You always tell lies. Whenever she's near you, she seems to be a different person.

CLEMENTINE: You think Olga loves you. Olga has no heart.

CHRISTIAN: She is not like you.

CLEMENTINE: So take your Olga.

BEROTTER: Don't get your neck all twisted again. Do they have to fight because of you? Don't annoy me with that look.

CLEMENTINE: She'll keep haunting us.

BEROTTER: What happened with the dog? Did you watch?

OLGA: You want to beat me?

BEROTTER: When was the last time I beat you?

OLGA: That was a long time ago. And I know what a relief it is for you.

BEROTTER: Don't make me sin against my blessed Anna.

OLGA: Go on, beat me, and you'll beat my mother in me.

BEROTTER: I can't do it. Listen to me when I talk to you, flesh of my Anna. (*He falls down.*) Look at me lie here: It is he who was so harsh with his Anna. The children must know.

CLEMENTINE: I can see she is getting away with it again.

BEROTTER: You're no angel either.

OLGA: Am I right?

BEROTTER: You are right. Everyone is always right. Only I am not right.

CHRISTIAN: Don't embarrass yourself in front of your children.

BEROTTER (*to all his children*): You shouldn't always leave your father out. I want to know why we don't have anything to say to each other.

OLGA: I can't always show it.

BEROTTER: Now that's my good girl. If only Anna were here.

CLEMENTINE: Do you like Olga better than me?

BEROTTER: You must have a lot of time [to waste]. Here you stand. What about Christian's collar? Does he have to ask for it again?

CLEMENTINE: That's all I am good for.

BEROTTER: You know what you have to do.

CLEMENTINE: Olga doesn't have to do anything.

BEROTTER: She doesn't feel well.

CLEMENTINE: What kind of illness could that be?

BEROTTER: You be quiet.

CLEMENTINE: I know you all hate me. Everybody hates me.

BEROTTER: Now she's starting too!

CLEMENTINE: They always want to gag my mouth. Mother looks down on me. She sees how you treat her child.

OLGA: You really believe that?

CLEMENTINE: She's my mother.

OLGA: I didn't want to do anything bad. She mustn't think that of me.

CLEMENTINE: You ran away from her when she was dead.

OLGA: Could you let her know that . . .

CLEMENTINE: She won't help you. Mother looks straight into the heart.

OLGA: I didn't want to kill it. It's not human yet. That's what they told me. So it won't be hurt. The catechism teacher says they go to another place.

CLEMENTINE: You're scared.

OLGA: I didn't steal a soul from heaven. It had no soul. It was too small for one.

CLEMENTINE: You won't get to heaven. You'll have to burn in hell, and I'll be lying in Abraham's bosom.

OLGA: And you won't even know me.

CLEMENTINE: I won't hear you scream. The distance'll be too great.

OLGA: It's your child. That's how the pious are.

CLEMENTINE: What is it that you are?

OLGA: Keep hitting my head against it. That's what never ends.

CHRISTIAN: You want to be someone else?

OLGA: I wouldn't like that either. I can't ever know for sure.

CLEMENTINE: Roelle is here. He is coming up the stairs.

BEROTTER: Stop jumping around in front of my face. He didn't come for you.

CLEMENTINE (*to* OLGA): You want to take him away from me too?

OLGA: Did I say I want him?

ROELLE (*enters*): Greetings everybody.

CHRISTIAN: Politeness personified. Why don't you turn right around.

BEROTTER: Christian, please. Let him come in first. Why don't you keep an eye on our oldest, young man? She is so unpredictable. It must come from chlorosis. She felt sick today.

ROELLE: Yes, of course. I, for my part, am more than willing.

CLEMENTINE: Here I see a beautiful young man bright and early in the morning.

BEROTTER: You come along, Clementine. Young man, you behave yourself now. (*exits with* CLEMENTINE)

CHRISTIAN: Sissy! In front of an adult he shows a completely different side.

ROELLE: You'll never understand the subtleties of dealing with people.

CHRISTIAN: Olga doesn't want you.

ROELLE: Let her tell me herself. Get out of the way. (*He pushes him aside.*)

CHRISTIAN: Wimp!

ROELLE: There's my signature! (*He hits him.*) My father sells snuff. That's the kind of father I have.

OLGA: I never said that.

ROELLE: In front of the Lutheran church. You said I stink.

OLGA: I was a child then.

ROELLE: It's an import business.

CHRISTIAN: He never produces a bill. He just shows his yellow face.

ROELLE: We don't stink. I want you to say that.

OLGA: You'll have to wait a long time.

CHRISTIAN: You just dare to come over here. I'll show you my grip. Open your collar so nothing restrains you!

ROELLE: My dear lady, let me give you an overview of the situation. You look at me; you don't see a dog with his tail between his legs. You don't see a creature filled with fear. But what do I see when I turn to you? Before my inner eye you stand there like a bundle of misery.

OLGA: Something irritating must've gotten in your eyes.

ROELLE: I won't blush over someone like you. You are a real beauty. Good thing I know. It's time to spread the news.

OLGA: What can you do to me?

ROELLE: I know from Mrs. Schnepf. It's not bad for me. It's only bad for you.

OLGA: I don't know the woman. I was never in her house.

ROELLE: You were seen.

OLGA: I don't understand.

ROELLE: Maybe you thought Mrs. Schnepf would keep quiet for you. The woman doesn't have to be afraid of anything.

OLGA: I don't even know what you're talking about.

ROELLE: She doesn't do it anymore. That's what she told my mother. It's against the law. She's fed up with it. And then she went on about who had asked her to do something like that. A talk between women, straight and plain—you should take a closer look at the people you deal with.

OLGA: You—monster!

ROELLE: So, what are we going to do now? Can't you guess? Come here. Just one more tiny step. (OLGA *moves unconsciously toward him.*) Now tell me what you've learned.

OLGA: You are running an import business that doesn't stink.

CHRISTIAN: Olga! You let him do this to you?

ROELLE: Your sister doesn't want you.

OLGA: Christian, where's your courage?

CHRISTIAN: Congratulations—to that bloated neck! (*He exits.*)

ROELLE: May you be miserable through me. That's what I begged on bloody knees. Now you are paralyzed.

OLGA: You are wearing such tight collars. I want to look up to you again.

ROELLE: That's nice. I'm much obliged to you. Could it be you feel remorse? Are you beginning to see? Someone told me I stink, my flame, so to speak—perhaps it was you. I won't talk about my feelings. You went swimming, and the others came along. I saw you from afar, me, the fellow who stinks. But it was Horn who followed you, and he said, "Has she got legs." You didn't even bother to slip your stockings back on at night. And Horn wasn't any older than I. But I stood at the wall as if my skin was different from the others.

OLGA: You had bad thoughts in your head.

ROELLE: I had brought a matchbox, and I waited until you'd pass. I held it in my hand. My neck was bloated. I thought, In a minute I'll set her skirt on fire. You should have said, "Man, you're so pale." "Horn," you said, "don't go with him." And I was disgusted with myself.

OLGA: I had no idea.

ROELLE: Today no skirt'll be set on fire. The moon crosses the window. From my room I can see the light in yours. But it doesn't matter that I stink. It won't kill me—not from someone like you. There is vengeance. With your permission I'll light one now. It calms me down.

OLGA: Do you know how to smoke?

ROELLE: I always did. (*He smokes.*)

OLGA: I want to walk arm in arm with you, in front of the whole town.

ROELLE: I don't want to be seen with someone like you in a dump like this. I prefer my untouchable skin.

OLGA: What do I have to do for you to . . . be quiet.

ROELLE: I, too, can have power for once. . . . you don't get it, do you? I think she wants to be nice to me now because I might tell the whole town, everything—the way I want to. Did you change? You are the same. You'll treat me the same again.

OLGA: What do you know of me?

ROELLE: I ask you, as your father confessor: This child of your maculate conception—what is it to you, object of love or hate?

OLGA: It is no different from my enemy.

ROELLE: I ask you as your father confessor: Can you deny that you wanted to do away with it?

OLGA: If only my mother had done it with me!

ROELLE: So she goes and beats it to death, so to speak, with some kind of tool.

OLGA: You are so sure that you are right. But you don't say what's to become of the child. And of me.

ROELLE: That's something you and your neat friend Peps should have thought of before.

OLGA: You try and think! When everyone's always coming after me and one longs to be free—and freedom comes in a beautiful shape and it's crashing down all over you—

ROELLE (*approaches her*): You mean—like this? (*She shudders.*)

OLGA: There he comes and wants us to sin together.

ROELLE: I say bend your knee, and she shall bend her knee and shall be as a woman in bondage before me.

OLGA: What are you doing with your greasy head so close to me?

ROELLE: Neck and arms are mine. Something to hold on to.

OLGA: Your voice is cracking!

ROELLE: So what? I don't care.

OLGA: I don't want to. It's sickening with you.

ROELLE: He does it. He does it not. He does it.

OLGA: Get away!

ROELLE: Oh no. We'll end up in hell no matter what.

OLGA: How dare you! Just touch your head! Go ahead! Feel what's sitting on your shoulders!

ROELLE: I hear what you're telling me. When I show my face among people, it makes a sick dog howl with laughter.

OLGA: Splash your forehead and get back to reason.

ROELLE: No water.

OLGA: Can you stand up straight?

ROELLE: You always have to insult me. That's all you do.

OLGA: I guess I should've slapped my mouth.

ROELLE: If you've more to say, do it fast—I am leaving.

OLGA: You won't see me fall on my knees. I'll send Peps after you.

ROELLE: Why don't you ask him if he'll marry you?

OLGA: I did already.

ROELLE: He's worse than I. I'm warning you.

OLGA: He can't just do what he wants either. He says, I have to be the smart one of the two of us.

ROELLE: Easy for him to say. He's praying his rosary while he's doing it with Hermione. (*He exits.*)

OLGA: I knew it.

SCENE 2

Later the same day. OLGA, PEPS, *and* HERMIONE *still backstage. Dialogue backstage.*

ROELLE: I don't want it. I won't be forced.

PEPS: You have to. (PEPS *pulls in* ROELLE *forcefully.* HERMIONE *follows. To* OLGA): Did he ask your forgiveness?

ROELLE: I can't do that. It never comes out right with me.

OLGA: What's wrong now?

PEPS: Olga, you just don't know.

HERMIONE: He went to confession and they wouldn't let him off.

ROELLE: I don't think that's so bad.

HERMIONE: It certainly is.

ROELLE: I'll just go to another priest.

HERMIONE: You'll have to confess that, too, if the first one didn't absolve you.

ROELLE: I'll never go to confession again.

PEPS: Then what do you do if you have to come up to communion with your whole class?

ROELLE: That's my business.

HERMIONE: People who don't go to confession go straight to hell.

ROELLE: I can achieve perfect repentance.

PEPS: You can't. Only saints can do that.

HERMIONE: I wouldn't want to know what he's got to confess to have this happen to him.

OLGA: What do you want from him? Leave him alone with what he has to confess.

PEPS: Olga, you just don't know. He filled the confessional with talk about you. He mentioned your name and dragged you through the dirt.

ROELLE: That's a lie.

PEPS: I stood close by and pricked my ears, young man. I heard everything.

HERMIONE: You should always be aware of that.

ROELLE: You can't reveal this. It's under the seal of confession.

PEPS: I'm not a priest.

HERMIONE: He's not bound by the seal.

ROELLE: You found out sinfully.

PEPS: Do you know what you did? You ruined her reputation in front of the priest.

ROELLE: I had to tell. It is a sacrament.

OLGA: You could have left my name out.

PEPS: He didn't need a name.

ROELLE: I'll leave it out the next time.

HERMIONE: So, you'll be going to confession again?

PEPS: He'll learn how to do it.

HERMIONE: He can't even genuflect properly.

ROELLE: Who could compete with you!

HERMIONE: Boys never know what to do with the sacraments.

ROELLE: I went in there with the best intentions.

HERMIONE: Did you have cramps?

ROELLE: No.

HERMIONE: I wouldn't call that the proper remorse.

ROELLE: Cramps are more for girls.

HERMIONE: Did you hold the missal close to your face?

ROELLE: No.

HERMIONE: These are rules one has to follow. I'm very strict that way.

PEPS: Hermione and pious!

OLGA: She carries on with Peps long after the church bells stop ringing.

HERMIONE: Who says I have to avoid him like bad company or a sinful opportunity?

OLGA: It's not because of me.

PEPS: Be quiet. You always were the smart one.

OLGA: You have become a completely different person.

HERMIONE: He just doesn't want to anymore. He's probably found someone else.

OLGA: Then I'll send out our engagement announcements next Saturday— just so you know.

PEPS: Guess how much Hermione's dowry is worth.

OLGA: I have to stop right here. I have to wait for my beloved to recognize me.

HERMIONE: He really would be stuck with you.

PEPS: She'd have her man get up first in the morning and grind the coffee quietly.

OLGA: Mother, you told me so.

HERMIONE: That's what you get for being so smart.

PEPS: For once it didn't turn out the way she imagined it.

HERMIONE: She thought she could always get her way.

ROELLE: That's no way to treat Olga. She was a child.

OLGA: Roelle is the only one.

ROELLE (*to* HERMIONE): All of this is your viciousness.

HERMIONE (*standing next to* PEPS): Have you gawked long enough at the chemical reactions between the two of us?

ROELLE: To me, Olga has a face like John, the favorite disciple.

HERMIONE: I'll smash your stinking halo. What happened to that dog?

ROELLE: What do you know! It isn't easy to close a dog's eyes. When he howled, it felt like my own soul. Olga understood.

HERMIONE: He admitted it. You are my witnesses.

ROELLE: Bitch.

HERMIONE: I'll tell the teacher. These are bad seeds; they must be thrown out of school.

ROELLE: You have no say in that.

HERMIONE: I'm going to get him hanged today—right now. (*She exits; ROELLE follows her.*)

PEPS (*stares at* OLGA): Is it gone?

OLGA: No.

PEPS: Why not? I gave you the address of Mrs. Schnepf.

OLGA: She doesn't do it anymore.
PEPS: You lie. You haven't been there.
OLGA: Cross my heart—I was there. She refused.
PEPS: You must have acted silly.
OLGA: She said she had done time for it. They keep an eye on her. She said we couldn't pay her enough to do it.
PEPS: Then you'll have to find someone else. I don't need a child.
OLGA: You don't like me anymore.
PEPS: Do something about it, or you'll really get to know me.

* * *

SCENE 3

A deserted, tree-lined street. PROTASIUS. OLGA.
PROTASIUS: It's so strange. You, of all people, walking all alone through this deserted street.
OLGA: Hey, you are following me.
PROTASIUS: Relax, relax, Miss Olga.
OLGA: If you don't leave me alone, I'll scream.
PROTASIUS: Timidity is an urge. It rises irresistibly in certain people. Let me tell you something. If I were you, I wouldn't want to be alone with some tough, low-class fellow in this deserted street. It's different with me. You know, I am an unbloody person.
OLGA: Begging's allowed only on Fridays in this street.
PROTASIUS: Thank you very much. I am familiar with that kind of cruelty. But I am not the needy beggar you take me for. I am sent by my doctor, Mr. Haehnle, who is an important man. Handle me with care, like an egg.
OLGA: You are bothering me.
PROTASIUS: Roelle is quite attached to you. I know that. You have the most influence on him.
OLGA: If you want something from Roelle, it's Roelle you should see. Why do you bother with me?
PROTASIUS: I am forced only by necessity, Miss Olga. I shall explain patiently. Because his mother, this hardened woman, wouldn't let me near him anymore. Even though he promised.
OLGA: Why should I care?
PROTASIUS: You are a possible detour to my goal.

OLGA: I don't understand.

PROTASIUS: Detour or escape route. Because my doctor always sends me on the difficult missions, and my Doctor Haehnle is not a patient man. Now, you see, I would have told you all that nice and slow.

OLGA: Why are you after Roelle?

PROTASIUS: Because he no longer comes on his own. That's why I have to get the boy. Because he won't do it voluntarily, because he's asked so many questions, and people keep taking notes about his inner life.

OLGA: I wouldn't want a doctor looking into my life.

PROTASIUS: That's supposed to be good for the eventual healing process.

OLGA: Is something wrong with Roelle?

PROTASIUS: What have I been talking about? There is sufficient speculation, and, if it is correct, there's something not quite right with that boy.

OLGA: But he doesn't know it.

PROTASIUS: He mustn't get excited, says Dr. Haehnle. But I think that's such a general statement; it holds true for anybody.

OLGA: Then why don't you leave him alone?

PROTASIUS: Because he's let us down. He's let science down.

OLGA: I am sure Roelle has his reasons for not going.

PROTASIUS: He doesn't have the perspective for that. It's just that this is the way it works: Whenever something happens with the boy and we can observe that, he can be written about. Those are the rarest people, says Dr. Haehnle—the ones that can be written about. And, if this boy stays away out of some silly resistance, where can I get a similar substitute?

OLGA: What could he possibly have to offer to you?

PROTASIUS: You surprise me. Through your self-absorption, you can't see what's right in front of you. This boy is a dark heathen, and he's involved with magic.

OLGA: Now don't get insulting. I'm leaving.

PROTASIUS: You can't do that to us. We've barely touched the surface with that boy; that's not enough for us. We do our research on him.

OLGA: And what am I supposed to do?

PROTASIUS: Make it clear to him that he has to come, that he is doing it for science.

OLGA: That'll go to his head.

PROTASIUS: Well now, that would be an advantage.

OLGA: I don't even know what kind of a person you are and where he'd end up.

PROTASIUS: I am inseparable from my doctor. I am his headhunter and
his spy. Don't think lowly of me because of that. I get him the people
who are right for his immortal discoveries. Without me, he'd be lost, I
tell you.

OLGA: I see you are exploiting the boy.

PROTASIUS: We exploit him, and we skewer him, but we guarantee him
a kind of immortality.

OLGA: This is getting very eerie.

PROTASIUS: It's the eeriness that makes us so precise.

OLGA: I don't want to tell him, that's all. It has to be his choice.

PROTASIUS: The boy doesn't have a choice.

*   *   *

SCENE 4

Sideshow at a country fair. Behind a Gypsy cart. ROELLE, TWO ALTAR BOYS.

1. ALTAR BOY: Ingolstadt's my kind of place
    They have a fine track for a race
    But one of the horses won't move
    the other one's got a cracked hoof
    The coachman looks like an ape
    and the wheels are all bent out of shape
    And when it gets started at last
    the cart cracks right down in the dust.

ROELLE: Will you stop that stupid noise!

1. ALTAR BOY: Listen to him. We aren't supposed to breathe.

ROELLE: You know I have to prepare. I have to listen for the voice deep
in here; I have to go way inside myself.

2. ALTAR BOY: Stop showing off. You need us to hawk your audience.
Without us, no one would give a damn.

ROELLE: Well, then, it just won't happen. Because I never can tell what
day or hour the spirit'll come over me.

2. ALTAR BOY: You stay right here. No running away now. You claim
you are a real saint; now you have to prove it. That's all.

ROELLE: Angels come to me.

1. ALTAR BOY: And they shall carry you so your foot shall not hit a stone.

2. ALTAR BOY: If you have friends like that, you have to show them to poor folks like us.

ROELLE: But it doesn't always work. I never know in advance when it'll work. The angels are there, or they aren't. I can't call them down just like that. The angels have to take me by surprise.

2. ALTAR BOY: You just have to try a little harder. We've told the people, and now they want to see real angels for once.

ROELLE: You can't see angels. You can only hear them.

1. ALTAR BOY: Tell that to your audience.

ROELLE: Oh, you are blind and deaf.

2. ALTAR BOY: We don't understand you, we know.

1. ALTAR BOY: How could we understand him? We are not his disciples.

2. ALTAR BOY: We are sick and tired of piety. We have too much to do with that stuff already.

1. ALTAR BOY: Believe me, I polish off the sacred wine in one move. (*makes gesture of drinking*) Because an altar boy knows what tastes good.

2. ALTAR BOY: Dominus your biscuit.

1. ALTAR BOY: What would they do without us?

ROELLE: I'll pray for you to figure it out . . .

2. ALTAR BOY: Karl, we are being transfigured. Let us give up to him our own holy spirit, our alcoholic spirit.

ROELLE: Have you ever heard of the active power of love?

2. ALTAR BOY: I don't get to the movies. My father takes the money I make as an altar boy.

ROELLE: It changes you. Beyond recognition.

2. ALTAR BOY: Is that so?

ROELLE: Saulus becomes Paulus.

2. ALTAR BOY: That's not too visible in you. I'd say you got worse.

ROELLE: What do you think the old Roelle would have done?

1. ALTAR BOY: He'd have taken off and yelled from behind a street corner, "They are all too low for me."

ROELLE: And the new Roelle?

1. ALTAR BOY: What does he do?

ROELLE: He stands right in front of you, looks you up and down, and says yes; he says, you are the poor in spirit.

2. ALTAR BOY: It is exactly the same in my book. Because you are proud and we are too low for you.

OLGA (*coming around the cart*): I've been running all over the fair grounds.

1. ALTAR BOY: I almost whistled just now.

2. ALTAR BOY: A candle's lit on the second floor
        She might slip in her slip and slip through the door.
OLGA: Roelle, come on, let's go behind the cart.
2. ALTAR BOY: What if we come with you behind the cart?
ROELLE (*to* OLGA): No one'll hurt you.
1. ALTAR BOY: Isn't she the bashful one.
2. ALTAR BOY: She needs to be pushed into it; that's when she gets hot.
ROELLE: Go, hide; I see the glow in her face.
OLGA: In mine?
ROELLE: One can die from it. The light from heaven.
2. ALTAR BOY: You can't fool us, you crazy devil.
1. ALTAR BOY: Religious maniac!
2. ALTAR BOY: You can't sell her to us for an angel. She's known all
    over town.
ROELLE: She's come for me. Be reasonable. Leave us alone, will you.
1. ALTAR BOY: She's come for him. And what do poor altar boys get?
2. ALTAR BOY: Come on, Karl, let them flirt. It doesn't matter.
1. ALTAR BOY: Let's get out of here.
2. ALTAR BOY: But we won't go far. We'll keep you under observation,
    you understand. You know what's waiting for you.
ROELLE: Fine with me.
2. ALTAR BOY: Ding dong klick klick
        the priest fell sick
        the sexton rings the bell
        the billy goat starts to yell
        meh meh meh
(*The* ALTAR BOYS *exit.*)
OLGA: I've come.
ROELLE (*strokes* OLGA's *forehead and face*): You must be completely open
    to me. You must respond to the most subtle emotional signals coming
    from me.
OLGA: I thought there was more to the story.
ROELLE: Would you like to become a saint?
OLGA: Come on!
ROELLE: Do what I tell you.
OLGA: But I don't want to.
ROELLE: It's too much for you; I can see that.
OLGA: Most people don't want to be completely open to another person.

ROELLE: Still, we are together, aren't we?

OLGA: Just don't think there is more to it. (*She watches him.*)

ROELLE: Your unrelenting scrutiny is about to wreck my mood.

OLGA: I have eyes. Can't I look?

ROELLE: But you are putting me in a bad mood.

OLGA: I look at that twist in your face.

ROELLE: One can't choose one's face.

OLGA: I say there's something not quite right about you.

ROELLE: What's not quite right about me?

OLGA: That's how physiognomy works. The instincts show right up there, even though they're hidden.

ROELLE: I never noticed that.

OLGA: Why don't you move? You are like an animal that pretends to be dead.

ROELLE: I'm always clumsy before such sharp eyes.

OLGA: You have to move; your movements will show me what I don't yet know.

ROELLE: When you stare at me that way, I can't think my own thoughts.

OLGA: Then I don't know if I should sit down with you at all. I want to find out something.

ROELLE: Who or what am I to you?

OLGA: That shouldn't matter to you.

ROELLE: But it does matter to me.

OLGA: You were right about Peps. He doesn't like me anymore. He is getting so mean.

ROELLE: He is no great loss.

OLGA: But I'm having a child.

ROELLE: That's the way it is.

OLGA: My belly's getting fat.

ROELLE: You mustn't abort it. The child is already alive, even though it isn't conscious.

OLGA: Thou shalt not kill.

ROELLE: That's what I thought. The child was created in love. Perhaps it's a beautiful child.

OLGA: Most certainly.

ROELLE: It should be allowed to live, even if it isn't beautiful.

OLGA: But what am I supposed to do?

ROELLE: You won't let me help you. Even if you don't want to admit it,

I am the important man in your life. Do as I tell you. You have to go
to the country, before it shows. You have to give birth to the child where
nobody will know you.

OLGA: That costs money.

ROELLE: I guarantee you, I'll come up with the money.

OLGA: You?

ROELLE: I'd love to have a beautiful child.

OLGA: You don't have to have it.

ROELLE: But I want to have it.

OLGA (*bitter*): And me with it.

ROELLE: It shouldn't turn out like its father.

OLGA: You are meddling in something—

ROELLE: By it becoming human, it makes humans of us.

OLGA: A person can't lean on anyone else. It won't do any good. (*She
runs off.*)

ROELLE: That isn't true at all!

MOTHER (*enters with a soup container*): I finally caught up with you,
spoiled brat. You just do what I tell you now.

ROELLE: You can't come after me with your stupid soups. You don't know
what that does to me. Let me tell you slowly.

MOTHER: You eat now. I have to tell you that every Thursday! You don't
just leave your oatmeal soup. You can sit here for an hour; I won't leave
till it's gone.

ROELLE: Mama, I'm trying, but I really don't feel like it at all.

MOTHER: And that delicious egg in there. Do I have to force it into you?

ROELLE: The way you treat me today.

MOTHER: Just wait, I'll lock you up in the cellar and let you scream there.

ROELLE: That's a classic threat. Look, Mama, now can you see how I force
myself? But that's for the pigs! It's cold.

MOTHER: I poured it in here the way you left it. Eat it now.

ROELLE: And that's supposed to make me strong?

MOTHER: Do I have to count? (*She takes the spoon and feeds him.*) There,
this one is for Saint Joseph; this one is for your dead little sister. Now
close your eyes. This one is for your guardian angel; you never know
when you'll need him. This one is for all the poor souls in purgatory—

ROELLE: Man doesn't have to eat.

MOTHER: How are you going to grow up? You'll starve to death.

ROELLE: Maybe that's what I want.

MOTHER: You abuse yourself. I'd be scared, too.

ROELLE: It *is* pretty scary.

MOTHER: They should've never thrown you out of school. It's eating inside you.

ROELLE: I do what I must do.

MOTHER: You got that from your father. Jesus, Jesus! I'm just a simple woman.

ROELLE: The teachers decided together that I am no good.

MOTHER: As if others don't get into trouble when they are young! It's something to outgrow.

ROELLE: I'm the only one they are after; the others get away with it. I don't know why.

MOTHER: It is unfair, son.

ROELLE: They said I'm a pest.

MOTHER: Don't take it to heart so much.

ROELLE: I'm not a pest. They'll see.

MOTHER: We are not the dregs.

ROELLE: And they don't know it all. They'll be surprised.

MOTHER: There are schools in other towns. I'll just have to spend the money. I'll send you to a boarding school.

ROELLE: I don't want to go to a boarding school.

MOTHER: But you can't finish here. You need to finish.

ROELLE: I want to stay here. Olga hasn't left either.

MOTHER: You'll drive yourself completely crazy over that person. Do you want to cut off your life?

ROELLE: Nothing comes easy with me. The crown of thorns is for me. I know that.

MOTHER: So get pricked. Really work on it! See if you like it!

ROELLE: You can't follow me, woman. I'm telling you, something is calling me.

MOTHER: Son, just don't go too far.

ROELLE: They'll see. I'll pull myself up by my own hair from the bottom of the swamp.

MOTHER: There are no miracles. Everything advances step by step.

ROELLE: They don't know who I am. Maybe I've made up my mind to become a saint.

MOTHER: Keep dreaming!

ROELLE: That's right. One just has to think big. And then one has to do something about it. Others have done it, why shouldn't I?

MOTHER: You do that!

ROELLE: One just has to have willpower when it gets difficult. Not eating, for example.

MOTHER: Not eating, not eating! Until light can shine right through you? Until you get every possible illness? Who'll want you then?

ROELLE: You have to eat so little that supernatural visions will come in bright daylight.

MOTHER: I don't think that's healthy. I think it's dangerous.

ROELLE: It can be done. I've tried it, and it's possible. It pushes you beyond your limits.

MOTHER: Aren't you terrified of your own daring?

ROELLE: It is terrifying. That's why I stopped.

MOTHER: You see.

ROELLE: But now I'm starting again. I hadn't gone far enough. I wasn't a saint yet.

MOTHER: It's gone to his head. Jesus! Jesus!

ROELLE: You can't stop me, woman.

MOTHER: Son, I don't want you to be a saint.

GERVASIUS (*appears behind the cart*): This time we caught him. He is just a mama's boy.

ROELLE: You have no business here.

GERVASIUS: You should know. I am everywhere.

ROELLE: You're shortsighted. You didn't see everything.

GERVASIUS: I've been standing back there the whole time, and I enjoyed it. This one is for Saint Joseph—just keep working on your willpower.

ROELLE: I don't want to say what you are.

GERVASIUS: So what am I?

ROELLE: You are a misguided soul.

GERVASIUS: I kept thinking, Should I come out and embarrass the boy for all eternity? At first I felt sorry for you, but then I felt more like embarrassing you.

ROELLE: That shows your filthy character.

GERVASIUS: Because now I can tell it in the schoolyard, where you find the better boys. I have a notion those boys will show no mercy to a mama's boy. One more spoonful. That one's for your guardian angel; you never know when you'll need him.

ROELLE: Go ahead, run to your dirty schoolyard. They all know who you're after. I can also hint to the police what you're up to, and they'll be waiting for you.

GERVASIUS: You'll have to prove it first. (*He exits.*)

ROELLE: Gone—like a skunk.

MOTHER: Jesus, I got the shivers.

ROELLE: You see now how embarrassing you are?

MOTHER: Yes, and I stood there like eternal misery in pain and remorse.

ROELLE: Are you going to chase me with that soup again?

MOTHER: I'm cleaning it up, I am. I suppose this is the cross I have to bear. (*She exits.*)

ROELLE: Now let's get ready for sainthood. I get stuck all the time.

CLEMENTINE (*comes around the cart*): I would have talked to Mrs. Roelle, but she was all confused. She didn't even see me.

ROELLE: My mom is quite peculiar about whom she does and doesn't see.

CLEMENTINE: Not with me. She once said, Clementine, should there ever be something going on between you and my son, I would have nothing against it because you are such a hard-working girl, and that is like a capital investment. She is right. The entire household rests on my shoulders.

ROELLE: Well, I pay a lot of attention to my mother's judgment. I tell you, she lived and learned.

CLEMENTINE: She has lived her life, and that's what I want to do too. How did Olga's bow get here?

ROELLE: The wind blew it.

CLEMENTINE: It wasn't the wind. That's her wide one, and it's not ripped. I don't understand you. You're after her. How someone can be so wrong about a person!

ROELLE: I wasn't following her; she came on her own. And she also left on her own.

CLEMENTINE: I must say, Olga is something. And I feel sorry for anyone who is after her. From the side she looks like a man.

ROELLE: You see everything.

CLEMENTINE: You've known me since I was a child. Now that you're a man, you can't play stranger with me.

ROELLE: I'd never compare you to your sister.

CLEMENTINE: I have to get away from home. It's no place for me.

ROELLE: I'm not the dregs. I can show myself to a woman.

CLEMENTINE: You'll know yourself who is better for you. Olga can only lead to misery.

ROELLE: Just let me get through this day.

CLEMENTINE: You won't regret it.

1. ALTAR BOY: It's time: People are waiting for your appearance.

ROELLE: Out of the question.

2. ALTAR BOY: Some people were inclined to call it a hoax, but I got them inspired.

1. ALTAR BOY: Hermione Seitz complains the loudest.

CLEMENTINE: What's he gotten himself into now?

ROELLE: We won't tell.

2. ALTAR BOY: He didn't elaborate for the other one either.

1. ALTAR BOY: He just means that you're already the second one today.

2. ALTAR BOY: The face she made, she should get stuck with it. (CLE-MENTINE *exits*. ROELLE *tries to leave*.) Don't let him get away. Roelle tries to avoid the crowds.

ROELLE: Now we're getting somewhere. I'm being assaulted.

1. ALTAR BOY: You must go there.

2. ALTAR BOY: You are the beginning of everything.

ROELLE: I'm not prepared.

2. ALTAR BOY: Think up something on your way over.

1. ALTAR BOY: Your followers want to welcome you; your enemies do too.

2. ALTAR BOY: You can't run away.

1. ALTAR BOY: Your Olga's waiting there, craning her neck.

2. ALTAR BOY: Your teachers are standing there, your classmates.

1. ALTAR BOY: And they all want to see what you have in store for them.

ROELLE: Have you drawn the chalk circle?

1. ALTAR BOY: We forgot.

ROELLE: First a chalk circle must be drawn because I have to step inside it.

2. ALTAR BOY: It will be done as soon as you get there.

ROELLE: And you expect it to work that way? Does everyone know that they can't talk to me?

2. ALTAR BOY: Let's go.

ROELLE: You can lift your hand like this. It can also be lifted like that.

1. ALTAR BOY: You want to show yourself like that? Good luck.

ROELLE: I call it an unusual posture.

(*A few students pass by.*)

1. STUDENT: We came the wrong way.

2. STUDENT: This way. You can go through this way.

3. STUDENT: Half the school's supposed to be there.

(*They exit. Some girls pass by.*)

1. GIRL: Here's one who believes it.

2. GIRL: They are not like other people. They don't live long, people say.

3. GIRL: Come on, I see him every day walking by the ravine.

2. GIRL: The organs, the inner organs can't take it.

(*The girls exit. A student comes around the cart.*)

STUDENT: They don't want to wait any longer. When is this odd savior supposed to come?

2. ALTAR BOY: We have to walk him around the square three times so he can concentrate.

1. ALTAR BOY: Three is the sacred number

(*The student exits.* PROTASIUS *and* GERVASIUS *pass by.*)

PROTASIUS: What do you call it, whatever it is Roelle is doing?

GERVASIUS: Don't start with Roelle, or I'll get nasty. That rotten bastard with his spiritism!

PROTASIUS: What did you say? Say it for me one more time.

GERVASIUS: Spir-it-ism.

PROTASIUS: Aha!

GERVASIUS: It's got nothing to do with alcohol. That man'll think up any obscenity.

PROTASIUS: Half a year ago someone did that kind of nonsense in the beerhall, just to make something happen on the podium. I assume that's where he got it. It's something with ghosts. They materialize, you understand.

GERVASIUS: That's too esoteric for me.

PROTASIUS: They look out of the medium, they look out of his throat and tell you things you don't know yourself. And you have to believe them; otherwise, the ghosts will strangle you.

GERVASIUS: And that's what Roelle is trying to imitate?

PROTASIUS: You can get famous that way. All you need is someone from the university to get interested, and he'll make something out of you.

GERVASIUS: You're kidding.

PROTASIUS: And you're jealous of the boy. I can see it.

GERVASIUS: That fellow should be arrested. I'll arrest him right now.

PROTASIUS: I doubt you can get away with it.

GERVASIUS: Have you never read in the papers: The perpetrator, showing signs of mental disturbance, was taken into custody?

PROTASIUS: Do you have a stamped photograph?

GERVASIUS: I've never needed one.

PROTASIUS: If you don't have a stamped photograph, you can't arrest anybody.

GERVASIUS: Says who?

PROTASIUS: You have to show it every time you do something in the name of the law; otherwise, the police'll get you.

GERVASIUS: It's really a strange thing, your education.

PROTASIUS: And then you need handcuffs that lock automatically because he isn't going to come with you voluntarily.

GERVASIUS: Wouldn't you know! I'd have arrested him.

(*They exit. Unrest and voices.*)

1. VOICE: Where is our promised angel? Let's get that angel up here.

2. VOICE: We want to see that angel.

MANY VOICES: Get that angel! Get that angel!

2. ALTAR BOY: They're ready. Let's go. Throw yourself among them.

ROELLE: I can't. I can't.

2. ALTAR BOY: You have to.

1. ALTAR BOY: I'll die laughing. What a fiasco!

(*The* ALTAR BOYS *drag* ROELLE, *who is behind the cart trying to resist, up onto the platform.*)

2. ALTAR BOY (*offstage*): Ladies and gentlemen, in these times of unbelief, an ordinary young man managed to make contact with real angels. Let me introduce to you a man who is visited by his angel, just like that. Without charging you admission and only to shake up the skeptics, to shatter the nonbelievers, my man here will show you this creature from heaven. May I have your utmost attention? I ask you not to startle this man with shouts or cheers; they could cause a fatal crash. Contact with an angel is life-threatening.

VOICE: He's sweating already.

VOICES: Shhh.

2. ALTAR BOY: Quiet back there. Absolute quiet. Otherwise, he can't get hypnotized. It's difficult.

VOICE: Be quiet, he's becoming hypnotized.

VOICE: But we don't see anything.

VOICE: Quiet, it's coming.

VOICE: Stupid tricks.

VOICE: Just hands and feet.

VOICE: He stands there like an idiot.

VOICE: What a flop.

VOICE: Swindler. Cheat. Police.

VOICE: What he is doing is a sacrilege.

VOICE: It's the devil in him.

VOICE: Down with him.

VOICE: Stone him.

VOICE: Watch me stone him.

(*Rocks are thrown. Some roll under the cart.*)

VOICE: I hit him.

VOICE: He's dead.

VOICE: Everything's just hocus-pocus.

(*Some students pass by.* OLGA *tries to pull* ROELLE *away.*)

Intermission.

* * *

SCENE 5

BEROTTER's *house. Balcony between two buildings.* ROELLE *wears a bandage.*
OLGA, CLEMENTINE, CHRISTIAN, PEPS, HERMIONE. *They are drinking wine.*

PEPS: Maybe he finally learned his lesson.

HERMIONE: Not him. If anything, he'll get worse.

ROELLE: I am different. I stand out in a crowd.

PEPS: Just don't come to me when you've hit rock bottom.

ROELLE: It turned out I have a few followers.

PEPS: More enemies than followers.

ROELLE: That's nothing yet. There's one fellow, I just have to approach him with my slow tiger's gaze, and he turns white as a sheet.

CHRISTIAN: I'd like to know who he is.

ROELLE: Why don't you go and ask for him? His name is Crusius.

CHRISTIAN: Never.

ROELLE: Crusius fell on his knees and asked my forgiveness; he didn't recognize me.

CHRISTIAN: I don't believe it.

ROELLE: He said, Roelle, man, mercy, he said. You weren't there. That's your problem.

CHRISTIAN: Then why didn't you get your book back when he took it right from under your eyes!

ROELLE: That was when he had no idea who he was dealing with.

OLGA: You better take Roelle's word for it. You weren't there.

(CHRISTIAN *moves further away from them and sits down again.*)

HERMIONE: Oh, how precious.

PEPS: And it's such a great night for getting drunk. Cheers.

ROELLE: Olga understood me. I let them smash a hole in my head.

CLEMENTINE: Was that necessary?

ROELLE: Can you believe it? Believe it, if you can.

OLGA: With Clementine, it's just envy.

CLEMENTINE: He didn't do it for you. It was for his own self-importance.

ROELLE: Angels do come to me, but they only come in solitude. They don't come to the market.

OLGA: They don't know, that's all.

HERMIONE: We don't believe it.

OLGA: You are the stubborn ones. You'll see how you end up.

HERMIONE: How will we end up?

PEPS: We are the ones you can't scare.

OLGA: I believe in angels.

PEPS: Now look what you've done, Roelle.

OLGA: I can't bend my little finger without being watched from heaven.

PEPS: That's what you would like, wouldn't you?

CLEMENTINE: And I have to wash the dishes all by myself.

HERMIONE: We didn't see you at mass.

OLGA: I don't need to be at a specific place.

CLEMENTINE: Won't Roelle soon be fed up with Olga aping everything he says?

OLGA: My Roelle can't be shaken.

CLEMENTINE: Don't always say he's your Roelle.

OLGA: I know what I know.

HERMIONE: Oh, how precious.

CLEMENTINE: I don't want to talk about how Roelle went on about you. He wouldn't say it to your face.

ROELLE: She wants to ruin my honor.

CLEMENTINE: Even if he won't admit it afterward.

ROELLE: When did I say anything negative? Tell me now.

CLEMENTINE: I can't do it when he's looking at me so closely.

ROELLE: You better think before you say something.

OLGA (to CLEMENTINE): Big mouth!

CLEMENTINE: Which one of us is right for you? I want to know right now.

OLGA: Clementine, you never run after anyone who doesn't pay attention to you.

CLEMENTINE: I know, because my hands are rough; I have to stick them in cold water. I'd like to see Olga do that.

CHRISTIAN: Look what he did to you.

CLEMENTINE: I've had enough. Always Olga. Mother, when she was still alive, always favored you.

CHRISTIAN: Hush now, not in front of strangers.

HERMIONE: I won't tell.

CLEMENTINE: They always go after me. Christian and Olga and the rest. Now I want to talk. High school, all of that, I wasn't allowed to go.

PEPS: That's all we needed.

CHRISTIAN: Get out of here. Scram!

CLEMENTINE: I just want to cry, and you can't stop me. I'm crying.

OLGA: Come now, Clementine. Let's wash your face. They don't have to see you like that.

CLEMENTINE: I don't care. I am my own person. I stay because I want to.

OLGA: You're coming with me.

CLEMENTINE: I can't even cry. (*She exits with* OLGA.)

PEPS: Did somebody stick a fork in your fat neck?

ROELLE: Someone like her can end up a traitor. She takes one step and gets stuck in evil.

PEPS: Who doesn't?

(CLEMENTINE *and* OLGA *return.*)

OLGA: They know that Roelle's with us. When we turned on the light in the living room, they yelled up his name from the street.

CHRISTIAN: How dare they!

ROELLE: They are my adversaries.

CLEMENTINE: I won't leave through the front door. They'll break our windows too.

PEPS: They'll get tired and go away.

OLGA: Do they know what they're doing?

HERMIONE: That's what you get with your Roelle.

ROELLE: Nothing will happen to you.

CLEMENTINE: Don't stand there as if you're at home here. It would be better for you to leave now.

ROELLE: You can't chase me away like a dog. I let them smash a hole in my head.

HERMIONE: Let's put three fingers in it. He's got a wound, that's his excuse.

PEPS: We don't want to know any of that. We have no use for someone like him.

ROELLE: That's even better. You'll pretend I don't exist.

OLGA: God, I've had enough. I can't put up with him forever.

PEPS: It's up to you.

ROELLE: It's not fair how she stares right past me at a distant point. I am sick.

PEPS: Didn't you get it? We don't want anyone sick in here.

CLEMENTINE: He's turning green.

CHRISTIAN: If you're sick, go home.

ROELLE: I won't find my way all by myself. I'm dizzy.

HERMIONE: Wouldn't you be happy now if someone would hold your head up for you?

ROELLE: I won't be able to make it.

OLGA: Lie down if you feel sick.

CLEMENTINE: No, take him away. Get him out of my sight.

OLGA: Not me.

HERMIONE: We don't want to touch him.

PEPS: He has lost a lot of blood. Maybe it's too much.

CLEMENTINE: Sit up, you! Sit up, will you?

ROELLE: I didn't come here for your pity.

CLEMENTINE: I can't stand the sight of this man!

ROELLE: I have my weaknesses, and I always have to defend myself because of them. Look, among other things, I am afraid of water. I can't go in. I get nauseated. I have to cover my mouth when the water rises up my body.

OLGA: I find that quite disgusting.

HERMIONE: I can't stop laughing.

ROELLE: If she won't look at me, I won't let her go to the country.

PEPS: You don't even have the money.

ROELLE: Who wants some? Who needs some? (*He shows them his money.*)

PEPS: You stole that from your mother's store.

ROELLE: It's not stolen. Besides, the store's in our house.

PEPS: That's called a double theft.

OLGA: And you come to me and make me accept stolen money.

CHRISTIAN: He pulled it off pretty well.

OLGA: I am going to take it back to your mother.

ROELLE: Then I'll tell her it was you who took it out of her cash register. She'll believe it on the spot.

OLGA: I'm cutting off our relationship. You are bad company. (*She starts to leave.*)

ROELLE: That's one of those classic lines. I know it well.

OLGA: Do you know who you're talking to? (*She stops.*)

ROELLE: I'll be seeing you again. You are no different than I.

OLGA: I'm much better.

ROELLE: How did you do it? Stand there right in front of me waiting for me to have a seizure.

OLGA: Because I collect people like that.

ROELLE: If it were up to you, I might as well have died.

OLGA: To me you aren't human. You haven't got the nerve for it.

ROELLE: I made up the thing with my nerves, so I can just as easily take it back again.

OLGA: Oh? So there is nothing wrong with you?

(PROTASIUS *and* GERVASIUS *enter.*)

PROTASIUS: Looks like another eating and drinking orgy.

PEPS: Who let you in?

PROTASIUS: I am supposed to act as a kind of carrier for the sick man.

GERVASIUS: I am the other one. I help him carry.

ROELLE: No one's sick here.

PROTASIUS: I am delighted that things took care of themselves.

GERVASIUS: How come your head is bleeding?

ROELLE: I am not the one you are looking for.

PROTASIUS: You are a damned provocation.

ROELLE: I have recanted. You must leave me alone.

PROTASIUS: You can't get away from us. We come flying. We come swimming, if need be. But let there be no need for force.

GERVASIUS: Let the insects live, even if they sting you.

PROTASIUS: You wouldn't want a corpse in the gulley.

ROELLE: I won't let myself be kidnapped. I'm not coming. I'm not walking into your trap.

PROTASIUS: You have to do it voluntarily.

ROELLE: I'll never come with you again.

PROTASIUS: We know too much. Did I ever tell you, brother, how you can alter the sex of your children?

GERVASIUS: I don't want any children, and you are not my brother. You are only my tormentor.

PROTASIUS: That's what you need. If you don't want to know, I'll tell this gentleman, who isn't as tough with me and who, I hear, plans to get married.

PEPS: I'm interested.

PROTASIUS: I'll make it short and intimate: If you're really hot for your lady, it'll be a girl. That's because you'll be with her too much. A boy comes only after a longer period of abstinence. Abstinence regulates the sexes.

PEPS: I am converted. Let's drink to that.

PROTASIUS: I call such voluntary conversions a sign of intellectual adaptability. And, I say, without this kind of adaptability man is lost altogether. Take me, for example, where would I be if I weren't so adaptable, intellectually? You'd be able to look right through me for reasons of nutrition. But that's not the case. Come along, brother.

GERVASIUS: I am not your brother. I'm fed up. This town has nothing left to offer me. I've done most of it.

PROTASIUS: You've lasted a long time, all things considered.

GERVASIUS: You can't make things up about me, you snoop.

PROTASIUS: It's your own fault. You're colorless. You bore me. You're getting old. You have no more new ideas. You're too ordinary. Nobody'll shed a tear for you.

GERVASIUS: You all sucked me dry like vampires. And then you dumped me.

PROTASIUS: You're like the dirt on the road. Invisible. You're too ordinary.

GERVASIUS: You took all the pleasure out of me. I feel empty.

PROTASIUS: You have to do the taking. That's what counts. But you don't take anymore.

GERVASIUS: I still take the boys.

PROTASIUS: They don't need what's left of you. You are finished, finished, finished. You better hang yourself. Come on, you half-corpse.

GERVASIUS: I'm not your corpse either.

(PROTASIUS *and* GERVASIUS *exit.*)

PEPS: I don't trust these men.

HERMIONE: I can't see straight anymore. Maybe they weren't even here.

ROELLE: You just can't get involved with them. I know that. It's best to stay away from them.

CLEMENTINE: Would you prefer someone shy?

ROELLE: I don't like such general questions.

CLEMENTINE: Do you know how to convert a person even if he's very difficult?

ROELLE: I wanted to, many times. But how could I succeed with another if it doesn't even work on me?

CLEMENTINE: What if the two of us stick together really tight?

ROELLE: It can't come from the outside. The real help must be inside oneself. And in my case it's just not there. They say it's the curse of this generation.

CLEMENTINE: You have to be able to wait. It takes a long time to develop.

ROELLE: Just try it with confession. You confess the same thing over and over again. I've stopped believing in a movement upward a long time ago. It might even be better to do something really bad. Stealing, for example. And feeling good because you've stolen and you attacked somebody. And not being afraid at all because of it.

CLEMENTINE: Did you really steal?

ROELLE: As soon as I begin to comprehend what a person really is, I'd rather exit from this horrifying life. I want to renounce it.

CLEMENTINE: You can't do that, renounce something. If you've done something, it'll stay with you always, and, I say, it stares right at you.

ROELLE: That's the greatest injustice.

PEPS: I come to you with my digestive problems.

HERMIONE (*about* ROELLE): And suddenly he looks all transfigured again.

CLEMENTINE: A lot of drinking here, I see.

HERMIONE: Just pour it down your throat.

ROELLE: Are you also always feeling hot?

CLEMENTINE: That's the American heat wave.

HERMIONE: Man has five toes and one head. Man has five toes and one head.

CLEMENTINE: But man has ten toes.

HERMIONE: Man has ten toes and one head.

OLGA: Clementine, time to get ready.

CHRISTIAN: I've had it. The way Hermione carries on.

HERMIONE: I'm not a crocodile. I'm not a crocodile.

PEPS: And everything keeps turning grayer and grayer.

ROELLE: I'll take Clementine to where it is completely dark.

CLEMENTINE: Will you let your daughter attend high school?

ROELLE: I won't let you preach to me. None of you is a saint.

CLEMENTINE: We don't need Olga. In the starlight.

ROELLE: And what about your presumed innocence? You can tell me.

CLEMENTINE: A person doesn't talk about that.

ROELLE: She just does it. She's probably just like Olga.

CLEMENTINE: You'll find out soon enough.

ROELLE: First they make you do it; then they plead innocent.

CLEMENTINE: Christian, he's not nice.

CHRISTIAN: You'd better apologize.

ROELLE: She's asking for it, that's what I think. I know what you want.

CLEMENTINE: He wants to slander me right here.

ROELLE: Don't try to deny it. It's obvious.

CLEMENTINE: Then why did you follow me, and why were you mad at Olga? You made me believe it was because of your love for me.

ROELLE: It's not my fault you're so dumb.

CLEMENTINE: Did he always have his eye on her and just pretended it was me? Now you're really going to get it. He thought I wouldn't mind. You don't know me: I'll come up with something for you.

CHRISTIAN: Let's use him to set an example. I've always wanted to do that.

CLEMENTINE: We'll dump him in cold water.

ROELLE: You can't do that to me.

PEPS: Let there be enmity between you and the water.

HERMIONE: Now we've got something. Now we can really get to him.

CLEMENTINE: Someone has to keep him here. (*She exits.*)

CHRISTIAN: He knows he can't get away from us. We'll block him.

ROELLE: I don't want to, I don't want to!

CHRISTIAN: Stupid ass!

CLEMENTINE: Here's the tub. Let's take off his shoes.

HERMIONE: Why not more?

(*They start to undress him.*)

ROELLE: I'll never talk to you again.

CHRISTIAN: Look at us cry.

ROELLE: I have my guardian angel, so this foot shall not hit a stone.

OLGA: You think Olga will help? Olga won't help.

ROELLE: I seek refuge with you.

OLGA: Grab him.

ROELLE: What kind of world is this?

OLGA: The kind where your neighbor must die in misery.

ROELLE: I want to confess. I want to confess something important.

CHRISTIAN: What?

ROELLE: I am a bad person.

HERMIONE: We know that.

CHRISTIAN: You won't die, man. It's only water.

ROELLE: Hold it. I want to do it myself.

CLEMENTINE (*pushes him in*): There. Let's see you sit in there.

ROELLE: Olga shouldn't look.

PEPS: She's still getting to him. (*General sobering up. They give* ROELLE *his clothes.* CLEMENTINE *drags the tub offstage.*) Clementine disgraced herself the most.

CLEMENTINE: It's all Olga's fault.

CHRISTIAN (*to* CLEMENTINE): Because of you we have to face ourselves like this.

OLGA: We don't want to keep you in this place any longer. You probably won't mind leaving.

ROELLE: I was naked, and you did not give me any clothes. You have poured your scorn over me, and now it stares you in the face.

OLGA: Oh, that we fall every day into a world of viciousness, just as we fell into our bodies, and now we're stuck with them.

BEROTTER (*enters*): Are you leaving, Mr. Roelle?

ROELLE: I had a sweater.

BEROTTER: Now *he* wants to leave too. Look at me, children, is there something wrong with my suit? I was at the Café Ludwig, but I left right away. People gave me such strange looks and moved away from me. Then one after the other paid and left. Did anything happen?

OLGA: Father, I have something to tell you. I am expecting a child.

BEROTTER: Christ in heaven! (*He collapses.*)

PEPS: That's such a sad thing to hear about a daughter.

HERMIONE: Someone help me hold him.

CLEMENTINE: Let's go inside, but without Olga.

OLGA: Now he's having a fit again.

PEPS: I begin to understand: This man doesn't have a chance today.

OLGA: You don't have to come after me. I'm going to the quarry. (*She exits.*)

*　*　*

SCENE 6

Meadow at the bank of the Danube. PROTASIUS, GERVASIUS.

PROTASIUS: Olga Berotter, much to her credit, went into the water. But Roelle, in an incomprehensible bout of whatever, pulled her out.

GERVASIUS: You don't say.

PROTASIUS: I stood at the bank. I even helped with the final pull. I showed myself to be human.

GERVASIUS: Makes me sick to my stomach just hearing about it.

PROTASIUS: Afterward she got mad at both of us.

GERVASIUS: The thanks you get.

PROTASIUS: She wanted to drown herself to get away from it all, but Roelle wouldn't let her. She won't forgive him for that.

GERVASIUS: No sense of reality. And it's guys like us who could easily pay the price for it.

PROTASIUS: We simply can't be good. It always backfires.

GERVASIUS: It doesn't suit us.

PROTASIUS: We aren't cut out for it.

GERVASIUS: It fails automatically.

PROTASIUS: A tiny lapse, so easily avoided.

GERVASIUS: We can make up for it pretty fast.

PROTASIUS: That's why I got my story in the paper. I do things in writing now.

GERVASIUS: You—that's all they need there.

PROTASIUS: Don't say that. I have a domed brain; that's a sure sign.

GERVASIUS: They'll chase you to hell soon enough.

PROTASIUS: So I went with an empty stomach to the local news desk. The fellow who sits there never knows where to get the news for his column. I say to him, you have no information about the nocturnal drama at the quarry, but I was there. And here's the story, signed: A lifesaver. That's me, I say, and another fellow.

GERVASIUS: Was he thankful?

PROTASIUS: Oh yes. But it still has to pay off.

GERVASIUS: Did you name names?

PROTASIUS: That's the nice thing about papers: You can intimate that it was someone, and that someone can do nothing about it. The news has already hit the stands.

GERVASIUS: That's sure awful for the Berotter girl.

PROTASIUS: I'll say. Reading that about oneself! Now I'll make myself at home with the local newsman and work as his informer as well.

GERVASIUS: But never again as a lifesaver.

PROTASIUS: I have to stay alive for my reports. Anyway, I am not one for big gestures. To me it's more of an inner thing.

(PROTASIUS *and* GERVASIUS *exit.* CRUSIUS, FIRST STUDENT, *and* ROELLE *enter from the other side.*)

CRUSIUS: You forget that to your former classmates you are an outcast.

ROELLE: I gave you money. Every time I saw you.

CRUSIUS: Don't tell me you wanted to buy me.

ROELLE: I don't want to offend you, but you have to do something for me.

CRUSIUS: I already do you a favor by taking it.

ROELLE: But I have to steal it out of my mother's cash register. That's a real problem for me.

CRUSIUS: We just don't like you. You are not like everyone else.

ROELLE: How am I supposed to be?

FIRST STUDENT: What kind of face did they stick on your skull? The way he dangles his paws gets me in a rage.

ROELLE: I am not aware of it. I don't know what I do with them. I would change it, really. I just don't notice.

FIRST STUDENT: Wouldn't do any good. You are who you are.

ROELLE: I don't like being an outcast. I'll do anything if you take me back again.

CRUSIUS: Anything? Really?

(ROELLE *nods*.)

FIRST STUDENT: Now hold it. Not so fast.

ROELLE: And you will take me back eventually?

CRUSIUS: I'm already doing the best I can.

FIRST STUDENT: But we aren't impressed. To us you are not a man.

ROELLE: I am the father.

CRUSIUS: I told them already. But they don't like it so much.

FIRST STUDENT: A woman's slave. That's what he turned into. That's something to brag about!

ROELLE: She eats out of my hand.

FIRST STUDENT: We'd need a demonstration.

ROELLE: Shall I bring you the girl, so you can try her out yourself? It's nothing to me: I wave; she comes.

CRUSIUS: Would you spit at her in front of me to pay your way back in?

ROELLE: Will you sit down and break bread with me?

CRUSIUS: You'll be just like one of us.

ROELLE: I have to buy my way in. It's the only way.

CRUSIUS: You are exactly who I think you are.

FIRST STUDENT: Unbelievable. So this Berotter girl puts up with everything from you.

ROELLE: And she knows why.

FIRST STUDENT: She always acted so smart. Now she's got a child from someone like you.

ROELLE: You said it. I am the father.

FIRST STUDENT: You're in real trouble if you're telling stories.

ROELLE: I don't lie.

CRUSIUS: Can it be true? He's starting to cry.

ROELLE: I hate myself. You drag me down.

CRUSIUS (*referring to money in* ROELLE's *pockets*): You got some more in there? Give it here. And don't say I robbed you.

(OLGA *is being chased in the distance. She has been hiding outside for a few days now. Sound of whistles and shouts; someone cries, "Hold her!" A few students enter.*)

FIRST STUDENT: The twelfth-graders have caught her.

CRUSIUS: You hear that? Everything's ready. You don't even have to bring her yourself.

(*More students come running in.*)

FIRST STUDENT: Now we'll cast her out. Let's stand right here.

(*Other students drive* OLGA *and encircle her. Whenever she tries to push through, they push her back.*)

FIRST STUDENT: You can't pass through here, noble virgin.

SECOND STUDENT: Now you can take a good look at her.

THIRD STUDENT: Have you dried off from your swim?

FIRST STUDENT: Olga Berotter was stung by a wasp.

OLGA: Make room. I have to get through.

THIRD STUDENT: You want to see your Daddy, after you ran away from him and became the talk of the town.

FIRST STUDENT: Honeyman, the Turk will marry anyone. He needs no ad in the papers.

OLGA: Why don't you go home where you belong?

THIRD STUDENT: Is that the way to treat us?

OLGA: How do you treat me!

FIRST STUDENT: She belongs to Roelle.

SECOND STUDENT: Nothing's too disgusting for her.

FIRST STUDENT: She'll be cast out, just like him. Then they'll see what they've got in each other.

SECOND STUDENT: Maybe she doesn't even like him that much.

THIRD STUDENT: She let him sting her, didn't she?

FIRST STUDENT: From now on you'll always be alone. There'll be no girlfriend to keep you company.

THIRD STUDENT: They'd be afraid to come with you.

OLGA: You have no right to do that.

FIRST STUDENT: We just made it our right.

CRUSIUS: You deserve to be spat at. Now let's have the two confront each other. (*He drags* ROELLE *in front of* OLGA.)

OLGA: What's he up to now?

CRUSIUS: Look up to your special lady, if she can stomach you.

OLGA: You dragged me down with you.

ROELLE: Then pull me up to you.

OLGA: Get your nails out of my feet.

ROELLE: These are the only feet that get me on the ground. I want to lie right here. You don't need to kneel. You are forgiven for everything.

OLGA: I don't belong to him; he won't let me go. You can see that. Get him off me. I don't want him.

FIRST STUDENT: I am beginning to have my doubts.

ROELLE: I am not the father. That's the truth.

CRUSIUS: So you made it all up? You just wait!

ROELLE: I'll never say it again.

CRUSIUS: What you went through so far was only a harmless beginning.

OLGA: He pulled me out of the water, as if I haven't been through enough, and now he's like this. He couldn't let me out of my misery, and he plotted it all to the last detail. You should have let me float, let the water flow through my teeth. I knew why I went in. Everything would be over now. You too.

FIRST STUDENT: She doesn't belong to him. So we have nothing to do with her either.

SECOND STUDENT: You can have your brat with anyone else, we don't care. But don't get involved with him, or *you'll* get it too.

(STUDENTS *and* CRUSIUS *exit.*)

OLGA: And so it came to pass: I've seen him among his own. Yes, indeed.

ROELLE: Don't leave. I'll scream.

OLGA: Go ahead, scream.

ROELLE: I'm going to hold on right there. And here—here's a knife. (ROELLE *hands her the knife.*) Stab me until my eyeballs turn upward for good.

OLGA: Annihilation.

ROELLE: Salvation.

(OLGA *hesitates, then she throws away the knife.*)

OLGA: On a heap of revulsion we have mounted two faces so that they shall stare at each other for all eternity.

ROELLE: Can't you ever give me relief?

OLGA: Take your evil wishes off my branded face.

ROELLE: Kneel down.

OLGA: No.

ROELLE: Wait, I'll get you by the throat. I'll make you scream.

OLGA: No.

ROELLE: One nice word, just once. Nice Roelle, good Roelle, say it. Nod. You can't even nod. Nothing. Roelle! What do you expect?

OLGA: The only excuse I have for you is that I am right with you on the same level of purgatory.

ROELLE: I'm not the man who praises the Lord just for the privilege to breathe next to you. I can do without your feelings for me. (*He takes back the knife.*) Whatever I would do for you, you wouldn't care. For you I am scum. But I'll get you. I'll get you. If the priest's hands are too hairy, take communion with your eyes closed. From now on I'll come over you in an evil shape. You might as well know it: Angels stopped liking me a while ago; they haven't come to me in a long time.

Now I am visited by another. You'll find out soon enough who lives inside me. I am the devil. (*He points the knife at her.*)

OLGA: Animal! (*She hits him.*)

MOTHER (*enters*): Let me see her touch you in front of me.

ROELLE: Mother, can't you see you're in the way?

MOTHER: Look what you've done to him. My son is out of his mind. I saw it coming. I knew it, I, his mother. Yes.

ROELLE: This isn't meant for you. This is between us.

MOTHER: I know your "between us." And I don't like it, your "between us." I'll prevent it.

ROELLE: Mother, it's time for you to go home now.

MOTHER: Not without you, son.

ROELLE: You really are a cross to bear.

MOTHER: Look how frightened he is, and pale.

ROELLE: You're a big help! Building me up in public as this idol with a monkey face.

MOTHER: You are talking to your mother, son. Be happy you still have me.

ROELLE: I am punished enough.

MOTHER: You seduced him. It's you who dragged him into everything.

OLGA: They haven't cut his head off.

MOTHER: Who are the ones who torture my son? You're coming with me to the school right now. You'll report yourself and all the others by name.

OLGA: If you want to get names, stick to your son.

ROELLE: You won't get any names out of me.

MOTHER: Jesus, son, did they ever give you anything but bruises? But I am going to the teachers, and I'll tell them it was Boettcher and Wimmer, who will deny it, and then it'll all have to come out. I can pull that off. I'm still here to reckon with. I demand severe punishment.

CRUSIUS (*enters*): There are no informers among us. We stick together. Out of necessity.

MOTHER: You are one of them. What did you do to my boy?

ROELLE: Not he. He isn't one of them. That's Crusius. He wasn't there.

MOTHER: You are lying. What is he doing here, then?

CRUSIUS: Just passing by. That's the best way to see a lot. From a distance I thought I recognized the young lady.

MOTHER: Maybe when I'm in heaven they'll tell me what's so special about her.

CRUSIUS: Excuse me, aren't you the young lady who kept looking at me during mass?

OLGA: Don't give me your dumb talk.

ROELLE: You can see that she doesn't know him.

MOTHER: Boy crazy!—You want to get under her skirt too?

CRUSIUS: My apologies, I mistook her for someone else. It happens.

MOTHER: You didn't. She keeps her men warm, one right on top of the other.

OLGA: I don't have to listen to that.

CRUSIUS: I am quite embarrassed. I cast the wrong suspicion on the young lady.

ROELLE: So get the fastest way out. Now.

CRUSIUS: But now I do have to stay. Young lady, don't do this to me. Don't avoid my eyes. You might miss something.

OLGA: Control yourself.

CRUSIUS: There are young ladies who think every man's out to get them. What am I going to do to you, in bright gray daylight?

ROELLE: She is mine. Just so you know.

OLGA: You aren't like Roelle.

CRUSIUS: I am not like that one there. Things are different with me.

MOTHER: He just walked in, and she's throwing herself at him.

CRUSIUS: What are we doing afterward?

OLGA: I'm looking for someone who'll emigrate to America with me.

CRUSIUS: I don't quite understand—you? —To America? —That's far.

OLGA: I want to go to America because no one knows me there.

MOTHER: She should be my daughter.

(ROELLE *wants to protest.*)

CRUSIUS: If you want to be pigheaded, it won't work with me. Let me tell you right off, I believe in the spiritual strength of women.

ROELLE: What an egomaniac. If she goes with him, he'll drag her down completely.

CRUSIUS: That's no reason to shed a life-sized tear. America's no good. You weren't really serious.

ROELLE: I'd like to know how you know.

CRUSIUS: I just do. Why do you look so dazed? Cat's got your tongue?

OLGA: I should be home.

CRUSIUS: That's a revelation. So why are you standing there?

OLGA: I'm going.

MOTHER: I won't put in a good word with your father to make him let you stay.

OLGA: I can do that myself. I let him beat me. (OLGA *exits.*)

CRUSIUS: She's got airs.

MOTHER: I like how she stalks out of here and doesn't know what's in store for her at home.

CRUSIUS: She knows.

MOTHER: She might arrive just in time for a house search.

CRUSIUS: Why?

MOTHER: You may tell that to everyone. I had my suspicions about this person for a long time now. I always said, you can get in from the back. All she had to do was climb over the balcony.

ROELLE: Into our house?

MOTHER: But this time I tricked her. It was always bills. This time I wrote down the numbers, and I let the police know in advance. And I reported her too. And, sure enough, something's missing from the cash register again.

ROELLE: Mother, that was me, always. I took your money.

CRUSIUS: That's what they say.

MOTHER: God Almighty, it can't be true. My boy, what made you do it?

ROELLE: Because they're always after me. I have to give it to them.

MOTHER: I must go back right away and tell them I misplaced the money and found it. I have to make a retreat, that's all.

ROELLE: It won't do any good if Crusius tells.

MOTHER: What can he say?

ROELLE: He has the money. He took it out of my pocket.

CRUSIUS: You gave me that money.

ROELLE: You took the money. There were people who saw it.

CRUSIUS: We don't want a lying thief like you among us.

ROELLE: Then what happened to my book, which you took from my desk? I'll tell that too.

CRUSIUS: Why did you let me get away with it? Anyway, that was an experiment. (CRUSIUS *exits.*)

MOTHER: Jesus, boy, listen to me—

ROELLE: She is gone. That's my punishment. She never wants to see me again. Everybody took her away from me. You too.

MOTHER: Let her be gone.

ROELLE: I don't like you anymore. It's over between us. To me you are dead.

MOTHER: That's a sin, son.

ROELLE: To me you are dead. Let go of me.

MOTHER: He's possessed by the devil, that's what it is.

ROELLE: Yes! Make three crosses over me. Splash me with holy water from the cemetery. The devil is everywhere. Stay away! Why don't you stay away? Let go of me!

MOTHER: I don't recognize you.

ROELLE: When I die, I'll go to hell, and I'll be damned. I'll be with the devil and all the damned souls. And that will never end, never. How could there be anything more cruel than that.

MOTHER: Son, you mustn't even think such thoughts!

ROELLE: You want to know something? My God is the devil.

MOTHER: Let go of him, unclean spirit. Enter a swine, enter your swines.

ROELLE: Your prayers can't exorcise him. To hell with your prayers, whatever you're mumbling. You can't help me.

MOTHER: A priest. He must be saved. (*She exits.*)

ROELLE: I am in the state of mortal sin. I must confess. I've learned how, but I don't remember. I forgot how to do it. (*He takes out a piece of paper and reads from it.*)

"I, poor sinner, accuse myself in front of God Almighty and you, reverend fathers, that since my last confession how many months ago I have committed the following sins: against the fourth commandment, how many times? Against the sixth commandment, how many times?" I am afraid. "Against the seventh commandment, how many times? Against

the eighth commandment, how many times?" These are my notes to
myself. I could eat them. "Against the seven deadly sins, I ask for a
healing penance and your priestly absolution." I'll try that. (*He eats the
piece of paper.*)

The End.

Kerstin Specht

KERSTIN SPECHT WAS BORN in 1956 in Kronach, an area similar to the one in her play *Das glühend Männla* (The Little Red-Hot Man). She holds a master's degree from the University of Munich in Germanics, theology, and philosophy. In 1985, she began to study filmmaking and film theory. She has worked as an actor and as a film and television director for the Bavarian Broadcast System. *The Little Red-Hot Man* is her first play. True to the *Volksstück* tradition, the play is written in regional dialect. We have not rendered the language into a regional dialect here, since the social significations of regions differ vastly from country to country. But we have attempted to sketch in certain grammatical errors and agrarian idioms that suggest its tone. Specht's second play is entitled *Lila* (Purple). Also written in the *Volksstück* tradition, *Lila* concerns a Philippine woman who is bought in marriage by a local farmer. Specht is a new playwright, recently profiled by *Theater Heute* in their "Newly Discovered Playwrights" series. Three theaters are planning productions of *The Little Red-Hot Man* in their 1991 season.

The Little Red-Hot Man is streamlined in effect. Informed by Fleißer's work, as well as Kroetz's, Specht's *Volksstück* displays an economy of form— a minimalism in its construction. Where Fleißer develops and suggests, Specht omits or cuts off. This technique of abruptly ending the scene creates the suggestion of a tableau at each scene's conclusion. The final moment burns into the viewer's eye during the blackout. Specht's minimalism sculpts and isolates the social gesture (the *gestus*) in brief episodes. While the story unfolds, the numerous, hermetic short scenes resist the movement of the narrative, both intensifying and distancing the material.

Specht sets her play in the borderlands between the former East and West Germanies. The play begins with the image of a woman watching out her window—suggesting a domestic surveillance system that replicates the official one already in place along the border. The unfriendly face behind the curtain and the malicious phone call that opens the play are also reminiscent of an earlier "neighborly" surveillance—that of fascist times. Looking and being seen, social surveillance, is heightened by the sense of the unseen other on the other side of the border and the comparative frame for living that the border initiates. Judging appearances is a leitmotif running through the play. The mother judges the appearance of her son's girlfriend. In turn, the mother feels that her appearance, her dress, is judged badly when she goes out in public. As she internalizes the social humiliation she feels about her own public dress, she incites domestic brutality, resulting in the bound, nude image of her son.

Specht names her major characters according to their roles in the family unit: mother, son, grandmother. In this way, she foregrounds the structure of the family unit as the motor of the narrative. The divided land, the borderland, is thus internalized within the personal relations of the family. Rival systems, jealousy, competition, private property, and collective responsibility are played out around the grandmother's bed or in the image and activity of scrubbing the toilet.

Some of the most powerful scenes in the play are the grandmother's monologues. They create the sense that one can speak the internal monologue of oppression. The image of the aging woman on the border, deserted in her bedroom—the detritus of the sexual, social, and material economy—seems to most defy the dominant ideological images of how caretaking might happen in this society. The family unit, health care, and nationalist myths have nothing to offer the grandmother but abuse. Yet her strength of mind, her imagination, and her precise insight into the boy and the nurse bring a personal nobility to this character which the social order ignores.

At the other end of the generational spectrum is the young "red-hot" man, whose urgent sexuality and hopes for future employment bring him a sense of failure, bondage, and, ultimately, violence. Whereas outside of the system the grandmother can find a certain internal strength, upon entering it the young man is robbed of his dreams and self-control. The grandmother claims her own old age, while the young man loses his future. The mother stands in between, like the wall, a vector of violence and pain. Specht draws these characters in the context of the effects of pornography and other contemporary women's issues around domestic labor, ageism, class differences, and the critique of the family unit.

The title, *The Little Red-Hot Man,* is drawn from the folktale related in the play, suggesting the folk tradition as a backdrop as well as the sexual / gender politics of the male character. Yet, though Specht's play employs some traditional elements of the *Volksstück* (the use of dialect and references to folktales, for example), she reconfigures the sense of "regional" in a contemporary, political way. Specht sets up the border between the two Germanies as a kind of region with its own unique variety of village life.

The plays by Fleißer and Specht, along with the introductory material by Cocalis, organize for the reader the critical *Volksstück* as a form for the representation of women's experience within a distinctly German theatrical tradition. Readers in the United States may also find traces of this tradition in plays written after the early 1980s (when Kroetz enjoyed success in the regional theaters) which reflect this influence and translate it, in local terms, into plays for women. One excellent example is Maria Irene Fornes's play *Mud,* which sets the female protagonist within a rural, regional milieu and which utilizes short, episodic scenes, the sense of tableau, and the focus on the domestic as a site of gender / sex power relations.

Kerstin Specht

The Little Red-Hot Man

Translated by Guntram H. Weber

The play is set in the Frankenwald Forest.
Frankenwald is on the border.
The border cuts through the forest,
through the brook, through a kitchen.
The train still crosses it,
but for the people it is the
end of the line.
Many move to the city.
What remains is the subsidized border life
along the no-man's-land between East and West.

Characters

MOTHER	ANKE
GRANDMA	BERTHOLD
SON	NURSE

I
KITCHEN.

A window.
A corner bench and chairs.
A stove.
Close by: the toilet.
Everything clean and cold.

"What remains is the subsidized border life along the no-man's-land between East and West." (Photo by Max Specht.)

The MOTHER *is sitting by the window in partial shade, staring out through a pair of binoculars.*

MOTHER: The old bitch—what's she staring at
the whole day, sitting and watching.
She's even got herself a pillow.
Without a curtain, in the Lord's bright daylight.
I'll make her jump again a little.
To give her a little exercise.

(*The* MOTHER *dials a phone number, still looking through the binoculars.*)

MOTHER: Look there, look there, can't find her slippers in a hurry.
Go on, jump a little.
Make it snappy, hop to.

(*A breathless voice answers the phone.*)

VOICE: (*tentatively*) Yes. Hello.

(*The* MOTHER *is silent, then hangs up. Laughs.*)

MOTHER: Got her again, the old crow. Should get herself a longer phone cord. Wouldn't have to run so far then.

(*Blackout*)

* * *

2

KITCHEN.

The MOTHER *comes in and slams a black book on the table.*

MOTHER: That was the last time.
GRANDMA: But you don't go there for the people.
MOTHER: The way they stare at you.
When I went up for communion,
I felt their eyes on my back,
like a bunch of little pins.
Like a pin cushion, my back was covered with pins,
with a bunch
of little pins.

GRANDMA: You're worse than they are.
Sitting by the window like an owl.

MOTHER: I'm not going no more. That was the last time.

GRANDMA: With your sins, you ought to go every day.

MOTHER: I've got nothing to wear. I might as well stay in bed, anyway.

GRANDMA: All you want to do is buy, buy, buy.

MOTHER: I've got nothing else in my life.

GRANDMA: Well, Kurt only has a bare little shirt on, and he's lying in the graveyard.

(*The* MOTHER *hits her in the face.*)

(*Blackout*)

* * *

3
KITCHEN.

The MOTHER *and the* SON *at dinner. Eating silently for a long time. The* MOTHER *slices red radishes and tomatoes for him.*

SON: I ran into that guy Daddy used to work with.
Some stories he told me.

MOTHER: They're all lies. We've got no father.
You never had one.
You'd always bite me to the blood when I was nursing you.
I nursed you with my blood.
You're of my blood only.
We don't need no father.
Didn't have one myself.

SON: The other kids go to the soccer field with their father.

MOTHER: You don't need no soccer field. You won't hurt your knees; you won't tear your tendon; you won't need to go to the hospital. I bought you a flute, didn't I. Play your flute, and you won't need to play soccer.

SON: Didn't want one anyway. I'm not a girl.

MOTHER: You don't know yet what's nice. (*Strokes his hair*) You'll see how nice it is to play for me.

(*Blackout*)

* * *

4
KITCHEN.

The MOTHER *is unwrapping a chrysanthemum, rustling the paper. Wipes the dirt off the table at once.*

MOTHER: For Kurt, so folks won't say she never puts decent flowers on his grave.

GRANDMA: But there's going to be another freeze.
The flowers will go bad overnight.
You should have bought something that'll stand a frost.

MOTHER: I won't put any flowers on your grave at all.

GRANDMA: I wouldn't see them anyway.
Then I'll be rid of you for good,
that's the best thing about it.

MOTHER: Then hurry up and clear yourself out of here.

GRANDMA: The boy still needs me.

MOTHER: He doesn't need you; he's got me.

GRANDMA: But you still need my old-age pension.

MOTHER: But not you. What are you doing down here all the time.
Go up to your room and stay there.

(Blackout)

*   *   *

5
KITCHEN.

Berthold is standing in the door beaming.

BERTHOLD: From my bees. Pure natural power.

MOTHER: All right, I'll take a little bucket full again.

BERTHOLD: You got a drop?

(Sits down. The MOTHER *puts a schnapps in front of him.)*

BERTHOLD: Gunda Schmolzen just died.

MOTHER: Breast cancer?

BERTHOLD: (*nodding*) She's lying up there in the mortuary with a bald head. People say.

MOTHER: And with her going to get a permanent every week.

BERTHOLD: Are you coming to the funeral,
            her being your schoolmate?
MOTHER: That would be too hard on my nerves.
            There's this roar in my ears. At first I was thinking
            it's the cars.
BERTHOLD: Time's passing. You've got to make the best of it.
MOTHER: You get old and you get all stooped over.
BERTHOLD: Remember the two of us in the Nativity play. You being the
            angel. After church you'd let me peek under your nightie.
            Come on, what you need is a man bending you over the
            table.
            That'll revive your spirits.

(*Grasps her around the waist. The* MOTHER *screams and hits his knee with
the honey bucket as hard as she can.*)

            Ouch! You old bitch. He should have given you a decent
            beating, Kurt should have.

(*He flings the door open.*)

MOTHER: There, I'll give you your honey.

(*She hits him again.*)

BERTHOLD: No wonder your old man hanged himself.

(*He limps out.*)

(*Blackout*)

* * *

6

KITCHEN.

The MOTHER *is sitting on a kitchen chair, crying. The doorbell rings
again and again. There is a knock. She does not move.
Suddenly, the window is thrown open. The* SON *climbs through the
window, jumping onto the light floor tiles with clay-smeared shoes.*

SON: Why didn't you open the door?
            What are you crying for?

(*Crying, the* MOTHER *doesn't answer.*)

	Come on, tell me.
MOTHER:	It was . . . I've got . . . split toes. Athlete's foot.
SON:	That hurts so bad?

(*The* MOTHER *pulls him to her. Presses his head into her lap.*)

MOTHER:	Don't ever leave me. Swear to it.
SON:	Mom, I was just over at Buckreus's.
	I can't be with you all the time.
MOTHER:	Yes, you can. We're the only ones that belong together.
SON:	I'm going to bed now.
MOTHER:	Stay. I'll tell you a story.

(*The* SON *groans.*)

When I was your age, I was always afraid at night. Of ghosts. You know, for Bible class I'd always have to go past the creek. They used to say there's a horse running around there with no head and a little red-hot man. A horse white as milk. I used to laugh, but once I did see one for real. White as milk, he was.

SON:	But he did have a head?
MOTHER:	Well, yes.
SON:	Well . . . I'm going to bed now.

(*The* MOTHER *holds him by the arm.*)

| MOTHER: | I bought you your favorite juice! |

(*The* SON *exits.*)

Please!
Drink a little!

(*Blackout*)

* * *

7
KITCHEN.

The MOTHER *is sitting behind the window with binoculars. She is eating cookies.*

MOTHER: Trucking sand into his yard again.
             Building something again. The bastard.
             Won't rest a single Saturday.
             He laid those bricks for the factory owner, and he saw
             how it looks, so now he wants the same.
             And he doesn't even have a wife.
             Marble all the way down the basement steps.
             We only have bare concrete.
             Marble—could have gotten it cheap.
             What with the gravestone maker being his friend.
             But Kurt, when I married him, I knew he'd never go far,
             no farther than the bare concrete on the basement steps.
             Now he's got marble on his grave.
             As a lid. No use to nobody.

(The MOTHER *goes to the stove, puts water on, and pours a packaged soup into it. The doorbell rings. The* MOTHER *hurriedly puts the binoculars behind the curtain. At the door, a thirteen-year-old girl with a basket.)*

ANKE: Pastries.
             And my mother says hello.
MOTHER: Oh my, Anke! Going for confirmation so soon.
             You're still a right thin little girl.
             Didn't get anything for you.
ANKE: There's no need for that.

(The MOTHER *gets her purse.)*

MOTHER: Here's five marks, Anke. Buy yourself something.

*(*ANKE'*s face shows embarrassment since she was expecting more.)*

ANKE: There's no need for that.

*(*ANKE *leaves. The* MOTHER *hurries to the window and, biting into the pastry, watches the girl through the binoculars.)*

MOTHER: Some uppity name she's got. That's her mother. With her
painted face, walking around like a giraffe.
As if she was better than us.
The young one walks just the same.
Just don't stick your nose in the air too high,
or else you might fall on it.
See, there she stumbles.

(*Blackout*)

*   *   *

8

GRANDMA'S ROOM.

*Dark, old furniture. A bed, a table, two chairs. An old sideboard. A
radio. A crucifix.*

GRANDMA: Why don't you come up and see me anymore?
SON: Mom doesn't want me to.

(GRANDMA *cries.*)

GRANDMA: She's horrible!
So you don't like me anymore just because your Mom says
so.
SON: I still do. Can't you give me twenty marks, for a book?
GRANDMA: Right away. You can have it right away.
There. Fifty marks, but hold onto it.
SON: I've got to go back down.
GRANDMA: You coming to see me again?
SON: Sure.
GRANDMA: The way you used to tell stories from your books.
About the Rajas and the white tigers,
and, when we went to the basement, you'd never say,
let's go to the basement, you'd say, let's
go to the catacombs.
SON: Well, I was little then.
GRANDMA: It was so nice when you were little.
You had such pudgy little hands.
You were so nice and round.
Like a little doughnut.

SON: Got to go down, else there's bound to be trouble.

GRANDMA: The way you'd tell me everything that was in your books,
            and what you'd learnt in school.

SON: You wouldn't understand the things I'm thinking now.

(*Blackout*)

*   *   *

9
GRANDMA'S ROOM.

GRANDMA *is pouring the last coffee beans into the electric grinder, grinds
the coffee with a whirring sound.*

GRANDMA: Did you get me some coffee at the store?

SON: Didn't have no time.

GRANDMA: Take yourself some money from my purse.

(*The* SON *goes to the wardrobe, takes out some money.*)

SON: What are you sitting in the dark for?

(GRANDMA *sighs.*)

GRANDMA: Used to be, I could turn the crank on the coffee grinder
            when I had a worry.
            Now all there is is buttons.
            Buttons everywhere.
            At best, the lid will pop up.
            Otherwise, it's all automatic.
            Now they've bred back the aurochs that had died out. But
            coffee grinders have died out for good.

            Come on over here and let me give you a hug.

SON: Grandma!

GRANDMA: Just like a beetle under a stone.
            Like a stranger. Don't respond at all.

            Around her, everyone turns sour.

(*Blackout*)

*   *   *

10

GRANDMA'S ROOM.

GRANDMA *turns off the radio.*

GRANDMA: Two jet fighters crashed. Just before Easter. Another one is going to crash tomorrow. You can bet on it.
That's the way it is. But why? Do you know?
SON: No. Why?
GRANDMA: When I was little and would ask why, I was told "Just because."

(*The* SON *gets a round of sausage out of the cupboard.*)

Today is Good Friday—mustn't eat meat, only fish.
SON: Fish is meat too.
GRANDMA: There's tattletales outside. Good Friday the bells ring all the way to Rome.

(*The* SON *speaks with his mouth full.*)

SON: In the war they rang all the way to the front.
Bells ring along with anything.
GRANDMA: Is that what you learn at school?
Right bright you are, but don't you get too cocky.
That's not your father in you.
Cocky boys have a hard time getting a job.
SON: I'm gonna be a gynecologist. A doctor for women.
GRANDMA: Babyboy!

(*Blackout*)

* * *

11

GRANDMA'S ROOM.

GRANDMA *is holding a photo album on her knees.*

GRANDMA: How sweet you look in this photo.

(*The* SON *is searching her cupboard.*)

What are you looking for?

SON: Something.
GRANDMA: There's no more chocolate.
SON: What am I doing up here? With you out of everything.

(GRANDMA *sighs.*)

GRANDMA: He just loved taking pictures, your daddy did.
                Every Sunday.
                There, your mother. With a hat on.
                He was always taking pictures,
                because then everyone would smile.
                They all smile in the pictures.
                Even your mother.

SON: He took a picture of the car too.
GRANDMA: It's smiling too, because he polished it before.

(*The* SON *frowns.*)

GRANDMA: There's nothing of him. Not a single little picture.
                No wedding picture either. She burnt them all.
                I'm sorry for Kurt, I am. Poor little June bug.
                Like a June bug, he flew into the light.
                The whole village was dark when he came across
                the border.
                The only place there was a light on was in our
                house. That's where he went.
                Scared me to death knocking on the window. In his
                uniform.
                I thought, that's a Russian.
SON (*laughs*): A Russian.
GRANDMA: He stayed, and he took your mother.
                The people here, they knew her bad mouth well enough.

(*Blackout*)

*   *   *

12
GRANDMA'S ROOM.

GRANDMA *is lying on her bed. She turns the cover back, tries to get up.*
Kicks her legs awkwardly.

GRANDMA: Ouch!!

(*Holds her hip. She tries to catch hold of her stick, which is hanging on the cupboard behind her. She struggles and groans.*)

Aaaah.
Lordilord.

(*She groans and groans.*)

As if I'd been fighting someone all night.

(*When she finally catches hold of the stick, she falls off the bed with a heavy thud. She remains lying on the floor for a long time. Then she knocks on the floor with the stick. Harder and harder. Hits the enamel chamber pot, sending it spinning through the room. The* SON *is standing in the doorway.*)

SON: You're making more noise than a whole soccer team.

(*Blackout*)

* * *

13
GRANDMA'S ROOM.

GRANDMA *is sitting up in bed, leaning against two big pillows. The door opens, and a woman wearing a nurse's cap enters.*

GRANDMA: Who let you in?
NURSE: Your daughter sent me up.
GRANDMA: Pains in the hip. So bad I wouldn't wish them on my worst enemy. Can't move.
NURSE: But you've got it quite nice here.
           And you're not living by yourself, are you?
           You've got your daughter downstairs who can take care of you, right?
GRANDMA: Right, yes.
NURSE: There you see. Isn't that wonderful, having children in one's old age. I see you've got medicine. You know, I'm

	absolutely snowed under. Such bad cases and people
	without anybody to take care of them. Your case is
	different.
GRANDMA:	Uh-huh.
NURSE:	Babette Motschmann got cancer. You just touch her, and her

GRANDMA: Uh-huh.

NURSE: Babette Motschmann got cancer. You just touch her, and her bones fracture. Won't last long. She's full of water. She was supposed to get a disc X-rayed, and they happened to aim a little higher, so they saw it was all white in there. Imagine that.

And she hasn't got anyone in the world. That's the kind of burden that is on me.

But you, you've got your daughter and your grandson. He can do things for you, can't he? (*Shakes* GRANDMA*'s hand*) And keep this in mind: "Whenever I think I'm lost and alone, a light will come to guide me on."

(*Blackout*)

* * *

14
KITCHEN.

The MOTHER, *in a white gown and rubber gloves, is cleaning the toilet thoroughly and awkwardly. Scrubs so hard her head shakes with the motions. Shakes the plastic bottle.*

MOTHER: Out of cleanser again.

SON: Do you have to clean on a holiday?

MOTHER: You water the rim on holidays too, my little Peebody. Do you have to now?

SON: I have to go. Out.

(*The* MOTHER *closes the lid and sits down on it.*)

MOTHER: Stay home, won't you? That's best, isn't it?

SON: I promised.

Want to try out a new racket.

My old one is no good anymore.

MOTHER: I'll buy you one. The best.
            So you won't have to go to those strangers anymore.
            They'll come to you then
            when they need something.
SON: I'm going.
MOTHER: Bring them along, your friends.
            So I can meet them. The kind of company you keep. I can
            judge them better, you know.
            You don't know yet how mean people are.

(*Blackout*)

*   *   *

15
KITCHEN.

The MOTHER *is reading the newspaper. The* SON *is reading a book.*

MOTHER: A week ago, in Coburg, someone killed a . . . you know, one
            of those, and her ad is still in the paper.
SON: (*reads*) "Now I am dead to all desire.
            He threw it all in his big fire."
MOTHER: Don't talk like that.
SON: That's the advantage of a weekly rate.

(*The doorbell rings. The* MOTHER *answers.* ANKE *is standing in the doorway.*)

MOTHER: Well, if it isn't Anke. Come on in.

(*The* SON *stands beside* ANKE, *putting his arm around her.*)

SON: (*to* MOTHER) You wanted to meet my girlfriends, didn't you?

(ANKE *is embarrassed, laughs. The* MOTHER *gets angry.*)

MOTHER: Your male friends.
SON: Don't have any, just women.
MOTHER: Get out, you . . . peacock.
ANKE: (*hastily*) I just wanted to ask if my cat is over here . . .
            Blacky . . . , a black tom—
MOTHER: I won't have cats in my house.
ANKE: I mean, in case he happens to come by . . .
SON: He'll go some other place if he's smart.

MOTHER: And your confirmation, Anke?
             Did you get a lot?
SON: She's treating me to the movies with that money.
MOTHER: That's it today.
             All I got for my confirmation was a handkerchief. And a
             slip from my godmother, and that was one of hers.

(*Blackout*)

* * *

16
KITCHEN.

The MOTHER *is wearing multicolored curlers along her forehead.*

BERTHOLD: I just finished cleaning my gutters, so I was thinking, yours
             is stuffed up too, and having my ladder handy, so I was
             thinking I'd just ask.
MOTHER: That would be all right. It's full of leaves.
BERTHOLD: It is good to have a man around.
             Who are you prettying yourself up for?
MOTHER: When I was cleaning, the hand shower got me in the face.
             Made my hair all frizzy up front.
BERTHOLD: If you take the curlers out, you can come along to the Spring
             Fair. The priest from Untersberg is coming with his band.
MOTHER: With his band?
BERTHOLD: He's singing the old folk songs again.
             First they turned their backs on him as a priest, and now
             he's coming back to the village with his band wearing le-
             derhosen. "Here's to you!"
MOTHER: That's not right. That's not the right thing for a priest to do.
BERTHOLD: Would be better for them if they still had him. At least he
             goes to the bar with people, but the new priest is going back
             to his blacks in Africa.
MOTHER: The priest showing them the way to the bar!
BERTHOLD: Now you've got religion all of a sudden. You never go to
             church.

(*Blackout*)

* * *

17

KITCHEN.

The MOTHER *finishes a bottle of home remedy.*

MOTHER: He kept on running to the riflemen's association.
I had to brush his uniform all the time.
There was always a parade somewhere, with him marching
    in it.
Washing his stinking socks all the time,
his handkerchiefs.
Messed up everything with his snuff,
chocolate smeared all over his belly.
He left a trail of dirt behind him.
From his dirty life.
It hailed on my bride's bouquet that day.
A thunderstorm on Whitsunday.
That was an omen.

Little birdie fallen out of his nest.
He didn't step on a single mine,
a border guard can get across any border.
And now they say
it was my fault.

A bus trip, air-conditioned, that was all.
I'd had too much sun,
but he had his beer.
And then he spat his beer on me.
I don't need a man.
I have no need for a man.

But he didn't need to hang himself.
He did that just to spite me.
That's why he wouldn't have no heart attack.
A deserter, that's what he was.
Here as well as over there.

(*Blackout*)

*   *   *

18

KITCHEN.

MOTHER: Saw you again with that Anke girl.
SON: Spying again, aren't you?
MOTHER: She's no good for you.
            A dimple in her chin, the devil on her mind.
SON: Then you should have a dimple too.

(*Losing control, the* MOTHER *slaps him in the face. The* SON *doesn't even
flinch. The next second the* MOTHER *is sorry and pulls him to her.*)

MOTHER: My boy. You're the only thing I have in the world.
            Don't get hung up on girls like that.
            You still smell like my little baby.
SON: Don't you get hung up on me.
            I'm no clothesline.
MOTHER: She's bowlegged.
            Your mother's legs are still pretty. Look.
SON: You don't look so straight either.

(*Blackout*)

*   *   *

19

KITCHEN.

(*The* MOTHER *is peeling apples. Very thin, with a peeler. Then she grates
the peeled apples onto a kitchen scale.*)

MOTHER: Bohemian apple tart, that's what I'm fixing for you.
            Now I've got too much.
            Come here, eat it down to two hundred fifty grams.

(*The* SON *scoops up the gratings with a big spoon.*)

            Stop!
            Now there's only two hundred grams left.

(*The* MOTHER *pulls his sleeve.*)

            Stop! I don't have any more apples.

(The SON *eats the last spoonful. The* MOTHER *cries.*)

	I made the batter with eight eggs. One pound of butter.
	Now I can throw it away.
	Why are you so mean?
SON:	What do you want?
	It was all for me, anyway.
	All for the Babyboy.

(*Blackout*)

* * *

20

GRANDMA'S ROOM.

GRANDMA *is sitting up in bed reading a newspaper. She is holding it with outstretched arms because she is farsighted. Now and then she massages her sore arm. She coughs slightly; the paper rustles. After a minute:*

GRANDMA: "Hippo to become immortal. It's going to be stuffed." Berliners. 35,000 marks it's going to take. They've got money for that kind of thing.
"His remains, including a hide ten centimeters thick, await the taxidermist." Some kind of immortality, being stared at in a museum for an eternity.
When I'm dead, I'll want my peace and quiet. But nobody would want to stuff me anyway. (*She chuckles.*)

"Even hippos have their father-son conflicts. When he was only a boy, Nante (left), the son of Knautschke (right), wouldn't keep his mouth shut. When Junior grew up and humiliated his sire, Knautschke lost all interest in life."
You wouldn't believe it, even animals are like that. They have a thick hide, and it's still no use.

(*Blackout*)

* * *

21

GRANDMA'S ROOM.

GRANDMA *is lying in bed. The* SON *plumps up her pillows. She strokes his cheek very gently.*

GRANDMA: Like milk and blood.
SON: I'm already shaving.
GRANDMA: Please don't mess with girls yet. Not so soon.
SON: You should talk.
GRANDMA: Babyboy!
SON: You weren't so pure yourself when you were young. Mother says so all the time, you had no honor.
GRANDMA: Don't be bad now, boy.
SON: You had an illegitimate kid. At seventeen. Didn't you?
GRANDMA: You don't know a thing.
            About how it was. Him always chasing after me.
SON: It takes two. Or did he rape you?
GRANDMA: You don't know a thing about it.
            I went to the cemetery and plucked leaves from those trees and made a tea to get rid of it and prayed, but it was no use, and, when I fainted in church, the old women gossiped and said that's what it is.
            So then I had to leave the Rosenhof farm.
SON: You could have fought them if you were in the right.
GRANDMA: No poor girl ever had a right.
            I was so ashamed going to the farmer's wife to tell her about her husband.
            "The woman can cover the man's shame with her apron" is all she said.
            She was humiliated. So I had to keep quiet too.
            And I left, and all I took along was my big belly.
            And then I thought, someday I will be happy about the child.

(*Blackout*)

*   *   *

22
GRANDMA'S ROOM.

The SON *puts a plastic bag containing food next to the bed. Quite openly, he puts* GRANDMA's *radio into another plastic bag.* GRANDMA *tries to look into the shopping bag.*

GRANDMA: Did you get that crummy cheese again?
            A jellied herring is what I want. Something fresh.
SON: I'd have to stand in line for that.

(GRANDMA *looks at him for a long time.*)

SON: (*in a low scream*) The fish are poisoned, Grandma! And the
            ocean too.
GRANDMA: Your daddy. Looking out of your eyes.
            Just thinking of himself when he was standing under the
            noose. Not thinking of his child at all

            I was always thinking of the baby child.
            Put ribbons in her hair like big blue butterflies.
            She never had to do any dirty work.
            I was left with the mess.
            Conceived her in sin.
            Got to pay for it.

(*Blackout*)

*   *   *

23
GRANDMA'S ROOM.

GRANDMA: You tell me nothing. You don't say a word. That's alright
            sometimes. When you're with an educated person, then you
            shouldn't talk all the time. You should listen. Be quiet. Then
            you can learn something. But your grandma, she's already
            with the worms, and she ain't rich.

(*The* SON *gets on the chair, checks the top of the wardrobe. He rummages
in the drawers. Takes out two silver spoons.*)

What if there's nothing else to take?
Will you come anymore?
(*shouts*) Will you come anymore?

SON: I need a motorbike.

GRANDMA: Wild beasts are more decent than that.
            (*in a low voice*) You can't leave me.
            You're all I have.

            Come here. Take out my earrings. They're gold.
            What do I need the earrings for anymore?

(*He approaches her; she pulls him onto her bed.*)

            They'll be hard to get out.
            Had them put in at seventeen.

(*Blackout*)

                        *   *   *

                            24
                    GRANDMA'S ROOM.

GRANDMA *is lying in bed, pounding on the floor with her stick.*

GRANDMA: Nobody coming anyway.
            I've always been afraid of being alone.
            Do I have to learn that too?
            Get to be as old as a cow,
            and still no end of learning.

(GRANDMA *fishes around under her bed with the stick and with difficulty
manages to produce a newspaper, yellow with age.*)

GRANDMA: A good idea to keep everything.
            Read the paper all over again. You forget what happened
            half a year ago. If you don't know the people personal it
            doesn't matter when things happened to them. So you don't
            need new papers all the time. The weather report doesn't
            interest me anymore. Politics neither. It did, once.
            Many a time I'd sit by the radio for half a day. The
            Bundestag and all that.

But the bigwigs fix it all up among themselves. They do.
Working at the pub, in the thirties, and the keeper was
mayor. Some kind of Hitler he was.
And then there were four councilmen. They were Hitlers,
too. They sat in the kitchen eating, and the keeper's
wife bathed in the sauerkraut barrel in the back
room.
A stickler for cleanliness she was. The farmers only
bathed at Easter.
And I had to roll up my sleeves and scrub her back. With
the root brush. Until it was red.
And then the man came and said, "You can tell the folks
things will stay the way they are. I am mayor, and Gustl
is deputy."
With no election. And everybody kept their mouth shut.

(*Blackout*)

* * *

25
GRANDMA'S ROOM.

GRANDMA *wipes crumbs off her bedspread.*

GRANDMA: It all stinks. (*She takes a comb from her nightstand, tries to
comb her disheveled hair.*)

Willi, he would. He would comb my hair. He would. He was
four years older and played the king when we were little.
And I was Antsy Ant. But today he would comb my hair,
sure. He's over there in their Party. Thought he'd make his
fortune there. He could come over here, if only they'd let
him. Married a girl from Sonneberg. With a factory. Making
glass eyes for puppets. So he stayed over there. And then it
all vanished into thin air.
He would take care of me, Willi would. Brought me pears.
Stolen from the mayor's garden. Were they ever hard. Had
to keep them until Christmas. But then the juice would be
all over your face.

He did take care of me, sometimes. Maybe he was feeling guilty for knocking me over. Cradle and all. I ended up under the tiled heater. Mother often told me about that. And he just bolted and left me lying there. But today he would take care of me.

(*Blackout*)

*   *   *

26

GRANDMA'S ROOM.

She is fishing under the bed with her stick.

GRANDMA: Have I got a thirst. And heartburn. And there's nothing left.
Just a bottle of wine.
Still wrapped up. Pretty little pattern. Violets.
Who gave me that? Those people downstairs would only give me some home remedy. With no wrapping paper.
Maybe it's from old Brühl?
(*Taps her forehead*)
Like a sieve.
His boys. They were something. Turned out well, all of them. Went to college, all of them. Never wasted any time. I want them to make good use of their time, that's what he'd say. A fine man, he was. With a nice moustache . . .
And then he was run over. He was.

He painted nice pictures. When his wife was dead, all he did was paint. Could have been a real artist. He promised me a picture too. Of the woods over there. With the path through the meadow. Where I'd run up to gather strawberries. For lunch. They all praised me for that.
Really, he should have done that before he died.
Well, it would be gone now anyway.
The boy would have sold it. If there was a buyer.
Turks maybe? From the glass factory.
They buy everything.

Lord, give him peace. Brühl, I mean. Even if he was a
sinner. And killed himself.
But his wine. It don't agree with me.
Dear Lord.
Such a thirst.
Would you change the wine into water?
For my sake.

(*Breaks the neck of the bottle on the edge of the bed, drinks in long
draughts. Cuts her mouth. Bleeds. Keeps on drinking.*)

(*Blackout*)

* * *

27
KITCHEN.

The MOTHER *tears her dress off her body. Tries to stuff it into the small
opening of the stove.*

SON:	But it's silk.
MOTHER:	It's got to go.
SON:	Women.
MOTHER:	I'll never leave the house again.
	The way they laughed.
SON:	When you order from the catalog, there is a chance someone else will have the same.
MOTHER:	But she has everything done by the tailor. Tailor-made, everything. Hanging on all the men. The bitch.
	She's got her tailor, special. She looked prettier. She's thin. So I simply won't go out no more.
SON:	But I will. I need a motorbike.

(*The* MOTHER *does not react.*)

	This week.
MOTHER:	Are you out of your mind!
	Do you want your mother dead?
	Don't you know the things that happen?
	Death is lurking at every corner.

SON: Death is a woman.

(*Blackout*)

*　　*　　*

28
KITCHEN.

BERTHOLD: Hungarians, sixty of them.
              Our men were over there, last year. Our band.
              And now it's them who're coming.
              We've got to put them up. The village is not so big.
              So I was thinking, maybe you could take one too. For the
              weekend.
              They'll just come in to sleep.
              Wouldn't be much work.
MOTHER: We've got no room.
BERTHOLD: Come on. You've got more room than other folks.
              With you having no husband.
              This way you could find one.
              If you don't like me enough. (*tries to touch her*)
              A bird in the hand is worth two in the bush.

(*The* MOTHER *raises her hand.*)

              Watch out! Hit me one more time and I'll kill you. (*pulls
              out a pocketknife, snaps the blade open*)
              I killed an ox with that once.
              With that little knife.
MOTHER: Full of lies.

(*Lets her take the knife from him. Sits down at the table.*)

BERTHOLD: In the Tatra Mountains. Fleeing from the Russians. And noth-
              ing to eat. So we chased an ox into a tree so he got himself
              stuck on his horns and—(*makes a noise*)—I stuck him in the
              neck. We smoked the meat.
              A giant leg. Was that ever heavy. Man oh man. The young
              guys today couldn't stand up to that.

(*The* MOTHER *pushes him to the door.*)

MOTHER: I've got to be cooking dinner. My boy is coming home from school.

BERTHOLD: Your boy—I just saw him. At the war memorial.
He's going to be some kind of guy. Different from you.
Those floozies were wearing skirts that hardly cover their ass.
And it's spring.
The catkins are coming out. So he'll be looking for a piece of fur too, a soft little piece.

MOTHER: You're full of lies.
Not my boy.
Full of lies.

(*Blackout*)

* * *

29
KITCHEN.

The MOTHER *is looking out of the window through her binoculars, drinking her home remedy. She has cookies nearby.*

MOTHER: Now it's snowing. This late.
No one outside.
Now the Schönwald kids are staring out their windows too. The glass factory closed down. So now the only thing they'll be doing is staring.
Almost Whitsunday, and snow.
But the sun is strong. It'll be lapping it up.

Whitsunday we'd always be up into the woods. Us girls.
Did our May walk.
The boys setting up May trees at night. Sometimes they put the little birch trees all the way up on top of the smokestack. One time they took the garden gate off the hinges. And the chickens were all over Mother's garden.
Oh Lord. Ruined everything.
And one time they made a chalk trail from our house all the way to Unternberg. Me, I had to spend half a Sunday scrubbing the chalk off the sandstone steps.
In the end, my fingertips were raw. And they didn't mean

to get at me at all. Only at Marga.
She was living upstairs.
She was pretty. Prettier than me. Teeth shiny as pearls.
But she just laughed and went for a walk with her aunt.
"No, no," she said, "no one would be thinking of me. They probably have their eye on you."
And I had my pride.
I'd rather get down on my hands and knees on the steps.
Because I had my pride.
Even though I knew that nobody liked me.

(*Blackout*)

*　　*　　*

30
KITCHEN.

Full moon.

Cat noises outside.

The SON *lies down on the kitchen table on his stomach, rubbing up and down.*
He *bites his arm. Grabs a cushion off the kitchen chair, buries his head in it.*
He *upsets a small bowl. It rattles.*

The MOTHER *is standing in the doorway in her nightgown, looking at him.*

(*Blackout*)

*　　*　　*

31
KITCHEN.

The SON *is tied to a chair with a clothesline. From upstairs, a knocking can be heard, violent at times, then fainter and fainter.*

MOTHER: You're not going out there any more.
           Your broth is spilt, your porridge boiled over.
           That little birdie,

you can tell her bye-bye.
I'm telling you,
Mother's got some say in this.
The horoscope said: Be careful today.
I'll teach you to be bullheaded.

(*The* MOTHER *tears a letter into tiny shreds.*
A strand of hair falls out.)

SON: (*shouts*) That's for me.
MOTHER: May her teeth fall out, and her hair,
            so they won't tempt God.
            You're staying with me,
            my flesh, my blood.
SON: Thirsty.
MOTHER: I'll heat you some milk, some chocolate?

(*She puts a pan of milk on the stove, looks into an empty chocolate powder*
can.)

            Chocolate's out.

(*Looks at her* SON *with satisfaction*)

            You always were a crawly little bug. Restless.
            Had to put you in the playpen. I could leave you alone then.
            You'd look at a catalog, mail-order, you loved the watches.
            You were upside down in my belly. They turned you around,
            with the forceps.
            Three days I didn't see you. He's so blue, the little fellow,
            that's what the doctor said. Three days I was hoarse because
            I screamed so hard. Because of you.
            And when we went to the zoo the first time, you had a new
            little gabardine coat. And the red monkey, you didn't want
            to leave him. He was throwing himself against the bars all
            the time. And then he threw up and lapped up the mess
            again. Over and over.
            Horrible. I was sick to my stomach, and you not wanting to
            leave. Not on your life. You always had a will of your own.
SON: Now you want to keep me in your gingerbread house, you
            old witch.
MOTHER: Don't talk like that. While you still have a mother.

SON: See. Go upstairs, take a look at her.

(*The* MOTHER *cries.*)

MOTHER: There were times when I wished you'd have something wrong
             with you so you'd always need me.
SON: I've got to go to the bathroom.
             My arms are hurting.
             Do you want me to crap in my pants?

(*She unties him.*)

MOTHER: You staying?

(*The* SON *makes a dash for the door; she tries to hold him.*)

             Stay!

(*The* SON *takes the hot milk off the stove and pours it on the* MOTHER*'s
legs. She screams a short, high-pitched scream.*)

(*Blackout*)

*   *   *

32
KITCHEN.

The SON *shuts a book.*

SON: Syphilitic, all of it.
             Did you read him? I hope so.
ANKE: "When you go to a woman, don't leave the whip behind."
SON: That's the thing women notice, because that's what they want.
             To be forced. That shows a man is really interested. The only
             way.
ANKE: Don't say such things.
             You don't mean them.
SON: I'm a cynic, and I'll grow up to be a gynecologist.
             To look into black holes.
ANKE: Today, on a holy Sunday . . .
SON: Exactly. The spirit enters her. With strange tongues.

(*He takes her head and kisses her. She tears herself away.*)

ANKE: If your mother . . .
SON: "I am the slave of my Satanic lover who ruined the demented
          virgins."
          Go on, say it!
          Say it!
ANKE: Don't be childish.

(*Blackout*)

*   *   *

33
KITCHEN.

ANKE *is lying on the floor, dead.*
Staring ahead, the SON *is sitting next to her.*

The MOTHER *enters, her legs in white bandages.*
The MOTHER *shuts the door. She stands still for a long time.*

She bends stiffly and lifts up ANKE's *lifeless arm, drops it.*

MOTHER: Dilla, dilla, dilla
          Little goose had to lose her feathers
          (*enticing*)
          dilla, dilla, dilla
          Little winter goose
          was growing little breasts
          little breasts of a silly little goose.

(*The* MOTHER's *foot touches a knife.*)

          The knife.
          Berthold's knife.
          That's Berthold's knife, isn't it?
          His little knife. From the Tatry mountains.
          Everybody knows about that.
          You mustn't worry.
          Babyboy.

(*Blackout*)

*   *   *

Susan L. Cocalis

The Politics of Brutality: Toward a Definition of the Critical *Volksstück*

The critical *Volksstück*, which has been enjoying a new vogue on the West German stage, is a dramatic genre alien to the Anglo-American tradition, and, although recent English works like Bond's *Saved*, Harold Pinter's earliest plays, or dramas of the kitchen-sink school could be related to it, no one would call them folk plays.[1] The term *folk play* in English would rather designate unliterary, impromptu dramatic performances, like the mumming play, that are usually accompanied by song and dance (sword dance, morris dance) and given at village festivals by the villagers themselves. These plays usually treat the themes of death and resurrection, honor local worthies, or celebrate heroic feats.[2] Since this term does exist in English and does refer to a historical form of the drama, the German term *Volksstück* will be retained throughout this paper.

Moreover, it will be maintained consciously, despite recent challenges to the validity of designating as *Volksstücke* certain contemporary, socially critical West German plays written in dialect, cant, or media jargon and treating the problems of common people.[3] For although one speaks of a revival of the critical *Volksstück* in the late 1960s and early 1970s, although numerous dramatists have been named in conjunction with this genre,[4] and although some of these authors explicitly label their own works as such,[5] there is little or no consensus as to what actually constitutes a *Volksstück*. Some critics advocate dispensing with the term altogether and replacing it with *milieu play* or *dialect play*;[6] others suggest retaining it but restricting it to a historical usage;[7] and still others propose expanding its field to include East German works not written in dialect.[8]

This lack of consensus may be attributable to the paradoxical nature of the critical *Volksstück*. It is an antigenre, or *Gegenentwurf*, which cannot exist without the foil of the totally uncritical, traditional *Volksstück*; it purports to effect political changes by its very apolitical nature; it attempts to serve humanitarian ideals by its ultrarealistic chronicling of the inhumane conditions governing social intercourse; it utilizes a naive mode of speech to demonstrate how mass culture has deprived the common people of the ability to think or to express themselves naturally; and it appeals to the instinct, pity, or compassion of the audience in order to provoke critical attitudes. Hence it attempts to be both conventional and critical, popular and political, compassionate and brutal, linguistically naive and sophisticated. If the critical *Volksstück* is to be defined at all, it would have to be in terms of these inherent contradictions. The following is intended as a step in that direction.

The critical *Volksstück* emerged as a genre during the Weimar Republic in the plays of Ödön von Horváth and his contemporary Marieluise Fleißer, plays that were viewed as efforts to continue, renew, and politicize the traditional *Volksstück*.[9] The latter was a form of popular play that had evolved in the late eighteenth and early nineteenth centuries in the *Vorstadttheater*, i.e., theaters in the outlying districts of the larger urban centers like Vienna, Munich, Berlin, Hamburg, Frankfurt, and Darmstadt.[10] The *Volksstück* was generally a farce, fairy tale, or satirical comedy written by one author in prose, verse, or the local dialect, and it usually included musical numbers.[11] It had a simple, unified plot, drawn from the daily life of the common folk, that was expected to demonstrate the just order of the universe. The action was initiated by some deviation from the normal order of things; a series of complications ensued (often involving temptations, mistaken identity, and reversals of fortune); and the suspense mounted until an actual deity, an influential patron, or an unexpected shift in fortune (shipwreck, lottery, inheritance, disclosure of one's true identity) intervened to reward the beautiful and the good and to punish the deviant and the evil. The normative social order was represented here by an intact family unit formed by persons of compatible social standing who interacted in accordance with culturally sanctioned, patriarchal customs. This ideal universe of just rewards was presented in a realistic manner as the natural, and thus normative, order of things.

Within this ordered world, the life of the common folk was portrayed, that is, a bourgeois author's view of what that should be.[12] Often enough, this entailed postulating an intact *homme naturel*, in the philosophical tradition of Rousseau, whose character traits were derived as the antithesis of everything negative in *l'homme artificiel* of civilized society. The common folk were therefore thought to be particularly close to nature, as opposed to civilized; physically strong, as opposed to effete; intact in the balanced use of their physical and mental faculties, as opposed to specialized in their skills; humane, as opposed to brutal and self-serving; and naive and innocent, as opposed to sophisticated and immoral. And although there might be momentary lapses into uncouth behavior, these were interpreted as a sign of the common folk's natural vitality, which was not to be confused with obscenity. Bertolt Brecht later characterized this type of play as follows:

> Das Volksstück ist für gewöhnlich krudes und anspruchsloses Theater. . . . Da gibt es derbe Späße, gemischt mit Rührseligkeiten, da ist hanebüchene Moral und billige Sexualität. Die Bösen werden bestraft und die Guten werden geheiratet, die Fleißigen machen eine Erbschaft und die Faulen haben das Nachsehen.[13]

As such, the *Volksstück* evolved as popular entertainment in opposition to the more pretentious forms of the theater, and it developed its own set of institutions to accommodate its anticultural bias.[14] It did so, however, within the existing cultural apparatus of the state and within the limitations imposed by censorship laws. This form of accommodation, which characterized the genre from the start, had become one of its most salient features by the end of the nineteenth century and certainly overshadowed any element of satire or social criticism that might show itself from time to time.[15] As Ludwig Hoffmann has remarked in this context:

> Das Volksstück arrangiert sich mit den herrschenden Verhältnissen und bedient ein Publikum, das darauf Wert legt, politisch in Ruhe gelassen zu werden. Die Satire weicht einem klebrigen Humor, das Volk wird auf die "Volkstype" reduziert, an die Stelle des Gefühls tritt das Sentiment, Kraft wird "kernig," das Lokale borniert, und über allem schwebt eine idyllische Moral, die dramatische Explosionen von Knallbonbonformat zuläßt.[16]

Moreover, it provided the state with a ready-made vehicle for propagating a nationalistic ideology of the German *Volk* and *Volkstum,* which Wolfgang Emmerich has described as follows:

> Volkstum als metaphysisch-idealistische Personifizierung, die anders nicht mehr erfüllbare religiöse Bedürfnisse auffängt und säkularisiert; Volkstum als bestehende Herrschafts- und Produktionsverhältnisse verschleiernde Integrationsideologie, die gerade aufgrund ihrer psychisch

regressiven, atavistischen Tendenzen aktivistisch eingesetzt werden kann; Volkstum als biologischer Organismus, der das geschichtliche Wesen des Menschen auf die Stufe der Natur zurücknimmt.[17]

This tradition of the *Volksstück* has continued on into the twentieth century. For, despite the threat that the film industry and later television may have posed for the *Vorstadttheater*, the inherent compatibility of these media has been duly recognized and exploited, so that by today filmed versions of such productions have become a popular staple of the West German broadcasting networks.[18] This situation persisted essentially unchanged until the radical student movement of the late 1960s and early 1970s rekindled an interest in the critical *Volksstücke* of Horváth and Fleißer, and a new generation of dramatists began to explore this genre's potential for effecting political change.[19]

That is, the new form of political theater which they envisioned would focus on the authority patterns in families, instances of moral rigidity, intolerance, servility, and obsessive concern with virility and sexual domination,[20] and it would thereby demonstrate what Rainer Werner Fassbinder called "faschistoide Grundverhalten im Alltag."[21] In demanding a new form of drama, the younger generation of playwrights, including Peter Handke, Martin Sperr, and Franz Xaver Kroetz, rejected an explicitly political theater, which they found embodied in Brecht's works, in favor of what Adorno would call autonomous art.[22] For although these younger dramatists acknowledged a debt to Brecht, they found his form of epic theater inadequate to their own needs on several counts.[23] They felt that it was insincere for an author to portray proletarian figures as perceptive, articulate, and class-conscious as long as the social system held the lower classes in a state of ignorance and passivity; that the explicit dramatization of political solutions on stage allowed the audience to digest the political message as part of the evening's entertainment; and that by showing instances of humane behavior in even the most inhumane circumstances, an author reaffirmed the audience's faith in the just order of the universe. For these younger authors, truly political drama either would have to be removed from the theater entirely or would have to disappoint the theatergoer's expectations systematically. In the latter case, one could dispense with a traditional plot; one could directly confront the audience with the play's action; one could allow the duration of the action to correspond directly to the duration of the play in a manner that would eliminate all suspense; or one could shock the audience by confronting it with ultrarealistic slices of life in graphic detail.

Some authors, like Handke, turned to an experimental, plotless framework (*Publikumsbeschimpfung, Kaspar*) to challenge the theatrical establishment; others, like Sperr and Kroetz, turned to an ultrarealistic form of the drama that was modeled on the plays of Horváth and Fleißer.[24]

Although there had been various attempts to rejuvenate the *Volksstück* during the Weimar Republic—Carl Zuckmayer had celebrated nature, vitality, virility, and fertility and had flaunted conventional bourgeois morals in his *Der fröhliche Weinberg* (1925), for example[25]—Horváth and Fleißer purported to continue and renew the traditional *Volksstück* by consciously destroying it in both a formal and an ethical context.[26] Horváth tried to achieve this goal through a process he called "Demaskierung des Bewußtseins";[27] Fleißer through a form of "naives Sehn."[28] In both cases this entailed providing a brutally realistic chronicle of common life, in all its sordid detail, within the formal and structural conventions of the traditional *Volksstück*. The discrepancy between the audience's expectations of light entertainment and the heavy, often tragic fare it experienced here was supposed to produce a shock effect that would force it to recognize how the common person is manipulated by society and thus exploited.

In this context, Horváth chose to attack the forms of consciousness, character structures, and behavioral patterns affected by mass culture and to show how the cultural aspirations and pretensions of the petite bourgeoisie (and proletariat) served to neutralize any moral indignation at social injustices which might be aroused by a critical political message.[29] This process could entail taking a traditional *Volksstück* plot but showing how a happy ending had become impossible in the modern world; exposing idealistic, noble, moralizing, nationalistic, or leftist rhetoric as *Bildungsjargon*,[30] or empty phrases that bear little relation to the speaker's actual lifestyle; using dialect, which normally connotes naïveté or an intact nature, as a means of showing how the common people have been rendered dumb by mass culture; contrasting sentimental musical pieces with the sordid realities of the action; or concluding a tragic action with the travesty of a happy ending. For, as long as the common people are deprived of their ability to articulate their thoughts and feelings, they are reduced to a level of bestial intercourse in which every person looks out for his or her own interests. The ideals of bourgeois cultural ideology only serve to obscure this fact. Herbert Gamper has described this process of confronting cultural clichés with the brutal realities of life, as follows:

Solches Vorgehen ist nicht, oder erst sekundär, individualpsychologisch

motiviert; die Spanne, die Rede und Verhalten der Horváthschen Mensch-
en irrlichternd durchmißt, ist die zwischen Kultur und "Bestialität."
Durch eine Kultur, die nicht die ihre ist, repräsentiert durch die zur
Phrase veräußerlichte Sprache, wie durch Gesetze und moralische Max-
imen, die zu erfüllen ihnen nicht möglich ist, werden sie zurückgeworfen
auf ihre "asozialen"..., auf ihre bestialischen Triebe. Sie gehen zu-
grunde als zweifache Opfer: der Natur und der Kultur.[31]

According to Horváth, language, as the expression of consciousness and as
the medium of civilized social intercourse, would therefore play a crucial
role in determining the action of the critical *Volksstück:*

Um einen heutigen Menschen realistisch schildern zu können, muß ich
also den Bildungsjargon sprechen lassen. Der Bildungsjargon (und seine
Ursachen) fordern aber natürlich zur Kritik heraus—und so entsteht der
Dialog des neuen Volksstückes, und damit der Mensch, und damit erst
die dramatische Handlung—eine Synthese aus Ernst und Ironie.[32]

Through the medium of language and through the constant disappointment
of the audience's expectations, Horváth tried to expose the brutality underlying petit bourgeois existence and to show how the manipulation of
forms of consciousness contributes to the rise of fascism.

In this respect, Horváth's critical *Volksstücke* are comparable to those of
Fleißer, who recorded the provincial attitudes and atavistic behavior of her
native Ingolstadt with such unrelenting candor that Alfred Kerr was prompted
to refer to her as "eine kostbare Abschreiberin kleinmenschlicher Raub-
tierschaft im hießig-heutigen Mittelalter."[33] Fleißer's plays differ from those
of Horváth, however, in the scope of the reality she portrayed—that is,
while he sometimes broached broader sociopolitical issues, as in his *Bergbahn*
(1927-29) or *Italienische Nacht* (1931), she tended to focus on the relationship between the sexes or "... Sitten und Gebräuche an Hand von An-
lässen..." as a paradigm for the larger social conflict.[34] Furthermore, in
contrast to Horváth, with his ironical style, Fleißer cultivated a form of
"naive Sehn," that is, a reduction of the dramatic events to a point where
the relationships between cause and effect become transparent and are then
"displayed" to the audience.[35] She compared this process to the way in
which a child would draw a house: The child's stick figure would refer not
to any particular building but to the concept of a house per se.[36] This new
form of naïveté, which would reduce human intercourse to the bestial level

underlying the veneer of civilization and expose the inhumane side of human nature, would replace the more idyllic portrayal of naïveté in the traditional *Volksstück*. Here the characters search for happiness in the customary ways but become hopelessly dependent on one another without being able to communicate their needs or to escape from one another. The atmosphere of this provincial society is so stifling and the brutality so prevalent that there can be no hope of redemption, no happy ending, not even as a travesty of the traditional *Volksstück*.[37]

After a long period of neglect, the plays of Horváth and Fleißer were rediscovered in the late 1960s and early 1970s and became such a prominent feature on the West German stage that some critics began to speak of a "Horváth Renaissance" and a "Fleißer Boom,"[38] while others decried their works, and those of their younger followers, as "Bajuwaro-Brutalismo" for "Kinder der Cola-Kolonie."[39] In any event, they met the needs of a younger generation of dramatists and served as the models for a contemporary critical *Volksstück*.

Although numerous contemporary authors have been mentioned in conjunction with the critical *Volksstück*[40]—among them Peter Handke, Martin Sperr, Franz Xaver Kroetz, Rainer Werner Fassbinder, Wolfgang Bauer, Harald Sommer, Peter Turrini, Franz Buchrieser, Gerald Szyszkowitz, Felix Mitterer, Harald Mueller, Heinrich Henkel, Jochen Ziem, Karl Otto Mühl, Wolfgang Deichsel, Gerhard Kelling, Renke Korn, Yaak Karsunke, and Jürgen Lodemann—and although some would designate their own works as such,[41] not all of these authors, nor all of the works of any given author, should be thrown together under the rubric of the critical *Volksstück*. The works of these authors—despite the fact that they are written in dialect, cant, or media jargon and treat the problems of the common folk from a socially critical perspective—are far too heterogeneous to be classified under one heading. New criteria for defining this genre are obviously needed, or one should indeed consider abandoning it entirely. As suggested above, one possibility for deriving such criteria would be to define the critical *Volksstück* in terms of an antigenre. As such, it would have to maintain certain conventions of the traditional genre in order to raise the expectations it wishes to disappoint.

The critical *Volksstück* would therefore have to rely on a set of characters drawn from the petite bourgeoisie or the proletariat, a naturalistic use of everyday speech patterns, and a unified, dramatic action with a conflict that creates a certain degree of suspense and allows the audience to identify with the main figures or at least to share a compassionate interest in their fate.[42] I would therefore contend that dramas of the authors cited above that are set in an experimental or plotless framework (Handke's *Publikumsbeschimpfung* [1965] or *Kaspar* [1967], Bauer's *Party for Six* [1968], or Sommer's *Hure Gerhild* [1971]); in a series of loosely connected, revue-like sketches involving a different set of characters for each scene and not unified by a single action (Ziem's *Nachrichten aus der Provinz* [1967] or Deichsel's *Bleiwe losse* [1965], *Agent Bernd Etzel* [1968], and *Frankenstein* [1970–71]); in a surrealistic or science fiction context (Fassbinder's *Blut am Hals der Katze* [1971] or Mueller's *Großer Wolf* [1970]); and in a foreign or historical setting transcending a locally bound, petit bourgeois milieu (Kelling's *Die Massen von Hsunhui* [1971] or Karsunke's *Bauernoper* [1976]) should not be considered critical *Volksstücke*.

Moreover, since the critical *Volksstück,* as an antigenre, must inherently challenge the audience's wish to escape into an intact, ordered, and allegedly natural world, I would also contend that it should deliberately shock the audience through the deployment of brutal, violent, or obscene acts, which it would present as the truly natural, and thus sincere, basis for everyday life. The audience might reject such shock effects, but it would at least be forced to confront them and to think about why they were replacing the entertaining effects of the conventional *Volksstück*.[43] Turrini explains this process as follows:

Ich habe für diese Geschichte [*Sauschlachten*] die Form des Volksstückes gewählt, um das Publikum dort zu treffen, wo ich es vermute: in seiner Bereitschaft zur Unterhaltung, in der vertrottelten Mittelmäßigkeit des Löwinger-Klischees. Ich hoffe auf die Bereitschaft des Publikums, einen Weg, den es selbst gewählt hat, zu Ende zu gehen. Theater ist für mich vor allem Sinnlichkeit, Grausamkeit: ich will mich von den Gesetzen einer langweiligen, von Psychologie und Kunstfertigkeit durchsetzten Dramaturgie entfernen, um mich den Abgründen der menschlichen Natur zu nähern. Ich will das Publikum auf diesem Weg mitnehmen: Schock als Ergebnis und nicht als Selbstzweck.[44]

In comparison to the traditional light farces, the critical *Volksstück* would therefore present a serious treatment of brutality bordering on criminality, often relying on sensational accounts of murders (especially within a family), maiming, suicide, abortion, or sexual perversion for its plot material.[45] By showing how the mechanisms of brutality function on a microcosmic level, the dramatists try to enlighten the audience about how violence can be institutionalized in the greater social whole:

> Wie Gewalt sich anstaut und entlädt, wissen die Leute nicht. Gewalt-tätigkeit ist eine anonyme Kraft. Deshalb wollen auch viele zeitgenöss-ische Dramatiker zeigen, wie Menschen dazu kommen, in der Gewalt ihren einzigen Ausweg zu suchen. Mir jedenfalls geht es dabei nicht um die Verteidigung von Gewaltverbrechen, sondern um die Anprangerung der Gesellschaft.[46]

Therefore, plays like Henkel's *Eisenwichser* (1970) and *Früstückspause* (1971), Kelling's *Arbeitgeber* (1969), and *Die Auseinandersetzung* (1970), Mühl's *Rosenmontag* (1974), Kroetz's *Oberösterreich* (1972), *Das Nest* (1974), and *Der stramme Max* (1978), which all present conflicts that are resolved without acts of wanton violence, also would *not* fall within the province of the critical *Volksstück*.

Furthermore, because the critical *Volksstück* would have to retain the local setting of its predecessors, or at least create an atmosphere of provin-cialism as a form of internalized regionalism, plays specifically dealing with conflicts at the workplace between labor and management would also be disqualified. For provincialism, as Bloch has defined it, would consist of an ideological system derived from earlier relationships of production which lingers on to obscure the actual causal factors governing the socioeconomic contradictions of the present.[47] In the critical *Volksstück*, provincial attitudes create an atmosphere of brutality, resignation, and fear which may, for a time, be confused with the mysterious ways of fortune but which ultimately disappoint the audience's expectations of viewing a rationally ordered world.[48] In the end, the good are not rewarded nor the deviant punished, for good and evil suffer the same fate here. Since no answers are provided that would explain the action, the theatergoer is held in suspense while being drawn into the provincial world:

> Er [der Dramatiker] gibt explizit keine politische oder soziale Motivation, und das macht dieses Verhalten für den Betrachter nur desto bedrohlicher, da ihm nicht die Möglichkeit zur platten rationalisierenden Bewältigung, d.h. zur Ableitung der dargestellten Zustände aus anonymen, fern und äußerlich bleibenden gesellschaftlichen Gegebenheiten mitgeliefert wird. Der Bühnenvorgang erlaubt es nicht, aus ihm hinauszugehen, sondern zwingt den Zuschauer hinein.[49]

By locating the conflict at the workplace, or by portraying it in terms of easily identifiable socioeconomic factors that are also discussed within the framework of the play, the dramatist would, however, transcend the thought structures of provincialism and address the problem in terms of the contemporary contradictions between capital and the proletariat, private property and the relationships of production. A "socialist," "plebeian," or "proletarian" *Volksstück*—as some claim to have found in the works of Brecht, Peter Hacks, Horst Kleineidam, Horst Salomon, Jochen Nestler, Franz Freitag, and Helmut Sakowski—would therefore seem to be a contradiction in terms.[50]

Perhaps on the basis of the above, it might be more profitable to classify the critical *Volksstück* according to its relationship to the tradition. If one did that on the basis of thematic preoccupation, one might arrive at the categories that follow.

In plays like Horváth's *Bergbahn* (1927–29), Fleißer's *Fegefeuer in Ingolstadt* (1926), Sperr's *Jagdszenen aus Niederbayern* (1966) and *Koralle Meier* (1970), Fassbinder's *Katzelmacher* (1968), Turrini's *Sauschlachten* (1971), Müller's *Halbdeutsch* (1970), and Mitterer's *Kein Platz für Idioten* (1979), the authors demonstrate how provincial social groups react to an outsider or social deviant. Horváth introduces a North German hairdresser into a group of Bavarian laborers; Fleißer and Fassbinder show how adolescents in a small town join ranks to persecute the unwashed visionary Roelle or the Greek guest worker Jorgos; Sperr, Turrini, and Mitterer record how an entire village can be mobilized to hunt down a homosexual, a whore, an intellectual who can only grunt like a pig, and the village idiot; and Müller depicts how the inmates of a refugee camp gang up on a newcomer from the East. In all of these works the action begins in a casually realistic manner but soon escalates into a kind of ritual witch hunt, which intensifies until the foreign element has been purged from the ranks of the group. In some cases, the townspeople drive the outsiders to commit criminal or abnormal acts for which they are duly jailed (Sperr) or committed to an asylum (Mitterer); in others, the outsiders are driven to semisuicidal acts (Horváth) or are physically slaughtered (Turrini, Müller). The deviants, who are often treated like sacrificial animals, rarely fight or even question the system of social norms but, rather, strive to be accepted by their peers or resign themselves to their fates.

A variant of this type of critical *Volksstück* can be found in plays like Fleißer's *Der Starke Stamm* (1950), Kroetz's *Hartnäckig* (1971), *Lieber Fritz* (1971), and *Stallerhof* (1971), in which the more intimate setting of the family and friends serves as a microcosm for the larger social whole. Here, however, the deviant behavior generally entails misdirected sexuality: that is, Fleißer's widower Bitterwolf impregnates and then marries his son's girlfriend; Kroetz's Helmut Rustorfer, who has lost a leg during army maneuvers, still has pretensions of marrying and inheriting his father's business; Fritz, an exposure artist who has been castrated by the police, tries to marry an employee of his brother-in-law; and Sepp, an aging farmhand, seduces and impregnates his master's adolescent retarded daughter. In all of these plays, which adhere closely to the conventions of the traditional *Volksstück,* the situation labeled deviant by the microcosmic society is shown to be natural under the circumstances, but the social norms prevail, and this alleged deviancy is punished. Moreover, although the characters treat the deviant brutally, acting in their own interest, this brutality does not reach the level of violence found in the more anonymous setting of the community. That is, the deviant may be disinherited, disowned, or expelled from the group and the abnormal relationship may be forcibly broken up or seriously undermined, but the action does not end in tragedy or in the ritual sacrifice of one of the characters.

This nonviolent resolution of the action is not, however, solely attributable to the more humane atmosphere of the family, as can be seen in plays like Kroetz's *Wildwechsel* (1968), Sperr's *Landshuter Erzählungen* (1967), Buchrieser's *Hanserl* (1970), and Szyszkowitz's *Kainiten* (1969) or *Weidmannsheil* (1971). Here the generation gap has become so acute that the father-child conflict can be resolved only by patricide. As a rule, the father will try to manipulate a son by threatening to disown him or will try to humiliate him by attacking his sexual potency or intellectual prowess; he tries to control his daughter's morals and sex life, however, by making her feel guilty or by brute force. After a certain amount of harassment, the child retaliates with an act of violence: Kroetz's Hanni shoots her father; Sperr's Sorm and Buchrieser's Hanserl strangle theirs; and Szyszkowitz's figures murder each other ruthlessly in turn. Rather than the reaffirmation of the patriarchal family one would expect in the traditional *Volksstück,* one is confronted here with patricide; rather than the normative patterns of authority, one finds overt rebellion; rather then the myth of the family as the private sphere, as a haven from the conflicts of the world outside, one experiences the home as an arena for the survival of the fittest; rather than the convention of an unexpected inheritance, one learns how sons come by an expected legacy; and rather than the home as an inner sanctum, one sees it as a place of confinement. Here, in this microcosmic society, the patterns of authoritarian behavior are formed that determine the political constitution of the common folk; the message of this group of critical *Volksstücke* is that brutality fosters brutality, familiarity breeds contempt.

The themes of love, courtship, and marriage are also stripped of all romance in plays like Horváth's *Geschichten aus dem Wiener Wald* (1931) and *Kasimir und Karoline* (1932); Fleißer's *Pioniere in Ingolstadt* (1929); Kroetz's *Heimarbeit* (1971) and *Männersache* (1970); Bauer's *Magic Afternoon* (1968) and *Film und Frau* (1971); and Turrini's *Rozznjogd* (1967). In some cases, this entails coming to grips with a partner's masturbation, extramarital liaisons, impotence, homoerotic tendencies, or sadomasochistic fantasies; in others, it is directly related to inhumane or physically debilitating working conditions or to the psychological effects of being unemployed. In contrast to the relationships in the traditional *Volksstück*, in which romantic love always triumphs in the end and is rewarded by engagement, marriage, or pregnancy, these relationships almost all end in tragedy, sadomasochistic rituals, or a travesty of the traditional happy ending. Horváth's Marianne may become engaged to Oskar but only after she has been seduced, abandoned, jailed, and bereft of her illegitimate child; Kasimir and Karoline break up; Fleißer's Berta is mechanically deflowered and abruptly left behind by a soldier; Kroetz's Willy drowns his wife's illegitimate child, and his Otto and Martha end up taking potshots at each other; Bauer's Birgit stabs Joe after being crudely harassed by him and his friend Charly; Bruno ("The Bard") and Senta engage in bouts of "Shakespearean sadomasochism"; and Turrini's couple strip themselves of all of the trappings of civilized society before they are hunted down like rats in the town dump. Again, even if the characters are not physically slaughtered, they are treated so brutally that they will never recover emotionally. Where the traditional *Volksstück* would speak of love, these plays show a simulated, singularly unerotic sexual act or naked sexual dependency; where characters previously spoke of their frustrations, they show simulated masturbation or impotence; where lovers previously were totally consumed by their love, they mouth empty phrases and seem preoccupied more with mundane matters than with passion during the sexual act; and where pregnancy previously was celebrated as the proof of the man's virility and the woman's fertility, characters are obsessed with contraception, abortion, or infanticide. Here, in the battle of the sexes, lies the material for political drama, according to the authors of the critical *Volksstück*, and not in explicitly political issues. As Kroetz remarked in speaking of Fleißer:

Drama spielt sich nicht dort ab, wo Herr Weiss mit Herrn Hölderlin
darüber richtet, wer in einer sowieso utopischen Revolution der anstän-
digere und wirkungslosere Revolutionär gewesen sei, sondern dort, wo
ein Dienstmädchen sich eine Nacht hat frei machen können, um ihre
Jungfernschaft gebührend herzugeben, was sinnlos ist, denn die gesell-
schaftliche Situation läßt für derartig unproduktive Betätigungen nur
ein paar Minuten Zeit.[51]

Although much of the brutality here is implicitly attributed to the economic
system or to mass culture, the characters themselves rarely recognize this
and therefore vent their frustrations on themselves and their partners. If
they do realize how they are being manipulated and rebel against the system,
they are usually destroyed in the process.

In plays like Mühl's *Rheinpromenade* (1974) and Kroetz's *Heimat* (1975),
the manner in which the older generation is relentlessly shunted aside to
make way for the younger, more productive members of society is contrasted
to the respect accorded the elders in the traditional *Volksstück*. Instead of a
venerable patriarch who governs his family sagely with the absolute authority
vested in him by centuries of Western cultural heritage, one finds old men
who live in the custody of their families but are otherwise ignored by them;
instead of a vital and useful member of society, one finds the "seniors," who
have been pensioned off and thereby branded as dispensable and who no
longer fulfill any meaningful role within the family. These old men are not
physically abused like the group of patricidal victims, for no one takes them
seriously enough for that. It suffices to humor and to humiliate them: for
an unseasonable affair, for wetting the bed, or for pretending to have something meaningful to do. Thus, Mühl's octogenarian Fritz Kumetat incurs
social censure and is legally declared of infirm mind as he tries to leave part
of his savings to a young hospital worker, and Kroetz's Hugo is deprived of
the custody of his granddaughter after he loses his temper and strikes her
for taunting him. Although such figures are often portrayed as vital men at
the beginning of the play, they succumb either physically or mentally in the
course of the action. Since the audience would find these figures much more
sympathetic than their materialistic, self-serving families, their very capit-
ulation should convey the message that this situation, which prevails in
modern capitalist societies despite any rhetoric to the contrary—most recently
in the form of patronizing the "seniors"—must be changed.

Finally, there is a group of plays like Horváth's *Glaube, Liebe, Hoffnung*
(1932), Kroetz's *Wunschkonzert* (1971), and Bauer's *Change* (1969) which

show how common people can be driven to suicide when they are no longer able to cope with the feelings of alienation produced by mass culture. That is, instead of directing their brutal urges toward others, they abuse themselves and ultimately destroy themselves. In this way, they would represent an extreme case of the passivity and brutality of the *Volksstück* as a genre. The political message inherent in such behavior is, according to Kroetz, that the energies thus spent could be channeled into other forms of political activity which could be directed against the status quo to create a more humane society:

> Würde die explosive Kraft dieser massiven Ausnutzung und Unterdrück-ung sich nicht, leider, gegen die Unterdrückten und Ausgenützten selbst richten, so hätten wir die revolutionäre Situation. So haben wir nur viele Fälle von kleinen, törichten Selbstmorden und Morden, die selbst wieder nur affirmativ funktionieren: die, die so weit sind, daß sie die Kraft und den Mut hätten, "ihr eigen Leben in die Waagschale zu werfen," liefern sich selbst der Gerichtsbarkeit ihrer natürlichen Feinde aus. Damit säub-ern sie unfreiwillig die Gesellschaft, gegen die sie klagen. . . . Nur so ist es möglich, daß die unmenschliche Ordnung, in der wir leben, auf-rechterhalten werden kann und wir weiter darin leben müssen.[52]

Since the critical *Volksstück* purports to be a form of political drama, one must now ask how effective it might be as an instrument of political change. Although not all of the authors associated with this genre have political pretentions—Bauer, for example, denies any such motivation—most of them do consider themselves partisan writers whose implicit in-dictment of society would be far more effective than the more overt political message of writers like Brecht, Weiss, or Hochhuth.[53] In the critical dis-cussion on this genre, however, such assumptions are not taken at face value and have recently come under attack on several counts.

One charge leveled at the critical *Volksstück* contests the premise that it is autonomous art, according to Adorno's definition,[54] that is, art in which the total absence of any political message in a brutally realistic work could be construed as a political statement in itself, insofar as it would impel the audience to change an absolutely inhumane world. As Adorno has explained this phenomenon:

> Jedes Engagement für die Welt muß gekündigt sein, damit der Idee

eines engagierten Kunstwerks genügt werde, der polemischen Verfremdung, die der Theoretiker Brecht dachte und die er um so weniger praktizierte, je geselliger er dem Menschlichen sich verschrieb. Dies Paradoxon, das den Einwand des Erklügelten provoziert, stützt sich, ohne viel Philosophie, auf die einfachste Erfahrung: Kafkas Prosa, Becketts Stücke oder der wahrhaft ungeheuerliche Roman "De Namenlose" üben eine Wirkung aus, der gegenüber die offiziell engagierten Dichtungen wie Kinderspiel sich ausnehmen; sie erregen die Angst, welche der Existentialismus bloß beredet. Als Demontagen des Scheins sprengen sie die Kunst von innen her, welche das proklamierte Engagement von außen, und darum nur zum Schein, unterjocht. Ihr Unausweichliches nötigt zu jener Änderung der Verhaltensweise, welche die engagierten Werke bloß verlangen.[55]

Although the critical *Volksstück* as defined above would be related to this form of political art, insofar as the authors avoid any explicit tendentious message, it could not be classified as totally autonomous, since they often demonstrate noticeable compassion for the plight of the common people, which tends to neutralize the emancipatory potential of the play's brutality. By these means, this genre could ultimately reaffirm the status quo.[56]

Moreover, since the critical *Volksstück* is an antigenre, it must maintain and therefore perpetuate the very conventions of its traditional predecessors which it purports to undermine.[57] For, although the authors attempt to shock the audience in order to raise its level of consciousness, this process may be confounded in various ways. On one level, the authors turn to this genre in order to reach a mass audience but then place demands on that audience which it is unable to fulfill. That is, the viewers are called upon to assess the action for themselves, to become indignant at a society that reduces people to the level of bestiality and to demand some form of qualitative change in that society. The efficacy of the critical *Volksstück* therefore depends—at least to a certain degree—on the ability of the audience to recognize the subtle way in which linguistic idioms are used to show how the common people are being manipulated; to recognize the difference between the traditional and the critical *Volksstück;* and to recognize the problems presented on stage as social problems rather than individually deviant behavior.[58] This would presuppose, however, that such an audience possessed a level of linguistic sophistication and powers of theoretical abstraction which surpassed those of the dramatis personae.[59] R. P. Carl has described this dilemma as follows:

Die tatsächlich vorausgesetzte Fähigkeit zur Abstraktion, zur Übertragung, zum Wiedererkennen gehört mit zum Bildungsvorsprung derer, an die sich die Aufklärungsabsicht nicht richtet. Die Schichten aber, deren Verständnishorizont angeblich zugrundegelegt wird, werden weder als Theater noch als Lesepublikum erreicht.[60]

In this context, the only people truly capable of understanding the political message of the play might be the liberal, intellectual theatergoers who would not be in need of political enlightenment.

One could assume that the mass audience, which is routinely exposed to sensational accounts of brutality in the media, might not be shocked by the graphic portrayal of sex and violence in the critical *Volksstück,* and, indeed, that it might expect such fare as part of an evening's entertainment. Moreover, the mass audience, which has internalized an ideology of consumerism, might have difficulty distinguishing the conventions of the old *Volksstück* from those of the critical one on a different level. That is, since the acts of consuming products with "natural" attributes or participating in organized ventures to enjoy or conquer nature now fulfill the same functions previously served by communing with nature itself—insofar as the former now promise the good life, happiness, self-fulfillment, recreation, or even redemption—the distinction between the rhetoric of nature in the traditional *Volksstück* and the media jargon alienating it in the critical *Volksstück* may have become obscured beyond recognition.

Therefore, the mass audience may perceive the dramatic action as violent but may interpret that violence as entertaining—in this case, as tragic. The author's noticeable compassion for the dramatis personae could then be understood as a variant of the terror and pity associated with the Aristotelian concept of tragedy or as a form of the emotional involvement demanded by soap operas, and the characters' plight could be interpreted as their inexorable fate.[61] Thus, despite its political pretensions, the critical *Volksstück* has been attacked for ultimately perpetuating the political status quo. It has been censured, like the drama of German Naturalism which it resembles:[62]

bloße Zustandsschilderung, die dem Oberflächeneindruck erliege und die Dialektik von Wesen und Erscheinung verkenne, Unfähigkeit zu einer Ursachenanalyse jenseits von biologischem oder soziologischem Determinismus, Verzicht auf jede weiterweisende Perspektive und damit objektiv weitere Festigung der Zustände, auf die anklagend hingewiesen werde.[63]

Given the dependency of the critical *Volksstück* on the mass audience, one must now ask how its authors can avoid becoming a part of the very process of shaping mass culture which they impugn in their works. As Walter Benjamin cautioned in the case of Dada and *Neue Sachlichkeit*, the Western cultural apparatus is capable of assimilating great quantities of radical art and of rendering it effete, as long as authors choose to work within the established system and try to reform that system "from above." That is:

> daß einen Produktionsapparat zu beliefern, ohne ihn . . . zu verändern, selbst dann ein höchst anfechtbares Verfahren darstellt, wenn die Stoffe, mit denen dieser Apparat beliefert wird, revolutionärer Natur scheinen. Wir stehen nämlich der Tatsache gegenüber . . . daß der bürgerliche Produktions- und Publikationsapparat erstaunliche Mengen von revolutionären Themen assimilieren, ja propagieren kann, ohne damit seinen eigenen Bestand und den Bestand der besitzenden Klasse ernstlich in Frage zu stellen.[64]

Thus, despite nudity, simulated sexual intercourse, masturbation, sadomasochism, homosexuality, and brutality, these plays are produced in subsidized houses and broadcast on national television. Furthermore, some dramatists like Kroetz, Bauer, and Deichsel have begun to internalize certain conventions of the television medium by serializing their plays, adapting the length of their work to comply with programming restrictions, modifying the milieu to conform to the norms of television entertainment, or turning to detective or science fiction adventures.[65]

The question has therefore arisen whether these works can be politically effective in this form or whether they have been co-opted to provide titillating new thrills to a jaded medium, i.e., whether they perform a function analogous to that of the Norman Lear sit-coms like "All in the Family" or the soap-opera parodies like "Mary Hartman, Mary Hartman," which periodically add new zest to American television.

Although some critics feel the vogue of the *Volksstück* has passed—the period from 1966 to 1975 is cited as its duration[66]—a survey of the *Theater Heute* listings of the annual productions on German-speaking stages would attest to the continuing popularity of this genre in both its traditional and critical variants, or at least to the continuing popularity of the authors associated with this genre. The specific plays of these authors which are being produced now, however, are mostly dramas dealing with the nonviolent resolution of petit bourgeois problems (like Kroetz's *Oberösterreich* or *Das Nest*) or plays that would bear no relation whatsoever to a *Volksstück* (like Fleißer's *Tiefseefisch,* which documents her ties to the Brecht clique in Berlin during the 1920s). As such, these plays would fall outside the sphere of the *Volksstück,* as that was defined above, and would tend to substantiate the passing of the vogue. The recent attempts of younger playwrights like Mitterer to realize the original aspirations of writers like Kroetz and Sperr in a form of peasant theater could also be understood in this context.

In conclusion, the very provincialism of the critical *Volksstück,* its reliance on a subtle use of language, and its dependence on certain audience expectations would all serve to make it a type of play which does not travel well. Indeed, a translation of such dramas into a foreign language generally necessitates a total transposition of the action into analogous regional circumstances with the ensuing adaptation of plot details and dialect. This form of transposition has to be repeated with each major move. And, though such a process was undertaken for the German versions of Bond's *Saved* or Arnold Wesker's works,[67] the English productions of Horváth or Kroetz have suffered from a noticeable lack of context. Sometimes they are presented as sentimental farces, sometimes as naturalistic tragedies, sometimes as political theater, and sometimes as sensationalized events. And, indeed, the critical *Volksstück,* as an antigenre, seems to be all of these things at once: popular and political, conventional and shocking, compassionate and brutal, naive and sophisticated.

NOTES

This article was first published in *Modern Drama* 24, no. 3 (September 1981): 292–313. Reprinted by permission. All translations are mine.

    1. See Ernst Wendt, *Moderne Dramaturgie* (Frankfurt/M, 1974); Moray McGowan, "Sprache, Gewalt und Gesellschaft: Franz Xaver Kroetz und die sozialrealistischen Dramatiker des englischen Theaters," *Text + Kritik: Franz Xaver Kroetz* 57 (January 1978): 37–48; and Rainer Taëni, "Revolution oder Rebellion? Über Arnold Weskers 'Die Freunde,'" *Akzente* 18 (1971):319–30.

    2. "Folk Play," *Oxford Companion to the Theatre,* ed. Phyllis Hartnoll (London, 1951), 269.

    3. For general information on the critical *Volksstück,* see Wend Kässens and Michael Töteberg, "Fortschritt im Realismus? Zur Erneuerung des kritischen *Volksstücks* seit 1966," *Basis: Jahrbuch für deutsche Gegenwartsliteratur,* ed. Reinhold Grimm and Jost Hermand 6 (1976): 30–47; Günther Rühle, "Von der Politik zur

Rolle: Rückblick auf ein Jahrzehnt (1965–1975)," in *Positionen des Dramas: Analysen und Theorien zur deutschen Gegenwartsliteratur,* ed. Heinz Ludwig Arnold and Theo Buck (Munich, 1977), 170–99; Hellmuth Karasek, "Die Erneuerung des Volksstücks: Auf den Spuren Marieluise Fleißers und Ödön von Horváths," in *Positionen des Dramas,* 137–69; Peter Schaarschmidt, "Das moderne Volksstück: Sprache und Figuren," in *Theater und Gesellschaft: Das Volksstück im 19. und 20. Jahrhundert,* ed. Jürgen Hein (Düsseldorf, 1973), 201–17; Walter Dimter, "Die ausgestellte Gesellschaft: Zum Volksstück Horváths, der Fleißer und ihrer Nachfolger," in *Theater und Gesellschaft,* 219–45; Gerd Müller, *Das Volksstück von Raimund bis Kroetz: Die Gattung in Einzelanalysen* (Munich, 1979).

4. See below for a complete listing. For more descriptive partial listings, see Rühle, "Von der Politik zur Rolle"; Karasek, "Die Erneuerung des Volksstücks"; Schaarschmidt, "Das moderne Volksstück"; and Dimter, "Die ausgestellte Gesellschaft."

5. For example, Horváth, Fleißer, Sperr, Kroetz, Bauer, Turrini, Mitterer, or Lodemann.

6. For example, Donna L. Hoffmeister, "Strategies and Counter-Strategies: Dramatic Dialogue in the Milieu Plays of Marieluise Fleißer and Franz Xaver Kroetz" (Ph.D. diss., Brown University, 1979), 1–18; or Thomas Koebner, "Dramatik und Dramaturgie seit 1945," in *Tendenzen der deutschen Literatur seit 1945,* ed. Thomas Koebner (Stuttgart, 1971), 451–53.

7. For example, Herbert Gamper, "Horváth und die Folgen—Das Volksstück? Über neue Tendenzen im Drama," *Theater heute: Jahressonderheft,* 1971, 77.

8. For example, Joachim Hinze, "Volkstümliche Elemente im modernen deutschen Drama: Ein Beitrag zur Theorie und Praxis des Volksstücks im 20. Jahrhundert," *Hessische Blätter für Volkskunde* 61 (1970): 11–43, and others who posit Brecht's works as a model for this genre, such as Hans Poser, "Brecht's 'Herr Puntila und sein Knecht Matti': Dialektik zwischen Volksstück und Lehrstück," in *Theater und Gesellschaft,* 187–200.

9. See Dirk Bruns, "Horváth's Renewal of the Folk Play and the Decline of the Weimar Republic," *New German Critique* 18 (1979): 107–35; Erwin Rotermund, "Zur Erneuerung des Volksstückes in der Weimarer Republik: Zuckmayer und Horváth," in *Über Ödön von Horváth,* ed. Dieter Hildebrandt and Traugott Krischke (Frankfurt/M, 1972), 18–45; Martin Greiner, "Carl Zuckmayer als Volksdichter," in *Theater und Gesellschaft,* 161–73; Rolf-Peter Carl, "Theatertheorie und Volksstück bei Ödön Horváth," in *Theater und Gesellschaft,* 175–85; Hajo Kurzenberger, *Horváths Volksstücke: Beschreibung eines poetischen Verfahrens* (Munich, 1974); Günther Rühle, "Leben und Schreiben der Marieluise Fleißer aus Ingolstadt," in *Marieluise Fleißer, Gesammelte Werke,* ed. Günther Rühle (Frankfurt/M, 1972), 1:7–60; Hansjörg Schneider, "Der Kampf zwischen Individuum und Gesellschaft," in *Über Ödön von Horváth,* 59–70; Wend Kässens and Michael Töteberg, *Marieluise Fleißer* (Munich, 1979), 30–42; and Hinze, "Volkstümliche Elemente," 13–30.

10. See Jürgen Hein, "Das Volksstück: Entwicklung und Tendenzen," in *Theater und Gesellschaft*, 9–28; Roger Bauer, "Das Weiner Volkstheater zu Beginn des 19. Jahrhunderts: Noch nicht und (oder) doch schon Literatur?" in *Theater und Gesellschaft*, 29–43; and Otto Rommel, *Die Alt-Wiener Volkskomödie: Ihre Geschichte vom barocken Welt theater bis zum Tode Nestroys* (Vienna, 1952).

11. For the following definition, see Hein, "Das Volksstück," 12–14, and Artur Kutscher, *Grundriß der Theaterwissenschaft*, 2d ed. (Munich, 1949), 119–23.

12. For a more detailed account of the evolution of *Volk* as a concept, see Wolfgang Emmerich, *Germanistische Volkstumsideologie: Genese und Kritik der Volkforschung im Dritten Reich* (Tübingen, 1968), 35–56, and his *Zur Kritik der Volkstumsideologie* (Frankfurt/M, 1971), 30–50; also Wendelin Schmidt-Dengler, "Das Kontrastschema Stadt-Land in der Alt-Wiener Volkskomödie," in *Theater und Gesellschaft*, 57–68.

13. Bertolt Brecht, "Anmerkungen zum Volksstück," in *Schriften zum Theater IV (Gesammelte Werke: Werkausgabe* XVII) (Frankfurt/M, 1967), 1162. "The Volksstück is usually crude and unpretentious theater (and learned aesthetes either kill it with silence or treat it condescendingly). . . . There one finds coarse jests, mixed with sentimentality, there is preposterous morality and cheap sexuality. The evil are punished and the good are married, the diligent receive an inheritance, and the lazy go out empty-handed."

14. See Hein, "Das Volksstück," 14–21; Bauer, "Das Wiener Volkstheater zu Beginn des 19. Jahrhunderts"; and Reinhard Urbach, "Raimund und sein Publikum," in *Theater und Gesellschaft*, 101–11.

15. For more information about the socially critical Volksstück, see Hein, "Das Volksstück," 14–21; Urbach, "Raimund und sein Publikum," 106–9; and Horst Denkler, "Volkstümlichkeit, Popularität und Trivialität in der Revolutionslustspielen der Berliner Achtundvierziger," in *Popularität und Trivialität*, ed. Reinhold Grimm and Jost Hermand (Frankfurt/M, 1974), 77–100.

16. Ludwig Hoffman, ed., *Volksstücke* (Berlin, 1968), 392. "The Volksstück accommodates itself to the prevailing situation and serves an audience that values being left in peace politically. Satire has yielded to tacky humor, the common folk have been reduced to stock characters, sentimentality has replaced emotions, strength has become "pithy," the local atmosphere narrow-minded, and everything is permeated by an idyllic morality that allows for dramatic explosions on the scale of a firecracker."

17. Emmerich, *Zur Kritik*, 49. (*Volkstum* as a metaphysical-idealistic personification, which acts as a receptacle for the religious needs that otherwise cannot be met and secularizes them; *Volkstum* as an integrating ideology that obscures the existing relationships of production and power, and that can be deployed as an active weapon because of its psychologically regressive, atavistic tendencies; *Volkstum* as a biological organism that revokes the historical dimension of humanity on the level of nature.)

18. See Hoffman, *Volksstücke*, 393; Hein, "Das Volksstück," 21.

19. See Rühle, "Von der Politik"; Karasek, "Die Erneuerung des Volksstücks," 144–45; Bruns, "Horváth's Renewal of the Folk Play," 109; Kässens and Töteberg, "Fortschritt," 30–32; and Dieter Kafitz, "Die Problematisierung des individualistischen Menschenbildes im deutschsprachigen Drama der Gegenwart (Franz Xaver Kroetz, Thomas Bernhard, Botho Strauß)," *Basis: Jahrbuch für deutsche Gegenwartsliteratur,* ed. Reinhold Grimm and Jost Hermand 10 (1980); 93–126.

20. See Theodor W. Adorno et. al., *The Authoritarian Personality* (New York, 1950), and the propagation of his theses during the student movement by Rudi Dutschke, "Die Widersprüche des Spätkapitalismus, die antiautoritären Studenten und ihr Verhältnis zur Dritten Welt," in *Rebellion der Studenten oder die neue Opposition* (Reinbek, 1968), 58ff.; and Kässens and Töteberg, "Fortschritt," 32–34.

21. Rainer Werner Fassbinder, stage directions to *Preparadise sorry now* in *Antiteater,* 1 (Frankfurt/M, 1970), 32.

22. As defined in Theodor W. Adorno, "Zur Dialektik des Engagements," *Neue Rundschau* 73 (1962); 93–100.

23. For the following arguments, see Peter Handke, "Straßentheater und Theatertheater," *Theater heute* (April 1968), rpt. in *Deutsche Dramaturgie der sechziger Jahre,* ed. Helmut Kreuzer (Tübingen, 1974), 124–27; Martin Sperr, "Was erwarte ich vom Theater?" *Theater heute: Jahressonderheft* (1967), rpt in *Deutsche Dramaturgie,* 65–67; and Franz Xaver Kroetz, "Horváth von heute für heute," in *Weitere Aussichten . . . :Ein Lesebuch,* ed. Thomas Thieringer (Cologne, 1976), 519–23, and his "Liegt die Dummheit auf der Hand? *Pioniere in Ingolstadt*—Überlegungen zu einem Stück von Marieluise Fleißer," in *Weitere Aussichten,* 523–28.

24. See Hans Macher, interview with Martin Sperr, Rainer Werner Fassbinder, and Franz Xaver Kroetz, *Donau Kurier* (Ingolstadt), 23 November 1971, rpt. in *Materialien zum Leben und Schreiben der Marieluise Fleißer,* ed. Günther Rühle (Frankfurt/M, 1973), 403–5; Marieluise Fleißer, "Alle meine Söhne: Über Martin Sperr, Rainer Werner Fassbinder und Franz Xaver Kroetz," *Theater heute: Jahresheft* (1972), rpt in *Fleißer Materialien,* 405–10; and Kroetz, "Horváth von heute."

25. See Rotermund, "Zur Erneuerung des Volksstückes," 22–45; Bruns, "Horváth's Renewal of the Folk Play," 114; Hein, "Das Volksstück," 22–23; and Jean-Claude François, "Brecht, Horváth and the Popular Theater," *New German Critique* 18 (1979), 146.

26. Ödön Horváth, "Interview mit Cronauer," in *Gesammelte Werke: Werkausgabe,* ed. Traugott Krischke and Dieter Hildebrandt, 2d ed. (Frankfurt/M, 1978), 1:7–16; and Horváth, "Gebrauchsanweisung," in *Gesammelte Werke,* 8: 659–65.

27. Horváth, "Gebrauchsanweisung," 660–61.

28. Marieluise Fleißer, "Neue Stoffe für das Drama?" from Herbert Ihering, "Das Theater von Morgen," *Berliner Börsen-Courier,* 31 March 1929, rpt. in *Fleißer Materialien,* 170.

29. Horváth, "Gebrauchsanweisung," 662–63; Bruns, "Horváth's Renewal of the Folk Play," 114–19. See Wilhelm Reich, *The Mass Psychology of Fascism*, 3d ed., trans. Theodore P. Wolfe (New York, 1946); Siegfried Kracauer, *Die Angestellten aus dem neuesten Deutschland* (Frankfurt/M, 1971); and Oskar Negt and Alexander Kluge, *Öffentlichkeit und Erfahrung: Zur Organisationsanalyse von bürgerlicher und proletarischer Öffentlichkeit* (Frankfurt/M, 1972), for background material on this topic. See also Kroetz, "Horváth von heute."

30. See Horváth, "Gebrauchsanweisung," 662–63; "Interview," 13.

31. Gamper, "Horváth und die Folgen," 74. "Such a process is not primarily motivated by individual psychological factors; the gap between the speech and the behavior of Horváth's figures is that between culture and 'bestiality.' Through a culture that is not their own, represented by a language that has been reduced to empty phrases as well as by laws and moral principles that they cannot obey, they are thrown back on their 'asocial' . . . , their bestial instincts. They perish as victims of both nature and culture."

32. Horváth, "Gebrauchsanweisung," 662–63. "In order to portray a person of today's world realistically, I had to let the *Bildungsjargon* [cultural and media jargon] speak for itself. The *Bildungsjargon* (and its causes), however, would naturally demand criticism—and the dialogue of the new *Volksstück* evolves in this manner, and with it the person, and only therewith, the dramatic action—a synthesis of earnestness and irony."

33. Alfred Kerr, "Marieluise Fleißer: 'Fegefeuer in Ingolstadt,'" *Berliner Tageblatt*, 26 April 1926, rpt. in *Fleißer Materialien*, 37.

34. Fleißer, "Neue Stoffe," 170; Fleißer also remarked: "Ich könnte natürlich immer nur etwas zwischen Männern und Frauen machen," in Marieluise Fleißer and Hans Fröhlich, "Etwas zwischen Männern und Frauen," *Stuttgarter Nachrichten*, 16 February 1971, rpt. in *Fleißer Materialien*, 349. See also Kässens and Töteberg, *Fleißer*, 37–42; Karasek, "Die Erneuerung des Volksstücks," 138–45; Rühle, "Von der Politik," 179–81; Schaarschmidt, 201–6; Dimter "Die ausgestellte Gesellschaft"; Hinze, "Volkstümliche Elemente," 18–25; and Rühle, "Leben und Schreiben," 50–56.

35. See Rühle, "Leben und Schreiben," 22, 51; Kroetz, "*Pioniere*," 525.

36. Fleißer, "Neue Stoffe," 170.

37. See Benjamin Henrichs, "Die Sprache verloren," *Süddeutsche Zeitung* (Munich), 22 February 1971, rpt. in *Fleißer Materialien*, 275; Herbert Ihering, "'Fegefeuer in Ingolstadt,'" *Berliner Börsen-Courier*, 26 April 1926, rpt. in *Fleißer Materialien*, 40–41; Kurt Pinthus, "Marieluise Fleißer," *Vortrag im Berliner Rundfunk*, 18 December 1928, rpt. in *Fleißer Materialien*, 370; Kroetz, "*Pioniere*," 524; also Susan L. Cocalis, "'Weib ist Weib': Mimetische Darstellung contra emanzipatorische Tendenz in den Dramen Marieluise Fleißers," in *Die Frau als Heldin und Autorin*, ed. Wolfgang Paulsen (Berne, 1979), 201–10.

38. See Kässens and Töteberg, "Fortschritt," 30; Hans Macher, Interview, in *Fleißer Materialien*, 403–4.

39. Fritz Rumler, "Einen Fetzen muß man aus euch machen," *Der Spiegel,* 9 March 1970, rpt. in *Fleißer Materialien,* 353.

40. See note 4.

41. See note 5.

42. See Karl Veit Riedel, "Volkstümliche Strukturen des Fernsehspiels," *Hessische Blätter für Volkskunde* 58 (1967); 47–67.

43. In this respect the authors would follow the example of Edward Bond, "Drama and the Dialectics of Violence," *Theatre Quarterly* 2, no. 5 (1972); 4–14. See Sperr, "Was erwarte ich?" and Martin Sperr and Peter Stein, "Wie wir Bonds Stück inszenierten," *Theater heute: Jahressonderheft (1967),* rpt. in *Deutsche Dramaturgie,* 67–72.

44. Peter Turrini, *Lesebuch: Stücke, Pamphlete, Filme, Reaktionen, etc.,* ed. Ulf Birbaumer (Vienna, 1978), 126. "I chose the form of the *Volksstück* for this story in order to reach the audience where I expected to find it: in its willingness to be entertained, in the imbecilic mediocrity of the Löwinger clichés. I am hoping that the audience will be prepared to go the whole way it has chosen itself. For me the theater is primarily sensuality, cruelty: I want to distance myself from the norms of a boring, psychologically and technically skilled dramaturgy in order to explore the depths of human nature. I want to take the audience with me on this venture: shock as consequence and not as an end in itself."

45. See Evalouise Panzner, *Franz Xaver Kroetz und seine Rezeption* (Stuttgart, 1976), 14–23; Franz Xaver Kroetz, "Soll der Kumpel Abonnent werden? Über das Volks- und Arbeitertheater," in *Weitere Aussichten,* 545–46; Rolf-Peter Carl, *Franz Xaver Kroetz* (Munich, 1978), 52.

46. Franz Xaver Kroetz and Helmut Walbert, "Die Lust am Lebendigen: Diskussion der Redaktion 'kürbiskern,'" in *Weitere Aussichten,* 603. "People do not know how violence builds up and is released. Violence is an anonymous force. Therefore many contemporary dramatists want to show how people come to the point that violence is their only outlet. At least in my case it is not a matter of defending violent acts, but rather of denouncing society." See also Kroetz, "Horváth von heute" and *"Pioniere."*

47. Ernst Bloch, *Erbschaft dieser Zeit* (Frankfurt/M, 1973), 113–23; Ernst Bloch, "Gespräch über Ungleichzeitigkeit," *Kursbuch* 39 (1979); 1 ff.

48. Kässens and Töteberg, "Fortschritt," 38–46; Renate Schostack, "'Pioniere in Ingolstadt' (ZDF)," *Frankfurter Allgemeine Zeitung,* 21 May 1971, rpt. in *Fleißer Materialien,* 266; Ernst Wendt, "Hartnäckige Menschenbeobachtung," *Theater Heute* (June 1971), rpt. in *Fleißer Materialien,* 288; Rühle, "Von der Politik," 181–82; Rühle, "Leben und Schreiben," 51.

49. Ute Nyssen, "Nachwort," in Wolfgang Bauer, *Magic Afternoon, Change, Party for Six: Drei Stücke* (Munich, 1972), 134. "He [the dramatist] offers no explicit or social motivation, and that makes this behavior all the more threatening for the viewers, for they are not provided with the possibility of easily rationalizing the

events away, i.e., of explaining the dramatized situation in terms of anonymous, distant, and superficial social factors. The events on stage do not allow for transcendence but, rather, force the viewer to enter into and remain in their world."

50. The categories are used by Hinze, "Volkstümliche Elemente," 26–39.

51. Kroetz, "Pioniere," 527. "Drama does not take place where Mr. Weiss and Mr. Hölderlin pass judgment on who was the more decent and thus effete revolutionary in a revolution that was utopian anyway but, rather, where a maid is able to get a night off in order to lose her virginity properly, which is meaningless, because the social situation leaves only a few minutes for such unproductive activities."

52. Franz Xaver Kroetz, Wunschkonzert, in Gesammelte Stücke (Frankfurt / M, 1975), 185. "[Franz Xaver Kroetz:] If only the explosive force of this massive exploitation and oppression would not be directed at the exploited and oppressed themselves, we would have a revolutionary situation. As it is now, we just have many cases of minor, senseless suicides and murders, which themselves serve to affirm the system: those who are that far gone that they would have the strength and the courage 'to throw their own life in the balance' are delivering themselves into the jurisdiction of their natural enemies. In this way they involuntarily cleanse the society that they are indicting. . . . Only in this way is it possible that the inhumane order in which we live can be maintained and that we have to continue living in it."

53. See note 23.

54. See note 22. Cf. Jean-Paul Sartre, What Is Literature? trans. Bernard Frechtman (New York, 1965); Horst Albert Glaser, "Formen des Engagements: Ein Beitrag zur gegenwärtigen Diskussion," in Tendenzen der Deutschen Literatur, 139–56.

55. Adorno, "Zur Dialektik," 106. "Every political commitment to the world must be renounced before the idea of a politically committed art can be realized, including the polemical alienation that the theoretician Brecht conceived and that he practiced all the less, the more he believed in humanity. This paradox, which sounds contrived, is based—without much philosophizing—on the most elementary experience: Kafka's prose works, Beckett's plays or the truly shocking novel 'The Nameless One,' are effective in a way that makes the officially partisan literature seem like child's play; they evoke the fear that existentialism only discusses. By stripping reality of all appearances they burst art open from the inside out, while self-proclaimed partisan art, working from the outside and therefore only for appearance's sake, remains in the service of that art. The inevitability [of autonomous art] necessitates those changes of attitude which politically committed works merely demand."

56. See Kurzenberger, Horváths Volksstücke, 113; Panzner, Franz Xaver Kroetz, 16–23, 25–26; Kässens and Töteberg, "Fortschritt," 39; Carl, Kroetz, 29, 164; Michael Töteberg, "Der Kleinbürger auf der Bühne: Die Entwicklung des Dramatikers Franz Xaver Kroetz und das realistische Volksstück," Akzente 23 (1976),

169; Pinthus, in *Fleißer Materialien*, 367–68; Kroetz, "Horváth von heute," 519–21; *"Pioniere,"* 526; "Über DIE MASSNAHME von Bertolt Brecht," in *Weitere Aussichten*, 574–75; "Meine MÄNNERSACHE," in *Weitere Aussichten*, 556; "Ich säße lieber in Bonn im Bundestag: 'Theatre heute'—Gespräch," in *Weitere Aussichten*, 589; "Die Lust am Lebendigen," 596.

57. See Theodor W. Adorno, "Zur Musik der Dreigroschenoper," in *Bertolt Brechts Dreigroschenbuch: Texte, Materialien, Dokumente*, ed. Siegfried Unseld (Frankfurt/M, 1960), 186; and Kurzenberger, *Horváths Volksstücke*, 111–13.

58. Carl, "Theatertheorie," 176–77.

59. Carl, "Theatertheorie," 177; Kässens and Töteberg, "Fortschritt," 31; Kroetz, "Bücherdeckel—Sargdeckel? Über den Versuch, sozialistischen Realismus in westdeutsche Volksromane zu packen," in *Weitere Aussichten*, 537–41, and "Soll der Kumpel Abonnent werden?" 541–47.

60. Carl, "Theatertheorie," 177. "The ability for abstract thought, transposition, or recognition that is actually presupposed here belongs to the educational advantage of those at whom the didactic element of the play is not directed. The segments of society, however, whose level of understanding allegedly forms the basis of the play, will be reached neither as a theatergoing nor as a reading public."

61. Carl, *Kroetz*, 39–41; Panzner, *Franz Xaver Kroetz*, 24–25.

62. Carl, *Kroetz*, 27–28, 40, 48–51; Panzner, *Franz Xaver Kroetz*, 21–22, 36.

63. Carl, *Kroetz*, 28. "Merely the description of a condition which succumbs to superficial impressions and fails to recognize the dialectics of essence and appearances, inability to determine the causal factors beyond biological or sociological determinism, renunciation of any perspectives that lead further, and therefore an objective stabilization of the conditions that were decried."

64. Walter Benjamin, "Der Autor als Produzent," in *Versuche über Brecht*, ed. Rolf Tiedemann (Frankfurt/M, 1966), 105. "That to supply an apparatus of production without changing it . . . is a highly questionable procedure, even if the material that is being supplied is of a revolutionary nature. We are confronted with the fact . . . that the bourgeois apparatus of production and publication can assimilate and even propagate amazing quantities of revolutionary themes without seriously threatening its own existence or the existence of the property-owning classes."

65. Kafitz, "Die Problematisierung," 98–102, points out Kroetz's awareness of this medium. See Riedel, "Volkstümliche Strukturen," for a more detailed analysis of the popular structures of television programming.

66. Kässens and Töteberg, "Fortschritt," 30.

67. See Sperr and Stein, pp. 67–72, or the German version of Arnold Wesker's plays, *Gesammelte Stücke* (Frankfurt/M, 1969).

Else Lasker-Schüler

Born in 1869 into a family of middle-class Jews, Lasker-Schüler began writing poetry at age five and distinguished herself, primarily as a poet, throughout her life. She married and moved to Berlin in 1898, without a university education. In Berlin, she disassociated herself from her husband and joined a circle of artists united by their antibourgeois stance. After her divorce from Lasker, she married the editor of the central Expressionist publication, *Der Sturm*. As a kind of proto–performance artist, Lasker-Schüler lived as two characters from her fiction: Joseph, the prince of Thebes, and Princess Tino of Baghdad—both of whom appear in full orientalist costume—perhaps as a way of marking herself as Semitic.

Twice divorced, living in costumes (one of them cross-gender), bisexual, and a bohemian artist, Lasker-Schüler flaunted customs and taboos. Her first play, *Die Wupper* (The People of Wuppertal), is her most famous. Published in 1909 and premiering in Berlin in 1919, it concerns what may be considered the "asocial" elements and factory workers in Wuppertal at the turn of the century. The play is a classic of a certain kind of social drama in Germany, staging class conflicts, strikes, and the effect of social conditions on personal relationships. In 1931, Lasker-Schüler won the coveted Kleist Prize for Literature. In that same year, however, she was beaten up by Nazi thugs and fled to Switzerland. Harassed by immigration officials and out of step with the local Swiss-Jewish community, she emigrated to Palestine. She later returned to Switzerland, but, in 1940, Swiss immigration officials refused to issue her another visa. She returned to Palestine, where she lived in abject poverty (often without food) and, again, out of sync with the local community. Martin Buber, a prominent Jewish man of letters, refused to acknowledge her work; thus, in a sense, it was accepted neither as German (an identity denied to her as a Jew) nor as Jewish. In 1945, after

Else Lasker-Schüler dressed as Prince Yussef. (Courtesy Kösel Verlag and the Else Lasker-Schüler Archive, Jerusalem.)

a long illness, she died in Jerusalem. Only recently has she been reclaimed as a Jewish poet. *IandI* was written during her exile in Jerusalem and registers the later contradictions and impossibilities in her life.

IandI

In this play, there are many religious, seemingly spiritual references. In contrast to the religion in Fleißer's drama, which stands for the oppressive role the Catholic church played for women in Bavaria, Lasker-Schüler's Jewish references, at this time politicized by the Nazis, stand for the opposite—a socially transgressive religious identity. Here was a religious identity that caused ostracism and death. Thus, a play that is the undoing of the Christian, classicial story of Faust and Mephistopheles—with Old Testament figures on the one hand and Nazis on the other—was, at such a time in history, a kind of political theater.

When I saw the Living Theater's production of the play in Berlin in 1990, directed by Judith Malina, I was most struck by the portrait of the playwright in the final act. In order to "read" the play in the context of a woman playwright, one might begin with act 6. The playwright is sitting in a garden in Jerusalem. Her own poverty, hunger, and isolation as a writer are personified in the character of the scarecrow.

SCARECROW: I am . . . made of straw and broomsticks, the counterfeit of a higher being. My graying braid came out of a trunk dating back to Wolfgang's period, pure rococo.

One can read this character as a part of Lasker-Schüler's divided self: the starving woman as a cultural counterfeit of Goethe, tattered and wearing the now sullied wig of the rococo. As scarecrow, she claims to have walked with Goethe, even to have invented a famous poem, but she is not allowed any place in history or in art—she is merely failed, cultural waste. She cannot write from the dominant Christian German tradition. She cannot write the great play of damnation and salvation. Instead, as the scarecrow, she must confess her transgressive identity: "On holidays, I'm Abraham! Or Isaac! Occasionally Jacob. But sometimes when the ladies come to the lady's salon for tea, they call me 'Little Cohen.'"

Beginning with this scene, one can then read back to the first scene of the play, which sets up the dramatic action as the production of a play within a play: Lasker-Schüler's *Faust*. Here, the play itself, rather than the character Faust, has been led astray not by Mephisto, but by German history as Mephisto. The vacant Nazi stage is peopled by exiles. Max Reinhardt has returned from Hollywood to Jerusalem to direct the play, and the Ritz brothers, American vaudeville comedians, follow in his wake. The United States, the other land of exile, haunts the text. Judith Malina's staging of the Ritz brothers made interesting sense of their role in the play. A film clip of a scene played by the real Ritz brothers was repeated over and over in the background, while actors dressed as those in the film and repeating the same gestures played in front of it. This burlesque scene playing simultaneously with the Faust scenes undercut the impact of the great classic; its constant repetition and low, comic style disturbed the notion of "the eternal," as suggested by the Faust theme. Then, in the scene with Mephisto, the actors playing the Ritz brothers became the Nazis. The clowns turn into the evil ones, and history becomes a farce, as Marx suggested. At certain points in history, Lasker-Schüler suggests, the parameters of comedy and tragedy collapse inward, leaving only the obscene conflation of seeming classical idealism with brutal torture. After Auschwitz, as Adorno wrote, poetry is barbaric.[1]

In *IandI*, Lasker-Schüler has created a complex pastiche of characters, places, and themes, rather than a simple narrative structure. This pastiche effect serves to dramatize the historical intersection of fascism, sexism, anti-Semitism, imperialism, and the dynamics of desire. Act 3 provides a good example of this convergence. Martha, the 195-year-old sex object / servant, is waiting tables for the Nazis. She then seduces Goebbels on a terrrace overlooking the park of Hell, where there is a Cupid fountain in the foreground and the idol Baal behind, in the bushes—a classical European referent and an Old Testament, hedonistic one. Martha, who has trouble hearing over the fountain waters of Psyche, mishears that Hitler is called the "mighty cock," conflating his patriarchal power and his own sexual politics. Enter Van der Lubbe, a "weakminded devil" singing nonsense rhymes about Calcutta. He is identified by Martha as "the crown prince of Dutch India"—in other words, a symbol of male power in the colonies. As she and Goebbels begin their exit, Goebbels sees Naziland coming into view, and Martha catches her panties on some brambles, somewhere between Psyche and Baal. As they leave the park, Goebbels is attempting to get Martha to show him Mephisto's secret files.

The accumulation of cultural tropes and political figures makes the play implode, rushing inward through German classic and contemporary history,

American movie culture, sexism, secret files, a Nazi obsession, classical gods, Old Testament idols, and the entrance of colonialist idiots. As a political play, this form contradicts Brecht's notion that the Epic should pull things apart, clarify contradictions, and reveal practices. Instead, the formal elements and social critiques are all swallowed up in a vortex of oppressive relationships, in which all of the pressures collude. The play is postmodern in its quotational pastiche style. It careens through history and the imaginary, stopping at the end on the image of a scarecrow in the garden in Jerusalem. *IandI* is the self that split—the divide of home / land that cleaves the playwright's skull.

Lasker-Schüler, like Fleißer, invents another version of the Epic form. In her Epic style, Lasker-Schüler takes on the classics as Brecht took on *Antigone*; foregrounds the conditions of theatrical production, putting the director and playwright onstage; and speaks her historical moment (the invasion of France, for example) and its material conditions (the Nazis' need for petroleum). The accumulation and acceleration of elements, rather than their isolation and careful iteration, governs her composition. Furthermore, since identity becomes the base for Hitler's fascist oppression of Jews, the play moves through the lyric—a marking of subjectivity and emotion on representation. In contrast to Brecht's scientism and his use of the pedagogical, Lasker-Schüler's play moves inward, to the IandI, rather than outward to labor conditions or the manipulation of markets. One might term this kind of dramatic construction the proximity effect—the reverse of Brecht's distancing device. Through a proto-sense of the politics of location, Lasker-Schüler employs the *mise-en-scène* as both a subjective and historical topography of identity. The feminist critic familiar with Minnie Bruce Pratt's "Identity: Skin / Blood / Heart" recognizes, in *IandI*, how identity politics and the system of representation intertwine. Lasker-Schüler's creation of the proximity effect offers a revolutionary new form of feminist theater.

IandI stages a specifically German identity politics for women in the times of fascism and anti-Semitism. In its construction, it dramatizes how gender and sexuality may intersect with national identity and interrogates the stage for its productions and the canon for its patriarchal and anti-Semitic values.

NOTE

1. Theodor W. Adorno, *Prisms,* trans. Samuel and Shierry Weber (London, 1967), 34.

Else Lasker-Schüler

IandI

A Theatrical Tragedy in Six Acts, a Prologue, and an Epilogue

Translated by Beate Hein Bennett

Characters

BAAL	A SCHOLAR
KING SAUL	MARINUS VAN DER LUBBE
KING DAVID	HERMANN GÖRING
KING SOLOMON	JOSEF GOEBBELS
THE POET	VON RIBBENTROP
FAUSTUS	HEINRICH HIMMLER
MEPHISTO	ALFRED ROSENBERG
MARTHA SCHWERDTLEIN	VON SCHIRACH
THE SCARECROW	RUDOLF HESS
THE RITZ BROTHERS	ROBERT LEY
DIRECTOR MAX REINHARDT	ADOLF HITLER
THE BUSINESS MANAGER	(THE FÜHRER)
THE THEATER DOCTOR	NAZI SOLDIERS
THE CRITICS	DEVILS
EDITOR SWET	KARL HANNEMANN

The first five acts take place in Hell, actually a theater in Gehenna, or the Infernal Regions, a place below the David's Tower in Jerusalem. The sixth act takes place in the garden of an eye doctor's house in Jerusalem.

[Several of the characters are silent presences. The above order is according
to the playwright's script and has nothing to do with the characters' order
of importance or appearance. —Trans.]

PROLOGUE

(*The* POET *can be heard talking to a companion on their way to the*
theater.)

POET:
   Ten years ago, or more, I fled
   Berlin, that god-forsaken Nazi city—
   invisible inside a golden ball
   suspended high above the murderous cries
   of the enslaved people of Berlin.
   Since then I see myself as one
   who has a more enlightened view of life
   than the cynic citizen imagines me to have
   in all this plumage. (Beware, you feather thieves!)
   This vulture's quill with which I write
   on rusty leathery paper
   was dipped in blood.
   I would rather write my manuscript
   on the yellowed pages of my heart—
   though people then might think I'm up for sale.
   I could accept that judgment
   if readers bought my books to adorn their shelves.
   For then we would be bound as book relations.
   Oh my dear friends up front and you back there
   who only can afford the cheaper seats, I am so tired.
   I know one cannot spend a lifetime in some nest
   stuck to sheer rock, battered by November storms,
   mercilessly teased by scoundrel spring and ripped apart
   at last by the daggers of July.
   . . . My destiny has led me to a heavenly vision— . . .
   and you may wonder why, having drunk from the silver cup,
   I return home to your earthen box.
   True, your narrow world cannot contain

a poet's boundless dream.
Forgive my overbearing pride, dear friend.
After all, I live a higher kind of life. —
Lightless nights are kindled by my joy
and stars have risen from my very eyes.
I lived upon this earth light years ago
and found only my poetry was not illusion!
So follow me through these narrow alleys.
Let's leave the modern city earlier than on working days.
Besides, the tower clock is slow, as is my watch!
Billboard dreams are glistening on the houses,
their sparkles flashing right to left
exchanging light like doggerel rhymes.
A witch's sabbath slaps me in the face,
just as I compose an image in
my poem, mystically.
Come, take a seat, mein Freund, and watch
this hellish play of my poetic art
straight from the theater of my heart.

(She whistles softly, with emotion, the end of "Must I go, must I go, must I leave my little town, while you, my love, stay here. . . ." While a hurdy-gurdy repeats the last verse, the curtain opens.)

ACT I

A place near the David's Tower, which native Palestinians call the Infernal Regions. In the crumbling stones of the ancient royal loggia, the three kings, SAUL, DAVID, *and* SOLOMON *sit on splendid thrones, uncannily immobile, painted brightly and gilded like the figures in a Panopticum. In the director's box:* MAX REINHARDT, *who has been invited from Hollywood to Jerusalem to direct this play. Across from him are three American comics,* THE RITZ BROTHERS. *The* HOUSE DOCTOR *just makes it to his seat. The* CRITICS, *arms folded, greet one another before the play begins.*

The Players:
THE DEVIL

DOCTOR FAUST

MARTHA SCHWERDTLEIN

VOICES from the audience: EDITOR SWET, TWO YOUNG WOMEN, etc.

THE POET

NAZI LEADERS AND THEIR GANG

BAAL

(*The* POET *who wrote this daring tragedy steps in front of the audience.*)

POET:

    Out of a quiet, timeless place,

    that neither word nor deed can manifest,

    I step into a world of your creation—

    at home, zum weekend, heute . . .

    Your world, dear people, is a bitter pill to take.

    Here I come, like a wet poodle,

    slouching home in secret—

    straight into the jaw of lukewarm phrases—

    my lips flashed stars—

    and all for what—

    all for humanity.

    But that is not our only purpose, my dear friends.

    For God's own reasons, the human soul

    (indeed, all souls still shackled to the body)

    cannot find peace in heaven

    which is not really very far from earth.

    Of course, the poet's inspiration longs to rise

    up out of the realm of the cold word

    into the blue of heaven.

(*Suddenly the barrel organ begins to play loudly.*)

    Listen, people, to this murder story

    which I committed in the dead of night!

    Trust me, I tell the truth when I poetize,

    you must suspend your disbelief—

    Just before the break of dawn, I split myself in half

    No, it was no hallucination—

    I and I, we broke apart!

A WOMAN from the audience: What a bore!

POET:

    When face encounters profile

and the profile encounters its full face—
I still bleed from that violent act.
After a life of futile calling,
I freed myself from endless solitude.
In my entire lifetime, I and I could never meet
but now my halves agreed to this courageous rendezvous.
The audience will shortly see
our miming talent is sublime.
Though unmingled in my dark and narrow body,
we will face each other on the open stage.
Between our virtue and our sins,
we declare the union of the I and I,
as it was surely intended to be
in the ancient testament's decree.

(*A short pause*)

Attention!
This is dedicated to my dear mother,
a great admirer of Goethe.
She is the guardian of my divided self.
Poor audience, united in a single yawn—
true, why should the overture be loaded down
with all this poetry?
Get the news straight from me:
Satan, the devil of devils, has surrendered!

(*The* POET *tries in vain to continue.*)

SWET: The report's a hoax! Where are the facts?

(*The* POET *makes another attempt to continue.*)

SWET: It's for the birds!
POET: Editor Swet, this is the second time you've interrupted me.
WOMAN in the audience: Aw, come off it.
POET:
    In life as on the stage,
    I speak the truth, the plain and naked truth,
    in verse as well as prose . . .
SCHOLAR: Verse, if you please . . .

VOICES from the audience: Holland's lost, Belgium gone, France, Denmark, Norway . . .

SWET (*calming the audience*): My newspaper *Haarez* would have reported the facts by now, if they were true.

POET: Mr. Swet, you are mistaken in your guess about what I have not said:

Satan, the devil of all devils, has surrendered.

Yes, indeed, he has!

Before God in Heaven, in the fourth act!

KING DAVID (*arises, unmoved*): Baruch ata adonai eluhenu, melekh haolam. . . . Blessed be the Eternal, King of the Universe . . .

(*The curtain falls but rises again immediately. The real play begins.*)

MEPHISTO (*leaning against a vine-covered balustrade on a terrace of his Infernal Palace*): Although I did not compose my satanic verses in iambic or trochaic measure, I was the one who put them on the stage.

(FAUST *remains unmoved.*)

MEPHISTO: Have I embarrassed you in front of these romantic philistines, Doctor Faust? Tell me, Henry, what was it you disliked so much? Is it the pompous style of this infernal scenery? Sit down, my friend, I'm nervous. It's time I knew the reason for your rancor.

FAUST: Those devils that you sent into the world report that both parts of my drama, one and two, were burnt in Weimar in the marketplace amid a howling crowd.

(*Short pause*)

MEPHISTO: I smelled it. I rather relish the stench of burning books and your charred verses, I savored from afar. (*Short pause*) No use complaining. God's Testament was burnt as well, the Bible, first and second part.

FAUST: Yes, late at night while praying, forgive me, I questioned if Earth and Heaven and Hell were really God's creation or if they did not somehow form themselves according to a prior pattern—

MEPHISTO (*cynical*): Most everlasting—

FAUST: The world exists, it seems to me, only through the human genius. What does the audience believe? It would be fantastic if it were only human fantasy. Human fantasy?

MEPHISTO: When Adam's homeless children were driven out of Paradise, they sought to live in a world of their illusion.

FAUST: And you, Mephisto, sinister man?

MEPHISTO: You ask mich selbst? I was the first to crawl across the plan of the Eternal and made my home in darkness. (*Boasting*) And God's earthly kingdom died from my serpent's sting.

FAUST: Now I'm really lost, my prince.

MEPHISTO: You're not alone. Billions of people, confused like you, go round in circles and cannot find their way.

FAUST: And the Eternal One, is He still firmly on his throne?

MEPHISTO: I'm not too sure of that. (*Short pause*) But let me ask you, Doctor Faust, with all due respect, why He created me, the Devil, from slime and scorn to live forever?

FAUST: I feel sorry for you, Mephisto.

MEPHISTO: Yet man created from a richer mix is no more savory. Just looking at him gives me indigestion. You and I, we all had to take a bite of that same sour apple. (*Short pause*) It tasted good to Adam Kadmon and does so even now, after deluge, death, and destruction—

FAUST: and darkness everywhere, and nowhere light—

MEPHISTO: Nowhere! And I have searched for it, like you! For, after all, I am a man like you!

FAUST (*amazed*): "And if you come in the final hour," says the Lord— the Lord (*with a sign of relief*).

MEPHISTO: The world prepared for its redemption before it was even born.

FAUST: You wicked ancient cynic, you . . .

MEPHISTO: who remained true

FAUST: to your godforsaken nature.

MEPHISTO: A faithless counterfeit of God's own image like yourself, my friend, belongs beneath my cloven hoof.

FAUST: Why this evil game, Mephisto?

MEPHISTO: Do you perhaps regret the vow?

FAUST: I am no match—

MEPHISTO: For God's sake! Who would not like to buy a home made of cement? It's cozy and most likely permanent! Man is a midget who hates the elemental for he's afraid of all that's monumental!

FAUST: Your words make me ashamed, my prince—

MEPHISTO: I strongly hope creation's unresolved debris will stall you only temporarily.

FAUST: I am ashamed—

MEPHISTO: I feel your heart's pain, and, like that maiden in a certain play,
Henry, the cheeks of my heart blush with you, coy but ready . . .

FAUST: Satan, is this an unkind slur on Margarete?

MEPHISTO (*two-faced*): You are mistaken, Faust.

FAUST: My God, I never could resist temptation.

(MARTHA *enters the room.*)

MEPHISTO (*his back to* FAUST): I could spit into his pious face. Martha
Schwerdtlein, read page F from my ledger.

REINHARDT: Listen, Mephisto. Give me a more scornful reading of that
last line: "I could spit into his pious face," etc.

MEPHISTO: I could spit into his pious face. Hey, old lady, how about it?

MARTHA: (*mumbling, as usual*): "Soup gets cold, no doubt about it."
Patience, Sir Satan,
it's not easy to find
and Sir Satan knows,
Martha is getting old and blind.

MEPHISTO: By the way, Margarete, quite in vogue, paints her Cupid lips
each night with lover's red. Her milkwhite body, though seductive still,
has gathered rolls of fat which she pours carefully into a trim corset.

MARTHA: Sir Satan knows, I'm going blind— (*She reads from the ledger
like a schoolgirl who has just learned to read.*) "The maiden weakened
Faustus's senses,
so he asked Satan,
how to bring down her defenses." (*Exits*)

FAUST: My Gretchen. . . . (*to* MEPHISTO, *indignantly*): You hid a trap
inside my senses!

MEPHISTO: But then you reached far greater heights than I—

(MARTHA *enters again, practicing her curtsies.*)

FAUST (*wistfully*): Her smile, a bubbling brook—

(MEPHISTO *laughs mockingly.*)

FAUST: Devil!

MEPHISTO: Do not forget, my friend, I am your personal devil, your very
own.

FAUST: What substance were you made of? Surely not of human salt nor the dust of long-forgotten dynasties.

MEPHISTO: The doctor's wrong! Those few angelic beings who deny that they resemble me are hardly enough to constitute humanity.

(FAUST *sinks to his knees.*)

MEPHISTO: What has come over you, my poet laureate?

FAUST: I beg the Lord, I, His child, I beg Him on my knees for—light.

There is a weeping in the world,
As if the dear Lord God had died—
And the shadow falls like lead,
resting heavy as the grave.

Come, draw closer, let us hide—
life lies in our hearts
as if in coffins.

Let us kiss deeply, you and I—
There is a yearning
throbbing in this world—
and surely we must die . . .

MEPHISTO: He doesn't hear you. . . . This Hell in which you find yourself is modernized and hardly God's domain. The fires of purgatory were invented by some monk to be the miserable sinners' court of law.

FAUST: There is no reference to that in the testament. Perhaps you found some lost fragment? (*A short pause*) Else He would come and help me as I before Him bow . . . (*Chanting*) as I before Him bow . . .

MEPHISTO: I am His witness—God is here! His curses sent me packing out of Paradise! And not a single grain of corn was left unturned! The first woman broke me with the first fruit from the tree! (*A short pause*) Take comfort, Henry, and turn your suffering into song—yes, sing, sing more fervently the old chorale—while I forge my sword on the fiery anvil!

(MARTHA *reappears on the terrace.*)

MARTHA:
Sirs, permit me to announce, dinner is served.
Those tender angel wings are burning to a crisp.
(*She counts the number of guests on her fingers.*)

What am I saying?
One, two, three guests? Four guests in all
await Sir Satan in the banquet hall.

(MEPHISTO *rises full of bluster.*)

REINHARDT: May I ask, Mephisto, that you make less noise getting up?
A more majestic rising up.

MEPHISTO: It's not my style to play Goethe without some hyperbole.

REINHARDT: I respect your right to disagree with me, Sir Devil. (*He notices
the actor* KARL HANNEMANN *in the wings.*) Why don't you take over
this leading role? Your late father, may he rest in peace, though later a
producer, made his fame and fortune playing Mephisto around the world.

POET: Gin Charly...

(MEPHISTO *hands over his devil's beard to his colleague* HANNEMANN *with
restrained regret.*)

HANNEMANN (*to* REINHARDT):
The devil's beard is on my chin.
I'm afraid, it's old and thin.

REINHARDT (*archly*): No time to grow a new one for tomorrow's premiere.
(*He gives the signal for the play to recommence.*)

POET (*forgets theater, stage, and players*): Oh Gin Charly, sing me that
aria by Grieg: I love you, I love you!

MEPHISTO: I love you, I love you...

ALL ACTORS: I love you, I love you...

REINHARDT: Ladies and gentlemen, before we proceed with our play, I
assume it is clear to you that Mephisto and Faust are a pair of twins!
Yes, fundamentally, they are and always were one person.

RITZ BROTHER ONE: It's clear!

RITZ BROTHER TWO: It's clearer!

RITZ BROTHER THREE: It's clearissimo!

REINHARDT: And, furthermore, you should know that Faust encountered
himself for the first time while riding a black and white dappled stallion.... And, moreover, ladies and gentlemen, every individual has almost always the power to overcome the evil impulse with the good. But
rarely can the good prevail.

RITZ BROTHERS: It has to fail. It has to fail.

(SATAN *and* FAUST *rise and take bows. They exit through the curtain,* FAUST
giving the DEVIL *right of way. The curtain falls in the shape of a heart.*)

End of act 1.

ACT 2

In the Banquet Hall of the Infernal Palace. The Players: MEPHISTO, FAUST,
MARTHA, GÖRING, GOEBBELS, HESS, VON SCHIRACH, MALE AND FEMALE
SERVING *and* DANCING DEVILS. *Ballet of flames.*

The guests rise when MEPHISTO *and* FAUST *enter. They do not recognize*
SATAN *until he turns directly to them.* FAUST *hesitates in the center of
the hall.*

MEPHISTO: To what do I owe this honor, gentlemen? (*Without waiting
for their answer*): Please, make yourselves at home after your long trip
down here to the underworld. (*He invites the guests to sit down at the
dinner table.*)

(*Devils show the guests their places according to a seating chart. The smallest
devil dries the sweat from* GÖRING'*s forehead and cheeks with his tail.*)

MEPHISTO (*pointedly to* FAUST): Please sit across from me, my noble friend.
SCHIRACH (*impertinently to one of the serving devils*): Who is that pale
man he just called his "noble friend"?
GOEBBELS: Man, you are dreaming! Shut your fat trap!
SCHIRACH (*to* HESS): Pale as Rosalinda's marble bust—it seems he came
with us on the bus.
GOEBBELS: The tragedy, part three!
GÖRING (*reproachfully*): Go, take a pee!
MEPHISTO (*signals to* MARTHA *to begin serving*): It is the custom at my
court that every guest, invited or not, discuss his business affairs with
me at dinner over a glass of wine. I assume, gentlemen, we're talking
about tariffs . . .
GOEBBELS (*under his breath to* GÖRING): What tariffs is he talking about?
The swine!
GÖRING: Shut up, pig shit!
MEPHISTO: I must urge you, in the interest of my limited time, to be
brief and to the point. I assume your concern is petroleum to be delivered
fresh from the source here in hell.
FOUR GUESTS: Heil Hitler! For Germania and for Rome, your Excellency!
FAUST (*correcting the gentlemen*): Your Highness!
FOUR GUESTS: Your Highness!

(*The serving* DEVILS *fill the goblets of the banqueters.* MEPHISTO *fills*

GÖRING's *goblet with satanic laughter. Flames shoot up out of the wine, sizzle, and he is beclouded by the fumes. In the reflection of the fiery wine,* GÖRING *pales as he recognizes the burning Reichstag building on the wall of the banquet hall. To be done with the aid of film.*)

MEPHISTO (*raises his goblet majestically*): Honored guests from the Germanic orders, I thank the Führer Adolf for his trust and faith in me . . .

GUESTS: Heil Hitler!

MEPHISTO: And for the honor of sending the Marshal himself and the bravest of his ranks. (GÖRING *rises and bows unsteadily before* MEPHISTO.) The four-leaf clover of his Germanic realm. Quite soon, his mighty troops will face England on the battlefield. Belgium, Poland, and the Netherlands were three easy tricks I've played into his hands.

La France

was taken in a trance,

but if you mate her with the German race,

I would consider that a big disgrace.

FAUST (*distressed by the manner of his satanic friend*): Satanas! (*Out of control*) You, who are dark and wild by nature, why do you tame the howling jackal in your heart with courtesies to them?

MEPHISTO:

Here's why: My roots do not go back to some low cult.

I am of old and noble vintage.

Noblesse oblige, that is the problem.

Henry, friend of my heart—

in Paradise I did not lunch on royal game,

nor did I quench my thirst from the blue veins

of Eden's primal human pair.

So shall I now excite my senses

at the rotten discharge of these heirs?

No, a better grade of wine shall quench my loathing

—a noble loathing.

(*He turns to the Nazis again.*) Since ancient times Paris has been the main source of sinners to fuel my flaming dungeon. (*Ironically*) The Führer should not drive his brave troops so blindly into this seething hellhole. The first drop of rotten blood dripped from the Jewish veins!

GUESTS: Heil Hitler!

MEPHISTO: From the highest peaks down to the Seine,

it's nothing but one madeleine!

(*Signals to* FAUST) The old lady with the goatee, the one whose picture is on my writing desk, she's our common grandma! Adolf and I are blood relations! (*Short pause*) The two of us, he and ich selbst, inherited a tendency for subversion from this hellish lady... only England seems to block her victory! But go ahead and drink a toast to us two devils. I'll warn my cousin against waging transoceanic battles. Yes, gentlemen, I fear that your Führer, because of his greed for victory, will finally lose the world that he stole in war.

GUESTS (*automatically*): Heil Hitler!

MEPHISTO: Assure him that I am altogether at his service, even though my hell is close to being burnt out too. The purgatorial ovens in which the sinners are roasting shall be put at his disposal for the little Cohens.

(*The serving* DEVILS *look up from their steaming pots, somewhat amazed. They are wearing long yellow frock coats and hold napkins between their arms and their sides.* MARTHA *is helping them serve.*)

MARTHA (*sweetly seductive*): Wings of fallen angels, crisp and tender...

MEPHISTO: That's what she calls those question marks of meat—we must forgive the lady and her idle chatter! By the Christian calendar she should be more than one hundred ninety-five years old.

SCHIRACH (*impertinently*): My old man kicked off at fifty!—
There seems to be a privilege in hell—
by promoting man to devil
the flame of life is newly fanned
and, unrestrained, continues without end.

GÖRING (*stuffed*): Nonsense! (*He roars like a tiger.*) Alright? Goddamned in hell! I got to open my belt. (*Very drunk, to* MEPHISTO) I beg you humbly for petroleum!

HESS (*sober, he interrupts*): Your Majesty, we request exclusive delivery rights of petroleum from hell to be granted to the German and Roman cartel.

MEPHISTO: And in return I'll take that arty little Eifel town? What was its name? What did you call it in your poem, Henry?

GOEBBELS (*affectedly*): Whatever the name, no doubt the Führer will deliver it, lock, stock, and barrel, down to the last rat, in gratitude to his Great Majesty.

SCHIRACH: As generous as the Führer is, Goethe always was too Christian for him. And he noted besides that *Prometheus* was created on commission.

MEPHISTO (*to* FAUST): I'll dig up your *Hermann* and your *Dorothea* before the light of day.

GOEBBELS: Those two badly baptized Jews, long dead? (*Totally drunk*) Just let them graze with the heavenly flock of sheep. . . . Woe to the race of Germans who polluted their German blood with Jewish seed, woe to the Jews!

SCHIRACH: Germany arise! Down with the Jews!

GUESTS: Woe to the whole Jewish race! Heil Hitler!

(MARTHA *returns to the banquet hall.*)

MARTHA: Forgive me, Sir Satan and gentlemen diners. There's some little fellow, Grynspan by name—he's so pitiful; we all are sorry for this little man. Poor fellow, he comes with his shaved head under his arm to beg Sir Satan for mercy!

GOEBBELS: Lady, drag in the crippled little son of Moses, right here before the throne of hell. I always relish watching a bit of Jew baiting.

FAUST (*stunned*): God gave him strength for a courageous deed. That same holy strength that He gave the great prophet down in Egypt's land.

GOEBBELS: Hey, you pasty face!

MEPHISTO: Don't insult the noble poet!

GOEBBELS: Is there no wall in hell to put him up against?

SCHIRACH: Himmler would pull his tongue out by the roots!

GÖRING (*totally drunk*): Up against the wall, up against the wall, fire!

A DEVIL (*accusingly*): And bury him in the sand, just as Moses buried me, for my sin against his people.

MEPHISTO: But like a roasted rabbit, he ran to me, anxious to repent.

FAUST: The slave driver's whip is still in his hand.

(*The* GUESTS *laugh diabolically. Flames shoot out of the goblets up to the ceiling.*)

GÖRING (*pointing at* MEPHISTO): You dirty devil!

GOEBBELS: He paints . . . he paints the devil on the wall. (*In dialect*) I'm doin' OK in this helluva state. Schirach, old shithead, whaddaya think? I leave ya with the kraut heads, an' me an' Satan, piece in hand, we'll close the deal.

SCHIRACH: Like Adolf said, once we got the world in our lap, we shoot straight fer hell!

(MEPHISTO *laughs with interest.*)

HESS: What's that creep giving away?

GÖRING (*wakes up*): Shut your mouths, both of you, or you'll be six foot under before the day is out.

GOEBBELS: Five times a hundred thousand devils came into the world.

SCHIRACH: Oh yeah! Those poor devils didn't have a bloody cent!

GÖRING (*falling asleep again*): Then said Little Pipifax (*points at* GOEBBELS)—

GOEBBELS: You're as dumb as they come. I alone, I alone am a devil made to order!

ALL GUESTS: I alone, I alone am a devil made to order!

MEPHISTO (*rises in noble indignation and disgust.* FAUST *does likewise. They lean against one of the pillars. Wild flames shoot out of all corners. From everywhere Satan conjures up dancing* DEVILS *of both sexes. Ballet of Flames*): Your Satan has a hell of a good time with this Nazi race.

FAUST: As in the year 1800, Devil—beyond all measure and proportion!

MEPHISTO: That's how young Henry saw it at the time!—Oh, if only our poet could still consult his mother, Madame Goethe, whom he quite forgot—on account of this pretty little goose—Madame was on his back or anyhow still clinging to his ruffled neck. But I, dear Henry, I admit, I added fuel to the flame. And Madame Goethe played into my hand. She had nothing against, she said, a brief affair, perhaps a weekend marriage. But Henry, experience shows a middle-class marriage, albeit short, has never done a poet any good. I refused to give my blessings! That's all I have to say!

MARTHA (*daring to approach* FAUST): My dear Sir, may I be so bold!

FAUST (*to* MEPHISTO, *perking up*): I thought I just heard Margarete's blond young voice, as if from heavenly spheres, Satanas . . .

MEPHISTO (*to himself*): My Faust, now a wiser man, won't be destroyed by this mere girl. . . . (*To* FAUST) Take her hand and lead her in a minuet. Come to your senses, Henry, don't turn glum just because her grandma's lacy shawl adorns her bosom. Go to bed a little sooner and slurp down the soup and tea which she made for you so lovingly.

(*The flames die down. It grows dark. The curtain falls. The hurdy-gurdies play the song "Enjoy life while the lamp still glows . . ." accompanied by the wild rough voices of the Nazis singing "Five times a hundred thousand devils. . . ."*)

End of act 2.

A scene from Act 4 of *IandI* by Else Lasker-Schüler, directed by Judith Malina, The Livir
Theatre, New York, 1990. (Photo by Ira Cohen.)

ACT 3

MEPHISTO *and* DOCTOR FAUST *are playing chess on a terrace overlooking the park of Hell. Below the terrace,* MARTHA *spins at her spinning wheel. Nearby is a fountain with Psyche in the center surrounded by little Cupids pouring water from jugs into the basin. In the foliage to the right of the fountain stands a huge stone idol of Baal.*

The Players:

MEPHISTO

DOCTOR FAUST

MARTHA SCHWERDTLEIN

GOEBBELS

VAN DER LUBBE, a dim-witted young devil

GOEBBELS (*having remained in Hell, now sneaks through the park and approaches* MARTHA'*s bench*): Madame, may I be so bold to venture that you love to spend the morning hours sitting quietly by the fountain. But look how these Cupids work themselves into a sweat pouring water over Psyche's feet to keep them wet. I would say she is a little thin though . . .

MARTHA: But with her little helpers she brought us love in hell. Just look at the water falling in the shape of a heart and see that small one dimpling her chin. (*Short pause*) Last night's still dancing in my head. I never saw so many brilliant jewels.

GOEBBELS (*pointing to the frightful idol in the foliage*): And who's this monster and the little demons that support his clubfoot?

MARTHA (*frightened*): Hohoho! . . . His name comes of an ancient noble breed, and his mind is of a very worldly bent, says Doctor Faust. (*She strokes* GOEBBEL'*s clubfoot.*) In fact, our Baal could resemble you, Mister, if he were made of flesh and blood. Sir, be patient—I will tell you his name—

GOEBBELS: This crumbling stone god is ceaselessly mirrored in the pond.

MARTHA: On every blank page, in every leaf in hell, our Baal is reflected as befits the time, Sir Nazi.

GOEBBELS: Yes, yes, this is quite interesting. But it would interest me still more if one could put Germania's God, our Führer, in his place.

MARTHA: The Savior? (*She looks uneasily toward the terrace.*) Our—Jesus—Christ?

GOEBBELS: As if Madame were just born yesterday—that old Jew is quite passé!

(MARTHA *is astonished.*)

GOEBBELS: The Führer shipped that Jewish preacher and his New Testament back home to Bethlehem, where he was born, first by the executioner's train, then gently by barge across the water . . .

MARTHA: That seems very hard . . .

GOEBBELS: We Aryans are well rid of him. Heil Hitler!

MARTHA: What is the name of your god?

GOEBBELS (*sarcastically*): Adolf Hitler!

MARTHA: And the Madonna who gave birth to him?

GOEBBELS: She looks just like you, Martha Schwerdtlein, as alike as two peas in a pod. (*He sits impudently beside* MARTHA.)

MARTHA: This all seems mighty strange to me—hmm. I never heard of this man till today—but, then, I'm not an expert in such matters.

GOEBBELS (*takes a photo from his wallet*): I always carry him with me, our Aryan God. In the good old days, the Germans called him "Wotan." Madame, look again at this new Wotan, our mighty rock.

MARTHA (*has ever greater difficulty hearing*): A mighty cock?

GOEBBELS: Haha! A cock?

MARTHA: A handsome man—

GOEBBELS: Handsome man. (*Sarcastically*) A noble profile! Heil Hitler!

MARTHA: What did he used to do before he took up being a god?

GOEBBELS: Hahaha! A mighty cock!

MARTHA: As I live and die, just minutes ago he strutted right by me all puffed up with pride, his ruffled tail spread out.

GOEBBELS: The cock of the walk!

MARTHA: A little excited, I thought.

GOEBBELS: The Führer. (*He breaks into a loud laughter.*)

(*The two chess players look up from their board for a moment.*)

GOEBBELS: A mighty cock! A mighty cock! Madame must be hard of hearing?

MARTHA: But I'm still young. This blasted water splashing makes it hard to entertain.

GOEBBELS: That's right. That's right.

MARTHA (*coyly*): Dear Sir, move a little closer. . . . I—I accept your—offer—with pleasure.

GOEBBELS: Enchanting lady . . .

MARTHA (*coquettish*): Just don't break my pretty tortoise comb . . .

GOEBBELS: You'll find me gentle as a lamb, sweet thing.

MARTHA: Dear boy . . .

GOEBBELS: You look gorgeous when you blush—

MARTHA: Sweetheart, we could chat more comfortably over there, in that jasmine-covered nook. (MARTHA *points to the window of a small garden house deeper in the park.*)

GOEBBELS: But, my dear child, in the dawning hours of the day—even hell would call it sin.

(MARTHA *sulks like an adolescent girl at this rejection. The weak-minded devil* VAN DER LUBBE *dances across the lawn and sings, accompanying himself on a wooden board shaped like a fiddle, scraping on it with a saw, always repeating the same song: "In Cutta, Calcutta, the rajah, maharaja . . .")*

GOEBBELS: Who have we here?

MARTHA: Our little dimwit devil—

VAN DER LUBBE: The rickshaw, rat-show, rick-rock, the daddy raja papa . . .

GOEBBELS: I've seen that fellow somewhere before . . .

MARTHA (*straining to hear*): Who?

GOEBBELS: Him.

MARTHA: This crown prince of Dutch India. If he weren't here with us in Hell, he'd be sitting in Vampur near Calcutta on his daddy's cushy throne, says Doctor Faust.

GOEBBELS: It seems to me, he's doing pretty well right here—

MARTHA: Yes, if he didn't have to bathe in the flames every day, the crazy fool, till he hasn't got a shred of skin left, roasted like a chicken, to do penance for his murders.

BAAL: For your soul, asshole!

GOEBBELS: Who said that?

BAAL: I, Baal!

MARTHA (*fearful*): How vulgar . . .

BAAL: You asshole, be damned!

GOEBBELS: Who said that?

MARTHA: That idol there with the clubfoot.

GOEBBELS (*looks at his own foot with embarrassment*): You swollen, lazy, swinish idol. How dare you curse me, like the Jews—me the minister, Satan's honored guest!

VAN DER LUBBE: In Cutta, Calcutta, the rickshaw, rat-shoe, rick-rock, daddy raja papa. . . . (VAN DER LUBBE *disappears down a side alley, but the melody lingers on.*)

GOEBBELS: Madame Martha, I hope I was mistaken—

MARTHA: Why not complain to Satanas?

GOEBBELS: Let's escape by the garden gate.

MARTHA: I'm really sorry for this interruption—but follow me, my darling, and don't be shy; we'll be past this monument in no time. (*Affectedly*) Heil Hitler!—

GOEBBELS: Past Psyche's fountain and past the idol of Baal together— divine lady, I'll follow you from life to death, you, my soul and my inspiration!

MARTHA: How did all this happen?

GOEBBELS (*lying*): How could it happen right here in the midst of hell? . . . I can't believe it—(*He puts his hand above his eyes to see more clearly in the distance.*) I see our Naziland come into view . . .

MARTHA (*getting stuck in the brambles*): Oh dear, my panties—caught!

GOEBBELS: How poetic . . . come, come along!

MARTHA: Darling, it's not the moment now to go so far; we can't get past the guards.

GOEBBELS: May I be so bold as to take you away from your kitchen and your household chores. I would be very happy, my darling, if you could show me around here a little, perhaps even the inner sanctum of the office files!

MARTHA: Inner sanctum of the office files?

GOEBBELS: I'd like to learn a little more about the business.

(*Both hear again the melody of Van der Lubbe's song: "In Cutta, Calcutta. . . ."*)

MARTHA: It's paradise up here, dear friend, compared to what goes on down there. (*She points to the side road leading down to the troops.*) This hillside leads to purgatory fires. Devil fathers and devil sons practice their firepower there, and, often in the heat of battle, they burn themselves to cinders. All this since the Nazis armed and changed the face of humankind—as Doctor Faust, the friend of the devil, teaches us— and deformed the world.

GOEBBELS: Oh, this infernal magic delights me—oh, you witch of witches!

(*Both disappear down the hill. The sun rises in a fiery glow bathing hell in its light.* MEPHISTO, *lit in scarlet light, leans over the balustrade of his veranda.*)

BAAL: Come, little lark, come settle on my thumb and rouse me with your youthful song.

End of act 3.

ACT 4

Two DEVILS *are about to raise the blinds on the terrace.*

The Players:
DIRECTOR MAX REINHARDT
MEPHISTO
DOCTOR FAUST
MARTHA SCHWERDTLEIN
BAAL
VAN DER LUBBE
GÖRING
GOEBBELS
SCHIRACH
LEY
NAZI SOLDIERS

(*By the dawn's light,* MEPHISTO *and* FAUST *are playing chess.* HITLER *is seen in the distance, accompanied by* RIBBENTROP, HIMMLER, ROSENBERG. *From afar the sound of continuous marching, muffled at first but later rising to an unbearable pitch.* MEPHISTO, *distracted, raises his head, then leans way back into his precious armchair.*)

FAUST: You're not paying attention today, Satanas; perhaps last night's green wine is making you a little groggy?
MEPHISTO: Instead of sun, those grapes soaked up poisonous fumes. Down here in Hell we all live in a toxic stench.
FAUST (*listening*): What's that hollow noise?
MEPHISTO: It's the soldiers up there in the blood and sweat of war: tin soldiers, barbarians, and slaves from Belgium, Holland, Poland, France, and all the other plundered nations.

FAUST (*forgetting where he is*): The devil take that brownshirt trouble-maker! Forgive me, Satanas, but you could take him on, couldn't you, if you tried?

MEPHISTO (*smiling*): I'm about to do just that! They're halfway to Hell already and will arrive in two and a half days. I'm sure down here the whole thing will collapse.

FAUST: This never-ending uproar will get lost in space.

MEPHISTO: God is the guardian, and Satanas (*boasting*) stands guard! We will not let our (*ironically*) Cousin Adolf disturb our game of chess.

FAUST: Your Highness, what can you possibly expect from this man of flesh and blood?

MEPHISTO: He speculates on usurping my throne! But my hand guides the game; it is my only passion in this exile.

FAUST: Do you think of your own hell as your exile?

MEPHISTO: Only eternity is not exile! To find your way there, Henry, you traversed the world—not always virtuous, but you remained immaculate in that land of . . . sins.

FAUST: The wind is silent in the linden trees tonight, the violet has wilted in my vase, and you, my friend, if I may call you friend, why have you grown so pale?

MEPHISTO: Henry, your lyric talent is amusing, and I'm touched by it:
"Tweet tweet
All in the hills lie still,
In every bough
You sense—
barely a breath . . .

Tweet tweet
The birds are silent in the woods
But stay,
Soon enough
You too will lie silent and still.

FAUST (*after a pause*): You're a master at recitation, Satan; I'm surprised at you. Every word you touched on goes straight to my heart. But why this obsolete old poem? Why not something more life affirming from my youth?

MEPHISTO: Still so vain, my Faust, after a hundred and fifty-five years? But pity we that poet man
whose poetry will never scan,

For ever since he was a youth.

Ratatata, tatatata. He wants to steal my wisdom tooth.

Ratatata, Tatatata.

FAUST: Ratatata

Tatatata!

MEPHISTO: "C'est un homme!" Here is a man, said Napoléon of you
while your mother, Madame Goethe, waited anxiously at home for her
distinguished son.

POET (*quietly to* MEPHISTO): Pardon me, Charly, please pronounce the *m*
in *home* more like an *n* so it rhymes with Napoléon . . .

REINHARDT: Sh . . . sh!

MEPHISTO (*consents with the* POET): Well, then: Thus were you honored
by Napoléon, while mother waited anxiously for her distinguished *son*.

(REINHARDT, *script in hand, shrugs his shoulders in amazement.*)

FAUST (*sings*): My sovereign, my sovereign in chains! . . .

REINHARDT: Gentleman, with more indignation, please: My sovereign,
my sovereign in chains!

MEPHISTO: When Heinrich Heine, that noble Jew and author of this song,
would sing it for the first time with his melancholy friends, I was there
bubbling in the Moselle wine they drank.

FAUST: Bonaparte was a falcon who parted the clouds and swooped to
earth. He led his army in person.

MEPHISTO: And shared the soldier's oath with all his men. (MEPHISTO
leans over the chessboard.) My friend, let's not get lost somewhere in
the backwash of history. From manhood you grew into old age and got
waylaid by that young thing. I lent you my magic wand, my devil's
member—and, being abstinent so long, I've fallen on hard times.

RITZ BROTHERS: Shocking . . .

FAUST: Hard times?

MEPHISTO: I myself buried the old caprices of my heart long ago. But you
just shed your outworn skin when lust pricked you and grabbed greedily
at those worldly goods. And now you'd bury me in the cloak of your
sanctity? But I cannot be transformed—I cannot be corrected.

FAUST: I am not about to undertake such a correction. Besides, the thorns
in my heart would puncture my prayer.

(*Pause*)

MEPHISTO: Doctor Faust is quite right, and I'm not sticking to the point.

The federal bank up there in the upper world is putting the crunch on us. I fear I will be bankrupt soon. And yet the devil has survived more serious setbacks, playing black against white and white against black— at the same time. (MEPHISTO *picks up a chess piece, somewhat distractedly.*) But what concerns me more is how the powers of the state and the powers of the stars always underlie these matters of economy and war. We heard the Archangel Gabriel singing on the Sabbath of our Lord. (FAUST *is moved.*) Angelic voices that very much offended me.

FAUST: Offended?

MEPHISTO: I cannot deny it! The devil by nature urges toward divine morality.

(*The last chess pieces vanish from the chessboard.*)

FAUST: Oh, Satanas, and will you come in the final hour? . . .

MEPHISTO: Mankind comes tumbling down. A new round begins! And yet the game is always played by the same kings! While the moon is high, my friend, let's repopulate the chessboard for another match. (MEPHISTO *leans swiftly across the chessboard, grabbing his king.*) "Checkmate to the Eternal One."

(*A heavenly white light encircles the chess players.*)

FAUST (*shaken*): Who was that?

MEPHISTO: Ruach! A fire wind from the Eternal One!—

FAUST (*passionately*): Satan, don't tread upon the ground where the deluge rose—Oh God, forgive him—(MEPHISTO *challenges him.*) Oh God, forgive him whom I love more dearly every day—forgive him his sinful spite, which turned his life to hell.

(*Soft thunder follows lightning, then a light rain; a rainbow emerges.*)

FAUST: Behold the arc of peace at the horizon. Our Father extends his fatherly hand to you.

MEPHISTO: I played this kind of colorful lasso trick much better in my youth.
The ordinary man must follow established rules.
No matter how much he has to suffer, and he does,
he does not veer from the familiar path
nor venture into deeper darker ways.

FAUST: And does not lose his equilibrium.

MEPHISTO: But I blow my top when I get drunk and scorn the
rules and regulations of society. I spit the devil's
spite into the face of life as it gives birth to
death, snuffing out the light of life. . . .
I like to paralyze the elements or, for a whim, whip up a storm.—
My friend, the tower clock strikes noon.
Who is to say, it isn't midnight yet,
perhaps it's timeless time?

FAUST: Eternity?

MEPHISTO: Once I heard the primal cuckoo's call
on the bright morning of creation's earliest day—
the Urcuckoo, newly hatched, sounding his first cuckoo call.

FAUST (*eagerly*): Go on, go on, Satan, what happened next?

MEPHISTO (*thoughtfully*): Countless centuries later, Henry, remember I
rescued you. . . . That cute little woman was just what I needed to wrench
you free from middle-class life. Good old Satan knew what he was doing.
When I found you, her hand and yours entwined,
the poisonous devil rustled through the leafy grove.
Henry, I love you . . . you are my faith.
Swept along by youth's ecstatic dreams,
You lured a butterfly, a young girl's ready heart,
into your net like a boy shouting with joy.
And I committed an unforgivable sin for you:
I crept behind you into the church's holiest hymns—
and worshipped you while bells sounded
the silvery day throughout the land.

FAUST (*after a short pause*):
My laughter tore itself from me,
my laughter with those children's eyes,
my singing, springing laughter
turned your night into day.
It tore itself from me and entered into you,
to kindle joy within your darkness.
But now it suffers from a lack of youth
and smiles an aged grin.

MEPHISTO:
I recognized in your drunken boyish song our origin,
our inspiration and significance—

You, like the devil, sprang from immemorial time!
And when you speak, I hear myself,
as when I was a child.
From afar you watched impatiently wild clouds approach.
You tamed the storm, that maddened bull.
And yet you wandered lost between eternity
and custom's comfort and finally settled down between the two.
I rattled at your gate with all my might, my brother.
For thanks you call me "devil."
Now every man and every brute bid me welcome
with this traditional rhyme.

FAUST: Satanas, no one has ever said such things to me. My mother did not even dare knock at my door when I slept late. She dared not let a friend in, not even dear Bettina, who always liked to wish me a good morning.

MEPHISTO (*imitating* MARTHA): Hohoho! But she had some interest in a certain Mynher, a lens grinder of Amsterdam, and, even if that gentleman did not kiss a lady's hand, he gave her plenty nonetheless. Soon enough the storm broke loose . . . an old story, old wine in old bottles! (FAUST *smiles in confusion.*) Cheerfully, she starched the ruffles on your shirt herself, the good and clever woman. I see it in my mind's eye still: With a satin ribbon she lassoed you and caught you by your silver powdered wig. But once there was a dreadful thunderstorm, and her madcap boy would not stay home but mounted his dappled horse. . . . That's when I—the devil in the flesh—I encountered him, encountered you, my bosom friend, and holding firmly to the reins, together we restrained the black and white runaway horse.

MARTHA: The devil in the flesh encountered our Henry in distress? Is that right, Director Reinhardt?

MEPHISTO: Overwhelmed by this mystical encounter, fearful and anxious, you longed for married bliss and the safety of the parental house and hearth. Only much later, you lifted up your pale courageous eyes to the unlimited spheres and abandoned the slave galley of your married life. (MEPHISTO *rises majestically and, in imitation of the Creator, he draws a circle through the white hot air of Hell.*)

(*Sounds of hissing and bubbling. The ground begins to smoke and soften to a mass of lava.* NAZI SOLDIERS *and their leaders sink into it up to their necks as they march through the gates. They scream.*)

THE HEADS OF THE SINKING NAZI SOLDIERS: Heil Hitler!

GÖRING (*stepping through the gates, he is fatally engulfed by the flood*): This is the devil's work!

BAAL: Look how mankind lays his evil at the devil's door—that he may rest in virtue with his neighbor . . .

(*Dawn grows brighter and illuminates the event.*)

FAUST (*seeing the situation clearly, he admonishes* MEPHISTO): Eternal life belongs to him who knows how to speak of "Love." . . . Only the one who loves can rise again!—

MEPHISTO (*sarcastically*): Hate imprisons us, how ever high the torch is held. (*He points to the lava bed.*) My one regret is losing all that tasty clover, which my cattle enjoyed so much in summertime.

FAUST: My heart can't bear the wailing of the soldiers, Satanas.

MEPHISTO: I bet their murderous drive will come to nothing, though for Doctor Faust it is an unsolved riddle. The answer to the riddle: rightful annihilation melts Doctor Faust's German heart.

FAUST: Like the deluge, the dreadful sea storms and bleeds . . .

MEPHISTO: Not even I, Satanas, ich selbst, can stop the world in its course, and so you, Doctor Faust, must accept that your turtledove heart will be a little wounded.

FAUST (*urgently*): But the world was good—"and He saw that it was good."

MEPHISTO: How then could such an evil horde overrun the rest of humankind?

FAUST: Which was created in His own image.

BAAL: The face of earth, imbued with God, rotted when it turned from its Creator.

MEPHISTO (*pointing to* BAAL): Here, Henry, from the mouth of time turned into stone, the primordial speaks.

BAAL: What is man without god? Without obeying the law of God?

KING DAVID (*rises*): He is in life as he is in death!

BAAL: Untouched by God's smile, he will lose his balance.

MEPHISTO: Like Cain, he kills his brother!

FAUST (*to himself*): And drags the world down with him.

MEPHISTO: Listen how this ancient stone rages with the fury of an avalanche.

FAUST: I thought I heard the voice of God. (*After a pause*) Aren't you related to Cain? Or was it a joke?

MEPHISTO: Of course, I wrote a flaming warning—"Mene mene tekel"—

on the walls of my Hell. I assumed that Doctor Faust would catch the joke. How could I, God's little devil, be related to Cain? His little devil whom the Lord formed with His own hands while the world was still bubbling in ecstatic chaos—related to Cain!!! (MEPHISTO *laughs furiously.*)

FAUST: You legendary creature—capricious man and brooding, sensual reptile lurking in the tree's dark womb.

MEPHISTO: Behind a blind crescent moon (*speaking as if to a child*), little Satanas was carried in Eden's unsuspecting womb. But this crazed son of earth was born of a nation in a fit of murderous lust, in some dingy railroad waiting room.

FAUST: Satanas, calm my wild pulse. . . . I cannot bear the fate of Germany.

MEPHISTO: Close your eyes as you used to do in the gray mornings when you stretched out in bed after a long night of drunken carousal in your student days and dream sweet dreams of Lotte and of Friederike; the present is about to fall asleep, in any case. Madame, bring us your golden vintage; we have a few songs left in our throats. (*Both start singing.* MEPHISTO *invites the audience to sing along.*)

Eat, drink, and be merry
and join in our song.
Who doesn't go along
is always wrong.
Edite, bibite, collegiales
Post multa saecula, pocula nulla—
Post multa saecula, pocula nulla—
Post multa saecula, pocula nulla!
I was a wild one in Paradise, my friend.

FAUST: Tell us about your mischievous pranks, devil.

MEPHISTO: I was a rascal. I stole some unfermented matter from the Lord to have some fun while He was resting on the Sabbath day. One drop was quite enough to spoil the chemistry. . . . Suddenly, good God, the gentle winds began to roar—sin did not yet exist—and yet they tore at His golden gate, and I stood laughing at my joke in the sugarcane. So young and, oh, so bad! And God, our Father, never forgave me that I spoiled His rest. I was no more than seven, and, when it turned cold in autumn, I would wear green leafy trousers and padded my backside with moss to soften the fall. . . . What I liked best was sitting with some frogs on a water lily pad, and, every now and then, I'd help myself to a juicy bite of frog leg while our dear Father watched over His first pair of humans and His other animals. But, in the apple blossom where I hid myself after my misdeed, greedy Eve discovered me and would not leave me untasted. She plucked me, poor little naked devil, from the bough, and, when it snapped, it woke me from my noonday nap— ruined my weekend. Since this incident, this cagey woman secretly denounced me to Michael and Gabriel, and their brother angels—

FAUST: Fearing that the Father would find out that His little devil son and—

MEPHISTO: Exactly—had done this mischief. So I snuck away with the unhappy couple into their exile.

(FAUST, *moved by Satan's story, embraces him enthusiastically.*)

MEPHISTO: Once when the world was young,
  I hung from a golden cloud.
  And our God, still a young father
  rocked my cradle—hey!
  through the blue ether.
  My curly hair danced in ringlets.
  I teased my grandpa, the moon, in his rocker
  and nibbled at Grandmama's sunshine—
  I locked up Papa God in heaven
  and locked the world into His halo.
  And God went bumpity-bump!
  And the winds whipped up a furious din,
  but later Father had a thunderous laugh
  with his angels over my—cardinal sin. . . .
  I'd give ten thousand happy lives on earth
  to live once again in that godly realm,
  in the midst of the heavenly host,
  as when I was God's own little devil!

(*Pause*)

FAUST (*enthused*): It does not matter if this event ever or never took place under God's roof. God Himself recites the story on holidays wearing His blue heavenly robe. A genuine golden ruby will cling till doomsday on your dark brow, Satan.

MEPHISTO: Even as one flees the devil, one calls him back from that same filth where a human heart is only capable of evil. Place in an envelope my brittle hair, which once fell in ringlets fair!

Brother dear, you roused my heart,
my veins, my blood,
and were my eyes not turned to stone—
and never cried!
I, Satan, would have wept—
FAUST:
Give me a little drop of time
to celebrate our unity
in tender, chaste embrace.
Oh, I would gladly die for you,
ally and companion of my road.

(*The droning sounds of the Nazi army drive all the devils to the upper spheres of Hell.* SATAN *leans over the balustrade. At a sign from him, the devils gather into a procession, which moves in an orderly fashion up a hill and disappears like an unending file of people which fades off into the clouds. The last one is* VAN DER LUBBE, *fiddling his song like a psalm on his wooden fiddle.*)

MEPHISTO (*to* FAUST): And who took this poor boy in? I or your God? At whose table did he dine on bread and fish? (MEPHISTO *looks at* FAUST *questioningly.*)

FAUST (*hiding his head in his hands*): It is not proper to question the actions of the Eternal One.

MEPHISTO: This Sunday school wisdom wouldn't impress Zebaoth, the Lord of the Stars, Faust.

FAUST: Wouldn't the Father of all living things someday forgive you? . . . I have attached my life to yours—if we agree in peace to enter heaven together harmoniously.

MEPHISTO: Your faith in God's love, Henry, hasn't got a leg to stand on. Often, dear child, you've let me lead you astray, though I was never far from God's thought. God is here—God is here! But I don't really love very much—this Unseen Presence. Tell me, dear friend, after the original Fall, who took you in?

FAUST: It is not for us to understand God in His mysterious ways.

MEPHISTO: You little preacher! That answer would cause God—and I know Him well—great annoyance.

FAUST (*listening*): Oh God, this murderous marching sound grows louder!

MEPHISTO: They too abandoned God and His wide heaven!

FAUST: Scorned Him—

MEPHISTO (*testing and challenging* FAUST): Conditions being what they are, I could be tempted to equip Adolf Hitler hellishly well and accompany him to America before his black star sinks. (*Short pause*) What do you think of that, Doctor Faust?

FAUST: Satanas, devil, forgive me, a man of flesh and blood. But I have never heard your majesty so frivolous.

MEPHISTO (*taking* FAUST's *hand*): Do you still offer the Evil One the Heavenly Kingdom for his reward? (*Short pause*) Henry, you are immortal, preserved for the world in marble monuments. But I—I cannot die. Can you imagine the situation—the devil up there in heaven? (FAUST *is silent, embarrassed.*) A dove with a charred branch in its beak. The devil's weakening; the Creator will not pardon him. My Hell, isolated from the stars, orbits darkly in the cosmos. Neither man nor prophet could extinguish it and bring it down. It still lives on today—though for theatrical use only—in our worldly fantasy.

End of act 4.

ACT 5

The Players: The same as in the preceding act. Two DEVILS *are opening the blinds.* MEPHISTO *and* FAUST *return to the terrace.* MARTHA *enters the terrace at the request of* GOEBBELS, *who stays hidden in the foyer at the entrance of the terrace behind a marble bust of Doctor Faust.*

MARTHA: Pardon, Sir Satan, when the Nazi heroes entered our Hell Garden, they. . . . (*She places her hand behind her ear so as to hear more clearly* GOEBBELS's *words, which she repeats impatiently.*)

GOEBBELS: stepped into a trap . . .

MARTHA: fell into the crap . . .

GOEBBELS: While you were busy with your game of chess, Highness.

MARTHA: While you were dizzy with your flaming mess, Highness, you missed—what?

GOEBBELS: Stupid cow.

MARTHA: Stupid cow—what?

FAUST: What?!

MARTHA: Help, help, Sir Satan, help, or surely they—

GOEBBELS: Will drown.

MARTHA: Will frown! They frown!

MEPHISTO (*amused*): Where were you hiding this morning?

MARTHA (*feigning ignorance*): What?

MEPHISTO: Madame, this is not the mating season.

MARTHA: But the Aryan God has laid an egg!

FAUST: My, my! The woman's pulling your leg!

MARTHA: What I really wanted to say, gentlemen.... (*She turns toward* GOEBBELS's *hiding place.*) The other Nazi gentleman, they called him Hermann—what? The sun, the moon, the stars shine on his chest— what? A facade and ... what a shame, what a shame, what a shame, just how, just how, just how, hohoho!

MEPHISTO: He's drowing in front of our Baal. Enough, Madame, be glad and get out of here! Why's that rotten clubfoot still stomping around in Hell? His intellect is limping far behind, and, if this raving slave won't break his neck, at least he'll break his leg on the way to Walhalla.

(*A bloodcurdling scream rings out from the entrace to Hell.*)

GÖRING (*calls out to* SATAN *from the sea of lava before his head sinks into the sizzling stream*): Let him croak up there on the steps of hell; he was always in my way!

MARTHA: Help, help, oh Satan, hurry up, or all is over with my darling!

GOEBBELS (*lifts his torso with difficulty, angrily*): Heil Hitler! My hope—

MARTHA: Hohoho!

(*New Nazi troops are heard approaching.*)

SCHIRACH: Adolf, Adolf, why has thou forsaken me?

LEY: As sure as my name's Ley, he will have his turn, by and by!

(MEPHISTO *restrains* FAUST, *who is about to get up and warn the approaching Nazi troops.*)

MARTHA: No one cares about my misery—

FAUST: I want to go down into death with the soldiers! (FAUST *scatters the chess figures all over the board.*) Like this game, my heart, my mind, my very guts are shattered. I implore you, Prince, stir up the flames of Hell and let me die there—I, the son of German poetry, I, the son of Germany—let me die together with my people!

MEPHISTO: Oh, this world made by man! Were God not God, he'd lose his mind! (*To* FAUST): You've seen horrors far worse than this and accepted them as the world's enigma. (*To two* DEVILS) Please get this rabid beast off my veranda! Throw him down the sewer with the other heroes. (*To* FAUST) You know how I love horses, but, when I see an abomination such as this, my own dainty, well-shaped hoof delights me.

FAUST (*preoccupied with verse forms*): I would hardly have expected such precise rhythms and such brand new metrics, even from my dear friend Friedrich Schiller, who escaped with elegant phrases from the stodgy path of the old poetry.

MEPHISTO (*visibly flattered*): As a child, I loved to spin out verses, but I leave the creation of true poetry to you. And, if the price of writing paper should go down, why it would give me the greatest pleasure on earth to be eulogized by you—especially to impress the spiritual authorities. Your song is my dance . . .

FAUST: Satanas, don't play blindman's buff with me.

MEPHISTO: But Satan's blind, blinder than you. If death could strike me down, then I could answer you, transfigured and illumined, as one whom God's mercy has absolved. The moon and its stars, Henry, are the poet's only prize. You are immortal, and I cannot die. No heirs await the sale of the estate. Your kingdom is not of this world. Even here in Hell, you live in dreams, in wish fulfillments, in seventh heaven, in the blue.

FAUST: That's what my professors told me at the university.

MEPHISTO: I scorn the learned professors; they have lost the sense of playfulness. See how playfully we are carried along by rhyme. The professors, on the other hand, dryly teach of roads they have never traveled. But every student's prattle rattles his little can with soupy stars and primal broth for dinner with his girl back home.

BUSINESS MANAGER (*hardly audible to* REINHARDT): Five percent of our subscribers are professors, and many get free tickets . . .

REINHARDT: I ask you all, please, scream a bit more melodiously; we are performing, as you can see, outdoors. (*To the* POET) Will you let me cut those last few lines?

POET: You ask the stars . . . better, ask the devil; he likes to answer questions of that sort.

OLDEST RITZ BROTHER (*to his brothers*): Heads or tails? (*He takes a silver dollar out of his vest pocket.*) I'll bet he says no.

MEPHISTO: No! As an expert in such matters, I say no.

OLDEST RITZ BROTHER: OK!

MEPHISTO (*returning to the play*): I repeat, my friend, you are immortal, but I cannot die. Once in a while, they call me for a Punch and Judy show, but, in a broken puppet's body, I am tossed into the gutter by the smallest street urchin. . . . Yet, in the days of your descendants, I prospered again and became a big shot. Disgusted, I made my escape by forging my hand into a Faustian fist and pushed my way into the darkness of my broken underworld. Your favorite son stood up in front of the circle that I left behind, sipping hot chocolate from mother's fancy china—your clown, the most insolent and ill-behaved at your poetry recitals; he rose, all dressed up in stiff collar and lacy cuffs, holding his grandfather's golden lorgnette and taking his father's noble restrained posture, reserved for court; he recited your solemn elegy by the light of a thousand candles for this aunt and uncle crowd.

All the hills lie still—
in every bough
you sense
barely a breath.
The birds are silent in the woods, tweet, tweet,
but stay.
Soon enough
you too will lie silent and still . . .

(FAUST *cries.*)

MEPHISTO: And, now that I am confessing, Doctor Faust begins to bawl? On the first day of our ressurection.

FAUST (*hiding his head in* MEPHISTO's *hands*):
I cannot find my self
In this alien eternity—
And feel I am worlds away from myself
between the first night and the primal fear.
I wish some pain would erupt
and hurl me down!
And clasp me firmly to myself.
I would that the creative urge
might take me home again
to rest at my mother's breast.

MEPHISTO: Your motherland has lost its soul. . . . No roses bloom there in the sultry winds.

FAUST: What I want is a lover.

MEPHISTO: And bury myself in her flesh.

FAUST (*looking painfully across earth and Hell*): Satanas, please lift my eyes far, far away from the past.

MEPHISTO: Yes, this is a trick I learned from God! To lift one's eyes from times gone by. . . . But, brother, once again we find ourselves afloat on the river of life! So, let's sing our happy student song!
Fill the jug and let's carouse!
We're two thirsty fellows,
two survivors of the apocalypse.
(*To* FAUST) Let's get down to business!!!
Eat, drink, and be merry,
Join in the song,
who doesn't go along,
is always wrong.
Edite, bibite, collegiales,
Post multa saecula
Pocula nulla!
And so we're off again, as in our student days, wandering over the rainbow in the kingdom of the Lord!

(MEPHISTO *and* FAUST *rise at the same time and seem to grow into gigantic human figures.*)

MEPHISTO: Dear brother, come closer, lean on me, so that you and I can really touch each other. (MEPHISTO *gives* FAUST *a dagger.*) And plunge this dagger into my heart. . . . Go on, kill the monster! (FAUST, *appalled, rejects the deed.*) Now that I want to separate the devil from him, he shows sympathy for the devil!
FAUST (*smiling*): I'm on the road to heaven; my senses are brightened, my heart is enlightened, through all times and all climes. (*Crowns of clouds form around the brows of* MEPHISTO *and* FAUST.) Now Paradise begins to shine on us.
MEPHISTO: The world of vain illusion is sloughed off like a spider's web by God's true world.

(*Moans and curses are heard from the drowning Nazi soldiers.* HITLER, *in full armor, stands at the Gate of Hell with his bodyguard and* RIBBENTROP, HIMMLER, *and* ROSENBERG.)

HITLER: Where's he at?
RIBBENTROP *and* HIMMLER: Where is Satanas?

BAAL: Gentlemen, dressed as you are in your barbed wire uniforms, why don't you bathe here in this lap of luxury?

HITLER (*to* ROSENBERG, *filled with fearful premonition*): Bathe in this lap of luxury? What's this fat lip up there talking about, Rosenberg? Bathe in a lap of luxury?

BAAL: Adolf, get in here! Satan has surrendered!

HITLER (*beaming with megalomania*): Hear that! He surrendered!

BAAL: I mean: surrendered to God, the Lord of the world!

(HITLER *and his gang step through the gate, and a rising tide of lava engulfs them, and they sink helplessly into the lava stream.*)

BAAL: Gentlemen, twist and turn, cringe and burn, feel free to enjoy your meal in the slimy sea.

MEPHISTO (*lays a fatherly arm around* FAUST's *shoulder*):
He poisoned the vintage of our German blood.
Lacking courage in battle himself,
He incited the youth to murder.
He's a false note of cowardice in humanity's harmony!
He leaves no ashes, not even a pile of dust!
This antichrist and anti-Semite must die an unredemptive death!
—Yet I, this primal, divided creature, this self offers me a new life—
As I and I unfold and evolve again and again,
I come redeemed and renewed to myself!
I advise each one of you in the audience, try this royal pattern on yourself.
It leads to clarity like a fine fugue! Let's first empty our glasses for the Redemption of the world! —Patience, dear audience, the last line of the fifth act will soon be spoken. I'm in no hurry. The one who laughs last, whether angel or devil, is the one who laughs best. Let's fill the glass once more and drink to the "dear audience"!
Down through the gates the past flows away,
I am at one with myself in blissful harmony
. . . such distant music. . . .
Between war and peace,
I raise my eyes and see: pyramids—
which is a vision beyond the bounds of time.

(*The Psyche of the fountain, with the aid of her Cupids, gives* BAAL *a funeral wreath made of lilies and reeds.* BAAL *tosses it onto the* NAZIS *in the slime.*)

BAAL: Rest in peace in your black mausoleum!

FAUST:
Loving angels in heaven are weaving
angel-wing dresses—for us. . . .
Soon we'll reach Heaven's blue pastures—
and look back on the world we left behind.

MEPHISTO: How will they bury you, my heart's companion, and me?—

FAUST: Both of us—simply bonded in one body: IandI

MEPHISTO: And enchanted by the noble torments of our reconciliation, the clergy will preach sermons in the original tongue: Old Hebrew.

FAUST: But we are through with earthly life; we're through! (*Both* MEPHISTO *and* FAUST *sing softly to the audience*)
"Enjoy life while the lamp still glows,
ere it wither, pluck the rose . . ."

End of act 5.

ACT 6

In the garden of an ophthalmologist's house in Jerusalem.

The Players:
THE POET
THE SCARECROW of the garden
EDITOR SWET, editor-in-chief of the daily *Haarez*
An AUDIENCE MEMBER

AUDIENCE MEMBER (*followed the* POET, *unnoticed, to the gate of the tropical garden*): Excuse me, my dear poet, allow me a brief question: Did you . . . write . . . this play . . . all by yourself?

POET (*imitating* BAAL's *thunderous voice*): That's a laugh!

(*The perplexed audience member quickly leaves the entrance to the garden. The exhausted* POET *enters the garden and sits down on a bench at the edge of a wide lawn. The* SCARECROW, *dressed in bright colors, comes loping toward her and stops in front of the* POET.)

POET (*after a short pause*): Setzen Sie sich, bitte.

SCARECROW: You get tired on this gravel. Besides, I'm hungry in English and French as well as in Hebrew. Other gardens have fruits and vegetables.

POET: I've got a box of chocolate cat tongues left—

SCARECROW: Give those to the street urchins! I like the taste of turnips, radishes, lettuce, and I am crazy about all kinds of watercress. What's the wife of the great eye doctor thinking of? Does she imagine that a scarecrow needs no food? Standing out here day and night in bright sunlight, without sunglasses and no umbrella against November rains . . .

POET: I'll gladly keep you company—

SCARECROW: Perhaps we should go away for Easter? Escape the gossip— I'm in the mood for romance and could turn the world into a fairy tale.

POET: We're in the same condition. We're both poor children of Israel, still trudging through the desert sands.

SCARECROW: Allow me to ask: Where were you all this time? Before they turned the light off on the world?

POET: William Tell invited me to Switzerland before I made my way here.

SCARECROW: And, in Weimar, Madame von Stein hid me under her great petticoat!

POET: How funny!

SCARECROW: But soon I went walking with Wolfgang, my intimate friend—

POET: Through the Eastern divan?

SCARECROW: Through the Eastern and Western divan—"ganz unter uns, mein Liebchen . . ."

POET: You traveled with Wolfgang von Goethe?

SCARECROW: Your doubt makes me blush. In those summer days, we used to stroll together, he and I, quite often through the Eifel valley. I was very jealous when Dorothea gave my friend a kiss in the twilight at the lake.

POET: Hermann's Dorothea? Oh!

SCARECROW: That's how women are . . .

POET: Oh!

SCARECROW: I was fuming with annoyance! But, in return, he let me borrow his muse for a few days. (*He sings heartbreakingly off-key*)
Do you know the land where the lemon tree grows?
Where in green groves the golden orange glows?

POET: So it was you who gave this song to the world? (*The* SCARECROW *puts his hand on the rim of his hat in a gesture that says yes.*) Looking at the brilliant curve of your chin, I trust you produced those elegiac poems. . . . (*The* SCARECROW *puffs up with pride.*) You seem well read,

Master Scarecrow. I've not read much in my life, because I can't stand the noise of turning pages . . .

SCARECROW: Nun gut, if I may praise myself, I'm a bookworm and love all the old trashy novels. (*He points to the ophthalmologist's house and winks at the* POET.) If the eye doctor's patient, half-asleep, forgets some classic volume on the table, I snap it up by the tail like a fish and educate myself like well-bred folk.

POET: That's why I usually ate alone because high-class people did not invite me, a semiliterate, to dine at their table . . .

SCARECROW: Don't cry, little girl, it's a long time since the scarecrow has been invited to tea and biscuits . . .

If only I had my fiddle

We could dance a minuet . . .

POET: In a dress made of this pure white garden mist . . .

SCARECROW: Then not only cats in heat would be caterwauling . . .

POET (*haughtily putting him off*): Oh . . .

SCARECROW: Never fear, honored poet, I am, as should be remarked to begin with, made of straw and broomsticks, the counterfeit of a higher being. My graying braid came out of a trunk dating back to Wolfgang's period, pure rococo. I am an ascetic, and, even if they drowned me in the River Lethe, what could I possibly forget?

POET: You, above all things, move me to pain—

SCARECROW: Yes, I—seduced you—

POET: Why me? Still, I would like to know your name. What do they call you?

SCARECROW: On holidays, I'm Abraham! Or Isaac! Occasionally Jacob. But sometimes, when the ladies come to the lady's salon for tea, they call me "Little Cohen."

POET (*sympathetically*): Your cheeks, dear Abraham, glow red—like the young poppy.

SCARECROW: But my blue, dove blue, cravat faded in last July's sun—

POET: But this (*Pointing to a gash in the* SCARECROW*'s forehead*) is really quite interesting—

SWET (*who had entered the garden unnoticed and overheard the last words*): This deep scar was inflicted by a rain-swept haw finch. . . . Finally, I find you here, my poet-princess, (*ironically*) and with a handsome "cavalier." Why did you steal away from the theater after such an ovation? Are you so modest?

SCARECROW: Don't insult me, Mister, but, above all, don't insult Madame, my Schwester.

SWET: On my honor, I had no such intention.

SCARECROW: Here in this garden, I'm the master and much more!

SWET: It was not my intention, your Eminence, to insult you ...

SCARECROW: Just try it! The creaky gate could stand some use.

SWET: I marvel at the welcome you extend to me, Lord of the garden.

SCARECROW: I was taught social manners by my uncle Flachsmann, who was an honorable member of the city council.

SWET: I beg you: Enough of that!

SCARECROW: Besides, I cannot tolerate such aggravation. Aber, excuse me, Sir Swet, my service here is very hard.

POET: Really, it's true. He works ten hours every day, plus overtime, to chase the sparrows from the seeded lawn.

SCARECROW: My sleeves are hurting, and my stilts pinch—and I have no assistants, like he does up there, and no time to rest.

SWET: Judging by your talent for expression, I think you should become a journalist. Let me commission you, Sir, to write an essay of about thirty lines on garden culture for the *Haarez*.

SCARECROW (*flattered*): The clock in the doctor's waiting room strikes twelve with its primal disharmonious gong. (*The* SCARECROW *totters off past his spot in the center of the garden, back through the gate and into the house of the doctor.*)

POET: He staggers, poor thing, as if he were drunk. I'm afraid he'll break his trouser legs.

SWET: He can always buy new brooms in the department store.

POET: But you can see he is of a superior nature ... and he was never little as we were.

SWET: Alright! And nobody will miss him. Once he's ruined by the autumn storms, we'll throw the old fellow out. (SWET *sits down at the end of the* POET'*s bench to tie his shoe.*) I hope, your friend, the scarecrow, will leave us alone a while.

POET: And what has brought you here, mein lieber Herr? You've come so far.

SWET: Alright! Your great play is of great interest to me.

POET: I'm honored, Mr. Swet.

SWET: But, between poetry and reporting, there is a difference, as night and day, dear poetess!

(SCARECROW *returns to the bench with an old top hat, carrying it carefully.*)

POET: I am so tired—

SWET: The reader of the newspaper, especially a friend of the theater, expects unadorned, objective, yes, even cold truth!

POET: Spiritless, lifeless, like our present lives.

SCARECROW: Look, Sir, the doctor feels his house is honored by your visit and sends you, as a gift from his antique collection, this hat from the Boer War.

SWET: Ohm's top hat?

SCARECROW: It suited your grandfather Kruger very well. I'll lay it in our poet's turtledove-blue lap. Or, better yet, why don't you put it on? It suits you, the grandson, excellently.

SWET: Mr. Scarecrow, I thank your doctor from the bottom of my heart.

SCARECROW: In my mind's eye, I can still see old Ohm Kruger standing there.

SWET: What?

SCARECROW: Oh, ja, the two of us went home zusammen after the elections, through the Mississippi valley. . . . I can still hear the water roaring.

SWET: Alright, come to the editorial office tomorrow, eight o'clock sharp; I'll be there.

(*The* SCARECROW *carves a heart into a tree near the bench. There is a short pause.*)

SWET: But now, dear Poet, do you believe your epic has solved the riddle of this world?

POET: No! As my counterpart already showed us in Part Two quite plainly, in order to assert the truth fully, I have to function on a higher level.

SWET: The riddle of this world will never be resolved completely in this world, not among friends, not in the everchanging IandI, not in the valley between summits, and not while waltzing in the lover's arms!

POET: Because it cannot be resolved in this world, Mr. Swet.

SWET: In wine, as in the River Lethe, there is residue.

THE DISEMBODIED VOICE OF KING DAVID: Residue remains in the golden goblet; even the royal one contains residue.

POET: And are there any other questions, Mr. Swet?

SWET: What shall I tell my readers, my spoiled and pampered readers, at their breakfast tables?

POET: Scarecrow, make up a rhyme! Perhaps even a smoother one than yours or mine.

SWET: It just might do as a filler.

POET: And might relax the nerves.

SCARECROW (*from the lawn*): Don't ask so many questions. It's all in the play, as it should be. Your grandfather, Ohm Kruger, was a statesman and a genius, and he bequeathed his art to you, Editor Swet. And his dignified top hat—put it on already; it suits you well.

(*The* POET *closes her eyes.*)

SWET: So tired?

SCARECROW (*about to approach the bench*): Dead tired, Sir.

SWET: I think she's dying . . .

SCARECROW: Her right eyelid is lightly fluttering—

THE DISEMBODIED VOICE OF DAVID: Little dove, swimming in her blood—

SWET: To annoy the tepid world even in death . . .

SCARECROW: She's so small—she could fit into the new mole hill—

SWET: We'll cover her with fine, quaking grass—

SCARECROW: Oh, if I could just move my feet as fast as you—

SWET: I'll snip a lock of her hair for remembrance—

SCARECROW: Look, and I'll cover her tiny hands with my *mouchoir.*

THE DISEMBODIED VOICE OF DAVID: She painted a golden band over her dark hair, like my poor son Absalom.

SWET: She's dying . . .

SCARECROW: Without clergy, rabbi, sheik, or pastor . . .

SWET: Fool—

EPILOGUE

(*To be spoken either by the* POET *or by an* ANGEL):
And here's the moral of this theatrical and hellish play:
The devil has returned to heaven to play the fool once more.
He came before God in His blue heaven,
with Faust at his side and I, God's poet, between them.
It was just before lunch.
And when the good Lord saw the dear boy,

his halo twinkled in His hair.
The little devil took note of that,
and, like a good boy, stroking God's worried face,
he gave back the unfermented stolen element
in that same long, hollow pipe.
What suffering it had brought into God's world!
What mad fantasies it put into humanity's head!
Then Faust and Mephisto leaped onto Heaven's ladder
and played with the great angels—horse and rider!
In Paradise, one is a child again!
But sometimes God, the Father, looks around:
"Bumpity bump! Bumpity bump!"
And sees His little devil break the Sabbath day
playing a finely carved pipe cut from that stalk,
in front of the sky-blue portals of the Sabbath Gate.
That mischief-making devil plays a psalm . . .

The play is over—
I know nothing more to say . . .
And yet I hear the question from the planet Earth:
"Do you believe in God?"

(*The curtain falls.*)

POET (*singing softly from behind the curtain*): I am so happy. I am so
    happy: God is here!

Else Lasker-Schüler

Excerpt from *The Theater*

Translated by Beate Hein Bennett

*To the magnificent Professor Max Reinhardt, dedicated with
Indian Love.*[1]

I love the theater. If, for my apartment, I could have just gotten a little pro-
scenium box, at least I would have known how to arrange myself, no doubt.
"For me, just to see a stage! Genuine theater would have to be played on it
all the time." Often more genuine theater is played in the playhouse pubs,
where my actor friends gather after a performance rather than before on
stage. Is there any place where you can still hear the horses stampeding,
thunder and lightning, hail and tumult? These kinds of plays are refreshing.
And I love scenery! Bare walls are for the birds! The effect of those aesthetic,
suave stages: a big yawn. Theater is theater! Theater isn't a lecture hall for
medicine or any other scientific discipline. And with symbolism, too, it's a
peculiar thing; to use the symbolic as a motif, as the content of the play, has
a dilettante effect. But a good play should *become* a symbol to the audience.
Of course, Strindberg, whose primary letter was a symbol, could allow himself—as he has often proven to us—to make the symbolic the content of his
drama. Air and vista—and a roving, emotional ellipsis—make up the breath
of a play and give it liveliness. Think of a fairground theater, even there
mixed in with the glitter spectacle—eternity. We do not want to go home
from a performance saddened or refined but rather shaken by the joy of sor-
row or even pleasure. Theater must remain theater.

(ca. 1924)

NOTES

Lasker-Schüler's letter to Max Reinhardt appeared in a collection of essays and poems
called "Das Konzert (1920–1932)," in *Gesammelte Werke* (Munich: Kösel Verlag,
1962), 2:635–38.
    1. Lasker-Schüler gave the title of Indian or Sioux to those men and women
she admired for their courage, spirit, and artistic integrity.

Judith Malina

Director's Note to *Iandl*

A German child, as I once was, learns early that Goethe's *Faust* is about the enigma of good and evil—and the mystery of the divided self. Like Else Lasker-Schüler, I learned of *Faust* at my mother's knee and learned, too, that the image of a Christian Devil in a German Hell is not exactly our Jewish image. But I struggled with the ancient duality, as each of us in her own way must do.

I lost all faith in Goethe when I read in an essay by Thomas Mann that, as an elderly Weimar magistrate, Goethe handed down a death sentence to a young woman condemned for Marguerite's crime, because, in Mann's words, "he so loved justice. . . ."

"Goodbye to literature," I replied, seeing that the poets themselves are not moved to compassion, not even as their poetry exalts it.

No, there is no question but that evil lives—I learned that early because I am a German Jew who narrowly escaped the great destruction and heard of the camps and of our own family's annihilation in the safety of New York.

How can I reconcile the existence of evil with the pacifism I espouse, with the way of Ahimsa—nonhurtfulness—which remains the bedrock of my political life?

The Faustian search is a lifelong one. When she was seventy-one, Else Lasker-Schüler confronted the eternal paradox of evil and wrote down for us in dramatic form her struggle with her own divided self—a German Jew in exile in Jerusalem (a Jew in exile in Jerusalem?!).

And—hallelujah!—she overturned all the canons of Faustian dramaturgy and theology. The Christian strictures mandate the overthrow of Mephisto: Faust must vanquish the Evil One in order to enter Heaven. But our Jewish Poet throws away the rules. Not only does Else's Faust enter Heaven but the Devil himself is transformed, transfigured, and ascends to Paradise in the loving embrace of his mortal alter-ego. At last, true forgiveness.

But . . . what about the Nazis? Alas, Else can only consign them to the flames that already blazed around them in Europe, although—don't forget— she has Mephisto condemn them before his metamorphosis, while Faust pleads tearfully for mercy.

And today, what are we to make of the punitive concept for which Hell is our model—of the inculcated notion that sinners must be punished? I asked the question of Dorothy Day thirty years ago, when we shared a cell in consequence of a peace protest organized by the *Catholic Worker.* "We know that Hell exists," she told me, "but we don't know that it isn't empty."

Friederike Roth

FRIEDERIKE ROTH WAS received in the early 1980s as one of the "new" women playwrights, who consciously foregrounded gender in their plays and wrote, from that perspective, about the relations between men and women. *Klavierspiele* (Piano Plays), was a landmark play and production in introducing this issue to the dominant theater producers and audiences. The accompanying interview with Roth introduces some of the issues around its opening.

Born in 1948, Roth earned her doctorate in 1975 in philosophy and linguistics. She worked as a university lecturer from 1976 to 1979 in anthropology and sociology. She has written five plays: *Piano Plays*, her first, in 1980; then *Ritt auf die Wartburg* (The Journey up the Wartburg) 1981; *Krötenbrunnen* (Toad Wells) in 1984; *Die einzige Geschichte* (The Only Story) in 1983; and *Das Ganze ein Stück* (The Whole: A Piece) in 1986. She has published several volumes of poetry, has had seven radio plays produced, and has translated into German two plays by Dorothy Parker and one by Jane Bowles. She has received seven literary prizes.

I have discussed Roth's work briefly in my book *Feminism and Theater* in reference to her play *Ritt auf die Wartburg*, which is about young women from former West Germany who take their vacation in East Germany. The play provides a unique perspective on the divided Germany through local, gendered settings (such as at the hairdresser) and activities (such as a local dance with border guards).

Piano Plays

Piano Plays represents the conjunction of genders: He and She, with the piano in between. Roth names her two major characters by their appropriate gendered pronouns, suggesting that the play is the interplay between genders. The piano signifies the bond and the bondage of their relationship. The piano belongs to Her, is played by Him, remains after He leaves, cannot be played by Her; yet She is unable to let it go. The piano is the apparatus—actually, a compound of social apparati: the producer of culture, sex, and the body. As a cultural apparatus, only He has access to the production of its music, and, as a sexual one, the piano assigns the role of her body. Like the piano, her body is an instrument upon which men (re)produce. Even when she "bangs" (pun intended) her body on the keys, humping and bumping them, it is only before a prospective male buyer. This indicates that even her tuneless banging of the keys requires the male gaze and is caught up in the economics of sexual difference, which, in this play, become literal.

She is a professional singer, who regularly earns money with her voice, but is promiscuous in her choice of styles. In other words, she can use her singing to earn money but finds no pleasure in the production of her voice, so she wanders from style to style seeking some satisfaction. Her ambiguous relationship to even the production of vocal music in the economy is heightened in scene 14. While she is caught up in direct sexual trade among several men in a bar (which is likewise promiscuous), her money is stolen by a man who hides it in his mouth. This is the money she earned from singing. Thus, the money that came from her mouth is stolen into his. This oral conduit of trade signifies the instant commodification of the cultural apparatus while also signifying the gender imbalance in access to culturization / commodification. The scene ends with a violent extraction of money from the man's mouth by other men in the bar, but She remains ambivalent about this retributive process.

In a sense, Her distance from this "restoration" is part of her general distance and cynicism throughout the play. While she experiences the anger and pain of her oppression, she works neither to rectify her situation nor to create any other alternative possibilities for herself. She is addicted to "love." Understanding her obsession with Him and her need for such a relationship as addiction is part of the feminist critique of an entire nexus of addictive behaviors by women in this society, from alcoholism and substance abuse to relational ones. While such an addiction is clearly depicted in *Piano Plays,* no critique of it is offered.

Beyond the image of the piano as cultural / social apparatus, the apparatus of the production of the play itself is laid out, so to speak, in its minimalism. The strong presence of composition is marked by the insistence of the style.

The elliptical, lyrical style is palpable in the severely contracted space of the language. This minimalism is unlike Kerstin Specht's, which suggests the "social gest."[1] Together with the creation of the cynical, masochistic character and the narrative of addiction, Roth's minimalism begins to feel like a gag on the woman character's / author's mouth. Like Beckett's minimalism, Roth's inscribes a contraction of possibilities at the base of composition. Some of what makes the play "mean," however, relies on what the reader / audience member fills in. A feminist audience, rather than that of a repertory theater, might receive the text in a more radical way than, say, the dominant culture. Yet its forceful portrayal of oppression clearly works on any stage, as the opening production, discussed in the interview, illustrates.

The piano as a symbol of cultural production and its relation to women has become a theme in the 1980s in other feminist works in German. Elfriede Jelinek (discussed more fully in the introduction) has written a novel entitled *The Piano Teacher,* which explores gender and authority in musical training and performance. Jelinek has also written a play entitled *Clara S.* (Clara Schumann), which focuses on piano music as the site where men make music and women, disciplined by practice, reproduce that music, in thrall to the cultural capital of "genius" which the men retain for themselves. Clara Schumann, in the Romantic tradition, is an apt historical figure for such an exploration. In a dark, brutal fashion, Jelinek dramatizes the situation as a sexual colonization along with a cultural one.

Given the traditional association of Europe, specifically Germany, with high culture, the critique of such composers and performers is vital to German feminists in undoing the politics of representation. In the United States, where popular culture dominates the market of representation, pop singer Madonna may seem more acute as a figure of women's participation in the cultural apparatus than, say, Clara Schumann. But Germany is still "attuned" to its concert halls and classical repertories, both economically and aesthetically.

NOTE

1. For a complete discussion of Brecht's creation of the *gestus* and the feminist uses of it, see Elin Diamond, "Brechtian Theory / Feminist Theory: Toward a Gestic Feminist Criticism," *Drama Review* 32, no. 1 (Spring 1988): 82–94.

Friederike Roth

Piano Plays

Translated by Andra Weddington

Characters

SHE	HE
1ST OLD WOMAN	ERWIN
2D OLD WOMAN	1ST BUYER
3D OLD WOMAN	2D BUYER
FRIEND	INSURANCE AGENT
WAITRESS (or WAITER)	THREE MEN
WOMAN IN BAR	WAITER

The stage: Grain fields, with poppies here and there. A sun. A few small tables, as in a bar. A bed, a piano, a small old table with two chairs, or the like. All on the stage at once.

I

I

Fields in high summer. SHE *and* HE *on one of those paths through a grain field which creates a feeling of exaltation in nature. With raging*

Translator's note: The German title of this play, *Klavierspiele,* carries a four-way pun. The word *Spiel* can mean "play" as in a theater piece, "play" as in having fun, or "play" as a musical instrument. It also means *game,* as in a structured conflict. From a linguistic point of view, the choice of *Piano Plays* as the title seems obvious. However, from a theatrical point of view, *Piano Games* seems closer to the mark in conveying the "feel" of the play.

sadness, SHE *whips poppies on the back of her hand, over and over.* HE *is trying, in a thoroughly touching way, to give the impression of being exhausted.*

SHE: The green and gold seem so serious to me now.

HE: Stop it.

SHE: What can I do in the face of nature. Way over there in the background, the landscape is sometimes blue. But that's a long way off.

HE: You're getting carried away with feelings for nature, and I'm sick of memories.

SHE: I'm going to die laughing. You'll do yourself in. Youth and innocence is long gone, my dear. Water over the dam and under the bridge. And, in the meantime, you're a fine, pure human being. Who simply never gets sick of anything.

HE: Stop it.

SHE: Families—and houses—and a crawling existence—I didn't invent them after all. —Everybody wanted to fly into the sun once. Until they noticed that it's the same sun that ripens the beans in their little gardens. (SHE *throws stones upstage, over her head.*) Come on. Let's go find some company. (SHE *disentangles herself, slaps him on the back like a comrade, and makes him get moving.*)

2

There are a few bar tables. The WAITRESS *sits at one, folding paper napkins into triangles, stacking them, and watching the customers. The two sit next to the regulars' table, order schnapps, and sit without talking. At the regulars' table, an old man,* ERWIN, *is enjoying himself loudly and unequivocally with three* OLD WOMEN. *They are pressing their corseted breasts against his arms with open impudence. All three* OLD WOMEN *have a ghostly, decrepit vitality.* ERWIN *speaks to the* 2D OLD WOMAN, *who is carefully dabbing real or imagined drops of wine from her high corseted bosom.*

ERWIN: I'm going home with you now.

1ST OLD WOMAN: You get that idea right out of your head.

2D OLD WOMAN: Why? Because you want him?

1ST OLD WOMAN (*shrill*): Me? I've got grown children and a grandchild on the way. I don't need any man.

3D OLD WOMAN (*with persistent, smiling tenderness*): Cheers, Erwin.

ERWIN: Forty years gnawing on the same bones.

2D OLD WOMAN: So gnaw on me now.

ERWIN (*suddenly and inexplicably turning to* HER): You see, Miss, when they're past the change of life, women, they give the greatest pleasure.

3D OLD WOMAN: Cheers, Erwin.

2D OLD WOMAN: Leave the young lady in peace. The market's over here.

ERWIN (*stubbornly, to* HER): When they get shaggy, that's the time to sail into the harbor. —You don't know anything about it.

1ST OLD WOMAN: Old fool.

2D OLD WOMAN: You think maybe you're any better?

3D OLD WOMAN: Cheers, Erwin.

ERWIN: Enough of that. The lot of you. I'm having a conversation with the young lady.

2D OLD WOMAN: And I'm going home. (*She goes toward the* WAITRESS.)

3D OLD WOMAN: Cheers, Erwin.

1ST OLD WOMAN: I'll buy us another glass of wine.

ERWIN: Forty years, the same bones. Guzzle your wine alone, you cunts. (*Roars*) Check!

1ST OLD WOMAN: But it's my turn this time.

ERWIN: Just between you and me, Miss, they've all got cobwebs between their legs. And you won't be the least bit better off.

(ERWIN *goes. The three* OLD WOMEN *break into shrill laughter, as if suddenly united.* HE *and* SHE *get out money at the same time. Both, but in their own ways, seem to be afraid of these women. They pay and go . . .*)

3

. . . to the piano. Next to it stands HER *pretty little old table.* HE *sits at the piano and opens the lid.*

SHE (*tired and abrupt*): No more.

(HE *snaps the lid shut again without comment.* SHE *gets wine and glasses: grim, silent, and looking for a fight.* SHE *opens the bottle, pours both glasses full, drinks half a glass resolutely—all this a bit too deliberately, as though* SHE *had something to prove but has forgotten what, after all.*)

SHE: The jazz virtuoso with the famous clean attack. I can't hear it anymore.

HE: Used to be, you could never get enough.

SHE: Used to be.

Used to be, one never got enough.

Used to be, you always wanted more.

And, of course, used to be, I was going to sing the "Queen of the Night" someday.

HE (*dryly*): So you made me your pet piano player instead.

SHE: So I should spend my whole life singing in the background with my all-too-unsuccessful voice. Just imagine this: One of these days you're sitting there, and it dawns on you, dimly, that maybe you're just a minor talent after all. (*Drawing* HIM *in a bit*) Your artistic endeavors are a bit laughable. You have the talent of a young girl . . .

HE: Stop it with these old stories.

SHE: That brought him out of it pretty quick. (*Imitating the* 3D OLD WOMAN *in tone and gesture*) Cheers, Erwin!

Oh, God. If I ever get that old. You grow black bristles on your face and brown spots all over your body. Then, of course, you get very compliant—Cheers, Erwin! —When you get old, you're not at your peak anymore. That's for sure. (*Again drinks deeply, heartily*) Your hopes are all dead and buried long ago.

HE: Don't drink so much.

SHE: These days I sing myself to sleep with my own song. I don't need a piano for that. And no musician. Certainly not you. (*Determined, but at the same time not at all convincing*) The piano has to go as soon as possible. (*Drinks*) I've just lost the melody. But that'll blow over.

HE: I never promised you anything.

SHE: Because you never ever make a promise you can't keep. No, you can't promise anything anymore. Just play the piano and take care of the kiddies.

Just once, a single beautiful lie from you.

I would have fluttered and rolled in the grass.

HE: Why lie? We're grownups.

SHE: At least that would have been a suitably sad illusion. It was nice, anyway. But I've never been happy. Lies are so much fun. They make people happy. The effort you would have had to make. To fantasize on my account. That would have been the high point. The razor's edge.

HE: But if it's lies—

SHE: You have to embellish life, my dear.

HE: I'd better go. When you start saying "my dear" . . .

SHE: Get out.

HE (*going*): See you soon.
SHE: And don't come back.

4

Night. And now SHE *is alone. An empty wine bottle and a nearly empty one are standing in front of* HER.

SHE (*not actually crying—furious, ironic, with the curious self-knowledge of the inebriated*):
I'm standing on top of the mountain. Me. And a mountaintop.
A mountain peak and me.
That is the high point. The razor's edge.
Alone, of course. On the mountain peaks you always stand alone.
And breathe in loneliness and a superior cold air.
That makes little icicles in your nose.
Hands off the mountaintops, honey.
You're just not made for the heights.
At first you want the peaks to storm and giggle and dance and sweat.
Then you're frightened of the shaky ground.
So it goes.

(*It gets dark.*)

5

The bar tables. SHE *and her* FRIEND *are sitting at the otherwise empty regulars' table, where in scene* 2 *two of the* OLD WOMEN *sat. The* WAITRESS *is sitting again—it should seem like she's never stopped—folding napkins into triangles and stacking them. The* FRIEND *is drinking hot chocolate,* SHE *a glass of wine.*

SHE: That brown, shriveled skin. How can anybody drink that stuff?
FRIEND: Stop making everything wormy.
SHE: Wormy. That's it. Something squashed and soft. And white crawling things all over it.
FRIEND: It was a passing affair. From the very beginning. And you knew it.
SHE: I saw an end from the beginning.

Then I didn't want to see anymore. An end is not really something to laugh about.

FRIEND: Did you sell the piano?

SHE: People these days don't know anything about pianos.

They're amazed at broken strings.

It makes me tired.

FRIEND: So have the strings repaired and get a good piano tuner. Then it'll sound like new.

SHE: I dreamed we got married. That was nice. Of course, the child was already stillborn. And there was a woman at the reception. She was a distant relative, and she was babbling about dark days and a few years burning at the stake with a husband who was actually neither stud nor mare. But he was her husband. And I would be just his current flame. And I would go along with it, and others would be upset, and she wouldn't stand for any more carrying on with her husband.

FRIEND: Don't make yourself crazy.

SHE: The distant relative was really his wife.

FRIEND: In your dream.

SHE: I was in a daze.

FRIEND: You're being stubborn and stupid.

Let's go for a walk.

SHE: Feed the swans. That's all I need.

FRIEND: Then huddle in here till you turn blue.

SHE: You don't turn blue that fast.

Do me a favor and come home with me. I don't want to be alone.

(The FRIEND *draws her finger almost tenderly along* HER *nose. They pay and go . . .)*

6

. . . and come in again and sit at HER *pretty little old table, on which there are ashtrays, already filled, and wine glasses, one for each. Smoke in the air, as though they have been sitting there for some time.*

FRIEND: Go to sleep now. It's late. And tomorrow morning is the rehearsal. If you go on smoking and drinking, you'll lose your voice.

SHE: In this chorus my voice doesn't matter anyway. I'll just move my mouth and take my feed with thanks.

FRIEND: You always like motets.

SHE: Motets. Motets. The way that sounds. Motets. I can't go on singing
"Ah welcome, Ah welcome" over and over.
An opera at least, if we've got to rehearse.
Full of tangled fantasies.
Something that takes you away from a bogus life.

(SHE *lies down on her bed while the sun goes down, and she becomes immediately more awake.*)

It smells like celery in here.
FRIEND: You're right. Celery sticks.
SHE: There you go again.
FRIEND: First you can't stand operas and you swear by madrigals...
SHE: That was operettas. The charming ones with pep and sweet melodies.
FRIEND: And then for months it absolutely had to be requiems. You want
to sing, and you don't. You want to sell, and you don't. You've got to
decide.
SHE: I want both.
A party, in celebration of nothing. That would be nice, a party like
that. Everybody making friendly gestures, but different from ours.
Hilarity. Giddy confusion. A few stylish women's heads singing dirges.
With stupid childish smiles on their faces. The lonely street lamp and
the old dog play important roles. A child playing and one sleeping. A
shadow and a cry from the wings. And lots of enchanting little creatures.
That giggle obscenely in tiny choruses and make dainty movements with
soft thighs and lightly arching feet. White on white.—
When it's over, it will be as if I had been king for a moment. (*Pause*)
It still smells like celery in here.
We just keep on singing the same old choruses.
You can just go on and go, if you want to stay in voice for it.
Of course, everybody has to do something for a living. And singing's
not the worst thing. But not the best, either.
FRIEND: I'm so tired now.
SHE: Yes. Well.

(*The* FRIEND *goes. It gets quite dark.*)

7

The stage is dark. SHE *alone, to the audience.*

SHE: My luck's run out.

An eternity lasts too long for me.

That was just another long hot summer with sparks in the air. And little storm animals floating in it. It drives out the memory of something that once was, that was unique, and wishes without direction. And you're leading yourself down the garden path if you think you've mastered the small talk. In the daytime it's beautiful weather, untroubled by our existence. Summer slugs crawl through the dry days. Blind cats howl in the sun. —Like a ruffled bird, beating its wings, I have tumbled through the nights where time goes by unmeasured. You know the glaring night-glow of the colors; it lets the stars come sliding down. Someone comes, steps in; then another comes and steps in too. I think I'll never be able to sleep again; not tonight and not tomorrow night and never any other.— Someone sits down with him, all tender and soft, a little feather. Her eyes are so bright, moths must gather on her. I see him kissing her, and how he runs his hand through her hair that makes a sound if you even look at it.—

Of course, that was his wife.

I've climbed into the mouth of autumn, it seems.

II

8

Afternoon, at the piano. The IST BUYER *actually has his shirt unbuttoned, to the last button above his trousers. A heavy silver chain dangles in the hair on his chest. The* BUYER *is playing a Chopin showpiece, powerfully, with lots of pedal, positively dazzling.*

SHE: For heaven's sake, stop.

IST BUYER: You can see for yourself, the thing's not worth anything anymore.

SHE: Of course not. If you can't play.

IST BUYER: I'm a piano teacher with the Musicians' Association.

SHE (*poisonous*): That's easy to hear.

IST BUYER: And I'm looking for a used piano for a student.

SHE: It's used. You can't argue with that.

IST BUYER: If it were only out of tune. But then the pedal is totally useless too.

SHE (*still hostile*): You gave it a lot of gas just now. You shouldn't run it all together into such a mush. Especially not the bright sharp pointed notes.

1ST BUYER (*unswerving*): Two of the strings are broken.

SHE: A piano teacher can't make the strings bounce.— He could.

1ST BUYER: Who?

SHE: And the way it sounds . . .

1ST BUYER: Excuse me. Your piano doesn't sound.

SHE: When a string breaks and gives up.

1ST BUYER (*comically pedantic*): No craftsman, who really is one, destroys the tools of his craft. Not even in revolutions. Anyone who destroys a piano doesn't deserve a piano.

SHE (*annoyed*): He was a flawless pianist. No two ways about it. He got runs like clear glass out of this thing. And destroyed pianos out of sheer delight. Seriously. And it was . . .

1ST BUYER (*formally*): Then might I . . .

SHE: I just meant to say, it was nice to watch. — (*Decided*) The piano has to go. But you first. You piano teacher, you. You don't need a piano. A cassette recorder, that's the right thing for you and your students.

1ST BUYER: Then might I . . .

SHE (*won't be stopped*): Music cassettes to whistle to. Between breakfast and the morning paper. Here the piano is not for a scrapbook, not for a student, not for family musical evenings.

1ST BUYER: Then might I . . .

SHE: Oh, just go. Skip the formalities. Can't you just simply go?

1ST BUYER: I may . . .

SHE: You may nothing. You'll have to do whatever you want.

1ST BUYER: I'd like to spend the night with you. (*Pause*)

SHE (*perplexed, but quickly decided*): Then stay.

(*He goes cheerfully back into the room and sits at the piano.*)

SHE: Keep your hands off the piano. But stay.

9

In the morning now. The same scene as the evening before, but all is in disarray. The 1ST BUYER, *looking rumpled, is sitting at the piano.* SHE *is in a bathrobe, hungover. Both are drinking beer.*

SHE (*determined and energetic*): Well. The piano has to go.
You mustn't think he gave me money for it. —
A piano just goes along with it. Believe me, a piano is one of the good
things, in spite of everything. —
I've even stopped listening to music in the mornings now. For the time
being. It's true. When the party's over you, put the flowers in the fridge.
In the morning, after the nighttime hunt, the spiders have disappeared
into their holes.
There's one in the bathroom, I just remembered. You'll have to kill it
for me, before you go.
(*He is leaning over his beer, silent.*)
When you come at closing time, they slop water on your feet and bring
down the iron grille. It's always the same.

1ST BUYER: You talk an unbearable amount of nonsense for a bright
morning.

SHE: This morning nothing's bright. —
No. Really. He's romping somewhere right now with his wife and kiddies
at the lake, rubbing little bodies warm when their lips turn blue.
I'm freezing.
The beginning is so small and secret. But an end. The whole affair is
an abandoned turd.

1ST BUYER: Let's get to the point. I'll buy the piano, for God's sake.

SHE: What kind of absurd boots are you wearing? I didn't notice that at
all yesterday. (SHE*'s grasping at straws.*) A person with boots like that
has no business having a piano.

1ST BUYER (*as if he understood something*): You're personally attached
to the instrument.

SHE (*hard and quick*): It's not an instrument. It's a piano.

1ST BUYER: Fine. Then I can go.

SHE: Don't you know anybody who's reasonable?

1ST BUYER: What do you mean?

SHE: And is looking for a piano. Just for himself, not for a student and
not for a woman and not for a son. And who understands something
about tone.

1ST BUYER (*smirking fatuously*): I'll send you somebody. Count on it. But
count me out of the game. (*He goes.*)

10

The bar tables. SHE *and her* FRIEND *at the regulars' table. The same
scene—with* WAITRESS, *chocolate, and wine—as in scene* 5.

SHE: That walk through the grain field that day was the end. I just didn't know it. Only a vague foreboding, full of anxiety. I already had a broken wing. I should have kept it light. With flying hair and frivolous conversation. —

I couldn't say a thing. The grain was trying to poke itself into the sky, and there was an itch in my hand, as if it lay between the grain and the sky. And it was all so quiet, no knowing where it came from or where it was going.

(SHE *takes another long drink of wine.*) When you get right down to it, nature is a great insolence.

FRIEND: Memories fade with time.

SHE: No. They don't.

FRIEND: And then they don't hurt anymore.

SHE (*irritable*): They do too. —

He gave me a poppy once. The fields were full of poppies. He had to piss, and he pulled off on the side of the road and stood with his back to me. And for the first time I see that he has bowlegs, and I'm almost stunned by emotion. There he stands, forgotten by the whole world. And then he takes a few steps into the field and gets me a poppy. (*Awkward pause. The* FRIEND *looks at her unbelievingly.*)

Well, OK. I called to him to bring me a poppy. Anyway he brought me one!

FRIEND (*ironic*): That at least. How good of him.

SHE (*with renewed determination*): Now I'm really going to sell the piano, once and for all.

FRIEND: You haven't sold it yet?

SHE: What does my piano matter to strangers? They go on living. Life goes on for them, happy, content. They only want my piano to play the accompaniment. Singing drunkenly, "It's a long way. Into the wide, wide world." Oh, well.

FRIEND: Do you want to sell it or not?

SHE: Of course, I want to sell it. But without these performances: Do you play yourself? Then why do you want to sell it? Doesn't it have a good sound? Is the tone gone? Are the pedals loose? Bad wood. The action's too soft. Ah, you don't play the piano? Then how come you have one? Fulfillment of a childhood dream, I understand. Then you really have no idea about pianos. Just between you and me, your piano isn't worth a whistle. (*Pause*) Nobody's gonna take my piano.

FRIEND: What then?

SHE: Never ever. —

What shall I do with the piano without him?

I know. I tell the same story over and over. Little kisses. Little kisses.

Again and again, the whole story from the beginning.

FRIEND: Oh, just stop it.

SHE: If only a wind would come. —

Be a dear and pay my tab. I want to get out of here. (SHE *goes very quickly.*)

II

With the 2D BUYER *at the piano.*

2D BUYER (*understanding*): It's not really about the piano.

SHE: It's only about the piano. What else?

2D BUYER: OK. Let's play the little game.

What did you have in mind?

SHE: I have no idea of the going price.

It's the first time I've done anything like this.

2D BUYER (*soothing*): There's a first time for everything.

Get us something to drink, honey.

SHE: Since when do you call me honey?

2D BUYER: I beg your pardon. I wouldn't want to get too familiar, my lady. A manner of speech in these situations.

SHE: Would you like some wine?

2D BUYER: Sure.

(SHE *goes. He stays alone for a short time—awkward and self-conscious. Then the usual opening the bottle, getting wine glasses, and pouring. They drink.*)

SHE: Am I right that you haven't the slightest interest in my piano?

2D BUYER: Let's get to the point.

SHE: You want to get to the point, and to me it's all cockeyed. Clouds are falling in my head and silly waves and children's little bodies and God knows what. (*Helpless*) If you don't want the piano . . .

2D BUYER: We can talk about your piano later.

SHE: And now?

2D BUYER: You're an attractive woman. Your charms put your piano to shame, if I may say so.

SHE: You'd better get lost.

2D BUYER: I'd really like to stay with you.

SHE (*mulish*): You don't want the piano at all?

2D BUYER (*determined*): Now don't make a scene.

SHE (*suddenly*): So get in bed. —

(*Resigned and ironic*) "Let's go to sleep," said the poet, and died.

2D BUYER: That's not exactly inviting.

SHE: You've got pennies on your eyes.

(2D BUYER *lies down on* HER *bed, fully clothed.*)

SHE: Yes. Indeed. (SHE *lies down beside him, also fully clothed. Pause. Then—hesitant.*)

He would go to sleep with his head on his arm. He would listen to me for a long time with his fingertips on his lips. Until he would just go to sleep.

He was so ordinary when he was asleep.

At night now I go back over the same ground as in the day. —

Just go.

2D BUYER (*almost gently and at the same time threatening*): I'm staying with you.

SHE: It's no use.

Love is rubbish. (*Pause*)

The photographs of fenced-in lakeshores . . .

2D BUYER (*impatient*): What about them?

SHE: Now he's telling other women how pretty they are. And it's almost winter anyway.

2D BUYER: Stop talking about my predecessor.

SHE (*sitting up, furious*): You're not his successor. Don't kid yourself.

2D BUYER: Don't make a scene. I'm telling you for the last time.

SHE: Get out.

2D BUYER (*slaps her*): I'm not a lightning rod for your fucked-up mental anguish. (*Hits her again*) And don't stare like that. And if I may give you a piece of advice, get out of the piano business. You're too high-strung for it, sweetie. (*He goes.*)

12

The bar tables. The same napkin-folding WAITRESS, *the same regulars' table. The* FRIEND *is sitting with a cup of cocoa.* SHE *enters with a swollen black eye, a bit tipsy.*)

FRIEND (*horrified*): How you look!

SHE (*offhand, matter of fact*): Somebody got mad.

FRIEND: Woman, take care of yourself. You're sliding into something.

SHE: I like it better than your soggy peace and quiet.

FRIEND: You don't belong in that sort of thing.

SHE (*more and more indignant*): Where. Where then.
Everything around me is huge and chilly and doesn't add up. Everything's running along smoothly. You might even understand the few lunatics who just can't learn for the life of them to take it easy like you do.
I need a schnapps.

FRIEND (*a touch too understanding*): Grain or fruit?

SHE: Grain. Of course.
Grain. (*The* FRIEND *orders the schnapps.*)
Nothing but dry thistles all around me. And wilted ferns. One gets so caught up in one's own daydreams. (*Pause*)
He gave me up so very willingly. For a visit with his in-laws, and to keep his wife in a good mood. She's just as quiet and soft as the rest of you. She mustn't know a thing. Mustn't upset the even-tempered. With me, he pounded on the piano with his fists. And then shoved me away. I don't understand it to this day, and I don't want to understand it.

FRIEND: That's just it. You don't want to get out of your misery.

SHE: Jesus. Don't get psychological on me. You'll be recommending therapy next. Group therapy, if possible. (*Quoting*) In two minutes we will scream our pain right out from the bottom of our souls. Nobody needs to feel embarrassed here. We all suffer. But we mustn't suffer; we must simply learn to deal with our pain. So let's all scream together. One, two, three, go. Thank you. Relax. (*Raging*) Until the day I die I will insist absolutely that shared joy is half-joy. That love sings and swings and makes you uncritical and doesn't deal in accounts paid in advance, like a greedy, shriveled-up old woman.

FRIEND: For God's sake, take better care of yourself. I can sell your piano for you.

SHE: That would be better. (SHE *starts frantically looking for money.*) I can't take it here anymore.

FRIEND: Keep your money.
Just go.

SHE: Right.
Well then.

(SHE *sways a bit as she goes.*)

13

Between the bed and the piano, an elderly INSURANCE AGENT *enters hesitantly.*

AGENT: Good day. You are ...

SHE: Come in. Come in. I know all about it. It's about the piano, so to speak. (*Giggles*) Be brave. Come closer. (*Whispers*) You don't sell pianos through the keyhole.

AGENT: Excuse me, but ...

SHE: Don't apologize. You're not the only one. (*Examines him*) Age isn't the decisive factor with pianos. (*Giggles again*)

AGENT: I don't know anything about pianos ...

SHE: No problem. Pianos aren't really very complicated.

AGENT: Pianos are furniture. That's not my department. My colleague in home furnishings ...

SHE: He can come, too.

AGENT: I'm here about your retirement insurance.

SHE (*puzzled*): What? Is that a marriage proposal, or what?

AGENT: I know, you're still young, and you're not thinking of old age yet.

SHE: Just what does my age have to do with you?

AGENT: You should be better insured. (*Starts to rummage in his briefcase*) You're a singer with a radio choir ...

SHE: I've sung with the state opera, too ...

AGENT: ... and surely earn ...

SHE: It's not a matter of money at all.

AGENT: ... a good salary every month. But if you were to get laryngitis, for example ...

SHE: Oh don't make it into such a production number.

AGENT (*irritated*): ... and if you were unable to work, you would receive an average monthly stipend of, let's say ...

SHE (*sits awkwardly in an unmistakable pose*): And just what would my average monthly stipend be, huh? Now I can't wait to hear that.

AGENT: Let's say two hundred and fifty—

SHE: Thirty days in a month. Two hundred and fifty divided by thirty, — that's about eight a day.

Just like Jakarta the sailor said after the seventh woman, and sank exhausted to the floor.

AGENT: What?

SHE: Let's cut the nonsense.

About the piano.

(*Goes to the piano and lies across the keyboard*)

You hear? (*Drapes herself, as best she can, over the keys*) Now, if that's not music. (*Moves, as in coitus, letting her buttocks hit hard and rhythmically on the keys*) Just listen to that. (*She is wearing out a bit.*) That's music with life in it, huh? (*Bangs roughly on the piano with obvious pleasure*) Man, that's the purest. It'll make you deaf and blind. (SHE *stops suddenly.*) Well. Don't just stand there.

AGENT: Yes.

But.

SHE: But what?

AGENT: You don't need that sort of thing.

SHE (*jumping up from the piano, aggressive*): What don't I need? Tell me now, just what am I not supposed to need? I don't need wornout old men's tales. I certainly don't need the music written out. Because I really need it all. Everything.

AGENT (*obstinately patriarchal*): It's a matter of the insurance. (*Business-like*) You should be insured. Against eventualities. Which always happen. Then you're stuck.

SHE: What does my security matter to you?

You really don't need a piano. Just the retirement insurance. Listen kid, when you're long underground, this piano will still be here.

You're not going to get one thin dime out of me. —

Go on, get out of here with your securities. (*He goes quickly.* SHE *pouts after him.*)

As if you were any better. You're all alike.

Cop a feel under the table.

And all so very proper on the surface.

14

At the bar tables. Must be dominated by the atmosphere of a third-class "pickup" bar, with appropriate music, lighting, nude photographs or porno films projected at random on the scenery. Instead of the napkin-folding WAITRESS, *a* WOMAN *is sitting at a table, with costume and makeup to fit the place. During the scene, she silently waves two or three* MEN, *who arrive one by one with large German shepherds, toward an area into which they silently disappear. After each one, she looks mechanically at the clock and makes notes. At the regulars' table of the earlier scene,* SHE *is sitting with a group of noisy men. One of the piano* BUYERS *is among them.*

SHE (*in high spirits*): That was a hot one. The Helgoland Lounge. I'm gonna go there again. (*Calls*) Check please . . . (SHE *discovers that her purse is empty.*) Oh God. Where's my money!

WAITER: We know that one. We're real fond of it.

SHE: I had it earlier.

IST MAN: You've still got plenty. (*The* MEN *laugh.*)

SHE: I loaned you a twenty earlier.

2ND MAN: She's right. She had a lot of cash in there.

SHE: How could that happen? Somebody snitched it.

WAITER: It's always the same story. Lady, you gotta come up with the cash when you've ordered the round.

SHE: Assholes. I haven't got it to burn. Why take it from me? Take it from the ones who burn hundred dollar bills in the fireplace. It's always the little guy that gets it in the face. I sing my throat raw, and somebody rips me off. (*Screams*) Who's got my money?

(*General searching and checking of wallets and protestations and trying to calm* HER *down.*)

SHE (*to the* WAITER, *trying to make light of it*): Money's gone. 'S all gone. 'N we'll never find it anymore.

I'll drink to that.

3D MAN: Two bottles of champagne and glasses for everybody.

WAITER: Who's paying?

3D MAN: I'll take care of it. Bring the champagne. Go on.

(*At the table, general puzzlement*)

SHE: Nobody was gonna be crooked here. Another kind of life here. I could die laughing again. You're a bunch of startled chickens here. Not even cocks.

(*The first bottle is opened and poured into the glasses.*)

Cheers. To all of us.

(*All but one* MAN *raise their glasses and drink.*)

How come you're not drinking?

(*The one* MAN *smirks, silently.*)

Cut the stupid grin. Cheers, Erwin, or whoever you are.
I'm drinking to you this time.

(*The one* MAN *keeps on smiling silently.*)

Cat got your tongue? I can see that.
What an enormous joke the whole thing is.
Don't worry about it. I'll live.
Anyway, cheers.

(*The one* MAN *is unchanged.*)

Drink with me now. Stop acting like you've got a mouthful of marbles.
IST MAN: He hasn't got marbles in there. He's got the money.
(*Laughter*)
2D MAN: Open your mouth.
SHE: Let him keep still. Leave him alone.
2D MAN: Open your face.

(*They jump on him. They hold both his arms, stretched out like a crucifix.*)

2D MAN: Open up.
SHE (*shrieking hysterically*): Shut up.
    Don't let them get you.
    Come with me.
    For God's sake, keep your mouth shut . . .
    (*Crying, as the* MEN *bloody his mouth, forcing it open.*)
    . . . and come with me . . .

(*The* MEN *pull bills out of the one* MAN*'s mouth. They throw the bloody money at* HER.)

III

15

The stage is dark. SHE, *alone, to the audience.*

SHE: I want to tell you, I'm coming apart at the seams. Quite without
    meaning to, I have thought through the stories that weave in and out

of one another without beginning or end. But too long. Sitting there, making up stories where everything fits together neatly—step by step, I have made solitude for myself, which you know as well. It's not the quiet calm we dream about in the high places which comes over us, the smile of a child. We stay down below, in dreams. The demons peek in through the windows; I brood and I tremble and I hear the bad old songs that try to shrink the great distances. And then sometimes I see ancient women, shamelessly lifting their skirts to show their legs with the blue and purple veins, and the wrinkled, shriveled-up old men with their quick, greedy glances. It all leads who knows where, and that's where I want to go. Once I'm there, I will know that my dreams didn't take me far enough. There will be a summer there, where the air lets me hear it. The blue wild chicory flowers and all the old stories will have withered. Snarling, hissing, twitching: all the wailing will have dried up, and I will be glad of nothing but the hot weather. Or how should I put it? But maybe it's winter, a white-on-white cold there, so that my face freezes. Then the distance comes a few yards closer and stays far away. The trees would be a long way off, —the way they are, otherwise, only in books. A now that has been would grow clear and intelligible and then disappear.
Both will come to be. Maybe.
You know how uncanny a single hen can seem in the evening when night is about to fall. So you know now that I really did come apart.

16

At HER *pretty little old table.* HE *is standing there again, after a very long time, and is trying, cheerful and untroubled, to act as if everything were in the best of order.* HE *takes his jacket off and hangs it across a chair, entirely too much as if everything were perfectly normal.* SHE *just watches.*

HE: So how are you? What've you been up to?
SHE: I want to go away.
Anywhere.
I just need a quiet place; that simply doesn't exist here.
HE: Just what are you looking for?
SHE: When I've found it, I'll know.
HE: North or south?

SHE (*annoyed*): I don't know. Where there's a sun and a moon. Where the sky looks as if it were the sea.

HE: Plains or mountains?

SHE: You're so dense.

Where everything whirls and swings, where it . . .

HE: You look dead tired. I don't think you're getting enough sleep.

SHE (*indifferent*): Waking, sleeping. Soon the fields will be harvested. And, before that, you dream well and without flinching of hawks and hairpins, crows, —I don't know what all. And everywhere there's life in it still. — (*Pause, then suddenly*) I like medieval paintings. Where they dance and drink and sigh, and afterward groan. Sturdy and thick-legged. There, at least, hearts are torn out and heads are struck off. The women's breasts are torn off with pincers.

HE: I kissed you once in front of the Barbara Altar.

SHE: Yes.

And?

HE: And nothing.

Just . . .

SHE: Just nothing. Only nothing and nothing and again nothing. A little taste of hell, that's all.

But, for God's sake, not hell.

Standing in a slanting rain and waiting for love and simply despairing. —

The daily business. This endless singing. —It blows the joy right out of me like stuffing.

HE (*almost lying in wait*): But, rumor has it, you're still having a pretty good time.

SHE: Worn out men prowl around my house at night. That annoys the neighbors, of course.

HE: You're in the old city almost every night, as I hear it.

SHE: You're going to have to hear quite different things. I can hear you screaming already: So little and all that blood. Everything, but not that. I can see you already, working out the touching gravestone. The death masks of dear little curly heads in stone. What a pity that stone can't be blond. You'd have to get hold of a very gifted artist, to blow the stone away from the little curls so gently that the impression of blondness would remain.

HE: Shut up. Right now.

SHE: What do you know! You can talk sensibly. I never would have thought it possible.

HE: Shut the fuck up. (*Softly*) I don't want to hit you.

SHE (*screaming*): You hit me all the time.

  The last scrap of song. When the child first sits on the wooden horse, no music plays. Even the stars are just sharp.

HE: It's no use talking to you when you're like this.

SHE: Yes.

  Even dreams don't work for me anymore.

(*It gets dark.*)

17

Night. SHE *is sitting with her* FRIEND *at her little table. Both are nibbling busily, continuously, on walnuts. Their movements have something bird-like about them. Their conversation runs along with this.*

SHE: It goes on like that, and I don't know how. He comes occasionally. We talk properly in the meantime, like civilized people: What's new? How's it going at work? That's a classy sweater you're wearing. Are the children well? Thanks, me too.

  Then we sleep together. When I lie beside him, it seems to me that we should introduce ourselves to each other. —Pleased to meet you. —The pleasure's all mine. —And when he goes, I laugh at him, friendly, in parting.

FRIEND: And, in the end, it really doesn't touch you?

SHE (*concentrating on cracking nuts*): You're right. You only find statues with misery pressed into their faces and wailing voices in the theater. And I've got to live.

FRIEND: Right.

SHE: Once the devil held a holiday for me.

  That was earlier.

FRIEND: Forget it.

SHE: Yes.

(*While they go on cracking nuts, the sun seems to rise over the bed* . . .)

18

But it gets dark again at once. HE *has come.*

SHE (*greeting him*): There's no end to it.—

  But it's nice that you're here.

HE: You could have figured it out, after all. Tonight there's going to be jazz and rock and classics. There are some poems in between, too, I think. In any case, text. I'm playing at the end . . .

SHE: Ah, yes.

(*Bitingly*) That fits so well. Business with pleasure, or how do they put it? (*Suddenly, without reason, overcome by giggling*) I'll get us an absinthe. Like in the old days.

HE (*as a diversion*): The piano is still here.

SHE (*indifferent*): You've left too many footprints. People don't want it like that. (SHE *goes to get water and Pernod.*) The usual?

(HE *laughs.* SHE *mixes. They both drink.*)

SHE: All quiet on the home front again?

HE: You could say that. (*Pause*)

SHE: I imagine your wife is soft and fragrant.

HE: That's right, exactly.

SHE: You're still no good at lying.

Surely she wears a shimmering gown like a goddess and, in the winter, a fur piece around her neck with sharp little claws.

HE: Now what are you getting at? It's the same thing here as it is there. Pure jealousy. By the way, she really does have a fur piece with claws. A black fox.

SHE: Pretty.

My head is so full. In the daytime, the buzzing air. At night, the swarms. I hear piano music all the time.

You make sand castles with the children. Some bygone Rome with underground passages. But I'm off to the side. And I carry on shamefully. All in all.

HE: My son. If you had ever seen him, you would have liked him.

You would have understood everything.

SHE: He has blond curls—I know, I know—and he's a dreamer.

So that everyone who sees him is touched. (*Laughs*) The devil's brat in an angel's robe.

HE: Will you stop that!

SHE: Oh, God. Your diligent little Lisa with the full lips. Who always wants to die laughing and can never manage it. Yeah, yeah, I know, nothing about your wife. Mustn't touch that. So let it go.

You're not the common crowd. They'd say the hell with the old thing. You wouldn't like that.

You'd rather get yourself a few expensive babes on the side, tender and reserved, with glistening shadows and helpless tics around their damned tired, dry eyes.

No. I want to be hateful now. (*Dejected*) I get so depressed about it. I want most of all to run as far as I can see. Where there's no cruelty in the morning light.

I don't want anything to do with love anymore. —

(*Pause, then suddenly coming briefly to life*) Somebody with a woman's hairdo keeps sending me roses now.

But they go black on me by evening.

HE: Who's that?

SHE: I want so much to go to sleep.

HE: And I've got to go. You're not coming?

SHE (*going with* HIM *to the door*): I've had enough of that. Too much. (*Strokes his face much too tenderly*) Play well. You must play well. At least.

19

Now SHE *is alone again.* SHE *lies on the bed and stays there a while. Suddenly* SHE *stands up and goes to the telephone.*

SHE (*on the phone*): Is that you? —

It's me. Yes. Come over here. —

I can't sleep. —

It's always the same thing. I lie there with my eyes wide open. I don't recognize anyone, and I stay silent, and I can't scream, and I see an open coffin with a child's corpse in it which has blond curls and looks innocent and is holding out flowers to heaven. I want to scream, heaven is lovely enough without your flowers. It has the whole field already. You just can't hear it rustle.

Just come over here fast.

(SHE *hangs up quickly so that no protest can get through. It gets dark.*)

20

Darkness. SHE, *alone, to the audience.*

SHE: The mean ugly days and the great fear of the night. We've been made into little movable people. Who age.

We think about the iridescent life that ours was once supposed to be, and we open the first bottle of wine.

Once it seemed like I had the sun on a leash. In those days, calling birds flew prettily through my head. I would have given heaven and hell the same value, and anything alien I would have simply sung away, as if it could never wear me down.

Once, it should have been like the beginning of the world or like the end of it. Or like a totally new beginning without compare. A new beginning: a nice idea, but old.

Heaven would have had to turn itself around and orbit Earth. But heaven's fire was dying away, and, at last, a white sun rose. White suns bring nothing, nothing but rain. I want nothing more up there now. Easily played out, it's all just whirring wildly in my head.

There are such lovely places in the abyss.

Who wants to know whom the birds kiss.

They fly light and easy, without mercy, far above.

(HER *doorbell rings a few times.* SHE *doesn't answser it.*)

Elisabeth Henrichs

An Interview with Friederike Roth:
Building Sentences, Ripping Out Hearts,
Knocking Off Heads

Translated by Wendy Arons

Elisabeth Henrichs: "And actually, in the beginning was not the word"—
that is from your poem "The Beautiful Body." What, for you, is the
beginning of a poem? Something that you've seen, something that you've
thought, something that you've heard "out of the mouths of people in
grave procession"? Or something that you've read, hence a word, which
"repeatedly transforms itself into a wonderful Word"?

Friederike Roth: Everything. I only know that I frequently observe, even
when I go into restaurants. All of a sudden my ear is lying on the next
table, and I'm listening to the people at it. There are sentences, whole
dialogues, which remain hanging in my head and which I write down
for myself at home. Actually, there's also a lot of reading material, because
I truly enjoy reading beautiful texts. And then there has to be a reason
for a poem. Suddenly then there's a theme, and I know: That's something
you can make a poem out of. I can recite almost word for word what
someone has said many years ago, but I have no memory for visual
details. Landscapes affect me in such a way that they make sentences
occur to me. When I drive over the Swabian Alps toward Ochsenswang,
I naturally think of [Eduard] Mörike, who lived there.

EH: Sometimes I go places only because the name sounds so beautiful—
Lipari islands . . .

FR: I do that in small ways. I'll turn off the road if there's a sign standing
there, like: ROTTENHARZ.

EH: And what would happen if you couldn't get rid of the words *Sargasso
Sea* or *Guadalquivir?* Would the word hang in your head, or would you
follow after it on the spot?

FR: No doubt, that's what I'd do!

EH: Borneo also sounds very nice.

FR: But there I would immediately concern myself with the culture.

EH: How long have you been writing? Even before you began to study philosophy and linguistics?

FR: I really first consciously began my studies with literature. I studied philosophy, of course, also classical philosophy, but I specialized in aesthetic theory and text theory. It had a lot to do with semiotics and mathematical aesthetics. That was very in vogue at the time, before 1968.

EH: Who was your teacher at the time?

FR: Max Bense, at the Institute for [Philosophical Theory] in Stuttgart. At the time I was interested in the question of whether or not it would be possible to find objective standards for the aesthetic order of a text. From the very beginning it was clear to me that it wouldn't work out, but I was very curious to see with which methods you would proceed. After a couple of semesters I felt a great craving to become synthetic, by which I mean I had the feeling: I want to make sentences myself now.

My first texts were the "minimal stories" that are no longer available today. Those were texts in the wake of concrete poetry. I wanted to know how one could arrange speech material, that is, words, so that they become exciting. After 1968 the whole thing began to bore me. I thought, this is leading to a deadend. The one who led me out of this deadend of the concrete was Ernst Jandl. Jandl was once a strictly concrete poet. For him it was similar—he also wanted content.

EH: What did you learn from this concrete phase?

FR: A sense of precision. An exactness for words and for their weight; that's also why I am so sensitive about small changes in the text.

EH: You finished university with a dissertation: "Aesthetic Theory in the Twentieth Century." Did your studies nourish your desire for poetry writing, or did they weaken it?

FR: I understand what you mean by "weaken." It could kill you. But I never let myself be influenced. Perhaps it's my Swabian bullheadedness. Certainly it has to do with my upbringing. I had a very simple home, but, when I was a child and couldn't sleep, my father used to sit on my bed and read me Hölderlin. That began when I was six. Of course, I didn't understand any of it, but I still have the Hölderlin rhythm in my ear today.

EH: Is your father still alive?

FR: Yes, he is very old, and, of course, I would like it if he lived to one hundred fifty. The texts that I write, he looks at them, and sometimes he shakes his head, and sometimes he says, "I like that sentence."

EH: In your poem "Suddenly a Mosaic Eye—In Ravenna Naturally" you write:

> *As if nature were*
> *the peacock*
> *the stretching of lily bushes*
> *the wild duck's throats, cat's heads*
> *very rare and pretext only for Art*

Do you deplore the fact that you must write?

FR: Naturally, no person must write. You can leave it. I want to do it, but I know that it's a pagan occupation. And, when I sit at a poem and know how it should be, and I sit there evening after evening, then sometimes I get into a fury, and I think, It would be better just to watch TV.

EH: In 1978 you published your first story, "Dreams of Order." Was this an attempt to free yourself from the necessity to write verse?

FR: No. I knew what I wanted to formulate, and it was clear to me: The theme is too big, it ruptures the form of poetry. The theme is the connection between order and nonorder and the simultaneity of order and chaos. On the other hand, it was also clear to me that I would never be in the position to write a traditional story. I tried to find a form that gave expression to this very inability, this reluctance to compose something fully. A disturbance in the face of closed totalities, closed worlds, closed views of life, should be made visible by the very fact that you rupture the form.

EH: Right on the first page of "Dreams of Order" is the sentence: "Without question I am a man." The I-narrator of the book is a "Mister" Pfaff. Would you rather have been a boy?

FR: I am happy now that I am a woman. I don't know how it was earlier. I only know that I should have been a boy. I should have been called Helmut. That my main character is masculine has absolutely nothing to do with psychology, only with the joy of experimentation. I wanted to invent a somewhat crazy man; it was play instinct, nothing more.

EH: Mister Pfaff is a "head-artist," a "thought player." His love is for the "conceivable," "the speculation over the possibility of the possible." Pfaff imagines to himself the development of the cosmos, the development of life. He asks: How would it be if "completely other forms of life had developed"? Is this Pfaff a document of that time when you were still completely identified with your mind and its work?

FR: Pfaff is a document of the opposite. I worked for a long time at adult education in order to earn money; I gave courses in philosophy. The questions of the people in these classes led to a point where I suddenly began to reflect on whether it was really so earth-shattering—what we were brooding on there. All of a sudden it became stranger and stranger to me that I really got a pleasure from the Kant readings and from Hegel. And I met people there who asked me, "So, what's the purpose of all this?" and this confrontation really irritated me. Pfaff is a document of this destabilization of my identity.

EH: Mister Pfaff sends his girlfriend, a Miss Schulze, away. Because she disturbs his order, because she doesn't grasp his chaotic head games?

FR: I had considered, How do I bring in an element that in a very crass way clarifies that what Pfaff constantly produces are chimeras—and suddenly it was clear to me: There is a woman, who disturbs him, and this woman—she embodies the reality principle.

EH: The "Dreams of Order" are made like a scientific work: a text with many footnotes and even footnotes to the footnotes. Do the books you cite actually exist?

FR: I shoved a couple of books in there that really exist, in order to give the whole thing an appearance of legitimacy. Otherwise, the footnotes are, without exception, invented. It was terrific fun to cite from a book of the nineteenth century which, of course, didn't exist.

The real reason was this: When I delivered my dissertation, the first draft, it had very few literary references. I was told that I probably hadn't worked enough. At the time I considered whether or not I ought to fake a bibliography. But it was clear to me that I could have been sacked from the university for such a forgery. But I knew that I would get revenge for it one day: use a scientific apparatus that I'd completely invented. The reactions proved me correct: There were many so-called educated people who made the accusation that the book was too cultured. There were many people who said they had tried to get these books in the library. And there were also those who claimed they had read these books.

EH: In 1980 you published your first play with Verlag der Autoren: *Piano Plays.*

FR: It was always clear to me that I wanted to write dialogue. Earlier I had written a couple of radio plays. It's connected with the method of my mind, with the way I hear sentences and store them up. What excited me was the attempt to transform dialogue into visible movements. The publisher's reader was completely dumbfounded and not very enthusiastic because Luchterhand has no theatrical publishing division, and I went to another publisher.

Man thinks—woman whores.

EH: In *Piano Plays* a woman occupies the center, a nameless woman. Herr Pfaff (in "Dreams of Order") thinks and thereby risks his head; "She" risks her body, she experiments in promiscuity. Real, or also as an artist of ideas?

FR: At least both were intended—in any case, not just reality.

EH: Pfaff, the man, thinks; She, the woman, whores. Do you sometimes feel self-hatred of your mother, hatred of women?

FR: Hatred of women—definitely not. I think that She is a very clever and very strong woman. Probably much more consistent than Pfaff. Pfaff is someone who prevents himself from action. The woman is someone who calls for action.

EH: Did you work out private conflicts with this play?

FR: Insofar as old experiences had become sentences out of jealousy. The play is a concentrate out of many observations, out of my circle of acquaintances, out of relatives. It strikes me that there are two ways of being old, especially with women: the resigned aged and the fighting aged. Strange to say, I have known more fighting old women than fighting old men. For many women there is a moment of revolt. When an older woman suddenly wants to grab a man, it violates every convention. But I know that this happens. I've heard of a retirement home where an eighty-eight-year-old woman cried out one night at 1:30 A.M.: I want a man now! And four hours later she was dead. It's against the rules for someone at that age, four hours before her death, to get such impulses.

EH: *Piano Plays* should have been staged in Hamburg by the director Gabriele Jacobi. Ms. Jacobi gave up the project three days before it was to open. Were you familiar with her work?

FR: Because I work in Stuttgart as a radio play dramaturg for Süddeutschen Rundfunk (South German Radio) I was only in Hamburg twice, the first time before rehearsals began and then four weeks later, at the first run-through. I'm sorry things happened the way they did. I had really wanted to see how a woman would deal with the text.

EH: Mr. Christof Nel then finished the work on your play, and twelve days after the missed opening date the premiere took place in the Malersaal

of the Deutsches Schauspielhaus. I photographed both productions. Interesting is this: The photos of the woman's production look clearer, more
peaceful; Mr. Nel's work brought disorder back to your text. Is this
disorder justified, since in your play it is stated: "I like medieval paintings. Where they dance and drink and sigh, and afterward groan. Sturdy
and thick-legged. There, at least, hearts are torn out and heads are struck
off. The women's breasts are torn off with pincers."

FR: That's about the Barbara Altar by Jerg Ratgeb. It was the medieval
pictures that brought the subversiveness in our heads into a very exact
order.

    If you engage in a play that works with sentences, then you ought
to make the sentences audible.

    Theater people will say, of course, you have to bring something onto
the stage, you have to have images. For me this was vulgarizing. The
play is not a crude play. I imagine it rather as calm. It is, of course, a
commonplace story, and I also imagined the woman as very commonplace.
But what I saw there was an exotic "theater person." I am bewildered
that Rotraut de Neve entered in the beginning dressed in tulle and
gradually stripped. I don't see it that way. I didn't see any work on the
language in the production, only costuming. If you read the play, you
notice that it is in language where She becomes more radical. The play
was denounced. I don't want to be tiresome. But when, for example,
"ladies" is said instead of "women," for me that's quite a difference. I didn't write a play in which a person who is admittedly strong,
but flipped-out, comes forward against a scolding male world. The
Schauspielhaus dramaturgs gave me the explanation earlier that this was
an interpretation that would exhibit the play but that was also malicious
and provocative. At the time I said I had nothing against it. This woman
has meanness, and she must be comic. But comedy is different from
ridiculousness.

EH: Did you like anything in the production?

FR: I sometimes liked Rotraut de Neve with her face, with the expression
on her face. I like what was hard there. I liked it, that the woman didn't
become teary-eyed. That is Rotraut's achievement. I can say nothing
about the men, because the men always came out just as "the men."
It's wrong that the men didn't appear as individuals.

EH: How do you explain that this play brought out so much aggression in
the actors?

FR: I hadn't expected this aggression. It is clear to me that it's difficult for an actor when he has a role in which he only enters and then exits again. I know that women do this in many plays, and that apparently it's never led to such aggression. I am very bewildered. I didn't think it was possible, this concentration of masculine actors: that they suddenly stood together and, standing together, loosed their anger upon me. It gave me the feeling that in the play I had actually described the men as being better than they really are. On opening night I gave each of the actors a book of *Piano Plays* with a different dedication for each. At the opening night party three of them gave me the books back with the dedication torn out.

EH: When, after the curtain call, one of the actors came to you and wanted to bring you on stage, your editor Karlheinz Braun stood up and explained to the audience that they hadn't seen a play by Friederike Roth but rather a paraphrase of it by someone who wasn't even in the program, by the director Christof Nel.

FR: The reaction of the publisher was correct. There had been no reflection on the play. And now I should've been thankful that they had "saved" the play. I know that they didn't have to save the play. I also don't know whether they wanted to save the play or only the leading lady, Rotraut de Neve.

EH: Shortly after the objection by Mr. Braun, Mr. Nel stood and slapped Mr. Braun in the face with brutal violence, knocked his glasses off his face. Afterward, at the discussion, the victims of abuse were there: you, the author; Mr. Braun, the one who'd been hit. Mr. Nel had disappeared.
—Friederike Roth, do you want to see this Hamburg production once again?

FR: No.

Erika Mann

BORN IN 1905, Erika Mann was the daughter of Thomas Mann and the sister of Klaus. She began her work in theater as an actor, studying in Berlin and acting in several theaters. She appeared at the Deutsches Theater under the direction of Max Reinhardt. In 1925 she played in Klaus Mann's lesbian drama, *Anja and Esther*. In 1926 for political and social reasons, she married Gustaf Gründgens, a gay actor and director. They divorced soon after. Gründgens went on to work in Nazi theater. His story was immortalized by Klaus Mann in the novel *Mephisto*, upon which both the film by István Szabó and the play by Théâtre du Soleil were based.

Erika Mann opened her cabaret, Die Pfeffermühle (The Peppermill), in Munich in 1933. She was the first woman to found a cabaret in the German tradition. The core members were: Erika and Klaus, Therese Giehse, Magnus Henning, and Sibylle Schloß. The ensemble was forced into exile soon after the first few performances. In 1935, Mann lost her citizenship and married W. H. Auden in order to gain British citizenship. Her cabaret toured Switzerland, Czechoslovakia, and the Netherlands from 1933 to 1937.

In 1937 Mann emigrated to the United States, where she worked as a journalist. She was sent as a foreign correspondent to cover the famous Nuremberg trials. During the years of the House Un-American Activities Committee (the late 1940s and early 1950s), Mann was denounced as a communist and returned to Switzerland, where she remained until death to work as her father's secretary and editor. She died in 1969 after nine years of illness. Currently, there is renewed interest in Germany in Erika Mann. The texts and documents concerning her cabaret as well as a collection of photos and documents surrounding the life of Erika and Klaus, which illustrate her lifelong practice of lesbian cross-dressing, appeared in 1989 in the volume *Beteiligt euch, es geht um eure Erde: Erika Mann und ihr*

Erika Mann. From *Beteiligt euch, es geht um eure Erde: Erika Mann und ihr politisches Kabarett die "Pfeffermühle"* 1933–37. (Courtesy Edition Spangenberg, Munich.)

politisches Kabarett die Pfeffermühle (Get involved, this is your earth: Erika Mann and her political cabaret The Peppermill) (Editions Spangenberg).

Mann's cabaret was antifascist, openly against Hitler.[1] Moreover, as the examples chosen here illustrate, its politics also satirized sexism, the reign of beauty, and anti-Semitism. Mann's cabaret played against the whole cabaret tradition, which, while political in some ways, was based on sexist jokes and gender reification. It was groundbreaking for a woman to take over this tradition and to play against its material. Also important was the acting of Therese Giehse. Giehse, a noted professional actor in Germany, chose to play in this popular venue in the acting tradition of physical comedy. Later, Brecht cast Giehse as his first Mother Courage. Her style of physical acting and comic timing were well suited to the Epic tradition and its focus on the physicalization of material conditions—a style derived from the cabaret tradition in the first place. Mann and Giehse illustrate an important site for women in theater through the tradition of physical comedy, which provides a radical use of the female body on stage, breaking with its usual sexualized or romanticized role.

The idea of physical comedy as a radical intervention for women was later narrativized by Gerlind Reinshagen in her play *Die Clownin* (The Female Clown). The play concerns a woman who abandons her life as a professional actor to become a clown. After playing the Amazon Penthesilea (in the play by Kleist) with her tortured love for Achilles, the actor decides to spend her life attempting to create a more gender-neutral actor, who is released from the sexism and the narrative trap of the text for, in her case, wordless acting. Reinshagen situates this clown between Emily Brontë, who is onstage writing (the woman writing the text), and Charlie Chaplin, the mute clown. In the end Reinshagen's clown balances on a tightrope over the audience and falls off. Chaplin picks her up and lays her at the feet of Brontë. Reinshagen dramatizes both the hope that physical comedy may provide a way for women to break out of the body bondage of the sexual object and to recover the text for their own. In the end of her narrative, she illustrates the trap within the dominant system of representation which still balances women above the audience's reception and leaves them there, to fall. For, as much as the physical comedienne may break with the system, she can never really operate outside of it.

Mann and Giehse used this comic, popular acting in their cabaret. The physical acting style provided these women with a kind of agency onstage as well as a way to materialize the effects of sexism and fascism. In other words, their politics spoke through their bodies. The setup of the cabaret as poor theater, with few props and sets, suited their performances in exile, when they were required to remain on the move. Unlike other authors in this book who address the classic tradition, Mann's was a theater of resistance in the popular form.

NOTE

1. For some discussion of this, and for a description of the depiction of the cabaret and Mann in Théâtre du Soleil's *Mephisto,* see Joel Schechter, *Durov's Pig: Clowns, Politics and Theatre* (New York: TCG, 1985). Also, for the subversive role in the cabaret tradition that Liesl Karlstadt played, see my "Introducing Karl Valentin," *Theater* 13, no. 1 (Fall/Winter 1981): 6–11.

Erika Mann

Lucky Hans

Translated by Katrin Sieg

Would you like to hear my tale?
Yes,—I am the Lucky Hans;
I'll entertain you without fail,
Let me therefore start at once.

I was a small boy long ago
Little Hans they called me then.
I knew no bitterness, no woe.
Famous was my happy grin.

My parents had a little farm
which they worked diligently.
The golden coins that they had earned
Lost their value suddenly.

The money vanished without trace
But I cried, Take my advice
Do not take this as a disgrace:
Poverty enriches life!

Aren't I happy,
Oh, aren't I glad,
I have more luck now than I ever had.
What a burden that money we had once,—
I'm rightly called the Lucky Hans!

Poems by Erika Mann from *Beteiligt euch, es geht um eure Erde: Erika Mann und ihr politisches Kabarett die "Pfeffermühle" 1933-1937*. © 1990 Edition Spangenberg, Munich 40. Translated by Katrin Sieg and printed by permission.

To find some work I went away,
So I could earn my keep.
Ten gruesome hours every day,
They got my labor cheap.

But, soon, the government decided
That some people should be chucked.
I told myself, I'd never liked it—
Lost my job but praised my luck.

Aren't I happy,
Oh, aren't I glad,
I have more luck now than I ever had.
What a burden that job I had once,—
I'm rightly called the Lucky Hans!

I was as free as wind and rain,
My companions from now on.
I thought my life was like a game,
Full of beauty and of fun.

I carved my growing gratefulness
On a concrete public wall.
To share my joy and to express:
"There is a swine in City Hall."

My friend called me in early morning
Told me of a certain list.
And he gave me urgent warning:
Hans, my name, they hadn't missed.

I crossed the border late at night—
Oh, how I enjoyed this trip!
My legs were running, right-left-right.
Exercise, it keeps you fit!

Aren't I happy,
Oh, aren't I glad,
I have more luck now than I ever had.

What a burden that home I had once,—
I'm rightly called the Lucky Hans!

They took my passport back from me.
That fulfilled my happiness
To give: That is my highest glee,
But I found I still possessed . . .

Such as, for instance, civil rights:
No one asked for my consent.
When they took those, I felt delight.
Thanks, beloved government!

Aren't I happy,
Oh, aren't I glad,
I have more luck now than I ever had.
What a burden those rights I had once,—
I'm rightly called the Lucky Hans!

The Witch

Good night, Witch Gruesome is my name.
I've made my way here to complain
And also for a little chat.
My home is in the dark, moist woods,
Amidst green leaves and tangled roots.
My only friend's my cat.

Through many a country and century
Have people always hated me,
And only for my ugly face.
They blamed me whether rain or shine,
Something went wrong—the fault was mine.
But that is not the case.

My crooked nose, my dark black hair
They pointed at me, it isn't fair!
It is my mothers' legacy.
Since they have called us Satan's wives
We lost in fires our lives,
That shouldn't trouble me?

From any person that I've met
I've suffered persecution, threat—
They steal the tea leaves off my shelf!
They pull my hair, they hide my broom
I'm sure that it will be my doom.
Don't dare defend myself.

Hands in my lap, I'm huddled there,
Think to myself, fate is unfair
And always was and always is.
The kitty purrs, the kettle glows
I pride myself in hair and nose

And blow myself a kiss.

I swear to you I'm without sin.
A scapegoat is what I have been.
For many hundred years till now.
You never get enough of me,
Because you need me urgently.
Peculiar somehow.

I have come here to chat a while,
The Good Witch Gruesome, with a smile,
I've told you of my grief.
I'm glad that now I get some rest
It lifts this burden off my chest:
The Jews are my relief.

The Cold

The year is born in wint'ry night,
It is so tender—take care of the child!
So many years have been lost like that—
And, nowadays, a cold sharp wind is blowing.

The snow, like razor blades, gleams blue and thin,—
The trees are freezing at their naked limbs.
Two hungry ravens circle in the sky,
And cows rub their cold sides while chewing rye.

Why does it freeze?
Why does it hurt us so?
Why? Soon the world will be
Nothing but ice and snow.

The world is cold,—pretends there don't exist
All things wrong, all things amiss.
This frosty pillow called Indifference,
Promotes the slumber and has many friends.

Who whines about injustice?
Of murder, and of torture as we've never seen it?
Leave me alone,—our steely skin gets tougher—
What do I care if other people suffer?

Why be so cold?
Why, since it hurts us so!
Why? Soon we will be
Nothing but ice and snow!

This is your earth! Get involved and fight—
It's you alone who has the might!
Go start a fire, bring some warmth and light

To our terrible, bleak winter's night!

For it is filled with horror and with cold—
As long as we don't stand up and be bold.
Defend yourselves and fight,—and then let's see,
Who the winner in this struggle will be!

I can't believe those specters are to win!
I know, the sun will vanquish in the end!
Why so? Because a light that glorious
Will surely be victorious!

(1 January 1934, Zurich)

Gerlind Reinshagen

GERLIND REINSHAGEN IS the most prominent German woman playwright of the contemporary era. Her plays chronicle the lives of German women from the Nazi era to the present. Always focused on the lives of women, the plays investigate a wide variety of experiences—from illness, to the experience of fascism, to ecological concerns after Chernobyl. Born in 1926, Reinshagen trained as a student of pharmacy. Her writing began with children's stories and radio plays. Since 1956 she has supported herself from her writing. Her play *Sonntagskinder* (Sunday's Children) (1976) was the first play by a woman in the 1970s to achieve major success. It played in several major theaters and was made into a film in 1981. It is the first play in a trilogy, which traces the German woman from the Nazi era to the present. The second play in the trilogy, *Frühlingsfest* (Spring Festival) (1980), concerns reconstruction after World War II and the so-called Economic Miracle, or the successful rebuilding of Germany in the 1950s. The third play, *Tanz, Marie!* (Dance, Marie) (1987) is about an aging, bourgeois couple and takes place in the present.

Reinshagen has written nine plays to date: *Doppelkopf* (Two-headed) in 1968, directed by the well-known director Claus Peymann; *Leben und Tod der Marilyn Monroe* (The Life and Death of Marilyn Monroe) in 1971; *Himmel und Erde* (Heaven and Earth) in 1974, almost a monologue, translated and directed by Carl Weber and filmed for television in 1976; *Sonntagskinder* and *Das Frühlingsfest,* directed by Claus Peymann at Bochum; *Eisenherz* (Ironheart) in 1982, also produced at Bochum, directed by Andrea Breth, one of the few women to work in the major houses; *Die Clownin* (The Female Clown) in 1985, produced in Düsseldorf; and *Tanz, Marie!* and *Die Feuerblume* (Fire Flower) in 1988. Reinshagen has had eleven radio plays produced, has published two novels and a collection of short stories, has had her plays anthologized by a major German publisher (Suhrkamp Verlag) and has won three distinguished literary prizes.

Although she denies that she is a feminist, Reinshagen's plays are consistently about women, who, within their material and historical circumstances, seek a certain subjective agency. Reinshagen's protagonists are those who imagine something else—the utopian possibility that something beyond oppression may be dreamed of and reached for. In various ways, this imagined alternative alters the "real" experiences of these women. This is not to suggest that Reinshagen is upbeat—far from it. If the woman always reaches, she does not necessarily attain, for she is caught within her historical possibilities. In *Heaven and Earth* she gains her own autonomy, her ability to die her own death, independent from machines that are her life-support system. In *Sunday's Children* the young girl attains, during Nazi times, the ability to imagine. The protagonist of *Heaven and Earth* does not escape her illness but gains some control over her dying; the protagonist of *Sunday's Children* cannot alter her historical moment, but she can survive internal destruction.

Reinshagen's plays emerged at the same time as the women's movement in Germany and reflect many of the concerns of the movement. *Sunday's Children* was written at roughly the same time as the emerging critique of women and fascism was being written.[1] It is important to note that the play opened in Stuttgart in 1975, while Ulrike Meinhof was on trial there. The questions of German identity, civil disobedience, and authoritarian structures were being raised in the courtroom at the same time as Reinshagen was putting the issues on the stage.[2] Set during World War II, the play concerns a fourteen-year-old girl—a playful, imaginative child, who, through the experience of fascism and war, becomes withdrawn, suppressing her own imagination and subjectivity. Reinshagen, however, does not portray women as the victims of fascism. Instead, like the feminist studies of the Nazi period, Reinshagen illustrates women's active complicity with fascism and details some of the ways in which domestic life mirrored its official structures. Likewise, *The Life and Death of Marilyn Monroe* mirrors early feminist concerns about the role of women as sex objects—in society and in their representation. *The Female Clown* dramatizes concerns around women who write and who work in the theater, a subject that is addressed further in this book in the section on Erika Mann and the cabaret.

Ironheart

As I have written in my book *Feminism and Theater,* the ability to write or to speak is of central importance in Reinshagen's theatrical world. No matter the case or time, having a voice and moving, through imagination, to something other than the status quo is always central to her plays. In *Ironheart* this agency is found not only in the heroine but also in the character of Billerbeck, who, on her hands and knees atop her desk—a monster produced by the collusion of class and gender systems that have closed her out of a satisfying sexual or emotional life—can still produce the long howl of oppression and pain; can still articulate the apocalyptic image of the woman who is disappearing somewhere along the seams of oppressive systems. Billerbeck can speak as Reinshagen can write. At the heart of this expression of oppression, as well as the dream that goes out beyond the margins, is the lyric. This is the lyric as it appears in the poetic monologue in *Ironheart,* and it is the total language of the play in *Fire Flowers*—the post-Chernobyl language of contamination. The lyric marks the agency of imagination.

Reinshagen expressed her belief in the political agency of articulation on a panel she shared with Ed Bullins in Seattle in 1983. At first the assertive black playwright and the shy German one seemed a strange pair. But when the topic turned to censorship, they spoke in agreement. For both, the greatest political danger to the playwright was self-censorship. This stance is similar to that of Christa Wolf's when she said that literature is "a means of self-assertion, self-affirmation." Wolf, the leading woman writer from the erstwhile German Democratic Republic, revisioned the romantic writers as "one of the first generations to feel torn inside by their inability to realize in action the possibilities which they sensed were there, inside them, very much alive and alert; which they rehearsed in debates and literary experiments."[3]

In other words, literature—or, in Reinshagen's case, the stage—is a place to rehearse social actions that are not possible in one's historical situation. The ability to imagine and to write out the imaginary is political in this sense. Reinshagen's women characters rehearse alternative possibilities on the stage, creating a social experiment apart from the dictates of the sex-gender diopoly.

NOTES

1. A film on women and fascism which was also groundbreaking is Helma
Sanders-Brahms's *Deutschland, bleiche Mutter* (1980).

2. I am indebted to Katrin Sieg for this idea.

3. Christa Wolf, "Interview with Christa Wolf," *New German Critique*, Fall
1982: 96.

Gerlind Reinshagen

Ironheart

Translated by Sue-Ellen Case and Arlene A. Teraoka

Could mortal lip divine
the undivelopped freight
of a delivered syllable
'twould crumble with the weight
      —Emily Dickinson

Characters

ELLINOR BUBLITZ, age 21

COUNTESS BILLERBECK, age 47

ADA, age 34

KOLK, age 26

ROSINSKI, age 49

LISSY, age 19

THE CLEANING LADY, age 38

Time: Now

Place: There are three stage areas divided as inconspicuously as possible, giving the impression of a single large room extending into the wings. Center: office A with four work areas, teletype, telephone, file cabinets, clothes closet, swivel chairs, a wash basin, etc. Right: a section of a packing room; and Left: a section of a lounge with a photocopier. There is a large window in the back wall of the office, through which a similar window of another building is visible. When illuminated, this second window reveals office B, a mirror image of office A. All sounds, silences, and light cues react to, answer, or emphasize the individual lines of the dialogue. They determine in a very essential way the feelings and actions of the figures.

Before the action begins, office A, then office B are seen for a few seconds without actors.

PART I

I

Lights up in office A. There is a large clock over the window. It is morning, two minutes before nine. BUBLITZ, KOLK, *and* BILLERBECK *are at their desks.* KOLK *and* BILLERBECK *are smoking, their feet on their desks.* BUBLITZ *checks her makeup in her compact. For several seconds the scene appears almost frozen. The clock ticks.*

BUBLITZ (*to* BILLERBECK): Well? What happened? Yesterday?
(BILLERBECK *is silent.*)
KOLK (*to* BILLERBECK): Nothing new under the sun, huh?
(BILLERBECK *is silent.*)
BUBLITZ (*scornfully*): Sunday. (*She begins to eat. Silence.*)
BILLERBECK: At first I didn't even open the curtains; made myself a pot of coffee—so thick the spoon stood up in it.
BUBLITZ: The worst thing is—you can't buy anything, can't go shopping for anything, anywhere.
BILLERBECK: Had the lamp on.
KOLK: In broad daylight!
BUBLITZ: The stores are all closed, it's like being on the moon. (*She drinks out of a flask, a kind of a glass hip flask.*)
BILLERBECK: Decided—if the doorbell rings, don't answer.
BUBLITZ: Like being dead.
BILLERBECK: It never rings anyway. (*Silence. The clock is ticking. Stage darkens. Lights up in the other window, revealing office B. A young man in an overcoat and cap is standing at his desk. He resembles* KOLK. *Cross-fade from B to A. The positions of the characters have changed slightly. Another day.*)
KOLK (*to* BILLERBECK): Well? The weekend? Yesterday? (*Silence*)
BILLERBECK: Garbage. (*Silence*)
BUBLITZ: Before, on Sundays, I always thought I died a little, Sundays. (*She looks at* KOLK.) That's over . . . thank God.
BILLERBECK: I had seventeen cups of coffee, I'm not exaggerating.

BUBLITZ: Thank God. (KOLK *and* BUBLITZ *look at each other.*)

BILLERBECK: I didn't go out all day. Can't do anything after a week like that. No energy.

KOLK (*to* BILLERBECK): And how long, did you say, that's been going on? Your Sundays, like that? How many years?

(BILLERBECK *shrugs. Silence.*)

BUBLITZ (*softly*): For a long time. (*Silence*) Maybe... for as long... as this cabinet has been standing here.

KOLK (*calculating*): That would be twenty-two times fifty-two, so more than a thousand, if I'm figuring right, one thousand one hundred Sundays, approximately?

BILLERBECK: Still remember the park that used to be here. (*Pause*) A mulberry farm.

KOLK: Amazing.

BILLERBECK: They raised silkworms for research.

KOLK: One thousand one hundred. That just can't be true. (*Silence*)

BILLERBECK: No, not quite, you see, it wasn't like that, it was more like... not the way you think.... (*She breaks off, Blackout. Lights up again immediately. The positions are changed. Silence. The clock ticks. Another day.*)

BUBLITZ (*to* BILLERBECK): Well? The usual again, Sunday, like always?

KOLK: Yes, what?

BILLERBECK: But, then, yesterday when I came home, for once had gone out on Sunday, stood at the door, a few minutes... when I saw the book again, open, the last word, and everything totally silent, you understand...

KOLK: Yes, what?

BILLERBECK: All of a sudden... something was there...

KOLK: I don't understand.

BILLERBECK: I mean, what I want to say...

KOLK: Still not clear.

BILLERBECK: Something... like a new... how should I say?... (*Silence*)

BUBLITZ: Sure, that's right. (*Silence*) In any case. (*Silence. Smokes.*)

(*Lights up in office B. The man has taken off his overcoat and cap and lights a cigarette. Blackout in B.*)

Isn't it today... Billerbeck?

BILLERBECK: What... today?

BUBLITZ: That certain day; you know!

BILLERBECK: What day?

KOLK (*to* BILLERBECK): Do you read? What do you read then on Sundays? In your darkened room?

BUBLITZ: You know what I mean, Billerbeck! (*Silence*)

KOLK (*to* BILLERBECK): Do you read Goethe? Or Schopenhauer?

BUBLITZ (*impatiently to* BILLERBECK): Isn't the time up—for him? (*Points to* KOLK.) His trial period over? Shouldn't Kastner come and tell us that they're going to keep him? (BILLERBECK *shrugs. Silence.*)

KOLK (*to* BILLERBECK): I bet you read Thomas Mann. (BILLERBECK *smokes, is silent.*)

BUBLITZ: Seems to me like he's been here forever, seems to me like a hundred years.

KOLK: A thousand! (BILLERBECK *is silent.*) I've been sitting here for a thousand years. . . . (*Pause*) My inner self is somewhere else.

BILLERBECK: Aren't you fortunate.

KOLK: Whether the time is up or not, whether Kastner comes or doesn't, that's as important as, say, the life of this fly. (*He catches a fly.*) Whether I let it go or squash it . . .

BILLERBECK: My God, where'd the time go? The thirtieth! We need to work at a smart pace, today!

KOLK: Of course, I could go back to school at any time. (*Silence.* BUBLITZ *looks at him.*)

BUBLITZ: Why can't Kastner come sooner? Maybe even before the deadline? (*She looks at* BILLERBECK. BILLERBECK *is silent.*) For example, you could speak up for him. (*Pause*) You did speak up for him, didn't you? (BILLERBECK *laughs ambiguously, is silent.*)

KOLK (*to* BILLERBECK): If you ask me, I think Thomas Mann is a charlatan. (*Silence. The kitchen timer on* BILLERBECK's *desk goes off. The office clock shows nine.* BILLERBECK *claps her hands, all stand.* BUBLITZ *checks the time on her wristwatch, shows it to* BILLERBECK.)

BUBLITZ: Your time is fast.

BILLERBECK (*looks at her wristwatch*): You're right. It's fast. (*She adjusts the timer. Immediately sits down again.*)

BUBLITZ: Four more minutes. (*Also sits down.*)

BILLERBECK: Yes. Four and a half. (ROSINSKI *enters, immediately joins in the conversation.*)

ROSINSKI: Four and a quarter. (*Pause*) Four heavenly minutes, ladies and gentlemen! (BUBLITZ *and* BILLERBECK *resume their relaxed position, smoke.* ROSINSKI *crosses to lay a packet of receipts on* BILLERBECK's *desk, pinching* BUBLITZ *as he passes. Meanwhile,* KOLK *begins working, noisily, opens the index file, takes out his writing materials, etc.*)

BILLERBECK (*smoking again*): I like to read the authors of the last century. The French. The Russians. But it all has to be wonderfully slow. Wonderfully slow and monotonous.

KOLK: Tearjerkers. Every day. Why do you need clocks when the chronometer is above your heads? The objective time is there! (*Points upward*)

BILLERBECK: The objective time! (*Laughs*)

ROSINSKI: The objective time! (*Laughs*)

BILLERBECK: The objective . . .

ROSINSKI: The ob . . . jec . . . jec . . . (*Both laugh hysterically.*) That's the way somebody talks when he doesn't know what work is.

KOLK: Amazing.

BUBLITZ: Rosinski, have you ever written anything like he did, have you ever written one hundred eighty pages?

KOLK: One hundred and eighty-seven!

ROSINSKI (*moves close to* KOLK): The crow-lk. He's black. Caws. Struts on pointed feet through the countryside. Smarter than the other birds.

BUBLITZ: Almost a real book, Rosinski, have you done that?

ROSINSKI: Have I ever written a book?

BUBLITZ: Then you can talk.

ROSINSKI: A hundred eighty-seven. (*Suddenly to* KOLK) When is your time up, anyway?

BUBLITZ: Been keeping your ear to the wall again?

ROSINSKI: If Kastner comes and you're allowed to stay on, you'll learn to do that too, little boy, work, work . . . (*Grins*) If Kastner comes!

BUBLITZ (*Upset*): What is that supposed to mean? Rosinski! (*Pause*) What have you heard?

(ROSINSKI *suddenly puts his finger to his lips, takes the hand towel from the washbasin, spreads it out on the floor like a rug, and watches* ADA, *who enters majestically. She strides over the hand towel to her desk, where she immediately takes out her makeup.* ROSINSKI *dances around her.*)

ADA (*looks at the calendar*): The end of the month here already. How it flies . . . how it flies.

ROSINSKI (*staring at* ADA's *cleavage*): Well? So? How was it? How did it go yesterday? (*Pause*) What pretty thing do we have here again today? (ADA *puts on her makeup, doesn't react.*) A kiss? A bite? Burnt skin? (*Silence*) A knife? Teeth? Cigarette? (*Cross-fade to office B. The man is now sitting at his desk, a young woman resembling* BUBLITZ *is combing*

her hair before a mirror. Cross-fade again to office A. Another day.) How
was Sunday, oh beautiful woman of my heart? How can I say, ladies and
gentlemen of God, look at that. It must've been a vampire. A full-
grown vampire! (ADA *goes to the wash basin, fills a glass with water,
takes a pill.* ROSINSKI *follows her, stands close to her.*) Look at that, a
vampi—(ADA *strikes at* ROSINSKI *with the hand towel, but* ROSINSKI
darts back to KOLK.) But if he comes, if Kastner comes now because he
has to, since he's already late . . . listen, he says, your accomplishments
are all well and good, my friend, all well and good, but isn't it, how
shall I say this, a bit, all a bit frivolous, little butterfly, he says? . . .
(KOLK *stares at him, is silent.*) Then there was that one guy we had, he
was a party member, brown or red, don't know exactly, they found out
about it, since, of course, there are lists, everything is on a list upstairs,
but whatever happens to you, sonny, they'll hand you an A-1 rating
when you go out the door, I'll swear to that by . . .

KOLK (*turning away*): You know, I've been wondering for some time now
how it would be if you went away for some new health treatment,
Rosinski?

ROSINSKI: What do you want, crow? Did you lose something here? (*Silence.* BILLERBECK'*s alarm goes off.* ROSINSKI *turns to go.*) If Kastner
comes. (*Exits. The three others cross to* BILLERBECK'*s desk and stand at
attention to receive their work orders.*)

BILLERBECK: Nothing can help us now. It's the end of the month. No
pleading tired. The desks will be cleared off. The drawers. Nothing carried
over into the new month. Unanswered inquiries. Complaints. Nothing
left in any corners. And remember: Money is expensive. (*She tosses a
package of scrap paper to each of them.*) Limited surplus. Take advantage
of the exchange rate whenever you can. Buy cheap, cheap! And: There
are sliding prices, think of that! Inventory these situations. Let me say
again: Nothing is to be carried over! The recall should be precisely . . .
what was I going to say? . . .

BILLERBECK (*she loses her train of thought*): Adjusted . . . yes . . . the recalls, all surplus goods have to go, Mr. Kolk . . . (*She holds her head in
her hands.*) What . . . was I going to say? My head . . . full of holes. . . .
Anyway, nothing accumulated, nothing, anywhere. . . . Remember it's
important, that it doesn't go over our. . . . (*She falters. The others remain
standing for a moment. Long silence.*)

ROSINSKI: (*coming back, takes the colorful knitted cap off* KOLK'*s head*):
Take off your hat, crow, or your brain will get hot! (*Leaves. Everyone*

goes to their places, begin to work, KOLK *sorts index cards,* ADA *double-checks figures with the adding machine.* BUBLITZ *orders the delivery receipts, eating, as usual, while she works.* BILLERBECK *checks the lists. Work noise, then, although the characters continue their activity, sudden silence.* ROSINSKI *comes back again.*) The latest news of the day: a) the building is getting a two-way P.A. system. (*Silence*) You can all talk through the walls. (*Silence*) Elisabeth is back.

KOLK: Elisabeth? (ROSINSKI *kisses his fingertips with great exaggeration. Leaves.*)

BUBLITZ (*after a while*): Lissy? But she just left.

ADA: Eight weeks. They granted her extension. And already sick before that.

BUBLITZ: So long...

ADA: Yes, an eternity.

BUBLITZ: It seems just like yesterday to me. (*Silence*)

ROSINSKI: (*Enters again, brushing past* ADA's *cleavage, shaking his head.*) That really does look mean. (*Leaves quickly after a glance from* BILLERBECK, *slamming the door behind him. Silence, very intense. In the background the ticking of the clock, suddenly very loud.* ADA *rummages through papers in her desk; for a while the only sound is the rustling of paper. Then* BUBLITZ *begins to type. Typing and rustling. Sudden silence. The phone rings;* BILLERBECK *is on the phone.*)

BILLERBECK: Of course. As always. Yesterday at the latest. Send a telly. We've got the picture. Only too well. Sell our souls for the company. Reply by teletype. Yes. Don't mention it. Thank you! (*Silence.* BUBLITZ *types, the typing slows, stops. Only the clock is heard; the ticking slows, seems to stop. The light in the room becomes brighter. Long silence. Everyone suddenly focuses on* ADA.) That really does look evil.

ADA (*Flattered*): Should I check only the current... or all the other months too?

BUBLITZ: In no way harmless, Ada, as it usually is.

ADA: Only February or the previous ones too?

BILLERBECK: It doesn't look like the normal Sunday marks.

BUBLITZ: Not the usual one. Ada.

BILLERBECK: Like her husband's—never.

KOLK: Not like the weekend activity of a civil servant. (*Blackout, then lights up again immediately. They work. Silence.*)

BILLERBECK (*Looks up, focuses on* ADA): Adaline, Adaline...

BUBLITZ: So today... (*Looks at* ADA.)

BILLERBECK (*shaking her head*): I can't help but...

KOLK: It damn well looks like a cut, Ada.

BUBLITZ: As though... somehow... ripped around...

KOLK: As though the knife was turned in the flesh.

ADA: So I check only the current month today? Or the entire year? Or what? (*Silence. Rustling of paper.*)

BILLERBECK: That almost looks abnormal. In a certain way...

KOLK: It looks obscene.

BUBLITZ: You could almost say...

BILLERBECK: It looks perverse. (*Silence. The other window in office B is illuminated. There are also four people at desks. In both rooms the light becomes brighter. Work noise. Blackout in office B. Lights in office A, as before. Silence.*) What can I say... dear God. (*Pause. Shakes her head.*) Every weekend the same story; there he sits at home, her civil servant, the poor devil, and she... she is who knows where with who knows whom in the bushes, or in a tent, running around, on a country road somewhere, in the woods, under a tree, in a third-class motel, but then: a curse, when he loses his nerve, when he doesn't stick it deep enough. And then one day: the catastrophe. (*Silence. In a commanding tone*): And, of course, you must check all the months—do I need to say that over and over again? You ask and ask, always the same thing, back to January, of course, dear girl, how often do I need.... (*Silence. Working. Typing.*)

ADA: There's no need for you to explain every detail, Billerbeck. Would really like to know, though, why and for what reason everyone comes up so close to me, every Monday, half the company, gets on my back; I only need to burn myself on the neck with a curling iron and everyone touches me, fingers my skin, my hair, my clothes, my pockets, my personal business, as though I had who knows what hidden somewhere. If you're so keen on detective stories, make some up for yourself, if you can! (*Silence*)

KOLK: But if it was just the curling iron, then why so... exposed, Ada? Why don't you come covered up on Monday morning? (*Blackout*)

2

ROSINSKI *in the packing room. Suggestion of a packing table with scale, roll of paper, tape, etc.* ROSINSKI *sharpens a knife.*

ROSINSKI (*singing*): Wait, wait for a little while... (*Pause*) Wait, wait for a little while . . . (*Pause*) Wait, just wait. . . . The rotten thing won't sharpen. Sharp. Sharp rotten thing. (*Laughs*) Cuts flesh. (*Pause*) And hair. (*Laughs*) Skin and bones. Stick! Stick it! (*He throws the knife into the door; it vibrates. He pulls it out, stamps a couple of packages, and then leaves the room with the knife. Blackout.*)

3

BUBLITZ *alone in the office. She eats as she figures the bills.*

BUBLITZ (*suddenly disturbed*): Somebody there? Who's there? (*Silence. BUBLITZ stops working, sits in a hunched position, arms wrapped around her knees, as though she needs to protect herself. The light outside appears silvery against the drizzling rain; the venetian blinds are pulled down before the window of office B.* BUBLITZ *changes.*) It's really nothing. It's quiet. Warm.
Silvery now.
What am I . . . afraid of?
Earth, it smells like earth outside.
But you have to ask yourself . . . (*Laughs*)
Rosinski is looking at the sun through a green bottle.
Ada has a summer dress on.
Snow white ribbon . . . ironed . . . pretty.
I ask myself, then, how and why is it
so cramped here . . . (*Laughs*)
But you're swimming,
Ellinor Bublitz,
In happiness? . . .
(*Softly*) Not alone anymore . . . (*Pause*)
What then? What then?
Everything, want everything, even closer,
Everything here to me, everything! (*Pause*)
Fear, Kolk says, is, what did he say?
Is the growing darkness in the mind . . .
I understand . . . see myself clearly.
Someday,
From a certain moment on . . .
Some day everything will be . . . real
(*Laughs*) Like gold,

So that people . . .
That they'll look over at me, to me here, all of them.
(*Afraid*) What is it
That's taking hold of me now
Hanging around my neck like a stone
Like a millstone, pulling, pulling
Like I don't know what.
(*She jumps out of her chair, stands in the middle of the room.*)
Is somebody there? (*Silence*)
Something creeping around? (*Silence*)
I know exactly . . . (*Silence*)

ROSINSKI (*leaps out at her with the knife, grabs her*): The Killer of Atlantic City, yeah!

BUBLITZ (*getting loose*): You'll give me a heart attack!

ROSINSKI: Not the worst way to die.

BUBLITZ: For you. Not for me.

ROSINSKI: You fall down, gasp a couple of times, suddenly . . . krrt, the eyes stare.

BUBLITZ (*crosses to her desk*): Rosinski, not that, not that again! For the hundredth time!

ROSINSKI: But some . . . rattle for a long time.

BUBLITZ (*working*): I don't hear a thing . . .

ROSINSKI: You turn blue.

BUBLITZ: I'm already behind schedule. You're holding me up.

ROSINSKI: Krrt, krrt. . . . Listen to me!

BUBLITZ: Billerbeck's dumped too much on my desk again.

ROSINSKI: Foam at the mouth. Cramps. Listen to me. He writhes. (BUBLITZ *holds her hands over her ears*, ROSINSKI *pulls them away.*) You listen to me! Listen to me! Then . . . very slowly: He suffocates. (*He pulls a bottle out of his jacket pocket.*) You don't feel well. (*Laughs*) Not well, little one. (*Looks at her*) But Rosinski is here.

BUBLITZ: You're holding me up. And I'll have to suffer for it.

ROSINSKI: I'll be here.

BUBLITZ: Because I always have to keep my desk clear; clear, I tell you, always! And not just on the thirtieth!

ROSINSKI: To your place, Rosinski—today, tomorrow, and forever and ever. Amen. (BUBLITZ *goes to* ADA's *desk, looks for somehting.* ROSINSKI *follows.*) Now and at the hour of our death. (BUBLITZ *returns.*) Rosinski has thought of everything. (BUBLITZ *working.* ROSINSKI *gets a water glass, fills it with Cognac, pushes it in front of* BUBLITZ. *She shoves it away.*) Nothing can happen, as long as Rosinski . . . (*He drinks, pours again, tries to force* BUBLITZ *to take the glass.*)

BUBLITZ: I can't, Rosinski, not again and again. Day after day—how many more times will I have to tell you: No, no more, I don't want to! (*Silence*) I'm through with that. (*She works. Silence.*)

ROSINSKI: Don't want to! Ah. All of a sudden. Don't want to anymore. As if she could decide that, an alcoholic! But me, I'm responsible for you! Where would you be, where were you, where have you been, what did Rosinski drag you up out of? In the gutter, done for, your arms shot full of holes, your liver a sponge, wouldn't have been much longer, you would've been selling yourself on the streets, if Rosinski hadn't been there . . .

BUBLITZ: OK, OK. A long time ago.

ROSINSKI: And if he wasn't still here, running around doing things, checking your pupils, worrying about getting you up on your feet . . . (BUBLITZ *works.*) So you can finally make it through. (*Silence*)

BUBLITZ (*loudly*): I won't touch it again. Not a drop. You don't want to understand that someone can change for the better. And at any minute the door here can. . . . Take your bottle and get out!

ROSINSKI: But a certain bird that's flown to you—he comes and goes, does what he wants; a persona grata. . . . I hear you two were at the movies for the second Sunday in a row.

BUBLITZ (*working*): I don't even have the day's transactions done . . .

ROSINSKI: But someone like that, won't help you, when you sink back into your misery!

BUBLITZ: The reports!

ROSINSKI (*holding her hand tightly*): You only work when I'm talking to you; otherwise, you just hang around. I'm telling you for your own good: This man, this certain person . . . won't lift a finger for you. (BUBLITZ *stops working, stares at* ROSINSKI.) Not that I expect gratitude . . . but a few words of thanks would be nice, if nothing else, for everything . . . that's happened, that I held you—don't you remember that anymore? Remember how you once said . . . how we stood together, the two of us, evenings in the pack room? If lightning should strike now, you said, we would both be dead, we would both die together at the same time. (*Silence*) That's what you once said . . . (*Silence*)

BUBLITZ (*working*): No. I never said that. That was you. You said that. (*Silence*)

ROSINSKI: This bird . . . (BUBLITZ *begins typing again furiously;* ROSINSKI *leaves, slamming the door shut.* ROSINSKI *returns.*) He won't pull you out of it, not out of anything, not him! (ROSINSKI *leaves.* BUBLITZ *types.* ROSINSKI *comes back but remains silent and looks reproachfully at* BUBLITZ.)

BUBLITZ: Go on, get out, and say hello to your wife and kids for me. (*She works. Silence.*)

ROSINSKI: The lackey is allowed to leave. (ROSINSKI *slips out. Blackout.*)

4

Lights up in office A. BUBLITZ *drinks the contents of a water glass in one gulp, fills it again from* ROSINSKI'*s bottle. Drinks again. She takes a third glass to the window. The neighboring window lights up; office B is now empty. Blackout on* BUBLITZ. *Blackout later in B.*

5

Office A. BILLERBECK, KOLK, ADA. KOLK *and* ADA *are standing, as in scene* 1, *at* BILLERBECK'*s desk to receive their work for the day. It's a little past nine. Another day.*

BILLERBECK: And remember: The day after tomorrow is the end of the month.

ADA (*combing her hair*): Dear God, how the time . . .

BILLERBECK: Be sure you clear your desks! Nothing is to be carried over into the new month. Or shuffled away. Must I say this again and again? The complaints, inquiries—don't forget them. Order, I say, order! We can never catch up; it's like quicksand. There's more of it every month. If I didn't . . . (KOLK *and* ADA *go to their seats.*)

KOLK (*parodying*): If you didn't do everything! We know what's up. Even without your assignments. (*Pause*) How would it be if just this once you'd swallow it? (*Silence. The clock is ticking. The rustling of papers is suddenly very loud.*)

BILLERBECK: Where would we be if at least one person didn't . . .

KOLK: Yes, where would we be? (*Silence*)

ADA (*changing the subject*): Beautiful weather yesterday, wasn't it?

KOLK: Maybe we would be even further along, most venerable lady?

ADA: Almost a bit like summer.

KOLK: How would it be if you let Ada and me divide up our work ourselves? (*Silence*)

BILLERBECK: When I finally retire...

KOLK: When?

BILLERBECK (*laughs*): Would you like to know where I'd move?

KOLK: No.

BILLERBECK: Far, far away, you see, to Martinique. (*Silence*)

ADA: That was a wonderful Sunday on the canal. With an old friend from the past. (*Stretches*) Ah, outdoors in nature...(*Silence*)

KOLK: Nature is a piece of trash. (*Silence*)

ADA: As if everything is expanding, so to speak. (*Silence*)

KOLK: Just don't try to fly too high. (*Silence*)

ADA: I saw a real black stork.

KOLK: I walked past a field they had fertilized and got a nose full of poison! Sulphur, quicksilver, cyanide.

ADA: Oh, will you be quiet!

KOLK: Yesterday I saw a fish swimming belly up. (*Silence. Then to* BILLERBECK): I asked you something, Billerbeck. You weaseled out of it. (*Silence*) You always weasel your way out!

BILLERBECK (*after a pause*): You're not a bad worker, Kolk. When you want to be, of course. So stay in your place.

KOLK: Would like to know, what's going on in your head.

BILLERBECK (*softly*): Stay in your place or be thrown to the dogs.

KOLK: Come on, come on. I want to know. (*Silence*) Answer me! (*Silence*) So. Nothing. Just as I expected. Nothing again. (*Silence. They work.*)

BILLERBECK: And the time has come to pass judgment, to reward your servants and to destroy those who have destroyed the earth. (*Laughs*)

KOLK (*turning around on his swivel chair*): So now...that was good. (*Silence*) Seems almost as if we've grown closer together. (*Silence*)

ADA: Working was different then. Back then...there was a little bit of Sunday in the whole week. The days were longer and yet somehow shorter. Didn't eat you up—the time at the office.

BILLERBECK (*laughs*): And the second angel set one foot upon the ocean and the other upon the earth and swore that henceforth there would be no more time.

KOLK (*to* BILLERBECK): Now you're really good.

BILLERBECK: You should read it over. Everyone, even those filchocrats up there.

KOLK: As if spoken from my own heart.

ADA: It's getting worse all the time with you, Billerbeck. Somehow—how should I say it? —destructive. Yes. As though you need to drag everything through the mud.

BILLERBECK: Even the mud isn't what it used to be.

KOLK: No longer natural, milady. (KOLK *and* BILLERBECK *laugh. Silence.*)

ADA (*to* BILLERBECK): Your clothes, the way you talk, everything is becoming more and more . . . rotten. Your thoughts. Yesterday we went to a village; there was an old house and written on it was, "May God protect us from injuries to our soul." . . .

KOLK: A psychiatrist would like it there. (KOLK *and* BILLERBECK *laugh.* ADA *works with obvious anger. Silence.*)

ADA (*furiously to* KOLK): And you! You always play the same old tune! Ever since you've been here! Stirred everything up, disturbed everything! Since you've been here, seems like she's gone downhill even faster. You should have seen her then. (*Points to* BILLERBECK) Do you know that she's a countess, a real one? And she looked like one then, always spoke softly, like this. But because everyone here respected her, of course, not because of her name, but because of the way she acted. . . . I can't remember when her ideas began, her crazy "apocalypse," which made her go soft in the head, softer and softer, her entire upbringing gone to hell, everything, and sometimes, I think, even her mind, you see . . . (BILLERBECK *has gone to the wash basin and holds her arms under water, without rolling up her sleeves.*) It hurts me to think of what she used to be and now so . . . low; it won't last, I think, not much longer . . . (BILLERBECK *holds her head under the faucet, getting her hair wet.*) It can't last much longer. (ADA *goes to the door of the lounge.*)

BILLERBECK (*stands up, completely soaked*): Pray, Ada, pray for us! (*Throws paper at* ADA, *screams*) And five copies of this and rather quickly, if you please! (ADA *goes into the lounge, slams the door shut. Silence.* KOLK *and* BILLERBECK *work. It grows darker, then suddenly light again.*)

6

BILLERBECK, KOLK. *The same situation as before.*

KOLK: I like you, really.

BILLERBECK: Not that, no; we shouldn't talk like that.

KOLK: Ada is too dumb. "Nature" . . . (*Laughs*)

BILLERBECK: And if we're mistaken? And we are the ones, it's we who . . . (*Breaks off*)

KOLK: But beautiful—that you'll have to admit.

BILLERBECK: We are the ones who are making things worse.

KOLK: We have our healthy minds.

BILLERBECK (*to herself*): Sometimes it seems to me that I used to know more . . . back then. When? Some time ago. (*Laughs*)

KOLK: But even if our minds aren't healthy—our intellect, of course, the judgments of our intellect . . .

BILLERBECK (*suddenly sharp*): Don't talk about "our" intellect!

KOLK: Listen, I thought you and I, the two of us . . .

BILLERBECK: The surplus stock . . . have you? Have you finished it?

KOLK (*works; after a while*): The judgments of our intellect, I mean— they can be falsified, verified, and finally what's left is unassailable, if not for long . . . if not—(*Silence*) I don't believe what people say about you.

BILLERBECK: And the recalls—have they finally been recorded? I see receipts for materials, mountains of receipts! (*Suddenly troubled*) What do people say? (*Silence*) A mountain, there, there, on your desk!

KOLK: You must hate this, I think, this work, these . . . people, the whole ridiculous penny-pinching.

BILLERBECK: A mountain on your desk, I said, getting higher and higher instead of smaller!

KOLK: You throw out a question, damn it, we talk about it, then you strangle it. Why the devil can't we finish something at least once?

BILLERBECK: Get to work! You don't understand anything.

KOLK: Yes, but . . . listen . . . (BILLERBECK *writes vehemently on the teletype, cutting* KOLK *off. Then a moment of silence.*) I think I'm going crazy. (*Silence. Work.* KOLK *stops during* BILLERBECK'S *monologue and listens.*)

BILLERBECK (*suddenly leaning back*): Yes, we lived in a castle, in a real castle. Almost like a fairy tale. But I hated it, everything there: the table manners and speaking in soft voices, and the hunting horns and evening concerts, and the hand-kissing, but only "gentlemen" in the innermost chambers. . . . I hated, hated the fancy phrases of the guests, the fancy phrases of the dogs, I hated it so much I could hardly breathe, until one day . . . the saving, though, came to me, yes, the insight that saved my life. During a celebration with the house full of people I went in and said, stated coldly, that I was expecting a child, which shocked them all so much, the whole clan, that they forgot to get to the bottom of the matter. Yes, I succeeded in getting away quickly, off to the city, a former servant took me in, in the nursery of a new apartment building, ten feet wide and ten feet long, where naturally I didn't stay, ran around then, as the saying goes, sank from one thing to another, quickly traded one man for the next, from one loser to another; it was the last one, a lottery collector, who kept me, that was the bottom . . . no, the absolute lowest was this, an office, the most despicable place in the eyes of my class. . . . It wouldn't have been any worse if I had worked on an assembly line, so they took my name out of the social register, erased me, and I forgot all of them immediately, as fast as one can forget, everything down the drain, until suddenly, one morning . . . Frank was at the door, Franki, the youngest one, the brother I had always dragged around with me like a doll . . . there he was with his little suitcase; he had come. (*Laughs*) Had taken his inheritance in cash and was standing there laughing! So we lived together for a while; that worked for as long as it lasted. No, for as long as we had imagined it would. It was always so quiet at home. Almost as quiet as it was at the office. We had time to think through a lot of things. (BILLERBECK'S *voice changes suddenly; she is herself again. Window B lights up; a young girl is putting on her makeup before a mirror.*) When I was alone again . . . I thought then it was over, life was at its end—thought I had learned everything, the most important and the worst . . . everything, and yet . . . in spite of everything, I still hadn't understood anything, not anything. I can't say when it was that I suspected something . . . a bit . . . perhaps only a glimmer . . . I suspected, everything always went its own way, but, while it was going, while I was thinking, I was just marking time, nothing was moving . . . no further, not one step, it must have been exactly then, difficult to account for in a "normal" mind, but I know one thing for certain: In every class—no matter how many there are—everywhere, everything is always possible. That's the miracle!

KOLK: The miracle? (*Laughs*)

BILLERBECK (*turns to* KOLK, *sharply*): Take note of that! (*Silence. Work. Window B darkens.*)

KOLK: A bit annoying, a miracle like that, isn't it? I've gone beyond that. A long time ago. And fundamentally! (*Silence. Work.*) I have seen a lot of the world, yes, all kinds of things, from Helsinki all the way to Nepal. But I have never discovered any great miracles! (*Pause*) I come in here from the outside world and find the same thing; you could see it yourself, could perceive it yourself, if you wanted to . . . (BILLERBECK *puts on her glasses, turns on the desk lamp, and shines the light on*

KOLK.) If only you didn't enjoy playing the ostrich here! I see with frightening clarity: There's absolutely nothing there. *(Pause)* Your miracle, it still hasn't happened! *(Pause)* My friends—*(Laughs)*—with their heads in the clouds, they go to the country; I see them hoeing in their small gardens; renovating their old farmhouses with their fathers' dividends or producing works of art. Works of art! *(Laughs)* I, who have decided . . . (BILLERBECK *stands up, comes closer with the lamp, studies* KOLK *as you would an insect. He becomes increasingly unsure of himself.*) I, who never close my eyes . . . I have discovered where the sickness starts and how it develops, I can lay my finger on the ulcer, I . . . I'll make it public, yes, indeed . . . me. *(Pause)* And if I should become infected, at least I would have a clean conscience.

BILLERBECK *(very close, ominously silent for a few seconds, suddenly points angrily to* KOLK*'s index files):* There . . . there . . . God . . . again! There's another mistake there, by God, one hundred seventeen, instead of one hundred seventy-one—he can't even write numbers correctly, and he wants to rattle the foundation! If that continues, they'll put a computer in his place, which would probably be the best thing; we'll continue with our paperwork, but let me tell you: Even the most degenerate, even the criminal, yes, even the white-collar workers can't be assessed by you, is incalculable, immense, that's what I have to say to you! *(Silence. They work.)*

KOLK *(holding his head in his hands):* I think I'm going mad.

7

Office. KOLK, *now alone, still in the same position as before,* BUBLITZ *arrives, a portfolio under her arm, goes to him, leans on him for a moment, sits in her chair, looks over at him, types three words on her typewriter, drinks out of a small bottle, eats, almost, as if out of embarrassment, looks again at* KOLK. *Silence.*)

BUBLITZ: What I actually . . . what I've wanted to ask . . . for a long time . . .

KOLK *(absently):* Eh?

BUBLITZ: Namely because, I thought . . . *(Silence)*

KOLK: What?

BUBLITZ: When I heard yesterday how they were yelling . . . *(Silence)*

KOLK: Who was yelling?

BUBLITZ: How they were yelling, yesterday, across the courtyard . . . they were yelling Adaline . . . (*Short silence*)

KOLK: How would it be if for once you managed to say a sentence, a single sentence, correctly, with a beginning and an end? (*Silence. Shouts.*) If for once you could just stop your eating, for example, can't stand to see you eat, without beginning and end, not one real meal but, instead, a little bit here and a little bit there. (*He suddenly stands up and sets* BILLERBECK*'s timer.*) We're going to practice that from now on. You'll eat when it's time. So there'll be a . . . contour to your life. So you can live like a human being!

(*Silence*)

Now what?

(BUBLITZ *is silent.*)

Can't talk now?

(BUBLITZ *is silent.*)

So say something. Speak, for God's sake, do it correctly!

(BUBLITZ *is silent.*)

All right, if you're not going to talk.

(BUBLITZ *is silent.*)

If you don't want to.

(BUBLITZ *is silent.*)

All right, then, I can't help you either.

(*Silence. The teletype begins to record,* BUBLITZ *goes over to it and pulls the cord from the outlet; moves decisively over to* KOLK.)

BUBLITZ: Give me a name, Kolk.

KOLK: A what?

BUBLITZ: Name.

KOLK: I don't get it.

BUBLITZ: One that's right. For me. A name.

KOLK: You have one, Bublitz.

BUBLITZ: Sometimes . . . there are people—Ada, for example.

KOLK: I don't understand.

BUBLITZ: Sometimes they call her Adaline.

KOLK: Still not clear.

BUBLITZ: Or Elisabeth . . . Lissy, that fits somehow. What I mean is, some people are called the right things, somehow.

KOLK: What nonsense is floating around in your head. (ROSINSKI *appears unnoticed in the door and listens.* BUBLITZ *speaks in a changed voice, while* KOLK *resumes working.*)

BUBLITZ: That's what I think . . . that it's not right what they call me, and all the time saying "Bublitz, Bublitz." . . . Stupid name, inherited from my family, but I don't want them saying it without thinking about it, without making any effort to really see me properly. . . . Giving people names that don't fit . . . is like being tattooed. . . . Can't get rid of it, or you tear off your own skin. . . . It's like a stamp, here, on your forehead, and maybe you've become a completely different person. . . . Maybe you're somebody else . . . but when they go to buy themselves a new dress, they look a long time for something they like and find just the right thing and wear it for as long as they like it . . . so, you see, they just have to . . . (*Turns to* KOLK) At least you should . . . (KOLK *moans.* BUBLITZ *softly.*) And maybe it also has to do with something else entirely.

KOLK: What century are you from, anyway?

BUBLITZ: With . . . somehow . . . love.

KOLK: Marble, stone, and iron can break, but our love . . . (*Laughs*) Love. (*Long silence*)

BUBLITZ: (*suddenly yells loudly*): And not once when we were talking, never, on any Monday, when they asked how it was yesterday did you ever mention "our" Sunday! (*Silence.* KOLK *begins running in a circle.*)

KOLK (*softly enraged*): From all sides, from all sides! You. The packer. Billerbeck. Her . . . especially. You think you speak the same language . . . nothing there. . . . It's a bucket of crap over your head!

KOLK: *Love,* when I even hear that word. (*Silence*) Do I need this? (*Pause*) Do I need this? (*Pause*) For a long time now. (*Silence*)

BUBLITZ: Forget it. (*Pause*) It's probably stupid anyway. (*Pause*) A new name. (*Pause*) I didn't say anything. (*Goes to her desk and begins typing quickly*) Must go on, dear God! (*Suddenly stops, looks at* KOLK) Eh, Kolk . . . OK? (ROSINSKI *loudly throws a packet of typing paper into the office. Both are startled.* ROSINSKI *disappears, slams the door shut. Blackout.*)

8

BUBLITZ *alone in office A. Lights up slowly in office B. A man is sitting there at his desk. Suddenly* BUBLITZ *crosses deliberately to the window and, with her lipstick, writes her name in big letters on the pane.*

BUBLITZ: That's my signature. That's me! (*The man continues working, doesn't look up.*) A lot to see in my signature. With my signature I say

everything. Everything is there: looks, age, my name. (*Startled*) Name?
(*Laughs*) Can't decipher that. You'd have to invent one yourself! (*Silence*)
Maybe, if you received our letters? . . .
If you received one of my letters? . . .
If you were the person who . . . (*Laughs*)
You would study my signature for a long time.
(*Softly*) You could see me.
(*Unintentionally at the window, she hides herself quickly.*)
(*Softly*) Can you see me?
(*Silence. The man continues to work.*)
Naturally we deliver anywhere.
(*A young woman appears at the window of office B and waters the flowers.*)
Who is that?
Doesn't matter. Only waters the flowers.
Your diligent little Lisa, makes the coffee . . . jumps when you crook your
little finger, eh? (*Laughs*)
It's clear: man who has understood my signature can never
(*The man doesn't react, turns his back to* BUBLITZ.)
never again bind himself to someone else.
(*Blackout in office A. The window of office B remains lit for another minute,
then goes to blackout.*)

9

(*Office A.* BILLERBECK, ADA, KOLK *at their places. Light focused on the
door:* LISSY, *a very beautiful girl.*)

LISSY: Hey! (*All look up.*) Are you all under a spell? You all look like
Sleeping Beauties. Just the way I remember you. Twelve weeks . . . for
twelve weeks I was sick and at the spa, and nothing, really nothing, has
changed here! Really uncanny, I thought, at the moment I came in.
(*Silence. Everyone except* KOLK *suddenly stands up and gathers around
her.*)

BUBLITZ: You're looking good.

ADA: Well, well!

BUBLITZ: And you got your extension?

BILLERBECK: What did they do to you?

ADA: How many did you make unhappy?

BILLERBECK: How many unbroken hearts?

BUBLITZ: Or families? (*Pause*)

ADA: But beautiful, she's still beautiful, by God!

LISSY (*slips around* KOLK): This is where Messerich used to sit. At first glance I thought the back of your head . . . (KOLK *stands up, moves closer;* BUBLITZ *creeps back to her seat.*) Will you be here a long time, or are you just temporary?

KOLK (*close*): Lissy, Elisabeth, a bad name. If you ask me, I, for one, would name you "Queenie."

LISSY: But I'm not asking you. (*Silence. Suddenly* BUBLITZ *starts typing madly. Everyone looks at her.* LISSY *leaves a package of paper on* BILLERBECK'*s desk.*) The guidelines from the boss. He asks us to get bids. As soon as possible! As many as we can. Final decision through Kastner.

KOLK (*flares up*): She can do that, too; Miss Billerbeck can make the decision just as well. Probably better. (*Silence. To* BILLERBECK): Now you say something. (*Silence*) People aren't allowed to use their heads! We don't move forward, not one step! (*Screams*) Do something, go on! A tiny step! (BILLERBECK *sits, has pulled her hair over her eyes. Silence.*)

LISSY: Oho! A revolution!

It was exactly the same way with Messerich . . . at the beginning. (*Pause*) Exactly the same. (*Laughs*) In that respect, nothing has really changed. (*Leaves*) (*Silence. They work.*)

KOLK: Twelve weeks . . . they don't usually send anyone away for that long unless it's necessary. Was she sick, or what? (*Silence*)

BUBLITZ: You could call it that.

(*Silence. The clock begins to tick louder and faster. Traffic sounds drown out the noise of the office. Loud airplane noise.* BILLERBECK *closes the window demonstratively. Office atmosphere. Long silence.*)

ADA: You see nothing. You don't notice anything. She still has herself in control. Hair, eyes, everything, eyeliner perfect. . . . You try to do the same. (*Silence*) She had a relationship with Kastner. For a long time. Until he moved upstairs. One day he said good-bye to her just like that. A small ring for good-bye and gone. When they ran into each other in the corridor . . . he didn't even look at her. Then she went out and took them, they found her in the warehouse. You try that sometime! But it wasn't the strong stuff. Only something for a headache. She was lucky.

Maybe it wasn't really serious. (*Pause*) Not dead serious. (*Silence.*
BUBLITZ *turns on her transistor radio: music. They all work. Blackout.*)

10

Another day. KOLK *and* ADA *are working. The teletype is running. After
it stops, the office is very quiet. Absently* ADA *pulls the comb from her
hair; it falls down over her shoulders.* KOLK *stops working.*

KOLK: Exactly why, my dear lady, why are you always trying to pull me
in?

ADA: Hello! A bad Sunday yesterday, young man, eh?

KOLK: You're constantly at it, trying to get me into your stories . . . (ADA
lights a cigarette.) With the old tricks, with the old tricks . . . (ADA *pours
cola into a glass, drinks deeply. Silence.*) Into the old stories! (*He tries
to work. Silence.* ADA *absently unbuttons her blouse partway.*) Into the
old silly stories. (*Silence*)

ADA: You're wrong, buddy. You already are in them.

KOLK: What you won't say. (*He works.*)

ADA: And you have been for a long time.

KOLK: Try and prove it!

ADA: You don't look at me when we talk. When I'm not working, you
get nervous. Clearing your throat. Drumming your fingers on the desk.
Rings, you make rings around me. Tight, tighter all the time. (*Laughs.*
KOLK *stands up,* ADA *shrinks back from him; he pursues her.*) Even
when I'm in another room, I feel it. Have an antenna for that. I can
feel it a mile away. (ADA *is backed up against the wall.* KOLK, *close
enough to touch her, stands before her, presses her still closer against
the wall, whispers.*)

KOLK: You! You are . . . something I could never imagine! No! Never! (*He
suddenly moves back from her; his arms drop to his sides.*) It's . . . the
waiting. Makes me sick. It drives me crazy. I practically . . . already
speak. . . . I speak in your language, don't know anymore . . . even the
weather outside. . . . Is it still summer? Or what? A blanket over everything. It all goes nowhere. But waiting. Waiting. . . . And if he came
today, Kastner, and set everything right, what would be changed? I would
still be waiting. We wait. You wait. They wait. It goes on and on, but
it comes to absolutely nothing. (*He moves closer again.*) Unless I play
a little game like you do. You, you spot your prey, you spin your web

around it, you take a deep breath and swallow it. Then you're satisfied for a moment, but a second later you throw it up, half-dead, half-alive, and then, then it starts all over again from the beginning. And nothing ever comes to an end; nothing ever goes anywhere.

ADA (*grinning*): You don't get anywhere, do you? Anywhere? Never get anywhere? (KOLK *brutally pulls* ADA *to him. The phone rings.* ADA *goes to answer it;* KOLK *follows her, stands leaning close against her.* ADA, *very calm*) Oh, yes . . . it's ready. Can be picked up. I'd have to check, yes. As for us, we take care of our business. Yes, we make it a point to make our deadlines. You should know that, sir. Nothing new under the sun, no. That's the way it is. (*Animated*) I'll forget I ever heard that, Mister! (KOLK *tears the receiver from her hand, slams it down, presses her against him.* BILLERBECK *arrives, sees what's going on, sits down, without a word, at her desk;* ADA *goes to the photocopier, works, the clock ticks;* KOLK *and* BILLERBECK *type frantically; the telephone rings; the teletype clicks; the sounds become unreal, oppressive. Blackout.*)

II

ADA *is alone in the lounge, standing at the photocopier; the door to office A is open; it is empty. As she works,* ADA *holds ice on her black eye and talks to herself.*

ADA (*laughs*): And the second angel set one foot upon the ocean and swore . . .
What a laugh!
Ruined, the earth . . .
There's no such thing as that! Some "God," or whatever you want to call it . . . who would ruin such beauty,
or whatever you call it . . .
(*She lets the photocopier run, leans against the wall, half-closing her eyes.*)

What I saw yesterday in the tent, how he stood up, Ali, I can see it . . . this . . .
(*She draws a line in the air with her hand.*)

from the shoulder up to the collarbone, against the light . . . very soft . . . a line . . . and in the mirror, as he comes at me, his face, it was broken, the mirror, a crack through the middle, in the half-darkened tent, because we didn't know where else to go where Albrecht couldn't find us, but

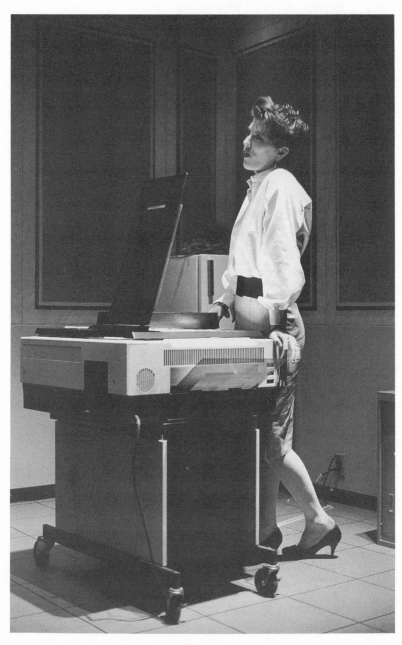

Ada at the copying machine. From *Ironheart* by Gerlind Reinshagen, directed by Sue Clement, University of Washington. (Photo by Mark Dalton.)

I see in the broken mirror how he's looking at me, as if I wasn't . . .
human . . . Like he's trying to . . . figure me out, the way he's looking,
I'm sure of it, surprised, because he loves me . . . really, if I could explain
it to Albrecht without him hitting me . . .
(*Runs to the empty desks*)
I just once I could . . . so that you both would understand (*Stands at the
photocopier again*) But I did once . . . (*Laughs*) I did see it.
(*The photocopier makes a loud noise. Blackout.*)

12

Office A. BILLERBECK, ADA, KOLK, *and* BUBLITZ *are working. The windows of both offices A and B are open. The teletype is running.* ADA
and BILLERBECK *stop typing. Similarly, in office B, four people are writing
at their desks. One closes the window.* BILLERBECK *stands up, also closes
the window, sits down again. The teletype is still running. Suddenly
quiet.*

BUBLITZ: Strange. (*Silence*)
ADA: Yes. (*Silence*)
BUBLITZ: Something wrong with my head today. (*Silence*)
BILLERBECK: Imagination. (*Silence*)
ADA: The hot wind. (*Silence*)
BUBLITZ: Doesn't sit right, here . . . something. (*Points to her breast*)
  Inside.
KOLK: Disaster weather today. The psychologists have claimed . . . (*His file
  cards fall to the floor.*)
ADA (*opens the window, leans out, stretches her arms*): Ah, storm outside,
  I always liked to be outside when there was a wind like this—only thing
  to do is to be out.
KOLK (*suddenly takes off his shoes and socks, walks around, as if in a
  meadow*): Can't concentrate.
BUBLITZ (*pulls a sheet of paper out of the typewriter, tears it up*): Once
  I do one thing wrong, I do everything wrong. Better to just go home.
BILLERBECK (*throws the shoes at* KOLK, *pulls* ADA *from the window, slams
  the window shut*): What does this mean? Now . . . especially now! Almost
  the end of the month. I have to say it earlier and earlier. It's only the
  twentieth, and I'm telling you: Think about it! At first it's only a few . . .
  just a couple of transactions left over which you push aside. (*Hurriedly*)

It bottlenecks, the list of expenditures, the surveys, quicksand, an ocean of quicksand . . . (KOLK *sits down on the floor, laughs without stopping.* BILLERBECK *sits near* KOLK.) You need to . . . keep your hand on the wheel definitely, a strong hand, so the damned business keeps running. You have to give it everything you've got, I tell you, because it's more than just "chicken scratchings," as Mister Schoolboy seems to think, not just "trifles" . . . (BILLERBECK *and* KOLK *look at each other.*) It was suggested that we extend your trial period . . . for three months. He said that, to be sure, not I. Kastner said that. (*Silence*)

KOLK: And how do you stand on this? (*Silence*)

BILLERBECK (*suddenly turning away*): I am alone! Alone, I have to do it all myself . . . maintain . . . (*She runs to the other desks, grabs their letters, file boxes, and accounts and piles them onto her own desk, also the contents of the wastebaskets, so that a mountain of paper is formed.*) If you leave me alone . . . I, I'll take care of your mess, all of it . . . buried up to my neck . . . (*She tries to climb onto the desk.* ADA *and* BUBLITZ *hold her back.*) Quicksand, faster and higher all the time . . . and no one, no one, the great bird flies lower and lower, I, alone, must do it . . . (ADA *and* BUBLITZ *shake her.*)

ADA: But we're here.

BILLERBECK: So that we can come out of it, come through it . . .

ADA (*puts her arm around* BILLERBECK's *shoulders, pulls her carefully down from the desk*): Come, good, good, it's alright; it's alright. (BILLERBECK *stares past* ADA.)

BUBLITZ: Here . . . me . . . it's me. My hand, you can take my hand, it's me.

ADA (*tenderly*): And me, Billerbeck! (BILLERBECK *stares.* ADA *brushes the hair from her forehead.*) It's us, we're here! (BILLERBECK *stares.*)

KOLK: We at least, if nothing else, far and wide . . . (*Laughs*)

BILLERBECK (*suddenly herself again, hisses at* KOLK): Quiet, you! Shut up! For God's sake! (*Loud*) Quiet, or you're out immediately! (*Softly, insistently*) Don't say it. (*Silence*)

KOLK: Your nerves, totally frayed, as I see it. You should get that taken care of. (*Pause*) So you've arranged this . . . extension for me. (*Pause*) I'll have to think about that. (BUBLITZ *drops a stack of papers all over the floor. Blackout.*)

13

Office A. BUBLITZ *and* KOLK *at their desks, far apart.* KOLK *stares straight ahead.*

BUBLITZ: It's nothing. No, really. It comes and goes. It's because she thinks: The world is going downhill, and this is only an interim, and the human race will destroy itself. They should examine her, with bands around her head or something, maybe some kid of lie detector; it doesn't mean anything; it comes and goes. But I've never, in the seven years I've been sitting here, known her to do anything crude. Not that she's like a mother—a mother is nothing—but if she wasn't here . . . (*She moves slowly to the door to take out some papers; suddenly* KOLK *stretches his hand out toward her.*) Want something? (*Pause*) That was like the first time. As though you had called my name. I've been waiting for that.

KOLK: Who ever . . . who has ever? Have always, stood aside, everywhere, for the sole reason that I saw through everything immediately. Always understood too quickly. But naturally they . . . they were aware of that. They knew I didn't care about their gossip. One look, and I knew, even without words. People are afraid of someone who sees through things. (*Pause*) They were afraid of me. That's not funny. Helms, for example, in my class, an odd guy, always bright and shining; I felt sorry for him, supported him with my last cent as they say. . . . He's a failure at math; I do everything for him, explain everything to him—vector analysis, everything . . . in the evening he goes to the others, alone, without me, has friends everywhere, familiar with the professors, drank with the assistants, never said: Come along! Didn't understand my language, not one of them, never, not even my parents anymore, I said "black," they understood "white," as though I came from another planet . . .

BUBLITZ: You can talk so beautifully . . .

KOLK: After a while couldn't talk with anyone, always sat and studied, finally knew too much, not too little, too much. . . . That was the reason I lost my nerve, the nerve to take the exams. A couple of times I thought I'd make amends, went up to them, approached them, but those people, as though they wanted to finish me, they built a wall in front of me, I couldn't come in, I was always on the outside, on the outs, even here, even among these . . . these . . .

BUBLITZ: Among who—these? (*Silence*) Who cares? You called, called me at least once. . . . Oh God, I'm happy.

KOLK (*lowers his hand*): You're happy? Eh? (*Laughs cruelly*) You're happy? (BUBLITZ *nods.*) Yes, when I'm finally down. (BUBLITZ *wants to go.*) Listen to me . . . Bublitz!

BUBLITZ: I'm listening. But you, you're listening with only one ear. (*Pause. Turns around suddenly to* KOLK.) And what would you think, Kolk, if they don't want you here, if we both left, together, and said good-bye on the thirtieth, and began again from scratch somewhere, and no one knew who we were?

KOLK (*laughs*): And after four weeks my name would still be Kolk and yours Bublitz ...

BUBLITZ: No one would know where we came from; you have to be able to create yourself, not into the future, anyone can do that, but going back, so that we'd be totally different, totally new ...

KOLK (*laughs*): Always be called Bublitz, for as long as you live, and you'll never get rid of it: your friends, your face, your new life, and you'll eat, again, constantly, and cling, again, as you always have!

BUBLITZ: That's twice. As if you can't do anything but beat somebody down! You beat people again and again, as always, the way you always have ... (*She wants to go. Silence.*)

KOLK: Don't go away, you, not like this. (BUBLITZ *moves to the window. Silence. A child appears in the window of office B, drawing figures on the windowpane.*)

BUBLITZ (*changed, under control*): Have to learn ... wait ...
You've always, for so long, everywhere ...
I'm used to it.
I was called twice,
and beaten back again twice.
Maybe I'll be called more often.
But if I'm beaten back again ...
Maybe then I'll be stronger
or harder, like iron (*Laughs*)
hard as iron inside
and not feel anyone's blows.
I wouldn't need any of your names then,
I would stand higher,
yes, "higher than a name"
hey, hey, I would stand on top of the radio tower
and spit down on names!
(*Softly*) What I think, no one can get at that!

KOLK (*stretches his hand out again*): Stay with me, Bublitz! (*Silence*)

BUBLITZ (*softly to the child*): Do you hear me, can you understand? (*The child in office B breathes on the pane, fogging it up. Blackout.*)

PART 2

I

Another workday. Noon. It seems to be very hot. BUBLITZ *alone in the office. She moves around restlessly, lifts her arms as though to express something: desire, joy. She lies down suddenly on the floor, breathes deeply, jumps up, takes a small bottle out of her desk but puts it away again, moves to the window, leans her head against the pane. Office B is now empty.*

BUBLITZ: FatherMotherMaryandJosephHendricksJoplinBobMarleyMaryhad alittlelambNowIcomeagainandagain . . . (*Laughs happily*)

ROSINSKI (*creeps up*): And . . . well? (*Silence*) Flickering again up there, eh? Here they'll all be crazy someday . . . (*He unscrews a fluorescent light.*)

BUBLITZ: It's one of those days today, a day, a day,
almost like before a holiday,
but somehow . . . crazy,
everything insane.
Already autumn and still hot.
But I won't drink.
Don't need any pills, nothing. (*Pause*)
No. Won't. Won't. Never again.
When I look out the window, suddenly it seems: I'm fantastically strong, as though I could shove the walls apart, or fantastically smart, everything just comes to me, as though I could . . . give a speech (*Laughs*) Me of all people . . . as if today I could grasp something. . . . Just a little bit further, I think, and I'll know it, I'll have it, be able to grasp it; either, I think, I'll get it or my head will explode. Either I get it or my head . . .

ROSINSKI (*working on the fluorescent lights*): You'll come to me again, back again.

BUBLITZ: And they can come a thousand times and say, how ugly the city is, I see it differently now, from today on let's talk about beauty instead, but I see everything double, as if suddenly I had another pair of eyes, . . . like . . . it starts to hurt all of a sudden, and it's good if it does, because then I'll be able to hold out; it's that way now, as if I can't see anything simple anymore and say: black is black . . .

ROSINSKI (*moves closer, whispering*): Yes, yes, will be again the way it used to be . . .

BUBLITZ: And maybe even Billerbeck is not what they say.

ROSINSKI (*still closer*): Like always, when you came, after work was over, and everything totally quiet, just the two of us, in the packroom, or that night when she, when Ella was in the hospital, it will be that way again . . .

BUBLITZ (*firmer*): I can do this or something else. I see lots of possibilities, all of a sudden . . .

ROSINSKI (*whispering*): Yes, and you won't always be looking around, all worked up, but instead you'll be quiet; you'll look at me, calmly, into my eyes . . . you . . .

BUBLITZ: And I could, could go away from here, just get up and leave, with him, because you know he, he believes that I could do it . . .

ROSINSKI (*still whispering*): And I'll always see your hands on the type-writer, the little blue vein on your forehead. (*Touches her carefully at the temple*) And you'll see, with your stupid eyes, what love is worth, rare as a diamond. (*Silence*)

BUBLITZ (*suddenly pushes him back*): Are you, are you crazy, Rosinski? . . .

ROSINSKI: What do you mean, crazy?

BUBLITZ: Babbling about love and at any moment . . .

ROSINSKI (*moves away*): Babbling? Yes. Why not? Maybe someone's interested in what I'm babbling about. For example, I could level with a certain bird, even tell him how I pulled you out of the gutter.

BUBLITZ: Nobody cares about that, not these days.

ROSINSKI: Or let a word slip that you're always ready for it, let yourself go with this guy and that guy.

BUBLITZ: That, when I explain . . .

ROSINSKI: And even with someone who's beneath you, just think: with a packer! I'd like to tell you about my friend. He has a dog, a mongrel, cross between a schnauzer and a St. Bernard—me, that's me . . . me against the rest of you, the packer they kid around with, the packer who fixes the toilets. I mean: Even you, kid, aren't worth anything. (*Silence*)

BUBLITZ: Who cares about worth when love's the case?

ROSINSKI: And right, there, that's exactly where it starts, when love's the case! It's a thorn in him; it will infect him . . . (*Laughs*)

BUBLITZ: It's over, Rosinski, over, over, past. Don't you see!

ROSINSKI (*pulls a note from his pocket*): And there's one other small thing. Just a note. The diagnosis. After three days in the hospital. Written in black and white.

BUBLITZ: Be quiet, Rosinski!

ROSINSKI: Rosinski, Herman—there, in black and white: shrunken, everything eaten away, here. (*He points to his liver.* BUBLITZ *holds her hands over her ears; he pulls her hands away. He gets an idea.*) And what if it's malignant?

BUBLITZ: I can't listen to that, Rosinski, stop!

ROSINSKI: Malignant, I tell you and you. (*He holds* BUBLITZ *tightly.*) You're not going to just take off, because that wouldn't be human. Just leaving somebody behind to die, not even the cannibals in the swamps did that; they never killed a dying man . . . so far as we know . . .

BUBLITZ: You're crude. A crude oppressor. And now it comes out! (*Pause*) Why . . . (*Pause*) and why don't you do something about it?

ROSINSKI: What?

BUBLITZ: Take . . . something . . . put an end to it. Quick, and it's over!

ROSINSKI (*softly*): Because you need the courage of a lion to do that. (*Pause*) Because . . . can't do it! (*Yells suddenly*) You, you pig of a woman! But you, I tell you, you'll never get old, with your new life, and because you're hot inside, and because we're the same, you'll fall again, if I'm not here, two or three short years maybe, then you'll be hooked on the needle, because you see, when people are the same they have the same fate a lot of the time; you'll fall apart just like me. (BUBLITZ *lays her head on the desk.* ROSINSKI, *softly, in a changed voice*): You'll rot on the inside, but your head will still be OK; the mind will function, but your living body will stink, and nothing will help anymore—no blank stare like the old people have, with your living eyes; you'll see yourself rot, every minute, every second, like you're buried; I hope it seems as long as a lifetime to you, all these seconds like hours, you'll hear your heart beating, your heart (*Makes the sound of a heart. Pause*)—a second lifetime filled with the fear of death! (ROSINSKI *puts the fluorescent light back in place, grins. Blackout.*)

2 HEARTACHE FOR LOVE

ROSINSKI *alone in office A, in the middle of the room. He drinks out of a flask.*

ROSINSKI: Cramp!
Pain. Here. (*Grabs his chest*)
What was that? What's the matter with me?
One girl out of millions, one, one, one!

(*Loud*) Hello, friends out there in the night!

(*Soft*) The little blue vein on the forehead ... (*Looks around, as if hunted*)
Everything black.

(*Blackout*)

3

Office, BILLERBECK *is working. The lunch break is just ending*, BUBLITZ
enters.

BUBLITZ: Excuse me. (*She sits at her desk.*)

BILLERBECK (*after a while*): It's getting worse. Tardiness. (*Silence. They
work.*)

BUBLITZ: Such hot weather today.

BILLERBECK: My dear girl, I won't have that. Not much longer.

BUBLITZ: Hot weather, enough to make you scared. (*Begins to work*)

BILLERBECK: It's not only that you always get back late from lunch; you're
not even doing your work anymore. When you first came, you were a
top worker. Now, ever since this man's been here ... (*Silence*)

BUBLITZ: Billerbeck, are you afraid of dying?

BILLERBECK (*continues to scold*): Pull yourself together! Mistake after
mistake! (*Tosses over a letter*) Unanswered! No notices about supplies.
Now even you. (*Silence. They work.*) Afraid of dying! Son of God! I
assure you: If someone should suggest to me, one day, if he said, "The
time has come," ... ha, I'd make a cross in the calendar, say a prayer of
thanks: God, I thank you, that it's all behind me ...

BUBLITZ: And why, if you see it that way, I mean, why not ... (*Pause*)
In the end you could finally.... If you see it that way ... (*Silence. They
work.*) I mean if I ever ... ever in my life came to the point where I
thought the way you do, I don't know what I'd do. (*Silence. They work.*)
At home our minister condemned it. (*Silence. They work.*) But I'll never
get to that point, I know that! (*Silence. They work.*) To lose hope is to
sin, he says ...

BILLERBECK (*on the telephone*): Yes, listen: Concerning article seventy-
three-dash-twenty, we need at least four hundred.... That's obvious!
Please!

BUBLITZ (*looks into her compact*): Do you think I'm pretty? (*Silence.
They work.*)

BILLERBECK: There comes a time, a time—or is it just a moment—when it's possible, when you could do it, and I ask myself whether, when the time comes . . . whether one shouldn't in fact do it? (*Silence, then in a changed voice*) For example, you walk through the office . . . and the idiots laugh behind your back. . . . They laugh more often now, don't they? You notice the way they grin, how they drool, but you walk on, as simple as that; you walk away very proudly, with head held high . . . must be very big, above it, child. (*Softly*) Then do it or don't do it. (*Pause*) And don't forget to leave food for the cats—enough for the next few weeks (*Laughs*) or the next few days . . . (*Silence*)

BUBLITZ: Recently read in the paper: Maybe someday the sun will be a giant red ball, because it will get bigger all the time . . . bigger and bigger until it explodes, then everything will be gone away, the earth and everything, only a small icy ball will be left. (*Silence*)

BILLERBECK: You've grown pale, child, these past few months, too pale.

BUBLITZ: Then no one has to beat their brains out anymore . . .

BILLERBECK (*moves over to* BUBLITZ): Get out for a little while, have a cup of coffee. I'll do that for you.

BUBLITZ: What then? Nothing like that has ever happened, something like that . . . and especially . . . when somebody changes all at once, they say . . . (BUBLITZ *stares blankly, leaves.*)

BILLERBECK (*alone, working*): The end of the month already and nothing totaled, the statistics incomplete, the balance isn't . . . (*Sits up straight*) the balance . . . (*Laughs wildly*) the balance . . . (*Laughs. Blackout.*)

4

Packroom. ROSINSKI *at the paper press.* KOLK *enters from the outside.*

ROSINSKI: Have a seat, crow. No sooner get back from the break and already deep in the dusty files . . .

KOLK (*sits on a crate*): Only too true.

ROSINSKI: Need some time, eh, to fall into step.

KOLK (*lights a cigarette*): My feelings exactly.

ROSINSKI: On the gate at the cemetery there's a sign: "Out of time into eternity" is carved there; is it like that, when you get back in here, something like that . . . right?

KOLK: Practically a poet, that's you, Rosinski.

ROSINSKI: Of course, could be the other way around.

KOLK: With the emphasis on *practically*.

ROSINSKI *(grinning):* Sometimes you're thrown back out of eternity...

KOLK: Compared to the blind, the one-eyed woman... *(Startled)* What's that supposed to mean, anyway?

ROSINSKI: Must get out of eternity and back into time.

KOLK: You're trying to say something! (ROSINSKI *is silent.*) What? What do you know? (ROSINSKI *works at the paper press.* KOLK *pulls him away.)* Who? What, man, out with it, or...

ROSINSKI: Or... what? Don't beat your wings. Everything's relative, crow. Let's assume they don't keep you, that doesn't mean: There's nothing between your ears, not necessarily, nah, could even be the opposite, yes.... Namely, that you're a clever man who will cause trouble... those people up there don't like trouble.

KOLK: That can't be true!

ROSINSKI: A troublemaker in the company, they don't want that.

KOLK: So those people, those swindlers, have been leading me on for all these weeks.

ROSINSKI: So, you see, crow, that's how it goes in this world: The smart ones get the ax; the dumb ones run the show.

KOLK *(doubles over with laughter):* Amazing!

ROSINSKI: Humanity, that's how it is.

KOLK: A misunderstanding!

ROSINSKI: As wrong as it is, humanity.

KOLK: A basic one! Hold your breath, Rosinski, I want to make this clear: If those people up there have decided something, Kastner and Co., I tell you, it's not a real decision. At best it's a reaction. Because, naturally, they smell a rat. Because, naturally, they're not so dumb that they don't notice what I'm thinking, my opinion of the company and all that. Hard for them to swallow it, right? —that the cart they're hitched to is a shitwagon with a broken axle. And if you want to ride on it, you've got to have a broken spirit. The question arises, my friend: Which came first, the chicken or the egg?

ROSINSKI *(rubs his hands, hops around, mimics* KOLK): Fantastic! The eggchicken! Phenomenal!

KOLK: And finally when your eyes are open you see; if you stay, you amputate yourself.

ROSINSKI: The lady without a head, haha! The man without a belly! *(Malicious)* All of them cripples, eh?

KOLK: And to hold on to the illusion that you can still change something, that's ridiculous.

ROSINSKI: Has you in its grip, it does!

KOLK: The only possibility is to believe you can get yourself out of it before too long, or...

ROSINSKI: Or? Or what?

KOLK: You'll kill yourself. *(Silence)*

ROSINSKI: Strange. *(Pauses)* Someone else just said that to me. *(Silence)*

KOLK: And you can't even really do that.

ROSINSKI: Cowards, eh? Don't take enough pills. Don't turn the gas up high enough. *(Slaps* KOLK *on the shoulder)* A cowardly, crippled race! *(Laughs)* But you, crow, praiseworthy! Take it with dignity. Rationally. As I always say, a man with spirit just can't be killed. *(They stare at each other. Blackout.)*

5

BILLERBECK, ADA, BUBLITZ *in the office, working. Sunshine. Silence.*

ADA *(looks up):* Now... the moment. *(Silence)*

BILLERBECK: Yes. *(Silence)*

BUBLITZ: Good today.

ADA: As if before I once had...

BILLERBECK: Like back then.

ADA: Should be more often...

BILLERBECK: Like sometimes on trips, suddenly you think: Nobody knows where you are...

ADA: No one can find you. *(Silence)*

BILLERBECK: As if it's always been this way. When we were still alone...

ADA: Yes.

BUBLITZ: Don't understand. *(Silence)*

BILLERBECK: It will never be again like it was before.

BUBLITZ: Oh, that's crazy! You talk...

BILLERBECK: We'll have to talk a lot from now on.

BUBLITZ: Your imagination.

ADA: You didn't have to say anything, before. To explain anything in a big way.

BILLERBECK: Everyone already knew.

ADA: Lots of times, we all suddenly did the same thing, sometimes at the same time, almost like an agreement...

BILLERBECK: The work got done almost by itself...

ADA: And while you were doing it, you could think in any direction . . .

BILLERBECK: Free . . .

ADA: Whatever you wanted.

BILLERBECK *(laughs):* Get started! Get started! *(The others look at her, irritated. Silence.)* Nothing will ever be the way it used to be.

BUBLITZ *(insisting):* What does that mean? What do you all want? As if it's all connected to him! *(Pause)* It's got absolutely nothing to do with him! *(Silence)*

BILLERBECK: Kolk will stay on.

BUBLITZ *(jumps up, runs to* BILLERBECK*):* Is that true?

BILLERBECK: Here. Between us.

BUBLITZ: Is that right? So you've spoken up for him? Oh let's celebrate, everyone. We have to decorate the room! With what? *(She pulls a few straw flowers from a vase, begins to distribute them, to stick them on the calendar, etc.)*

ADA *(stands up):* A party?

BUBLITZ: Very colorful, it should be totally different, so that when he comes . . .

ADA: But what? Now?

And maybe a big sign?

BUBLITZ: And write BEST WISHES on it.

ADA *(brings paper):* This?

BUBLITZ: Yes, this, that's good!

ADA: What should we write?

BUBLITZ: "To a long, happy . . ." what?

ADA: "Strength in unity?" *(Laughs)*

BILLERBECK: "Till death do us part"—how would that be? *(Laughs)*

ADA: Oh, do be quiet! So now, what do we write? (LISSY *comes in with a stack of files for* BILLERBECK. KOLK *follows her, dancing around her.* BUBLITZ *throws the flowers into the closet;* ADA *covers the sign.* ROSINSKI *appears in the door, listens.)*

LISSY: What's the matter with all of you? Such a strange atmosphere, as if something's in the air, everyone's ten feet off the ground; really, I'd be scared here.

KOLK: Ditto. If I weren't already leaving, Queenie, and hadn't turned my back on all of it, I'd get myself transferred to you.

LISSY: I wouldn't bet on that.

KOLK *(close):* Wouldn't you like that? *(Silence.* BUBLITZ *types furiously.*

Everyone looks at her. LISSY *and* KOLK *slip out again.* ROSINSKI *remains in the door.*)

ROSINSKI (*watching the two of them leave*): Like I always say: A butterfly. From flower to flower. Not picky. Would be satisfied with pigweed. But Lissy, if he gets involved with her, what would he have? Half a person, because nothing else can grow here. When he looks around, what does he see? Cripples, nothing but cripples, he says, their brains shriveled from lack of use. A dried mushroom, the brain. And finally the worker, a mongoloid you can't stand to look at. Not my words!

BUBLITZ: Did he ... say that? Rosinski?

ROSINSKI: Better if it had never been born, humanity. You should finally realize that, and blow yourselves up. . . . But you don't have the guts to do that, not even that, too uneducated. Everything half, everything half ... (*Silence.* BILLERBECK *types. Silence.*) That's what he said. (*Silence*)

BUBLITZ (*stands up, determined*): No matter how much poison you spit out and whatever you say, it's all yesterday's news. (*Silence*) We're all beyond that, Rosinski. (*Silence*) I'm far beyond ... (*She passes out straw flowers again frantically, screams.*) We'll celebrate, whatever happens! (*Blackout*)

6

Office A, toward evening: candlelight, wine bottles. The banner, a flower bouquet painted on it, hangs on the wall. BILLERBECK *and* BUBLITZ *wait.* ADA *leads* KOLK *into the room blindfolded, ceremoniously removes the blindfold. Radio music. Later* ROSINSKI.

KOLK (*after a pause*): I don't know. What should I say? I believe I owe an explanation. (*Clears his throat*) I believe I need to make a speech. It appears that I'm staying. (ADA *embraces him briefly;* BILLERBECK *shakes his hand;* BUBLITZ *stares at him.*) I, what should I say? (*He goes to his desk, places his hands on the typewriter.*) This is my typewriter. (*He opens card files, removes cards, flips through them, like a card game.*) The index cards. A short while ago, in the early morning, I woke up and could feel them, could almost smell the cards; it was somehow ... comforting, I thought, really, for a moment I thought: can't live without these cards ... (*Laughs*)

BILLERBECK (*goes to her desk*): It's the twenty-seventh, friends, and the workday's not over yet, not at all.

KOLK: I've been wanting to tell you that for a long time now.

BILLERBECK: One hour and fourteen minutes left.

KOLK: No matter what else I wanted to say. (*He approaches the window. Snow on the ground. The moon appears. Lights up slowly in office B. He speaks in a changed voice, stammering.*) I . . . I sit here . . . at the typewriter, I write on the cards, I make an effort to write clearly on the cards, my mark there on the cards. (*In office B the blinds are lowered.*) It's often quiet, almost like in space, yes, quiet, good, I think, here, I think sometimes, nothing can come in, no matter what comes . . . (*Laughs*) This is the ark . . .

BILLERBECK: Stop it, I say!

KOLK: But that's the truth!

BILLERBECK: Stop that!

KOLK: But I have to . . . say it . . . finally . . .

BILLERBECK (*hisses*): You're saying it, you're saying the truth, the way it's "written."

KOLK: As sure as I'm standing here. And so: It doesn't matter what happens, if the world should explode, that's fine with me. If the human race should become extinct, as Billerbeck predicts, we'll close the windows, the blinds . . . (*Pause. Laughs.*) So I'm one of you from now on. (*Blackout in office B. He takes* BUBLITZ *in his arms.*) And this is my bride, Rosinski!

ROSINSKI: Congratulations. (*Silence. He spits at* KOLK's *feet, goes to the door.*) He celebrates, no matter what happens. (*He stands in the door. Silence.*)

BILLERBECK (*begins to circle* KOLK *and* BUBLITZ, *speaks at first softly, then increasingly louder*): The truth! It's a lie! Stinks! "The truth!" That's the truth that stinks to high heaven!

KOLK (*turns away*): Suspected that. For a long time.

BILLERBECK (*runs around, pushing everyone aside*): This is the truth that becomes a lie!

This is the devil who speaks the truth!

The truth! (*Laughs in despair*)

It's just a silly, washed-up dame!

Everything's rotting, I tell you; the book of books:

a euphemism! None of it's right.

No angel will come from heaven.
No mountain will crumble to the ground.
The sun won't darken.
The ocean won't become bitter,
No blood will flow in the rivers.
The catastrophe, I tell you, the catastrophe has already happened.
(*To* KOLK) Devil! Devil!
(*She begins throwing files. The others huddle together.*)
It's the devil, he's destroyed everything with his glance.
One glance and you've got the mark on your forehead,
one glance and you're wounded.
The devil as a surgeon, gentlemen, countless glances
like knives, sharp,
that's the way he's cut the disease from our bodies,
the ulcer, yes, and the heart as well!
(*Softer*) What I thought,
what I thought possible, even possible, even yesterday,
possible for humankind,
is over, over!
(*Laughs, to* KOLK) Murderer! Murderer!
(*Points to* BUBLITZ) Look at her, the young bride,
she's alive, but doesn't have the strength to scream.
She bites off her tongue in pain.
She wants to die and can't do it.
She's not alone.
The end, however, if it should come, the end of the world
would be a child's game, a play, a beautiful one.
We could hold hands, we could look into each others'
eyes, and think perhaps as our last thought, it will be
green again, in another world somewhere, a quiet world
without people. . . . Then maybe we'll watch the sun fall
from the sky, all of us together, without fear . . .
If only it would happen, to save us.
But it won't happen.
The catastrophe already happened a long time ago.
(*She crouches in the foreground and, with a blank look, spills milk from
a milk carton into the empty flower vase and from there onto the earth.
Slow blackout.*)

7

Lights dim slowly in office A until the characters disappear. Lights up in office B. The young girl, who had earlier watered the flowers, now opens the window, and in a panic climbs onto the windowsill; it is obvious that she wants to jump. BUBLITZ *moves close, as in a trance, to the window of office A.*

BUBLITZ: Help!
But how?
How to go on, now?
Can't, of course . . .
Someone will come.
Have to . . .
So high!
Help! Help!
They have to come,
Now, right now,
have to in time,
Hurry!
Can't you hear?
Listen!
Don't panic!
Hold on!
Easy!
Ah, it's already . . .
Can't, of course . . .
You can't . . .
Someone . . . will come . . .
Everything will be . . .
(*The young girl jumps.*)
(BUBLITZ *screams.*) No! No! No!
(*Blackout*)

8

Office A. Dawn. BUBLITZ *enters quietly with two large bags; like a thief, she begins to pack her private effects: shoes, pills, a small bottle, mug, sweater, a novel, makeup, etc. She lays some files on* BILLERBECK'*s desk and puts the bouquet of straw flowers on* KOLK's *desk. She takes another look around, marks a small cross on the wall calendar, is just about to leave the room when* ROSINSKI *bursts in. He pulls open a drawer, sees that it's empty, and lets it fall to the floor. Step by step* BUBLITZ *moves away from him.*

ROSINSKI: Has it gone that far? Have we come to the end, the two of us? No staying on for you, that's clear. But out there, I swear, sooner or later . . . a standoff, eh? (*Tries once more to move closer*) Here, if you stay, you could at least . . . vegetate, even when I'm no longer here, live out your life, somehow. But out there you'll go from one guy to the next. (*Laughs*) Won't be able to hold your head up high again! You'll go to the dogs, the way you're built. (*Pause*) Could still come back, if you want. (*Pause*) (BUBLITZ *continues to move toward the door; she smiles suddenly.*) If you don't . . . the first week, without us, I swear, you'll either take something or jump off something. A pile of garbage on the sidewalk. (BUBLITZ *is gone.*) I'll swear to that by . . . (*He collapses at* BUBLITZ's *desk. The* CLEANING LADY *comes, begins to vacuum.*)

CLEANING LADY (*yells to make herself understood*): What was that girl's name?

ROSINSKI: Girl? What girl?

CLEANING LADY: The one who sat at the desk. (*She turns off the vacuum cleaner.*)

ROSINSKI: That one, if she had asked, asked for a name, I would have called her "Ironheart" (*Pause*) but she didn't . . . (*Blackout. In office B the first people arrive for work, sit at their desks, type, write, make telephone calls.*)

Anke Roeder

Theater as Counter-Concept:
An Interview with Gerlind Reinshagen

Translated by Angelika Czekay

Anke Roeder: The dramatic form was and still is reserved for men. By 1930 Marieluise Fleißer had already asserted: "The next achievement we [women] must produce is the play." Is there a dramatic form that you would call "feminine"?

Gerlind Reinshagen: I am allergic to the so-called feminine view. There is a feminine subject, which we know better than men. But, as far as the shaping of form is concerned, a short story, for instance, the structure must be very carefully formed. One of the best female short story writers I know is Katherine Mansfield. Besides, in drama, we haven't written closed forms for quite a while, but only "cocktail parties." We adjust the theatrical forms to the open social forms.

AR: In her book *Desire in Language,* Julia Kristeva provides a theory that differentiates between the feminine and the masculine as the semiotic and the symbolic. The semiotic is the mother tongue. The father tongue symbolizes the grammatical structure, the syntax, the social order. The feminine-semiotic is repressed but has not disappeared. In poetic language, it becomes effective again as a means of breaking with the system of order. Mallarmé called it the entrance of "music into the alphabet."

GR: This is an interesting theory. When a man writes a play, he will first think of its structure and then increasingly move into a state of mind in which he abandons this so-called syntax. A woman will start with the semiotic, from emotion, concern, fear, or horror, based on her own experience or her experience with others. During the process of writing she will incorporate the syntax. For any play it is absolutely necessary that she incorporate the syntax, as much as it is absolutely necessary for a man to abandon it, when he writes.

AR: The form is necessary, but in your notes to *Spring Festival (Frühlingsfest)* you mention a "different dramaturgy": "The main plot proceeds under the surface and erupts only from time to time." What do you mean by this?

GR: This corresponds to my idea of theater. When I go to the theater, I think it's time for a different dramaturgy. The one hundred eightieth violent porno movie from the U.S.A. bores me to death. It's the same with this new trend of cynicism in theater. When photography was invented, painters reacted very subjectively with impressionism and expressionism. In contrast, in this country people try to excel the suspense on TV, often even the special effects. The discrepancy between imagination and reality, the persistent pursuit of the inner image, and the failure of the original concept—for all this I would like to find a form. I have tried to do this in different ways—either by including dream sequences or through the appearance of a fictive dialogue partner or through intertwining different levels of language. I am thinking of Robert Wilson's image theater. He has brought a different style of narration into the theater, and we should find one for language.

* * *

AR: You talk about the "double existence" of characters, their efficient, organized lives, on the one hand, and their possible, fictive lives on the other. Is this tension stronger in the male characters or in the female ones?

GR: The women concern themselves more with their different roles. Their experimenting with their lives might be due to the old situation of being a love-object. I tried to show this in my play about Marilyn Monroe. I tried to unravel the myth about her, by trying to show her in different roles according to how the audience wanted to see her. In contrast, men's fantasies are directed to their desire to become something in the world, not to be an object of love for others.

AR: Are these variations of roles more positive in the female characters than the male, whose Janus-like double faces are exposed in your first play, *Doppelkopf? (Two-headed?).*

GR: With the men, the doublings are dictated through circumstances, while, with the women, they develop out of a playful desire to create. Perhaps you can compare this to an artist who makes innumerable sketches. A woman makes sketches of herself in the same way. With women, however, these sketches always relate to the women themselves, while with artists they relate to the world.

AR: You are an artist yourself. In your three major plays *Sunday's Children* (*Sonntagskinder*), *Spring Festival* (*Frühlingsfest*), and the published but unproduced play *Dance, Marie!* (*Tanz, Marie!*), you developed a history from the beginning of World War II through the 1950s, up to our time. But you don't do this by presenting facts, as in a documentary play, but, rather, from the inside of the people concerned. Does this mean that the plays are revolts against a pragmatic way of life?

GR: Yes, there is this strange contradiction. Many theater people ask where is the political play that explains our reality? I don't believe that the subjective production of theater, which is already a translation of reality, is apt for the portrayal of our material world. Drama is only a revolt if it moves away from this reality, if it forces people to think differently. I don't want to repeat the pragmatic way of life on stage. From my own political and sociological understanding, I do want to portray the reality of life, and the counter-concept at the same time. This must be possible in theater.

Renate Klett

An Interview with Gerlind Reinshagen

Translated by Angelika Czekay

Renate Klett: At first, I would like to ask you something general. For many years you have been the only woman in Germany who wrote plays and was successful at it. How did it feel to be the only woman within the male domain of contemporary drama? Were you frigntened of that or proud of it?

Gerlind Reinshagen: Well, I was rather frightened. I have always tried to explain why I was doing something, but then I felt that people wouldn't like a woman explaining things to them. Theater itself made me anxious. In Germany, for some reason, it's more difficult than in other places because there is always an expectation of how a play should look instead of a simple curiosity to discover: What is it *she's* doing? I realized that when I read the reviews from other countries, they referred much more to my intentions. In Germany the production of my first play, *Doppelkopf* (*Two-headed*), drew a lot of attention, but my second one, *Leben und Tod der Marilyn Monroe* (*The Life and Death of Marilyn Monroe*), in which I tried to do something different, was immediately attacked. Whereas today, fifteen years later, there are a lot of young directors who say, "I would like to stage this." So, in the beginning I was intimidated. I was not strong enough to say: "I'll do that in an even more radical way." Maybe I should have written a play like *Marilyn Monroe* four or five times until I had a clear idea of the form, like a painter who paints the same motif, maybe twenty times. I did suffer somewhat because people were attacking me with such strange arguments. For instance, if I consciously tried something new, they said, "She doesn't know how to write plays," or they said, "These plays are too epic"—that was a frequent reproach. Or, if I tried to create a certain atmosphere on stage—something that is very important to me—people said, "That's untheatrical; you mustn't do it that way."

RK: Yes, it's a familiar reproach that women are not capable of creating plays properly and that they can't master the construction of suspense, the formal structure, or the construction of meaning on stage. Marieluise Fleißer had to deal with this reproach in her time as well. Instead of this attack, one could ask whether this is really a lack of ability or perhaps just a different image of theater. It's the same as when women playwrights are asked whether they think they could describe a man or how they could possibly understand men's behavior in this or that situation. I assume nobody ever asked Mr. Ibsen if he had enough self-confidence to describe Nora. At the most, women are conceded the ability to create a female character, but with a male character they still have to justify themselves.

GR: Yes, I have had experiences like this. I did produce male characters, and I was asked exactly that question: How could you know this? That, however, was concerning a piece of prose, *Rovinato.* The character is an apprentice. First, I had to remember my own time of apprenticeship; then I thought myself into the character of a man; and then, as you suggest, I immediately had to face this reproach. Could I really do it? Perhaps one has to think more about a male character, throw all men you've ever known into a saucepan and stir. There are also roles that are so far away from reality that they clearly become fantasy characters, like Virginia Woolf's *Orlando.* Maybe it's easier to do it in that way.

* * *

RK: And so, what is it that you want to see in theater?

GR: A building made of language is what I want to see—no, experience. At first, I go into a theater, and the nicer, the easier it is, the better. But then, when it gets dark, I no longer want to experience this coziness, or toilets on stage, but a building made of language. This is difficult to describe. As a theater, perhaps a building of words like the texts of Calderon or Aeschylus or Lorca. This is the kind of theater I'll now try to create, for the first time.

RK: Then why do we still need theater at all? I could just read the text and create the theater in my head.

GR: No, that's different. Now wait a minute—that's a good question; I have to get this clear for myself now. Actually, it's the characters who make this building small or large. The playing out of their conflicts or their similarities. You can't imagine that in your head. And the characters live in a prison or in a castle or in a music hall, which you don't create with walls but only through language. This is actually how it was in Greek theater. There theater was a house made of language. Today it's a house of cardboard and painted clouds and wood, often a very nice house, but only a visual image decorated with language. And visual images you constantly see everywhere—in film, on TV, in magazines. Theater is really the last place where language can actually be experienced; it doesn't matter which language—you can experience curses or poems, but really experience them, with your eyes and ears.

RK: Yes, but an image doesn't necessarily prevent you from experiencing language. Theater is always an image, too, even if there is only one person on an empty stage.

GR: Yes, but the image must be related to language. For instance, when Klaus Michael Grüber did *Lear* at the Schaubühne, it had something of a language house in it. There the image was also very nice but always subordinate to the language. In that performance Grüber dared to do something unusual, and I liked that a lot. Normally, you see the classics, and either they are supposed to educate you, which is awful, or they are like a magazine, or the events are exaggerated and extreme. This *Lear* is totally different. I immediately tried to write a story about this. In *Lear,* the images are only a mirror of what actually happens, images of coldness, power, madness. And it is really exhausting; it isn't customary anymore to concentrate so much on language. Now it's more often sudden changes of mood, outside effects. Or, take Lorca, *As Soon as Five Years Pass By* (Sobald fünf Jahre vergehen). There all the strong images derive from language too. "An ocean in a glass," he writes; isn't that a great image?—and also one that you can only attain through language.

*   *   *

RK: Your last play before *The Female Clown* (*Die Clownin*) was *Ironheart* (*Eisenherz*), right? That seems like a rather big jump from *Ironheart* to *The Female Clown* if you compare language, form, and means.

GR: Yes, on the one hand, that's true, but, on the other hand, it isn't, because in *Ironheart,* you also have this situation of several people in isolation. Only the way in which the story is told is different. In *Ironheart,* I tried to work with fractures, which is rather difficult to show in theater; perhaps the fractures were not strong enough. I always cut off what people were thinking. On the surface, the office life goes its usual way, but suddenly someone says something completely different—also on a different level of language—expresses her thoughts, her image of herself, and then continues on as usual.

*   *   *

RK: Of all the characters you have created, which one is mostly you?

GR: The villains. I always think—as with the Nazi general in *Sunday's Children* or with the bookkeeper, who adapts himself to all situations— how I would act in such a situation. Would I really be good enough for a heroine? Would I really hide a Jew, or would I be too much of a coward? These characters, which you most identify with, are also the most interesting ones.

RK: Let's take *Sunday's Children*. With whom would you identify most?

GR: Well, actually with the girl, with Elsie, because I have seen many things through her eyes, but also with Metzenthin, the apprentice, who betrays somebody else to save the girl. Then also very much with Lona, the servant, who has this desire for freedom. I don't know; I can't really say. Maybe I also identify with the children. But then there is always a person who lives outside of everything—in *Sunday's Children*, that's Tilda, in *Spring Festival* it's Oda—who lives alone but manages to give this situation a positive direction. These are always the people who know much more about life because they have been treated in such a bad way. I know an innumerable number of people like this. Actually, Tilda is the character I like most of all; she is in all my plays, also in *Ironheart*. A person banished from society, who because of this has developed power and a contempt for the world. I would like to write a play about her; I just don't know how yet. That should also be a little bit funny because, unlike the rest of us, she is not afraid to be ridiculous. Really, who dares to be ridiculous? How does Sue-Ellen (in the television show "Dallas") move? One should actually have the freedom to be ridiculous.

RK: Like the "female clown"?

GR: Yes, that's why the result is a female clown. Penthesilea says, "Only this one [Achilles] is of equal birth to me, no other." And something like this would indeed sound ridiculous today because people are thinking in smaller categories. Nevertheless, this pretension to love and exclusivity is everywhere, wherever I look. It is so easy to ironize something like this, and more mendacious. It's the same with suffering. It's so important to live through your phrases of suffering. But today people try to avoid such experiences by running to the psychiatrist and trying to understand everything and being so incredibly clever that they become insufferable. But you go on if you face the situation, if you don't escape it or rationalize it. Actually, these are very old thoughts—Pascal's, Robert Walser's thoughts. However, they are still true; I have learned the same from my own experience. If I look at the state of this world, I don't believe in much anymore, but I believe that you need a critical attitude toward yourself for each personal action simply to go on existing. That's also true for each relationship between people, no matter if it is between men or between women or between women and men or in a friendship. For example, in the romantic period no one doubted that friendship existed. Whereas for us this doesn't exist anymore, if we constantly doubt it, if we constantly see all relationships only in a pragmatic way: "Does it work? Or not?" But in the moment in which you say: "I have a notion of a friendship, of a relationship, and I want to go in this direction, no matter how far I get," at that moment it exists, and that is important.

One should see more than simply that which one can use. But everything that can be a utopia, or a game, has been put aside, also in the theater. Theater as a play of possibilities—that hardly exists anymore. For instance, I would be interested in using a block of apartments in Berlin as a setting for the Phaedra material or a story of incest. Then this would include the great notions that people still have, even when they don't want to believe in them anymore. But today you can only present such a thing in an ironic way. And, actually, this is already a betrayal.

Ginka Steinwachs

APPEARING LAST IN this volume, Ginka Steinwachs represents the post-modern German woman playwright. Her playful attitude toward cultural composition, down to the root forms of the language itself, permeates her text. Impossible to translate literally, her words are playful pun composites of etymological and social allusions which detonate rather than resonate their strictures of vocabulary and grammar. The (re)creation of words is so central to Steinwachs's project that she is in the process of completing her own dictionary. In order to suggest the intertextual play in her text, I have included a few casual footnotes, which suggest her sources. Steinwachs also likes to play with her own name: she refers to herself as G.S., which suggests George Sand and Gertrude Stein; *Stein-wachs* itself means "grown from Stein."

Born in 1942, Steinwachs studied theology, philosophy, and comparative literature in Munich, Berlin, and Paris; then structuralism and poststructuralism with Roland Barthes at the École Normale, where she earned her doctorate in 1971. Steinwachs taught in the university but currently lives solely from her writing and her work as a performance artist. Her performances are well known in the underground circuits in Berlin and Hamburg.

One can feel how such performance work permeates Steinwachs's texts in the free play of images and the open sense of action. Also an excellent violinist, Steinwachs's sense of sound is central to her puns and allusions, rhythm and resonances. In her theoretical writings on dramaturgy, she calls her theater the "theater of the Palate"—the theater as *oral* institution in contrast to *moral* institution (a reference to Schiller's work on "The Stage as a Moral Institution"). Steinwachs performs this dramaturgical notion with a large pair of leather lips, to which she gestures with her hands in white gloves. The performance incorporates the text as text incorporates the body.

The sensual, material sense of language is the base of Steinwachs's word play, as expressed in her "palatheatre":

> This . . . this . . . this
> Shows the very in-essence of my personal poetics: the utopia
> of the fleshy word,
> of the full-bodied word, of the word that seduces you to
> handle and smell and touch it, of the sensual word which has
> a weight and exudes perfume, of the word that enlightens and of the
>   word that lives and delivers emotion.[1]

Steinwachs has published plays, poetry, theory, and prose. Seven of her radio plays have also been produced. *George Sand* was produced in 1988. *George Sand* has been published as a single text, and an anthology of her plays is forthcoming. A new anthology of feminist postmodern criticism, entitled *Ein Mund von Welt: TEXT/S/ORTEN* (A Mouth of World: Text/sGenres/Sites) is dedicated to her work.

George Sand

George Sand is a massive, book-length text. In working with Steinwachs, we decided to cut some of the scenes from the final section in order to make the length more manageable for production and inclusion in this anthology. Also, Steinwachs decided that, for the English translation, she would completely rework the "Homolulu" scene with me, in order to find references in the United States that would make the scene work the way she felt it should for the reader or the audience. Since Steinwachs revels in nonsense words, some of the choices in English were made simply according to the "feel" of cultural usage and sound. Her steep ascensions to high art, avant-garde techniques, and philosophical references—all cut short by deep dives into the ridiculous, or sometimes the simply silly—provide a fragmentary and unusual grammatical structure. Jamie Owen Daniel, Katrin Sieg, and I worked with Steinwachs to find the American equivalent of her text rather than a translation.

On the page *George Sand* is unique in its composition. Perhaps only the later plays of Heiner Müller make a similar use of the written play text. Whole capitalized passages interspersed with regular print and capitalized fragments create the sense of a text set apart, underscored in some way—

what Müller, in his work, has described as the final remains of the chorus. Capitalization creates the sense of voice speaking through, above, or under the text, as the chorus once interpreted, responded to, or contextualized the dramatic dialogue. The reader is prompted to ask what encourages this voice: history, as it moves, or the politico-aesthetic drift of the discourse? The capitalization prints out a sense of the emphatic—the resistance the figure of George Sand sets in motion.

Steinwachs's dialogue is a composite of poetry, prose, essayistic fragments, loose thoughts, historical details, rhetorical tropes, polemical assertions, and sometimes even a fragment of traditional dialogue between characters. Her scenic descriptions defy production. They are not calculated to set the stage but, rather, to work on the level of metaphor and image, requiring that the production team interpret, fantasize, and cocreate an environment suitable for such philosophical ruminations, feminist dares, sexual transgressions, flights of fancy, promiscuous characterizations of canonical authors, gender jokes, and banal expressions of the heart. Lois Weaver, Peggy Shaw, the Five Lesbian Brothers, and two members of Bloo Lips produced a staged reading of "Monsieur / Madame," Steinwachs's fragment of *George Sand,* at La Mama in New York. (The reading took place on 23 September 1991 and was sponsored by the Goethe House New York.) This experiment did not attempt to "act out" the text, but, rather, to produce a local version of it. Adding such pop, American texts as "Hey There, Georgie Girl," the production situated a Eurocentric text in the Lower East Side of New York. In a panel discussion the following day, Steinwachs said this was exactly the kind of performance her texts require. Peggy Phelan called it "the bliss of mistranslation."

George Sand does not present the character on whom its title is based but becomes, as a whole text, an icon configured as George Sand. Within the German feminist context, she marks an early hero of the social movement. A colossus of bigender, bisexual practice, she stands—as in G(E)ORGE VON FONTAINEBLEAU—astride the chasmic binary of dominant practice, one foot on each side. George is the woman who must earn her keep in cultural production, laboring, unlike the patriarchal, class-privileged dandies in the elegant men's salon; yet not laboring like Flaubert, the engineer of the puffing loco-motive of mimesis. In this play, art as imitation is abandoned early on, as the drunken artist staggers unevenly up the stairs to illuminate the frozen statues in his atelier.

Primarily, George writes; she is the woman who writes. She writes while historical and political forces twitter in the trees, looking for bread crumbs along the Rue de Revolution. She is written by Steinwachs, as her lesbian desire blooms in a hothouse, metonymically proliferating along wet, slipping wordplays of seduction, while the CONCEITED LADIES OF GOOD SO-CIETY fan themselves. The writing does what it can do as it moves through narrative assignments, showing off and rebelling, resisting the tradition of dramatic movement. After the hothouse of word-wachs, the super-8 zoom-in transmogrifies this synthesis of the social into the lyrical kernel of lesbian feminist activism: The quadrille of waiters from the Anita Bryant chapter of the Moral Majority rush in to provide aid, while George and Marie, moving through the moon phase of subject/object exchange (that is, into the utopia of intersubjectivity) pass over into EMPHATIC FLIGHT. Retaining the context of social, political, and historical forces, Steinwachs flips the narrative into the high gear of *l'écriture feminine* to take off into a flight from the dominant—emphatically exiting. Steinwachs does not stop this George Sand icon here, however, but proceeds on into the far-flung net of the legal system, on the one hand, and the French Revolution, on the other.

Steinwachs's synthetic achievement here is stunning. In an imaginative, playful, yet political textual practice, she has brought together psychoanalytic structures of desire and discourse contradicted by, but still overcoming, dominant repressive practices; historically specific class and gender politics at work in a woman's creative imagination; and the portrait of a woman caught in the contradictions of cultural production. On the formal level, Steinwachs employs a theatrical use of film technique, which also becomes a structure of meaning; late twentieth-century forms of performance, in which the performance itself may run along with the text but is not mimetically bound to it; and a semiotic approach to characterization. Sand is a *sign* in signifying matrices: her own imaginary one, her position in the dominant one, and Steinwachs's own. Sand is not a "self" in the old sense of the word, nor even a stable referent. Sand, like sand, runs through the fissures of text and performance, is fleetingly perceived in the net of the structures of meaning, and escapes in emphatic flight, only to run out into the channels of the law. She is the poor woman and the rich woman—a woman oppressed by society and liberated by revolution. Sand, the dynamic sign, is signified by her movement and her resistance at once. Steinwachs's text is a wordmap of textual/sexual/political experience.

NOTE

1. Ginka Steinwachs, "Das Gaumentheater des Mundes," in *Die Schwarze Botin* 21 (Berlin, 1983), 131–33. Translation by Katrin Sieg in "Women in Theatre: German Women Playwrights on Theatre" (Goethe House, New York, 1991, photocopy).

Ginka Steinwachs

The Twentieth Century Vox Female Voice Presents

George Sand

Archaeology of Female Consciousness:
Oral Theatre Overcomes with Fantasy
the Anorexia of Not Enough

Translated by Jamie Owen Daniel and Katrin Sieg, with Sue-Ellen Case.

I.
a woman in motion

Characters

GEORGE SAND, née AMANDINE-AURORE-LUCILE DUPIN; married name, THE BARONESS DUDEVANT, world-renowned author
CASIMIR BARON DUDEVANT, her husband

Photomontage from the Bad Godesberg production of *George Sand*, directed by Ina-Katrin Korff. (Photo by Stefan Ordy.)

ALEXANDRE MANCEAU, sculptor, her lover

JULES SANDEAU, provincial author, her lover

MARIE DORVAL, actress from the Comédie, her lover

ALFRED DE MUSSET, oral Parnassian, her lover

HONORE DE BALZAC, sensual writer of prose from the Comédie Française, here stoker of the fires of French literature, her lover in the realm of possibility

GUSTAVE FLAUBERT, silver syllablewright from the Schools, here locomotive engineer, her lover in the realm of necessity

MANAGER and SALES CLERK at the Handsome Horseman

EUGENE DUC DE GRANDLIEU and COMTE SIXTE DE CHATELET, characters from BALZAC

NEIGHBORING TABLE OF MEN—Also one of WOMEN QUADRILLE of the WAITERS in HOTHOUSE DE LA PAIX

ARISTOCRATIC TOMCATS and PROLETARIAN PUSSIES

*   *   *

I

ATELIER OF THE WALTZ DREAMS

SCULPTOR'S STUDIO IN PARIS IN THE VICINITY OF THE PLACE DE L'OPÉRA.

THE STUDIO IS HIGH ABOVE GROUND, AS IF FASTENED TO THE GRAY PARISIAN WINTER SKY.

IT IS NIGHT.

ALEXANDRE MANCEAU, AT THIRTY-FIVE THE YOUNGEST AND LAST LOVER, RANKED IN THIRTY-FOURTH PLACE IN THE SERIES OF PRETENDERS TO THE FAVORS OF THE ADORED AMANDINE AURORE LUCILE DUPIN, ALIAS GEORGE SAND, DRUNKENLY STRUGGLES UP THE SIX FLOORS OF THE APARTMENT HOUSE ON A VERTIGINOUS SPIRAL STAIRCASE.

UPWARDS. FROM THE DEPTHS OF THE WINECELLAR TO THE HEIGHTS OF THE SCULPTOR'S WORKSHOP. HEAVY-LEGGED, HE STRUGGLES UP THE STAIRS, LIGHT-HEADED HE HUMS A MUSETTE-LIKE TUNE. IT WAS COMPOSED BY FRYC SOPIN, KNOWN TO THE PUBLIC AS FREDERIC CHOPIN.

WALTZ MUSIC:

THIS IS STILL THE GOLDEN AGE,
THESE ARE STILL THE ROSE-FILLED DAYS.[1]
MANCEAU CLIMBS AND CLIMBS. HEAT PROVOKES HIM TO TEAR
THE TOPCOAT FROM HIS BODY. THERE SHE IS, SEEMINGLY
WITHIN REACH. CRAVING. PURE VOLUPTUOUS EXCESS.
MAN IS A PLEASURE MACHINE THAT INCESSANTLY DESIRES DE-
SIRE.[2] SIGMUND FREUD INTERPRETS THE BREATHLESS DREAM-
IMAGE AS FOLLOWS:
SEXUAL INTERCOURSE ON THE RISE.
FRUSTRATION. THE KEYHOLE OF THE DOOR. IS THE KEY IRREG-
ULAR? THE IRON STAIRCASE. THERE: A PRESSURE. IMPRESSION.
MANCEAU HAS FALLEN INTO THE STUDIO ALONG WITH THE
DOOR. WALTZ FOAM FROM A SCHMALTZY SPRAY OF NOTES. IN
THE STUDIO, CONTEMPORARY SOCIETY CONGREGATES IN
STONE. THE PROMINENT LADIES AND GENTLEMEN OCCUPY AN
ILLUSTRIOUS POSITION IN THE WAX MUSEUM.
SILENCE.
MANCEAU'S CREATIONS BARELY OPEN THEIR MOUTHS BEFORE
THE THEATER WORLD OF THE WORLD THEATER SHRINKS
DOWN TO THE SPHERE OF THE THEATER OF THE PALATE.
THE CREAM. THE SOURED CREAM SOCIETY'S FROTH FLAT. POPS
OF CHAMPAGNE CORKS.
MANCEAU DECAPITATES A BOTTLE OF VEUVE CLIQUOT. TAKES A
DEEP SWIG. PITCH-BLACK IN THE FOREST OF STATUES. HE
RUSHES BLINDLY TO THE LONELY ONES. THE MARBLE ALONE
WEIGHS A TON. WHOEVER CAN MERELY ASCEND THIS CO-
LOSSUS HAS ALREADY WON A BATTLE.
SIGMUND FREUD CHEERFULLY INTERPRETS THE DREAM-IMAGE:
SEXUAL INTERCOURSE ON THE RISE.
WALTZ MUSIC:
THIS IS STILL THE GOLDEN AGE,
THESE ARE STILL THE ROSE-FILLED DAYS.

*   *   *

ATELIER OF WALTZ DREAMS

CHOPIN WALTZES.
the curtain rises.

---

1. The lines are from a poem by Johann Ludwig Uhland.
2. The reference is to Gilles Deleuze and Felix Guattari, *The Anti-Oedipus*.

the stage is dark.
a sound like someone climbing stairs in the wings.
lyrical men's voices:
   I CLIMB THE SPIRAL STAIRWAY
   SIX STORIES OF EXERTION.
   SO STEEP, THE WAY I TAKE THEM,
   WITHOUT CURVE OR DIGRESSION.
creaking stairs. gasping for breath.
a long period of time passes with only musical accompaniment.
someone unsteadily strikes a match. LLUBIMOV-effect.
manceau enters:
   LET THERE BE LIGHT—
holds the champagne bottle he carried under his arm into light:
   AND THERE WAS LIGHT.
takes a drink, losing the key in the process:
   idiot.
attempts to pick up the key:
attempts to fit it into the keyhole:
   come on then.
turns it the wrong way:
   no monkey business.
one more time: wait a minute, if i first nimbly turn you—
seizing it: with both hands,
thinks: by the beard of the prophet
acts: take hold.
lets himself drop exhausted, strikes a match:
   I prophesy MONSIEUR ALEXANDRE MANCEAU, the 34th, ranked
   youngest and last lover, in the series of pretenders to the adored
   AMANTINE AURORE LUCILE DUPIN, alias GEORGE SAND, during
   the night of his 35th birthday—
gathers strength for a superhuman effort:
   Let's do it, darling.
throws himself against the door, the door breaks:
manceau: the great breakthrough.
strikes a match. light falls upon the statues:
   riffraff.
dances, the bottle embraced as his partner, from one statue to the next: ha,
upsurge of a spray of waltz notes.
distributes wax lamps among the statues, lights them:
   the cream, the soured cream of society.

I illuminate the LIGHT OF POETIC DELIGHT.
gallantly, with a bow toward his creations:
   MESDAMES, MESSIEURS, I have the honor of illuminating the greatest
   minds of our century. whoever has played a role in it I hew out of
   STONE(STEIN) or carve out of WAX(WACHS).
raises the bottle up against a woman's breast, titters:
   lululul, here's to you, most honored, noble MADAME D'AGOULT: how
   did you find such a fine feather hat dressed so uniquely with a feathered
   swan's neck. FEMME FATALE. not a PARISIAN of metropolitan blood, who
   doesn't begrudge the
   austro-hungarian parvenu his treasure. LISZT is who it is.
   FRANZ is the scoundrel's name.
passes his hand over his mouth, spins around:
   lalalal, there she burns, all aglow, the beautiful MADAME DORVAL.
   MARIE DORVAL from the COMEDIE HUMAINE, ah, pardon, FRAN-
   ÇAISE is in flames. BONJOUR TRISTESSE. MONSIEUR ALFRED DE
   VIGNY, poet, obligingly extends to her his arm. the high-born cavalier,
   the hot-blooded beast. ARISTOMCAT, PROLETPUSSY. lips hearts, oral
   craving, pure voluptuous excess. man as a pleasure machine that incessantly desires desire: an animal.
waltzes: THIS IS STILL THE BEAUTIFUL GOLDEN AGE,
   THESE ARE STILL THE ROSE-FILLED DAYS.
has hurt himself: tell me, you my charming creations, who was it that
   chose to credit me on the open stage as the master of sculpture?
manceau: the treacherous buffoon, the wretched fungus, the slimy snail,
   the repulsive one, the demon, who will suffer the juicy wad of rage in
   my belly.
makes a lunge toward the unlit section of the stage: briefly:
   i advance on my opponent with the blade of my bottle of VEUVE
   CLIQUOT.
very loud: make way. make way for the stonemason.
strikes out wildly around him: shadowboxing. land a blow.
snickers: gloom, gloom, on this dim side of the stage, there rustles the
   broom.
advances further: ha. i smell the stinking filth of the gentlemen colleagues
   of the sinecure of the most peaceful of all civil servants of the certified
   corporeal lovers of GEORGE SAND—
courageously: take the champagne bottle, MANCEAU. grasp the dagger.
   so. EN AVANT EN AVANT. and who do we have here? our rival,

CASIMIR DUDEVANT. we already know his empty stare. the blue-blooded ZERO is no more than a BARON. noble scion. mount your steed. how YOUR EXCELLENCY bares his teeth, protecting his own. this fine gentleman with the illustrious name aspires—

makes the sign of the cross three times: IN NOMINE PATRI ET FILII ET SPIRITI SANCTI after la dolce vita. AMEN. but I will turn the tables and turn it around—

presses the bottom of the champagne bottle, against the stone until it tips over, as if he were to uncork it: wumm. voluptuous pure excess. would that we had it here.

drinks: ah, man is a pleasure machine, that incessantly desires desire: an animal.

waltz: THIS IS STILL THE GOLDEN AGE,
THESE ARE STILL THE ROSE-FILLED DAYS.

lights a candle in the hand of DUDEVANT's neighboring statue: YOUR GRACE, if you will permit me, your neighbor: sensually smurfing MOUSSAILLON the FIRST. HIS MAJESTY THE SNOB shows only contempt for the MOB. valued MONSIEUR MUSSET, have the honor of the silver tabatière.

manceau has the statue of the PRINCE OF POETS give him a light with the words: ODI PROFANUM VULGUS ET ARCEO.

he rotates the statue in such a way that its gaze is directed toward the gigantic yet-unfinished memorial to the UNCHAINED TITAN: GEORGE SAND. manceau, who is blowing clouds of cigar smoke, has her recite:

TE VOILA REVENUE,
DANS MES NUITS ETOILEES,
BEL ANGE AUX YEUX D'AZUR,
AUX PAUPIERES VOILEES,
AMOUR, MON BIEN SUPREME,
QUE J'AVAIS PERDU.

YOU RETURN TO ME
IN THE STARRY NIGHTS,
BEAUTIFUL ANGEL WITH
VEILED LIDS,
LOVE, MY CHERISHED PRIZE
WHOM I HAD LOST.

manceau: ha, how in this poem, muse and MUSSET are interwoven and face to face. more greedy for triumph than for mercy, I place the ORAL

PARNASSIAN before the tribunal. the son of the muses will be buried with his face to the wall

gestures: and finished off in no time. your poet-latin is out, your shining lightlet is doused. off with you. who do we have here, then?

dances: one two three, five six seven, the MUSETTE was written by CHO-PIN. MONSIEUR FRYC, pregnant with tuberculosis, playing brilliantly on the lobes of his lungs. HIFI. dear lord in heaven stand by me, he's vomiting blood. whooping cough wracks him. I'll leave him be, the least breeze can blow him over.

giggles: at night in a boat, only hand-colored coloratura twitter machines are awake.

more solemnly: who or what is forming before my creative eyes? the avenue of statues. POET-PRINCES fidget along the roof ridges. UTOPIANS brush the spruces. headway is being made in the direction of SOCIAL REFORM. a signpost points the way toward NOHANT in the blue distance.

bowing and scraping: BONJOUR MONSIEUR, BONJOUR FLAUBERT. you, the very image of a blond NORMAN with a Flaubert photo beard, whose triply enveloped intellect simply didn't find its feminine counterpart here below. your torment true to life—so much so, it made of the world a vale of woe.

manceau: your work, on the other hand, will penetrate into even the most distant future on the strength of its golden pinions. a winged bicycle, with a silver syllable-wright friction. in general FLAUBERT has transformed the PEGASUS of antiquity into the iron horse of locomotion.

hisses in imitation of one: i in any case see him daringly driving THE 19th CENTURY OPERA-EXPRESS OF ART. literary hubbub. special outing. other poets have come along from the party. BALZAC stokes the engine with coal. STENDHAL tosses his autographs. fans throng around him. HUGO, wearing the vestments of the NATIONAL RAILROAD SOCIETY, takes the tickets. how sentimentally bovaryesque FLAUBERT is as he stays on the same track / in the same rut.

his IDEES RECUES seduce. the smokestack puffs away.

in the tone of an announcer: NORMANDIE PARIS / ICI PARIS, PARIS / BERRY PARIS. this FANFAN LA TULIPE has a tempo to it.

GEORGE SAND takes a go—

climbs up the G.-S. statue:

and springs onto it.

lyrical male voices:

I CLIMB THE STATUE
OVER THREE OF THE BODY'S MEMBERS.
SO STEEP, THE WAY I TAKE THEM,
WITHOUT CURVE OR DIGRESSION.
caresses the cold stone with his hot hand:
 a garden of lusts: breasts.
  here, in this place, I could still sculpt away a grain of sand. lakes, from
   which milk and honey flow. pitchers, that pour out white and red
   wine. beneath these: finely tuned, the clavichord of the ribs. SOPIN
   wrote his ETUDE FOR BLACK keys for it.
  his hand caresses farther down:
   beneath this, the equatorial belt line. whirling zinging pearls without
   end. the whiteness of the loins would blind the blind. hammer chisels
   shame, charm, swarm; swam over it.
deeper: the clitoral comb, taken by vaginal well.
watercourse in moss-covered ground. say, you experts, doesn't this stream
lead directly to the heavenly and multiple sex of women?
manceau's hand caresses further down:
 beneath this, thighs pressed: the columns of HERCULES.
further down: beneath these, calves, myriads of cells.
further down: beneath the ankle a proper wankel a proper root:
 the bare foot.
sobers himself up, arrives at the foot of the stage with a bottle of bubbly:
 no foolishness now.
grabs his tools, gets started:
 let's do it, darling.
WALTZ MUSIC:
 THIS IS STILL THE GOLDEN AGE,
 THESE ARE STILL THE ROSE-FILLED DAYS.

                                    II
            MY HORSE FOR A PAIR OF PANTS, SAYS THE
           HERMAPHRODITE CHILD OF SUN AND MOON

KLALAP. KLALALAP. MOVEMENT. A REAL WOMAN SPRINGS ONTO
 A HORSE OVER THE CHAMPS-ELYSÉES LEAVING THE GRAND
 AND PETIT PALACES AT SOME DISTANCE BEHIND. EASTER TIME.
 OUTING TIME. DRESSED UP TO GO OUT. MALE PASSERSBY, WHO

CHEW BRITISH TOBACCO, CURSE. FEMALE PASSERSBY, IN WIDE
STARCHED SKIRTS, DISPLAY THEIR CONCERN. ELECTRIC SPARKS
ILLUMINATE CROCUSES ON COBBLED PAVEMENT. HOOVES CLAT-
TER, FIRST NEARBY AND THEN FAR AWAY. THE REAL WOMAN
DETONATES THE ARC DE TRIOMPHE FROM WITHIN. AN OUT-
SIDER, TRULY UP ON A HIGH HORSE.

MALE PASSERSBY GET ON WITH THEIR DAILY AGENDAS AND RE-
LIGHT THEIR PROMENADE-CIGARS WHICH HAVE GONE OUT IN
THE INTERIM. FEMALE PASSERSBY HOP HIGH EXHAUSTEDLY/
EXCITEDLY FROM HIGH HEELS TO HIGHER ONES.

KLALAP. KLALAP. COMMOTION.

SOMETHING LIKE DISTANCED, FARAWAY MEMORY OF PREHISTOR-
IC TIMES: AMAZONS WHO'VE AMPUTATED ONE OF THEIR
BREASTS. GEORGE SAND HAS GROWN UP AROUND HORSES.
SHE COMES AND GOES ON HORSEBACK, ALWAYS AND EVERY-
WHERE ON HER HIGH HORSE.

THE TEMPO THAT IS SET BY THIS FANFAN LA TULIPE IS DICTATED
BY HER TEMPERAMENT. IN THE FORM OF A HORSESHOE IT FOR-
TUNATELY RUPTURES THE IDYLLIC QUALITY OF THE SCENE.
ALBUM PAGES FROM THE NINETEENTH CENTURY ARE DISAR-
RANGED ALCHEMICALLY ALONG THE THIRD SEX. THE HER-
MAPHRODITE CHILD OF THE SUN AND MOON SPELLS.
STEINWACHS SEEKS THE ABC'S OF THE EIN(STEIN) STONE. THIS
RESULTS IN A NOTICEABLE ALTERATION OF THE SEXUAL LAND-
SCAPE. TROUSERS VERSUS SKIRTS. A MAN'S ARROW FOR THE
WOMAN'S MIRROR. THE TRANSVESTITE, THE TRANSSEXUAL,
THE NEUTER OFFERS HIS / HER HORSE FOR A PAIR OF TROUSERS.
ISN'T THAT AN OFFER?

                    *   *   *

THE HANDSOME HORSEMAN

circus equestrian music:
     the highest form of happiness on earth, of course,
     is to be found on the back of a horse.
through the transparent door above the carpet-laden front entrance,
GEORGE SAND as an AMAZON from the great upper-class world enters

the secret world of male vanity, male luxury, and goal-directed thought. she leads her black stallion indolently by the reins. no clattering of hooves. her boots don't make a sound. only the feather in her hat moves rhythmically up and down.

manager: BONJOUR MADAME—

gives his salesclerk a wink: take the reins of the charming lady's horse—will you allow me, my lady?

guides her to the post: out of my hand

george hums:

> the morning sky bluing
> the morning dew falling
> four hooves beating,
> the day is breaking.

salesclerk, aside: curious, highly curious. a lady. a lady customer in THE HANDSOME HORSEMAN MEN'S TAILOR SHOP.

laughs: the beautiful horsewoman, member of the heavily endowed JOCKEY CLUB, to this AMAZON we lost a champion in our national horse racing competitions.

george: i won't allow this.

manager severely: Madame Baron? what request might i do you the honor of—

salesclerk, prompting: reading your lips?

george, monosyllabically: MY HORSE FOR A PAIR OF PANTS.

manager, ostentatiously: a pair of trousers made of nipponese silk for your husband, a pair made of chinese velour for your lawful spouse, a pair made of taffeta for the better half of ya?

salesclerk: we tailor everything in the materials and the design as it is preferentially worn at the courts of ST. PETERSBURG, LONDON, POTSDAM.

salesclerk: including striking outfits with brocade pockets, with chenille tassels . . .

george: a misunderstanding. the pair of trousers i require is not for CASIMIR BARON DUDEVANT, but for myself.

manager, insulted: we don't make trousers for women.

george: my horse for a pair of pants.

salesclerk, aside: you can't get any more monosyllabic than that.

manager: but, but, we now live in a world which has been perfectly tailored to the needs of men, whose privileges no one can touch.

george lets her riding crop whistle through the air, so that it cracks: I AM
THIS NO ONE,[3] i require them immediately—
hits upon the servile nature of both men:
gitty up, walk, trot, high trot, gallop.
manager and salesclerk get in step.
george: a pair of trousers that are tough, without pockets—the riding crop
whistles down. manager at a high trot, salesclerk at a gallop to the
storeroom.
george: with which i will be able to traverse the path i have mapped out
into the SOMEONE'S LAND OF MEN.
circus equestrian music:
the highest form of happiness on earth, of course,
is to be found on the back of a horse.

SUPER 8 FADE-IN: THE ELECTRIC HORSEWOMAN

DOUCE FRANCE. a herd of wild horses races through a thicket toward
the camera. GEORGE SAND as a young child lies in wait for a horse,
springs as teenager running headlong through the woods, and chooses
as a grown woman to run the obstacle race from the province of BERRY
to the national capital of PARIS. the AMAZON is brightly lit. saddle
and reins of her black stallion are decorated with light bulbs. her riding
costume itself is electrified. a pressure, impression: and there was light.
GEORGE SAND leaves the dark provinces behind her. before her lie the
suburbs of the capital. accordion music and the music of the spheres.
heaven's awning rolls out like a great dance floor, upon which the stars
dance to the hit parade. the AMAZON accelerates. this FANFAN LA
TULIPE sets the tempo. raging, she enters the sleeping city through the
PORTE D'ORLEANS. GEORGE SAND slows her gallop to a trot.
she looks around. what a stage set. in these buildings people live, love,
sow their wild oats. pleasure is earned. debts to the creditor paid on the
installment plan. She stops her entrance: here is where i want to live,
become a human being.
george: ah, the BOUL'MICH, the PONT SAINT MICHEL, THE SEINE,
experienced as i rode past them. the majestic crowns of the trees along
the banks of the SEINE offer shelter to the republic of the sparrows. oh,

---

3. The line is from Gotthold Ephraim Lessing's polemical *Briefe, die neueste
Literatur betreffend*, this one dated 16 February 1759.

to have SAINTE CHAPELLE, the PALACE OF JUSTICE, and the CON-
CIERGERIE at one's back. the renaissance clock with the inscription,
FLUCTUAT NEC MERGITUR guarantees my safety. in this space, the
drama of ST. JOAN played itself out: another HERMAPHRODITE
CHILD OF SUN AND MOON from the provinces. suffering creature.
her suffering was my body. how often have i sensed her historical warring
on horseback in the shadows of my beloved NOIRE VALLEY.

brrr, walk: now things are getting serious. The IMPRIMERIE NATIONALE,
the press quarter. the smell of printer's ink is oppressive on the rooftops.
imPRium of the JOURNAL MANDARINS AND PRESS CZARS, con-
sultors, controllers, coachers. how slimy it is here. water sprays. my black
horse wades up to the crupper in slimeballs. brokers. the mudclub of
crocodiles.

ZOOM IN ON THE BOOM:

a giant crocodile arises from the waters of the NILE. another one, then
many. the animals lie motionless on the surface of the water like pieces
of wood. only where they breathe do bubbles form and then burst. they
breathe impurely. foul water is made more foul. horny-grainy upper
snouts open, grainy-horny lower snouts close. the crocodiles act as if they
were in the training ring. it SNAPAPS. afterwards they close their vaulted
eyes deliberately and allow themselves to comfortably-sleepily drift back
into the mud.

george: the human being carries CROCODILE in his entrails;
the HORSE at the height of his chest.
the measure of man is cerebral output. unaware of
CROCODILE and HORSE.

eavesdrops: the hubbub of literature on the stock exchange of the art market.

snatches: golden rain: dollars, rubles. brr, brr. here, where value and lack
of value are represented as currency, i want to perform my COMBAT
TRAINING on probation in the affairs of printer's ink.

ZOOM IN ON THE BOOM:

a karate course for women. split britches. WOW.
one woman jumps. two other women hold a burning brick. eee-yah!
the burnt brick explodes.
the woman gently performs a roll. burnt clay crumbles, sand trickles.
SPIDERWOMAN. a long period of time passes with musical
accompaniment.
BLACKOUT.

* * *

Meanwhile, back at THE HANDSOME HORSEMAN, esq.
manager and salesclerk hurry, dusty, out of the storeroom.

here: our smallest pattern.
salesclerk: a pair of pants fit for a twelfth-grade schoolboy. snapap.
manager: your trousers, most valued and dear lady.
george, aside: in order to be a WOMAN in a manner appropriate to my
    class in PARIS, one needs an income of 30,000 francs annually. i re-
    peat: 30,000 annually. after my separation from house and home, i'll
    have scarcely 4,000. i repeat, 4,000 francs annually, and there will be
    the fees for the soup kitchen, tuition for MAURICE and the obligatory
    music lessons for SOLANGE. everything depends on me. if i'm as diligent
    as possible, a completely insidious hope: to be able to live by my own
    writing. question: how do i trade upon my misery with my contem-
    poraries? answer: eee-ya! George Sand, the 19th-century (female) fox
    proudly presents the fashion of women's trousers on economic grounds.
    split britches. i am merely poor and in no way impudent.
grabs her trousers: MY HORSE FOR THIS PAIR OF PANTS.
leaves the horse as deposit against her debt, hurries off, in the doorway of
    the transparent door collides with two famous BALZAC characters, whose
    conversation remains aristocratic skirmishing. EUGENE DUC DE
    GRANDLIEU, BEAU OF GRACIOUSNESS, enters on the arm of SIXTE
    COMTE DE CHATELET, who is known throughout the city as a pederast.
eugene: the cavalry, SIXTE. dear lady, i herewith seek your pardon on my
    knees.
sixte: the ALPINE, parcours, EUGENE. MADAME, i ask emphatical-
    ly: forgive the FAUX-PAS that has occurred.
george as she leaves the stage: the SOMEONE's LAND of men—simply
    ridiculous.
circus equestrian music:
    the highest form of happiness on earth, of course,
    is to be found on the back of a horse.
once inside the two famous BALZAC figures collide against the obstacle of
    the black horse which, as a result of the equestrian incapacities of the
    management, is still in the way.
eugene: the cavalier assault, COUNT.
sixte: the ALPINE obstacle course, DUKE.

eugene, melancholically:
THE ALP-ES, THE ELDERS,
THE OL-PES, THE OLDERS.[4]
sixte, maniacally: etcetera, etceteratata.
eugene leads the black horse into the background:
the BODYGUARD of his majesty NAPOLEON III.
sixte: don't encroach upon me.
eugene: first the DUKE, then the COUNT—a question of military ranking.
sixte: the old world of the PATRIARCHY is still unscathed: as it should be.
manager, dust-free: the cherished, the most cherished pleasure.
both men at once: we favor british fabrics. please guide us to the suits.
salesclerk leads the gentlemen to the sales table.
manager empties out the contents of a glass wardrobe. the management seems to have concerned itself with the sartorial well-being of its well-to-do customers to the point of breaking into a sweat. these customers are critical. they compare cuts, check materials. time passes with musical accompaniment.
finally:
eugene: i could accustom myself to the cream-colored silk suit.
sixte: i would like to acquire the velvet suit with silk lining.
manager, belly-laughing, opens two cubicles:
would HIS HIGHNESS and YOUR EXCELLENCY snapapa please—
salesclerk, prompts: like to try them on?
eugene bare to the waist before the curtain:
apropos, COUNT, what is your opinion of the gowns of the society women, how their colors flamed before us yesterday in the powder room of the FOYER OF THE PALAIS GARNIER OF THE PARIS OPERA?
sixte with hairy legs:
oh, DUKE, under the venetian chandelier, the ruby necklace of our friend DE MAUFRIGNEUSE burned blood-red.
eugene, with bare legs:
ah, in the light of the oriental candelabra, the white lynx DES ESPARD wore waxed as if in a fairy tale—none, however, i ask you, none more simply extravagant.
sixte, bare to the waist: ah, in the corridors, where the CABINET OF THE MINISTERS bow and scrape, DES TOUCHE

---

4. The reference is to Mayröcker/Jandl, from their record: "Gott schütze Österreich."

danced, her shimmering moon dress preceding her.
eugene passionately checks the feel of the silk against his skin:
    SIXTE.
    SIXTE?
    SIXTE! have you ever calculated the exact difference, i mean the enormous
    difference between a nappa glove and a nappapa glove?
sixte, all in velvet, shakes his head distractedly.
eugene, flustered: the difference ... between them ... is ...
sixte: i understand: nappa and nappapa gloves.
whinnying with laughter. the cash register rings.
manager and salesclerk join in bright golden laughter.

* * *

iii

G(E)ORGE OF FOUNTAINEBLEAU

KLIP KLAP. IN THE SPRING FOREST IN THE DOMAIN OF FON-
    TAINEBLEAU, A WOMAN IN MOTION WHO IS REALLY WEARING
    TROUSERS LEAPS OVER AN ABYSS, THAT OF THE GORGE, AND
    IN THE PROCESS ALTERNATES BETWEEN HER SUPPORTING LEG
    AND HER FREE LEG. RIGHT-LEFT-LEFT-RIGHT. THE ROSY-FIN-
    GERED THREATENS TO DAWN. AURORA, THE SUN RISES.
RIGHT LEG: THE INSTITUTION OF MARRIAGE (THE MARRI-ARCHY)
    BY EXTENSION THE CHURCH, THE MILITARY, AND THE
    FATHERLAND.
LEFT LEG: SO-CALLED FREE LOVE (AMOUR-ARCHY) BY EXTENSION
    ANARCHY, DEBAUCHERY, AND EXCESS.
RIGHT LEG: TRADITION IN THE SENSE OF ALWAYS ALREADY.
LEFT LEG: UTOPIA IN THE SENSE OF NO PLACE ON EARTH.[5]
RIGHT: THE ETERNAL-FEMININE-OF-YESTERYEAR OF ONE'S OWN
    SEX.
LEFT: THE NOVUM OF THE RISK OF BREAKING ONE'S NECK.
AURORA WITH LEGS SPREAD OUT OVER THE ABYSS OF THE
    GORGE, WHICH CAUSES HER VAGINAL LIPS TO OPEN. THE SUN

---

5. *No Place on Earth* is the English title of Christa Wolf's 1979 novel, *Kein Ort.
Nirgends.*

IS SHINING WARM FROM THE SKY. BENEATH HER THE HOLLOW GAPES.

AURORA, BESIDE HERSELF FROM ALL THE JUMPING BACK AND FORTH, CAN'T GO ON.

SHE TAKES A DEEP BREATH. THERE'S SOMETHING IN THE AIR. MONSIEUR/MADAME IS IN THE AIR. A WOMAN, WHO WITH ONE STEP BIDS ADIEU TO THE ANCIEN REGIME OF THE INSTITUTION OF MARRIAGE—SHE HAS IT IN HER LEGS—A MAN, IN WHOM GERMINATES THE LONGING FOR CHANGE IN THE RELATIONSHIP BETWEEN THE SEXES GERMINATES INTO SO-CALLED HUMAN RELATIONSHIPS.

WOMAN IS EARTH, MAN WIND, PEOPLE SAY.
LET THEM SAY IT. THERE SHE BLOWS.
THAT'S THE WAY.

* * *

G(E)ORGE OF FONTAINEBLEAU

the sun shines upon a stream. it flows into a meadow. this gives way to a pine nursery. this opens out into a rocky ledge with hollows and crevasses. crickets chirp. birds twitter.

GEORGE stands upon the rocky ledge. each leg comes to rest on another part of the crevasse.

GEORGE, while alternating back and forth between supporting leg and free leg:

a LIFELONG question as to whom i should now turn. HUSBAND LOVER LOVER HUSBAND CASIMIR JULES JULES CASIMIR.

remains standing on her supporting leg, balancing:

right. i only feel at home in NOHANT the family seat. i like the crackling fire on the open hearth, tropical fruits in the orangerie, my horses in the stable, the poor sparrow i found half-frozen and raised in the pigeon house, the four-poster in the room of my grandmother, MADAME DE FANCEUIL, in which i will die; and the journeys to the south with CASIMIR and the children and the great social events we host during the ball season; the appearance of half of the province in vibrant ball clothes on the parquet and the farmers and servants in the vestibule. i have need of the vegetable garden, use the park and grove. but if i may

speak frankly with you: i'd rather be alone, alone. CASIMIR has become
louder through the years of our marriage. he drinks brandy, yells in the
stable like a stable boy and clings to the servant girls like bad luck.
changes over to the free leg, which thus becomes the supporting leg:
   left: it will bring good luck. has good luck chosen me? in any case, i
   move away from the family seat during the winter. seven months here,
   five months there. i can't do it any other way. i have to write. where is
   my desk? miles away from sweet homey BERRY in an attic, with barely
   any light. walls, floors and ceilings, all close together. no suites, no
   flights of stairs. chandeliers and candelabra are lacking, as well as niches,
   and so i live and work right next to JULES SANDEAU, a journalist by
   profession. we speak PATOIS, his family is said to stem from LA CHATRE.
   our pinkish white ardor. we have no other choice and write about our
   lives for tomorrow's success. we travel in the right circles, frequent our
   colleagues who enjoy large circulations, and yet: we struggle to get by
   from day to day.
maurice, both hands full, a ball of string in one and a paper kite in the
   other, which he wants to let fly, runs from right to left across the meadow,
   exits.
george in thought:
   to the right the abyss of the other, to the left that of one's own sex.
solange, a butterfly net in one hand and a white parasol in the other, stalks
   from left to right across through the new foliage.
male voices:
   how nice, how nice
   a mountain minus ice
CASIMIR, BARON DUDEVANT, FEUDAL LANDOWNER, and JULES
   SANDEAU, JOURNALIST, each without the knowledge of the other or
   that of GEORGE, attempt to climb the GORGE. they are splendidly
   equipped like mountain climbers. CASIMIR, pathetically:

LES VOILA, CES SAPINS A LA SOMBRE VERDURE,
CETTE GORGE PROFONDE AUX NONCHALANTS DETOURS,
MES SAUVAGES AMIS, DON L'ANTIQUE MURMURE
DE MON EPOUSE AURORE A BERCE LES BEAUX JOURS.

you again, pines in dark silk
the silhouettes of caves who know the shadows.
my savage friends, whose antique murmurs
rocked my wife AURORA in her cradle.

casimir distributes kisses to the dear mild air.
jules, emphatically:

LES VOILA, CES BUISSONS OU TOUTE MA JEUNESSE
COMME UN ESSAIM D'OISEAUX, CHANTE AU BRUIT DE MES PAS.
LIEUX CHARMANTS, BEAU DESERT OU PASSA MA MAITRESSE.
NE M'ATTENDIEZ VOUS PAS?

the grasses of my youth rustle
like swarms of birds to the sound of my steps
charmed places, beautiful desert where my lover trod.
didn't you wait for me?

GORGE of FONTAINBLEAU tell me: where does my GEORGE await me?
jules looks to the skies in all directions.
george: but someone is there. they are breathing heavily. men's voices re-
sound from afar.
jumps, right leg: CASIMIR BARON DUDEVANT, decked out like a foppish
gallant, with every possible thing the nobility invents for itself as a
distinguishing characteristic: silk shirt, linen polo suit, signet ring which
his great-great-great-great-grandfather wore on his ring finger, help!: a
specter enters the bedroom, and then me immediately after—and puts
our love to sleep.
jumps, left leg: home sweet home, love in pairs.
JULES SANDEAU chews alternately on his fingernails and on his pen.
he hasn't put a single sentence to paper all the live long day. but a
JOURNALIST is paid by the line. where are the columns, where the
pages? not quite two in the morning, and he falls asleep over his work.
jumps: to the right, the contractually guaranteed use of the other sex.
jumps: to the left, the contractless dear vagabond life of the BOHEMIAN
without a penny.
solange pursues butterflies from left to right:
MAMAN, MAMAN, i have a PAPILLON!
(off)
george: to the right, the reproduction of the flesh—
maurice lets his kite fly again:
dip, glide until you rise up to the sphere of the wooly cirrus clouds.
imitate MAMAN's train of thought. some distant, very beautiful day i
will accompany them with lithographs etched by my own hand—my kite
should arise, arise on a mountain minus ice (exits).

george: to the left that of the spirit. ah, what i wouldn't give if that four-leaf clover MAURICE were to come flying straightaway to my heart.

male voices:

how nice, how nice

on a mountain minus ice

casimir has reached the summit and pleads breathlessly:

i love you truly and in a manner appropriate to my class, AMANDINE AURORE LUCILLE. let us renew our vows and extend to me your hand in order to strengthen our lifelong bond—

is interrupted by jules:

MADAME, i love you spontaneously and uncontrollably: humanly. in addition, i offer you the personal use of SAND, the first half of my surname. what a beautiful name for a WOMAN IN MOVEMENT—

casimir, brusquely: you mean, THE WOMAN OF STANDING.

george chants as a children's rhyme HUSBAND LOVER LOVER HUSBAND CASIMIR JULES JULES CASIMIR. the action shifts from the rocky crevasse to the meadow and stream.

solange from the left: where have you been so long, MAURICE?

maurice from the right: in the hollow. my kite got caught.

solange: look, and i've caught a brimstone butterfly. your kite, always your kite. i don't see it.

maurice: that could be because of the sun. my kite is swimming in the light.

solange: the heat is beastly. should we go for a swim?

maurice: yes, we could wade in the water.

solange takes off her clothes.

maurice: i'll just wind in the string and follow you.

solange: MAURICE, i have to pee.

pees into the water.

maurice: in the RIPPLING brook,

a weasel sat on a ROCK.

SOLANGE, me too.

pees from the meadow into the water.

solange: THE wiener SEES where it pees

UP TO ITS KNEES.

maurice: but i pissed farther, serves you right!

solange splashes her brother with water:

tale-teller, ha! i don't need a water cock.

i am the mouth, grab hold of it.

maurice jumps into the water to get closer to her.

solange: hm, dear brother, how good this will feel when i'm grown up.

maurice: my watering can—

solange, impertinently: is leaking.

casimir rises to his full height. the action shifts back to the heights: MAURICE, SOLANGE!

maurice and solange: PAPA!

casimir: come up here, my children, serfs of my flesh. your mother, who already found herself bored to tears with married life after the birth of MAURICE, has withdrawn here into the rocky world of divorce, as she puts it. i poured treasures into her lap, the diamond tiara, the platinum necklaces, one after another, and yet only her fantasy, her overheated fantasy, is responsible for her decision to leave me, my tomb. i know her. have you ever seen her when she's riding? as a sprinter, she is the best far and wide, and this while wearing a pleated dress. her hounds barking behind her, everyone in the vicinity of this province knows her, whether renegade thief or hunter. but be that as it may: i want to be a father to my two darlings. MAURICE, SOLANGE. come to me! how good that feels. wouldn't you like to praise your father? ah, you still must elevate further.

casimir: until the children get here, i'll proceed strategically and transform myself from an honest nobleman into a common lasso twirler.

throws his mountain-climbing line toward george's legs.

fine, the right leg snaps into the LEGALIZED INSTITUTION OF MARRIAGE.

maurice's voice: uncle JULES.

solange's voice: uncle JULES.

jules: i see how GEORGE torments herself. but in order to achieve my dream, i'll risk conducting myself in the open air as a womanizer.

sets such a clever trap for her that she is caught in it:

fine, the left leg is stuck in the trap of LIBERTINAGE.

maurice's voice: my kite.

solange's voice: his wing. my butterfly.

jules: if i might be honest, GEORGE. your brats, issue of my rival, send me into a rage. but i must come to terms with the hated urchins if i don't want to lose your love.

george, robbed of the free movement of her legs, abruptly falls, headfirst, into the rocks. CASIMIR and JULES, shocked by this sight, let go of the ropes.

george: HUSBAND LOVER LOVER HUSBAND CASIMIR JULES JULES CASIMIR what woman could reckon with men. their cold-blooded pursuit with ropes and swords is what they call passionate love. thievery is what i call the attempt to win a woman in this way. those who make such an attempt: criminals.

looks around: no matter, nothing broken, though i fell several feet. no broken bones. my praise extends to the horizon of the horizontal position.

takes up her notebook: i must record what happened to GEORGE at the FONTAINEBLEAU GORGE before BOTHO STRAUSS comes along and gets a hold of it.

contentedly lights herself a cigar: perhaps some far-off day my fall will ignite the fires of the woman's question?

smokes and writes.

iv

HOMOLULU: HOTHOUSE DE LA PAIX

CHOO, CHOO, CHOO. I'M COMING.

THE LOCO-MOTION OF NINETEENTH-CENTURY LITERATURE SPEEDS STEAMING INTO THE FOYER OF THE PARIS OPÉRA, A GREAT TRAIN STATION OF SORTS.

THE TRAIN IS ENGINEERED BY GUSTAVE FLAUBERT, THE SILVER SYLLABLEWRIGHT WHO HEADS TOWARD THE NORMANDY OF HIS CHILDHOOD. HIS STOKER IS HONORÉ DE BALZAC, THE BIG FAT "H" AND THE BIG FAT "B," WHO SHOVELS HIMSELF DEEP INTO THE "SCENES FROM PROVINCIAL LIFE."

TEMPORARILY ONE SINGLE PASSENGER: A MAN WITH THE TENDER COUNTENANCE OF A WOMAN, A WOMAN IN MEN'S CLOTHING: GEORGE SAND.

FLAUBERT: THE ARTIST SIMPLY MUST BE OF BOTH SEXES. GEORGE EXITS THE TRAIN BY WAY OF THE RUNNING BOARDS AND HURRIES OFF ON FOOT TOWARD HOMOLULU.

ON FOOT. ALWAYS AND EVERYWHERE ON FOOT. DIDN'T SHE CROSS THE ALPS ON FOOT? ALONE, WITHOUT MOTHERCHILDRENLOVERSOUL, TO MUSSET, TO VENICE.

IN HOMOLULU IS THE HOTHOUSE OF PEACE, A SURREAL COMBINATION OF GLASS, SUCCULENT GROWTH, AND A SEVRESLIKE PORCELAIN COFFEEHOUSE. WITHIN, CANNABIS PLANTS

OF ALL KINDS, ALSO REFERRED TO AS THE "FLOWERS OF
GOOD" IN THE CIRCLES OF DOPE-SMOKING WOMEN. SHE
WANTS TO BRING THESE TO HER LOVER MARIE DORVAL OF THE
HUMAN COMEDY—AH, PARDON, THE COMÉDIE FRANÇAISE,
AS A GIFT.
INSCRIPTION ON THE DRIED BOUQUET: INHALE.
INITIATIVE TO LEGALIZE MARIE-JUANA.

* * *

HOMOLULU: HOTHOUSE DE LA PAIX

a glass greenhouse (nineteenth-century ironwork construction)[6] with a fountain in the center (which can also be a WALLACE fountain.) Among the
lush vegetation of rain forest, tobacco, pot plants, banana trees, orchids,
irrigation units, and spraying equipment, are coffeehouse tables with
busts and inscriptions. along one glass wall the bar, on the other the piano. SIDE TABLE WITH MALLARMEBUST OF THE CONCEITED LA-
DIES OF GOOD SOCIETY, who fan one another with marabou and
ostrich feathers and while doing so recite poems with head on breast,
breast on head:
AILE, QUELS PARADIS ELIRE,
SI JE CESSE OU ME PLONGE AU
TOUCHER DE VOTRE PUR DELIRE,
MADAME MADIER DE MONTJAU.
wings that choose paradise,
if i stop fanning, oh!
the falling filling feeling pure delirium,
MADAME MADIER OF MONTJAU.
one woman has been fanning in french, the other in german. at the words
"falling filling feeling" the women emit a fountain of gurgles; at the word
delirium they become wet.
QUADRILLE OF HEAD WAITERS.
four gentlemen in tails who have grown together to form a single SER-
VANTMONSTER to the extent that each of them only moves as the stand
of a single serving tray:

---

6. The allusion is to Walter Benjamin's discussion of the nineteenth-century skel-
eton of the city as an "ironwork greenhouse," in *Pariser Passagen*.

delighted, delighted, extremely delighted.
   delighted on high, delighted to the highest.
inhale deeply:
   armchair, chair, and canape, so—
      knuckle, instep, and big toe.
go off, absorbed, to take orders.
SIDE TABLE WITH THE BUST OF AN INDIAN CHIEF OF THE WELL-
   TO-DO GENTLEMEN OF GOOD SOCIETY. BIG BEAR smokes a peace
   pipe; the gentlemen puff on expensive tobacco and play CANASTA.
first gentleman: i've drawn a lucky hand.
   now it's your turn.
second gentleman cuts the cards: my second deuce, a joker. it flows, everything flows away in transitions.
first gentleman: just take this HOTHOUSE with its irrigation units.
second gentleman: five, six, seven at one stroke.
sweeps the cards together: or the transition from the raw to the cooked.
first gentleman: or the passage from honey to ashes. it's warm in here—
jumps up and washes his hands, which are dirty from the card game, in the
   spray of the fountain: in this heat.
second gentleman: my second canasta!
first gentleman: bang, the GREAT BEAR has spoken. may i beg you on my
   knees for a light?
second gentleman: the discovery of fire took place on the first globe of the
   first world; that of tobacco, on the other hand, on the second globe of
   the second world.
first gentleman hisses: LADIES with LADIES. the here-and-now of lust.
second gentleman: BOYS with BOYS. it's beyond CROCODILEbelly—
first gentleman: HORSEbreast. man is brain-heavy, and his true nature remains unknown to him.
second gentleman: DUAL WORLDS THEORY OF PHILOSOPHY.
first gentleman: DUAL WORLDS OF SEXUAL PSYCHOLOGY.
second gentleman: the partial drives under the command of the genitals.
first gentleman: there she is.
second gentleman: la voilà, the polymorphous perversion.
QUADRILLE OF THE HEADWAITERS to the side table of the well-to-do
   gentlemen:
   that is simply comparative.
   that is doubly superlative.
they serve tea with white rum: don't get up.
   remain sitting quietly on your derrières.

the furniture A LA NAPOLEON III thanks you in the style of the SEC-
OND EMPIRE.

PIANO MUSIC:

heart, oh heart, what pain it knows,
even the thorn must wear the rose . . .

two waiters: tra-la-la-lay-lay-lay the pianist est arrivé.

two others: it's LISZT. FRANZ is the scoundrel's name.

they dance as if on roller skates, in the process displaying crystal-clear
laughter.

MAIN TABLE with a statue of BAUDELAIRE and the inscription:
PARADIS ARTIFICIELS.

JUANA MARIE DORVAL, her hair in perfumed ringlets, enters on the arm
of GEORGE SAND, who is wearing a top hat and dress coat. GEORGE
indolently lets her top hat whirl around on the tip of the spraying water
and gazes with pleasure upon the spectacle, while MARIE lingers near
the fountain.

george: my hat, it has three joints, three joints has my hat.
maui zowie, a thai stick, and panama red.

marie: a woman's breast and hawaiian dope.
cigarette butt and curling smoke.

george: three joints and two lips, this is my lesbian credo . . .

marie: maui zowie, as far as the eye can see. i want to fill my mouth with
a juicy joint.

GEORGE: go ahead—take your fill.

marie, in coming: how big, how strong, how decisive you are, and how
heavenly hard you make me, dressed in your leather boots à la butch.

GEORGE: with what fragility you cast down your eyes and how close to
our dear mother earth you bend your femmy form.

marie smokes, sits down: your eternal aura, AURORA (offers her some
dope).

george takes a joint and lights it from marie:
my telluric sunken treasure.

marie inhales: ON THE NATURE OF WOMAN AS ONE OF THE
HEAVENSTORMING ATLANTINS.

george: ON THE NATURE OF WOMAN AS A SEA-STALKING PIRATE.[7]

marie: GEORGE SAND. a member of the woman's weather underground—
my terrorist.

george: wherever the world goes to women's heads, it stands on its head.

---

7. The allusion is to Ulrike Ottinger's *Madame X*.

marie: i am exhausted from our seven-mile promenade over the body of
the city.

george: the way from the PALAIS DES LOUVRES to the beauties of the
TUILLERIES—a hop, skip, and jump. the name of your transparency is
seduction.

marie: you, however, sit haughtily like Alpine ridges.

george: i hear hammering and chiseling. is that from the drugs?

marie: not far from the PLACE DE L'OPERA, the ATELIER OF WALTZ
DREAMS of a certain ALEXANDRE MANCEAU is said to—

PIANO MUSIC:

heart, oh heart, what pain it knows,

even the thorn must wear the rose . . .

george: have opened.

george transfixed by the pianist: never heard of him . . .

marie: just wait, the—

george: who?

marie: the woman, the fisher of persons, will net him.

george in toxication: keys drumming, fingers knocking.

marie, also in toxication: arpeggios on eighty-eight atonalities. this smoke
is choking me.

george: me, too. i have, you have, we have smoked marie-juana, juana-
marie. the plural i, the singular we.

marie: piano music. LISZT at the PIANO. his touch, an intoxicating drug.

george: he can't be compared with CHOPIN, who holds his own.

marie: UP. the dark carpet of reality spreads out.

george: DOWN: the roof of glass, bright as the sky.

marie: in its reflection BAUDELAIRE recovered from the effects of space
and time.

george: it is written here, read it for yourself.

marie: PARADIES ARTIFICIELS.

george hums: LALALAL, the extraordinarily beautiful MARIE DORVAL,
MARIE DORVAL of the human comedy—ah, pardon, the COMEDIE
FRANÇAISE, my mistress.

marie: now, a poem: in the beginning was grass.

BAUDELAIRE convalesced as the poet albatross. the ancient mariner as
dross.

they enter into the phase of intoxication that stimulates a production of
the oral theater.

george: MARIE: criminal clitoral cannabis.

marie: GEORGE: critical clitoral credo.
george: the cradle of critical chaos.
marie: chaosmosis. cosmos.
marie: a clitoral oratorium.
george: PASSION FLOWERS in a minor key your passion blossoms to satiety.
   always, when i rush the outer limits of the primordial forest of emotions—
marie: the naked truth, the denuded-nudity—
george: then i say to myself, there is only one thing that counts as my
   lesbian credo:

IL S'AGIT AVANT TOUT
DE DEBROUSSAILLER
LES CHEMINS DU DESIR.[8]

ART, THE DESIRE
IN THE JUNGLE OF HUMAN EMOTIONS
TO EVEN OUT THE PATH.

george: special affects. the sound that knocks your socks off.
marie: i luff du.
george: i sink to mytelf, telf...
a part: venetian allusion: lipkiss.
SIDE TABLE LADIES OF AFFECTED GOOD SOCIETY spew forth poison
   and bile: lisbians lisp with lips.
SIDE TABLE GENTLEMEN OF CONCEITED GOOD SOCIETY spit chewing tobacco: lesbians rattle with rasps.
SIDE TABLE LADIES point with torches to the marijuana-intoxicated
   lovers: lesbians sting like wasps.

COME JOIN IN THE FUN AT THE
SUPER 8 FOCUS-INN:
marie in a transparent coffin as if transitorily embedded in death. george
   approaches her on a glass cothurnus to release her by means of cunni-
   lingus. now the coffin comes to life and moves on glass feet.
george: everything sprouts in HOMOLULU.
   i am a tree and you a bush.
the coffin enters the water and drives forward on silver waterwings.
marie: everything flows in HOMOLULU.
   i am a raft and you are the river.

---

8. See André Breton, from *L'Amour fou*.

QUADRILLE OF HEADWAITERS from out of the water: we are from the
    Anita Bryant chapter of the moral majority:
    did the ladies call for HELP?
serving: ONE BELOVED AURORE THERE.
    ONE BLOODY MARY HERE.
    WE WORK 25 HOURS A DAY.
george and marie walk intoxicatedly out of the moon phase that inclines
    toward the subject/object exchange, and pass over into the phase of
    EMPHATIC FLIGHT.

HEAD TABLE
marie: ALFRED takes a dim view of my nightly leaving to take my role as
    woman of interpreting the world on the stage. My new show features
    the only animal that makes love.
george: ALFRED or CASIMIR. i hate them all. DE VIGNY here,
    DUDEVANT there. you alone are the divine interpreter of CORNEILLE
    and RACINE, you alone elevated the audience to the point of riotous
    applause.
marie: i play nothing more than what i am: the entire grand family of
    "i's." rather than the "i," BERNICE and the "i," PHAEDRA and i
    would of course prefer the "i" INDIANA and the "i" LELIA to feel
    you, beloved MONSIEUR GEORGE, down to the base of the palate-
    theater of the mouth in the shallowness of modern inspiration.
george: my sacred oath. i will tailor a role for you upon your body. the
    vault where SHAKESPEARE, GOETHE, KLEIST, and BÜCHNER will
    lie.
marie: the theater is flying.[9] they are flying.
george: ROUSSEL, ARTAUD, and yet others.
marie: the theater flies. after them. after them.
george: after them.
pause.
marie: when will you leave CASIMIR,
    when will i be yours, my dear?
george: separation from the castle at NOHANT, from bed and board. a
    decision for a lifetime, no mere stroke of the pen.
marie, elegically:
    LA MAISON DE MON COEUR EST PRÊTE,

---

9. Here the allusion is to Ariane Mnouchkine's film about Molière, *Das Theater
fliegt, wir müssen hinterher.*

ET NE S'OUVRE QU'A L'AVENIR.
PUISQU'L N'Y A RIEN QUE JE REGRETTE
MON BEL EPOUX TU PEUX VENIR.[10]

the house of my heart stands wide open.
the future, its room full of roses
where i, with nothing to regret
sink softly into its marriage bed.

SUPER 8 FADE-INN:
george sits up in confusion.
she carries the somnambulistic marie in her arms.
marie transparently breaks through the mirror of the glass walls.
beating their wings, both women leave the glass construction of the greenhouse behind them. a great deal of time passes with musical accompaniment
until they have reached the head of the statue of APOLLO on the roof of
the great train station of the PARIS OPERA—a sort of infinity point of the
intoxication of love.

*   *   *

V

ATTIC OF LIBIDINAL PHASES

ATTICS. GRAY ROOFTOPS.
CAST-IRON BARS IN FRONT OF THE WINDOW. THE MAJESTIC
    CROWNS OF THE TREES THAT LINE THE BANKS OF THE SEINE,
    REFUGES FOR THE REPUBLIC OF SPARROWS. THESE, UNDER THE
    DIRECTION OF THE SPARROW WHO HAS TRAVELED FARTHEST
    (MOINEAU VOYAGER), ARE ABOUT TO SOUND A REVOLUTION-
    ARY CONCERT OF CHIRPS.

LIBERTÉ! EGALITÉ! FRATERNITÉ!

WINGED ONES OF ALL TREES AND BUSHES UNITE!
UNDER THESE CROWNS, THE ARISTOCRATIC STEMS. FAMILY
    TREES.

---

10. Another quote from André Breton, from *Nadja*.

ADJOINING THIS, CARRIAGES AND COACH HORSES OF STATE AND
DIGNITARIES WHO ARE ON THEIR WAY TO THE QUARTER OF
THE CITY FOR STATE DIGNITARIES (XVI. ARRONDISSEMENT,
BOIS DE BOULOGNE).
HORSE APPLES OF ARISTOCRATIC LINEAGE AS THE FOUNDATION
FOR THE LIFE OF THE SPARROWS. WHO HAVE SWORN TO UP-
HOLD THE COMMON GOOD? VIVE LA COURT! VIVE LE ROI!
AMONG THE TREE TRUNKS, IN THE EARTH, NEAR TO THE RIVER,
THE TREE ROOTS SUCK UP MOISTURE WITH THEIR BUILT-IN
PUMPS. THEY SCRAPE AND SUCK AT THE BASE FOR THE MAJ-
ESTY THE CROWN.
THE RIVER ITSELF NAVIGATED BY ITS BOATMEN AND
BOATWOMEN.
ITS MIRROR OF WATER, MIRROR OF SOCIETY, IS FRAGMENTED.
DISTORTING MIRROR FRAGMENTS AND BROKEN MIRROR, A MASS
OF SPLINTERS.
GEORGE SAND GLANCES UP FROM HER WRITING. TSS. TSSS. THE
PRESSURE OF THE BIOLOGICAL CLOCKS THAT SAND SMOKES
AWAY. SHE IS ALL EARS. CHR. CHRR. THE PRESSURE OF THE
RAVEN'S FEATHER QUILL ON THE MOUNTAIN OF PAPER. AN INK
SPOT.
THE PRESSURE OF EXISTENCE, HOURS, DAYS, NIGHTS TAKES A
HEAVY TOLL.
THE READY CASH MELTS AWAY LIKE BUTTER IN THE SUN.
HOW LONG WILL THERE STILL BE ENOUGH FOR THE LYCÉE? FOR
MAURICE AT THE PRESTIGIOUS HENRY IV SCHOOL: FOR THE
SUMMER VACATION BY THE SEASIDE? FOR SOLANGE TO TAKE
A CURE FROM THE BAD CITY AIR?
FOR HER LOVER? FOR A FRIEND IN NEED?
A COMPLETELY INSIDIOUS HOPE: TO LIVE FROM ONE'S WRITING.

* * *

ATTIC OF LIBIDINAL PHASES

george: to hatch the sentence. sweating ink. 30 sheets per day, 30 days per
month. 4,000 francs for me on an honorarium basis. spring, summer,
fall, winter. milk and bread, as well as my son MAURICE, sweeten the

drudgery. and the DIARY and the STORY OF MY LIFE and my COR-
RESPONDENCE. for this i could buy SOLANGE her dowry. oral craving,
pure voluptuous excess. man as a pleasure machine that incessantly desires
desire: an animal.
bones in her hands, she guides a great joint of poultry to her mouth:
everything flows past in transitions. just take the transition from the raw
to the cooked. the resurrection of the dinner in art. flesh in the spirit.
puts the gnawed-on joint aside, wipes her hands clean on a used piece of
copy paper:
the carbon copy of the copy of . . . for . . . rewritings of written copies.
taboo. a taboo. i am breaking my ambivalently promised long-held
silence and openly admit i have a certain ANAL TENDENCY toward
assiduity in the fulfillment of obligations. fastidious. MUSSET. how do
they come to him of all people? HIS MAJESTY THE FIRST, THE SNOB,
despises THE MOB, and is much too vain for a confession of this sort.
yes, from the soles of his shoes to the . . .
reaches toward the box for a DAVIDOFF, quietly smokes for a long while;
cigars are a matter of concern for the MEN'S TAILOR SALON "AUX
BEAUX CAVALIERS," or, THE HANDSOME HORSEMAN, to make
sure i don't soil my tough gray pants.
eavesdrops on the birds in the trees along the banks of the SEINE:
VOILA LES P'TITS OISEAUX.
CH'NTEZ LES P'TITS OISEAUX.
the story of the sparrows traveling in search of the best government.
votive animal. on the coat of arms of my mother's family, which dwelled
for a year on the QUAI DES OISEAUX, living on the prey caught in
their traps in the trees. my childhood in the CONVENT DES AN-
GLAISES. i had just arrived, already the leader of the pack, and during
the nights the worst of all the girls in the dorm. until my beloved
supervisor converted me to her viewpoint. through her alone i felt myself
called upon to become a nun. MADAME DE FRANCEUIL vehemently
opposed this. her granddaughter was not going to become the laughing
stock of the enlightened french nobility. . . . i, however, have never re-
tracted this stage of development in my puberty.
listens: klalap. klalalap. horses. the darlings of my father, proud of his
generations of forefathers—our family can be traced back to the germans
in the person of GRAND DUKE MORITZ OF SAXONY—who, at the
age of 35 and as the 34th successor in rank and sequence of the branches
of the dynasty's family tree, was fatally injured during an excursion into

the dark NOIRE valley. the wiles of fate. the malevolent wantonness of destiny. AMANDINE LUCILLE AURORE DUPIN DE FRANCEUIL bends under the blow and is morose for the rest of her life. the burial day. mother shimmering in black, wearing the latest paris fashion. her transparent gown glistens seductively. i have an aversion to the seductress. i am all alone. i have no one at all outside of myself. our pact to be a pair. i think about father crossing the ALPS with NAPOLEON's TROOPS. the infantry. the cavalry. leaders and groups. his life was a gamble from beginning to end. i want stability. ach, that there might someday be a dike against death.

dreamily: SCARCELY ANYONE WHO DOESN'T BURDEN HERSELF WITH THOUGHTS OF IMMORTALITY, WHEN DEATH TOLLS THE HOURS OF FATALITY.

listens: tooooooootoooooooot, a cargo ship. the walls tremble at their foundations. the ATTIC OF LIBIDINAL PHASES trembles. i swear by my art: HOW AND WHY FATHER LIVES ON IN ME!

carries her plate away, empties the ashtray:
death and life. floods, earthquakes, MOUTH OPEN, CLOSED. SPHINCTER OPEN, CLOSED. the way of the world. everywhere, something is functioning, everywhere.[11] sometimes with interruptions, sometimes without. what an ingenuous mistake to have said IT. there are machines at work everywhere.

with a glance toward the audience:
ÉCRITURE-MACHINES, READING MACHINES.
ACTOR-MACHINES, SPECTATOR-MACHINES.
in the ORAL WORLD THEATER OF THE PALATE everyone is an amateur. to each his own spherical disturbance of the peace and cosmic orgasms, you MOON-MOUTHS and SUN-ASSHOLES.

a sound in the wings like stairs being climbed:
I CLIMB THE SPIRAL STAIRWAY
OF THE APARTMENT HOUSE
SIS, SIX TO THE QUAI MALAQUAIS
OVER SIX STORIES of EXERTION,
SO HIGH, THE WAY I TAKE THEM,
DIRECT, WITHOUT DIGRESSION.

stairs creak and gasp.

---

11. This passage is taken from Gilles Deleuze and Felix Guattari, *The Anti-Oedipus.*

a great deal of time passes with musical accompaniment.

the door is furiously opened.

musset: to hell with your goddam diligence, george. parcels of paper tower before you, you sit as if you had been sewn down by your chaste backside and you neglect me, ALFRED DE MUSSET.

george: first comes work, then life.

musset: can't there be an exception?

george: YOUR MAJESTY is a pain in the neck to me: i am busy earning my daily bread.

musset: QUI NE GARDE AUX AMOURS SES PLUS BEAUX JOURS? EVERYTHING DEPENDS ON, EVERYTHING IS COMPELLED BY, LOVE.

george: first you must fill your stomach.

musset: the judgment of your court throws a wet washcloth in the face of every kissmouthpleasure.

george, angrily: don't say that. i call your idea-licking a simple nose-picking. ART DOESN'T COME FROM ABILITY BUT FROM NECESSITY.

musset: i hope you suffer for that.

violently sweeps the stacks of paper and the biological clocks from the table. i've had it. in the end you will die of bowel failure.

george boxes him on the ears: fragments. YOUR EXCELLENCY, whose burial will mark the end of a lifetime of drunkenness, will have to personally take this broom in your illustrious hand and sweep up the mess you've made in my retraite. mountains of paper. ink stains.

musset, bowing: J'ÉCRIS QUAND CELA ME CHANTE. i only write whenever the electric blue spark flashes and the VIOLET MUSE unfolds her COSMOGONY in me.[12]

george: oral parnassian.

MUSSET, SINGING:

POET, PRENDS TON LUTH ET ME DONNE UN BAISER,
LA FLEUR DE L'EGLANTIER SENT SES BOURGEONS ECLORE,
LE PRINTEMPS NAIT CE SOIR; LES VENTS
VONT S'EMBRASSER—

POET, TAKE YOUR LUTE AND MAKE A MOIST SIGN,
OF KISSMOUTH LUST ON MY FACE.

---

12. The lines are from the postwar Austrian surrealist Konrad Beyer, from "Der Vogel Singt, eine Kosmogonie."

THE HEDGEROSE IN THE BUSH IS BLOOMING, HOW
YOUR TENDER BUD'S SPROUTING.
THE SPRING AWAKENS, SOFT BREEZES EMBRACE,
AS SINGING, AS SONG, AS SINGING.

george: a romantic nightingale in search of its TERRA INCOGNITA
BEATA.

musset: GEORGE, i have something intimate to say to you. don't laugh
at me, don't consider my words commonplace.

pulls her passionately to the floor:
i love you unceasingly.

poetically: my alabaster star, APHRODITE springing from sea foam. my
thousand-times beautiful, my LORELEI.

george, prone:
my plum-sauce-brown SON OF THE MUSE MOUSSAILLON, my daytime gallant, my fall pheasant, my pearl-entwined red partridge.

musset: my arabian horse of gold with pure-blooded flowing mane.
my honey-greedy AMAZON. my mussel, mercurial, my lighting.
my illumination from a thousand and one nights.

george: my courtly courtesan, my heavenly carrot. intruder into the ice of
my heart.

musset: my apricot mimosa. my rose flora. my pulp muse.

george: my LIDO SWAN.

musset: that sounds downright venetian.

improvises on an imaginary mandolin while on his knees:
L'AMORE IS A ZOGO.
            L'E A LOGO.
            L'E A FOGO
            L'E A COGO
            L'E A VOVO
            L'E A LOVO.

X

DIVORCE-MARCH-TWO-THREE

TSCHENG DENG PENG.
THE DIVORCE MARCH TWO THREE:

OUT-OUT-OUT-OUT.

INTO THE STATE OF MATRIMONY AND—

OUT-OUT-OUT-OUT,

WHICH IN THE YEAR 1835, IN THE PROVINCIAL CAPITAL LA CHÂTRE IN THE PROVINCE OF BERRY IN THE STATE OF FRANCE AND EVERYWHERE, WAS FIRST PLAYED IN FRONT OF A SELECT AUDIENCE OF GAPERS AND APES FROM THE FIRST TO THE LAST NOTE, AND HAS SINCE BEEN REPEATED ON THE ORGAN OF THE LAW.

THE ORCHESTRA: A GRAND GUARD OF RHINOS, FOUR GREEN-MONKEYS AS DRUM-MAJORETTES, A CAPUCHIN-MONKEY AS CONDUCTOR WHO COUNTS PERSISTENTLY: ONE, TWO, THREE, FOUR, TURNING FROM THE JUDGE'S PODIUM TO THE WOODEN BENCHES IN THE AUDITORIUM, TURN LEFT, TURN RIGHT, TURN LEFT, TURN RIGHT.

BUT THIS FANFARE WAS THE VERY FIRST, AND OCCURRED AT A TIME WHEN A WOMAN (IN CASE OF A SEPARATION OF BED & TABLE) HAD NO CLAIM AT ALL ON THE RETURN OF HER PA-RENTAL INHERITANCE, I.E., A DOWRY, INTO HER POSSESSION.

JUDGES AS ASSES AND THE WOODWIND.

LAY ASSESSORS AS MULES AND THE BRASS.

ATTORNEYS AS WILDCATS AND THE STRING.

MAÎTRE THIOT DE VARENNES FROM THE ARDENNES AS BONVI-VANT: AMONG THE SMALL CIRCLE OF EQUALLY MINDED KNOWN FOR THE AUTONOMOUS INVENTION OF THE PHRASE "WINE, WOMEN, AND SONG"; IN CONTRAST, THE SHORT, STOCKY MAÎTRE MICHEL EVERARD DE BOURGES, A TALL GNOME, COVERING HIS BALDNESS WITH A HANDKERCHIEF, KNOTTED AT THE CORNERS, AND SPEAKING FLUENTLY IN ALL WORLD LANGUAGES OF A BOCCA DELLA VERITA.

THE IDEA OF EGALITARIAN JUSTICE: BREATHE IN, BREATHE OUT: AS A MARSEILLAISE-INTERNATIONAL.

THE DIVORCE-MARCH-TWO-THREE:

OUT-OUT-OUT-OUT.

INTO THE STATE OF MATRIMONY AND

OUT-OUT-OUT-OUT.

THE ADVERSARIES ROW AND SMOKE IN FRONT OF BLANK WALLS.

AUDIENCE AS APES & CYMBALS & BASS DRUMS.

A RUMOR CIRCULATES: GEORGE SAND IS ALLEGEDLY A LESBIAN

AND A WHORE RATHER THAN A WIFE AND MOTHER. WHAT
HER TROUSERS COVER IS MALE INSATIABILITY. NO LIGHT. NO-
WHERE IN SIGHT. THIS ACCUSATION ALONE UNDERMINES THE
TWO-WORLD-THEORY OF HOMOLULU AND HETOROGONIA IN
PHILOSOPHY.

* * *

Court room in the inferior court of the provincial capital La Châtre in the
province of Berry, France and everywhere.

DIVORCE MARCH TWO THREE:
OUT-OUT-OUT-OUT.
INTO THE STATE OF MATRIMONY AND
OUT-OUT-OUT-OUT...

the GRANDVILLEORCHESTRA of rhinos, with the support of four green-
monkeys as tambour-majorettes, conducted by a capuchin monkey, play
the march. one, two, three, four, turn left, the ORCHESTRA turns from
the courtroom of the STAGE into the auditorium of the THEATER. the
three presiding asses from the gray fraternity occupy the court desk. in
front of it, the attorneys confront each other. MAITRE THIOT DE
VARENNES holds the lion of the salons, CASIMIR BARON DUDEVANT,
on a leash; MAITRE MICHEL EVERARD DE BOURGES holds GEORGE
SAND the lioness on his leash. an anticipatory scratching spreads through
the audience of gapers and apes.

supreme ass yawns:
hee-haw...i proclaim the opening of the trial DUDEVANT vs.
DUDEVANT. i notice the presence of the entire population of the
MENAGERIE DES MUSEE D'HISTOIRE NATURELLE DE PARIS here
at the PALACE OF JUSTICE OF THE SCHOOL OF LIFE in our dear
community LA CHATRE in the PROVINCE OF BERRY in the DOUCE
FRANCE. dear lay-assessors, dear colleagues, the picture that presents
itself to me is beyond words. All languages. the first hungry gapers start
opening the first bags of peanuts. sleepy apes make themselves com-
fortable on banana peels.
the METRO GOLDWYN MAYER LION MICHEL EVERARD DE
BOURGES roars at the attorney's stand, not just for my ass's ears, the
black attorney-panther THIOT DE VARENNES hands out slaps with his

paws. at his side, the sleek lion of the salons, CASIMIR BARON DUDEVANT, known beyond the state borders as a TALL STREAK through the ink drawings of GRANDVILLE, stands up very straight.

supreme ass:

in contrast, the dolled up BARONNE DUDEVANT extends her hand in an illustrious and worldly manner to MICHEL EVERARD DE BOURGES (*snaps his hooves together*).

second presiding ass yawns:

hee-haw . . . (vehemently) OUT-OUT-OUT-OUT. not another note of the DIVORCE-MARCH-TWO-THREE. out of the courtroom with the GRANDVILLE ORCHESTRA of rhinos. let the trial begin (*rings the bell*).

third presiding ass yawns:

hee-haw . . . let it take its course within these four blank walls without further disturbances. a question regarding procedure? no questions regarding procedure. yes. there we have the CASUS. CASIMIR BARON DUDEVANT jumps up from his mat, his head is beet-red.

casimir roars: MADAME DUDEVANT is faking the appearance of a young man. she likes to have the HANDSOME HORSEMAN in the RUE DU FAUBOURG SAINT HONORE work for her. she gallops across the CHAMPS-ELYSEES, a female AMAZON, a horsewoman, and woe to the ear that this must hear, is a female member of the JOCKEYCLUB. her most recent tailor's bill amounted to . . .

first lay assessors mumbles: horrific, such a sum, a horrendous sum.

second lay assessor: a heap, a horrendous heap of money. that rumor must be spread.

first lay assessor: a fortune.

second lay assessors: such value.

first lay assessor: psst. quiet. de facto i can glimpse the caress of a BUR-GUNDY PURPLE RED dress.

second lay assessor: with slits.

first lay assessor: lower your organ. why this trumpet tone?

second lay assessor: PIANO PIANISSIMO. You ask, it's done.

casimir: she shed all feminine virtues:

MODESTY CHASTITY WILLINGNESS CLEANLINESS DOMESTICI-TY SUBSERVIENCE PROPRIETY OPENNESS VULNERABILITY and has no notion of the value of money.

supreme ass awakens from his officious sleep:

the value—

second presiding ass, likewise:
of money—
third presiding ass, likewise:
no notion!
first lay assessor: horrific—feat.
second lay assessor: horrendous feat.
george, seated, in a silvery voice:
HE has slapped me in public.
HE has cheated on me with kitchen maids.
HE has gambled with my palace in ROULETTE games.
Supreme ass:
stop, stop, in the name of the law. They attack each other with vile
words.
second presiding ass:
talons claw into a body with a soul.
third presiding ass: WOMEN TURN INTO HYENAS. trace of blood. torn
out strands of hair. streaks. all hell. glands, testicles and balls. i feel as
if—matrimony falls.
casimir roars: THE SILENCE OF THE DESERT IN US.
george silvery: i am personally occupied by reminiscences reaching back to
the PHARAOHS. a grand-style souvenir: THE ROAR OF THE NILE.
the audience comes alive.
the gapers hurl peanuts, the apes throw banana peels.
shrieks:
first lay assessor: my sight is dim. the contours swim.
SPECTACLE FOR THE JUDGE.
musingly: so that is what it's like when the THEATER WORLD OF THE
WORLD THEATER shrinks down to the ROUND OF THE PALATHEA-
TER OF THE MOUTH.
second lay assessor: everything i peruse is tinted in blues and double-
exposed.
addresses himself: THE DEBACLE OF CIVILIZATION.
supreme ass, commandingly:
film or sound recordings are not allowed. otherwise i am forced to exclude
the representatives of the MEDIA from the further course of the trial.
no ZOOM, no FLASH, no SHOOTING, no SNAPSHOOTING. i herewith give the word to the highborn MAITRE THIOT DE VARENNES
from the ARDENNES. MAITRE, your PLAIDOIRIE please.
thiot, imploringly:

my good name, traditionally representing the cause of the SILENT CON-
SERVATIVES IN OUR COUNTRY, is at stake here. i am appalled by
the general degeneration of mores in the SECULAR BATTLE OF THE
SEXES, and immediately take SIDE with all my might and phallic power
as the advocate of the male. the accusations against my client endanger
the ROLE OF THE MODERN MALE IN OUR SOCIETY PER SE. the
male is put against the wall of law and rendered dysfunctional. therefore
we, the BLACK PANTHERS from the FRACTION of the BLACK PAN-
THERS in GOVERNMENT, opine that there must be put a public stop
to this attack. we assume that DUDEVANT loved his wife, married to
him by laws of the church and the state, and can only be dissuaded
from this conviction by evidence, which has to be brought forth.
MESDAMES—MESSIEURS, dear audience of gapers and apes, believe
us: there was nothing but happiness for the young couple up to the rose-
covered, sweet-smelling, hedge-growing summer of the year 1831.
george, as in a trance: BIRDS CLOUDS WINDS.
casimir, hypnotized: ROSES HEDGES PERFUMES.
george: HORSES WOODS WEEDS.
casimir: HUNTS MELLOW AIR.
george: HEART, OH HEART, WHAT MORE DO YOU . . .
casimir: LIFE'S SUPREME HAPPINESS . . .
george: RIDING RIDING RIDING
casimir: RIDING RIDING RIDING . . .
george: i ride through the dear VALLEE NOIRE.
casimir: i follow you on BEBE QUOTQUOT COCOTON.
george, emphatically: follow follow follow.
casimir: BATTUE THE WILD BOAR.
george: hunt down the pig. the arrow hits home. went through his throat
    and through his air pipe.
the audience sits breathless.
gapers and apes follow the remembering of the past by the warring parties.
thiot: but the HAPPINESS did not last. because soon the SPLEEN and the
    MOODINESS of the baronness's disposition turned her against her
    spouse.
pours out the last of his accusations:
WOMEN IN DRAG WHO PURSUE THE MUSE, WOMEN ARTISTS
WITH AMBITIOUS VIEWS, are and will always be an abomination to
us, the BLACK PANTHERS of the FRACTION of THE BLACK PAN-
THERS in the GOVERNMENT. long live the PHALLUS. long live the

PHALLUS. down with the mannish women. fear our malice. genital supremacy. MAL DE SIECLE.

george staccato: THE MEASURE OF WOMAN'S FREEDOM IS THE MEASURE OF A SOCIETY'S FREEDOM. down with the MYTH OF VAGINAL ORGASM, with the male-dominated imagination of the cunt.

the GRANDVILLEORCHESTRA of rhinos, supported by green-monkeys and conducted by a capuchin-monkey, introduces the march from the auditorium to the stage.

DIVORCE MARCH TWO THREE:
OUT-OUT-OUT-OUT
INTO THE STATE OF MATRIMONY AND
OUT-OUT-OUT-OUT...

first lay assessor hisses: she really goes for it.

second lay assessor: oh man.

george: WHEN YOU GO TO MAN, WOMAN, DON'T FORGET HIS BOOT. i beg your pardon, RESPECTED MEMBERS OF THE COURT, but this had to be stated emphatically.

uproar in the audience.

everything goes topsy-turvy.

no one knows what's top and what's bottom.

the shifting of values is materially reflected by the throwing of peanuts and banana peels.

the three judges: TSCHENG DENG PENG. we can no longer suppress our malevolent surprise. one thousand francs in pure gold. THE PRICE OF THE GOLD FRANK IS RISING. THE PRICE OF THE GOLD FRANK IS FALLING. a severe warning in the form of a penalty for mrs SAND. that will cool the hotheads under those lioness wigs.

thiot indifferently: but so it came about that the SHE-PIRATE OF THE FEMALE SUBCONSCIOUS, as we have come to know her from INDI-ANA, the PIRATESS OF THE SOUTH EAST ASIAN SEAS OF FEMALE SOULS, as we have come to know her from LELIA, did not in the end find HAPPINESS. because HAPPINESS—

raises his voice, raspingly: cannot be found on the whole wide world other than in the true obedience of marital duty. derision and agreement from the audience.

gapers: a stove of one's own.

apes: morning time is ever fine.

gapers: WOMEN WINE AND SONG THE WHOLE LIFE LONG.

apes: twice a week, the average obligation.

supreme ass: hee haw . . . THE HIGH COURT thanks MAITRE THIOT DE VARENNES for his PLAIDOIRIE. our asses' ears seldom or never hear such substantial wisdom about FUNDAMENTAL QUESTIONS OF BOURGEOIS LEGISLATION. we now give the word to MAITRE MICHEL EVERARD DE BOURGES. MAITRE, we are short of time. please be concise.

de bourges gets up and roars:

A ROSE IS A ROSE IS A ROSE IS A—

elaborately wipes his glasses with his folded handkerchief:

DEAR-SHMEAR GRAY-BROWN JUDGES AND ASSESSORS, MY DEAR GAPERS AND APES. my motto: GINKA STEINWACHS, pardon me, GERTRUDE STEIN, pardon me, GEORGE SAND, G.S. for short, is the greatest poet in the whole country, and has long been known to you, as you are sitting here smacking and scratching. A WOMAN IS A WOMAN IS A—in other words: i, the OFFICIAL ADVOCATE OF THE LEFTIST JUNE-REBELS and other PROGRESSIVE, OPPOSITIONAL GROUPS, i am now advocating the female sex, conditioned to be left-handed so to speak. where are women encouraged and supported according to their talents, where will this stein reach the full extent of its greatness? my near-sighted eyes gaze at EUROPE, AMERICA, the globe. wherever i look, woman is a BALD SOPRANO.

de bourges: because of male domination over her property, the woman of today has no choice but to be disinherited. in the case of a separation, and because of the RESTORATIVE TENDENCIES OF OUR LEGISLA-TURE, this occurs almost always without a chance to protest on her part.

through the BOCCA DELLA VERITA:

but this woman here is a . . .

indiscernible: no common . . . but a . . . and what a . . . and i tell you: ominous . . . voluminous . . .

serious . . . monstruous . . .

in short: i am about to give you the EXAMPLE OF WOMAN'S NATURE AS A FORCE CAPABLE OF RECREATING THE RELATION BETWEEN THE SEXES.

derision and agreement from the audience.

the female apes begin again to check each other for lice.

they continue to peer quizzically into their neighbor's face as if it were a mirror, and proceed to beautify themselves.

female apes: A ROSE IS A ROSE—

gapers: A WOMAN IS A WOMAN—

female apes: here the silver box, there the sanitary napkin.

gapers: my stick, my tampon.

female apes: the measuring of emotional crevasses.

gapers: WOMAN IS A BALD SOPRANO.

female apes: there she blows. that's the way.

de bourges, well-mannered: i thank the LEFTIST PROGRESSIVE WING IN THE AUDIENCE for their spontaneously whistled VOTE. let me unleash the WOMAN TITAN. through my mouth, this colossal woman demands her economoral independence from her spouse's tutelage, and her right to have her property restored to her. what is at stake is predominantly real estate: palace and estate of NOHANT, and a pension for her own old age and the education of her children.

gestures: for this purpose, the FOREMOST LITERARY FIGURE OF OUR TIMES has rushed back from the deserts and steppes, in order to bow to the MAJESTY OF THE LAW in all her glory. CASIMIR DUDEVANT, you will not deny that in order to accompany a woman along a shared path through life it requires a certain power and intellectual ability.

REFLEXION. and who are you, i ask?

artificial puase: A HIGH-BORN ZERO AND NOTHING BUT A BARON.

george, before passing out:

i have lost the trial.

EVERARD is preaching to deaf ears.

first lay assessor: help, help. THE BURGUNDY PURPLE RED ONE pales.

second lay assessor: because for her, all hope now fails.

female apes and gapers: NEIGHBOR, YOUR SMELLING-SALT.

first lay assessor: CALL FOR THE RED CROSS, THE AMBULANCE.

second lay assessor: BRING A DOCTOR, GIVE HER A CHANCE.

first lay assessor: come to,

second lay assessor: come to, MADAME!

first lay assessor: THE WORLD WON'T STAY THE WAY IT WAS, ONCE TWO HONORABLE ASSESSORS—

second lay assessor: SIDE WITH THE NEW WOMAN.

supreme ass, absent-minded:

rejoice, rejoice:

sweet air grows moist.

second presiding ass, likewise:

orchids bloom, wafts of perfume.

third: explore the borders of the jungle of feeling its bottom its ceiling.

the GRANVILLEORCHESTRA of rhinos plays a final fanfare.

* * *

DIVORCE MARCH TWO THREE:
OUT-OUT-OUT-OUT.
INTO WEDLOCK AND—
OUT-OUT-OUT-OUT . . .

the MEMBERS OF THE HIGH COURT retreat to their chamber, wagging
their tails. CASIMIR attacks THIOT. MICHEL EVERARD DE BOURGES
bends over GEORGE. she awakes slowly from her faint. she has forgotten
everything around her, sees through things and people in a spell of clear-
sightedness:

george: FROM INFANCY I COULD NEVER BEAR DOMINATION OF
ANY KIND OR NATURE. IT WAS YOU ALONE, EVERARD MICHEL
DE BOURGES, BALD, WEARING YOUR KNOTTED HANDKER-
CHIEF ON YOUR HEAD, WHO I HAVE LOVED, FROM THE DAY
OF MY BIRTH AND THROUGH A NEVER-ENDING STRING OF
PHANTASMS. HAVE YOU EVER RECEIVED THE LETTERS OF A
TRAVELLER THROUGH THE FLOWER OF THE MAIL? I AM SO
GLAD YOU EXIST, MY BIG HUNCH-BACKED MANNIKIN, I AM
SO GLAD YOU EXIST.

faints again.

XI

PROGENY OF THE '48 REVOLUTION

PSSST. QUIET.
IT APPROACHES. A SOUND LIKE BATTLE DRUMS, TRUMPETS. SOL-
DIERS SINGING THE MARSEILLAISE AT THE TOP OF THEIR VOIC-
ES, INTONE THE INTERNATIONAL.
REVOLUTIONARY ETUDE:
CHILDREN OF THE FATHERLAND, HEAR THE SIGNALS,
THE DAY OF GLORY HAS FINALLY COME . . .
THE AIR HISSES. WHAT MAKES IT WHISTLE IS A POLIT-AESTHETIC
THRILLER. GEORGE SAND IS IN THE MIDDLE OF THE MOVEMENT.

SHE STANDS UPRIGHT UNDER THE CAVED CEILINGS OF HER
SON MAURICE'S ATTIC ROOM: 8, RUE DE CONDE, NEAR THE
QUAIS. SHE IS SOMEBODY. FOR INSTANCE THE RIGHT HAND
OF THE LEFTIST INTERIOR MINISTER LEDRU-ROLLIN. FOR IN-
STANCE THE INOFFICIAL EDITOR OF THE OFFICIAL NEWSLETTER
DE LA REPUBLIQUE, FOR INSTANCE THE SPONSOR OF THE PO-
LEMIC MAGAZINE "LA CAUSE DU PEUPLE," A FLAME SHE WILL
PASS ON TO JEAN-PAUL SARTRE.

PSST. QUIET.
THEY RETREAT. THE SOUNDS OF BATTLE DRUMS, TRUMPETS DIE
DOWN. SOLDIERS WHISPER THE MARSEILLAISE, HUM THE
INTERNATIONAL.
REVOLUTIONARY ETUDE:
INTO THE FINAL BATTLE AGAINST THE TYRANNY
INTERNATIONAL SOLDIERS ROAR WILDLY . . .
GEORGE SAND AS THE VIRTUAL MOTHER OF THE REVOLUTION
PRESSES HER EAR AGAINST THE CHEST OF THE EXTREMELY
PREGNANT ZEITGEIST. LABOR PAINS COME IN EVER SHORTER
INTERVALS. THE BAD THING IS THAT THE EMPIRICAL CONDI-
TION OF THE FRENCH BOURGEOISIE CANNOT YET ALLOW THE
BIRTH OF THE SPIRIT OF EGALITARIAN JUSTICE IN PRODUC-
TION- AND CONSUMPTION-BASED PARTNERSHIPS. EXPLOITA-
TION OF WORKERS. UNDERPRIVILEGED CRAFTSMEN. SOCIETY
WOULD RATHER BE UNCHRISTIAN THAN SOCIAL. IT REGARDS
THE MARIONETTE AS THE PERFECT IMAGE OF PEOPLE'S AGEN-
CY. HERE FANTOCCII—THERE BURATTINI. HERE THE COARSE
MATERIALS OF THE POOR MASSES—THERE THE FINE FABRICS
OF THE RULING CLASSES.

PSST. QUIET.
HERE IT IS: THE SOUND OF BATTLE DRUMS, TRUMPETS. SOLDIERS
SING THE MARSEILLAISE AT THE TOP OF THEIR LUNGS, INTONE
THE INTERNATIONAL.
REVOLUTIONARY ETUDE:
GO, GO, COMRADES, COLLEAGUES, FRIENDS, BROTHERS,
FORM BATAILLIONS FOR HUMAN RIGHTS . . .
THE EVENING'S PERFORMANCE AT THE PALACE OF NOHANT BE-
GINS IN FRONT OF MORE THAN 50 INVITED GUESTS. LISTEN

CLOSELY, IMPROVISORS AND EXTEMPORISTS. THE CURTAIN
RISES TO EXPOSE THE THEATER WORLD OF WORLD THEATER.
HISTORY, A BEAUTY WITH HAIR COMING DOWN AROUND HER
SHOULDERS, ENTERS AS A WHIRLWIND. WHAT A PACE SHE
HAS, THIS FANFAN LA TULIPE.
THE REVOLUTION PREPARES HERSELF FOR THE PARIS COMMUNE
OF '70/'71, THE GREAT OCTOBER REVOLUTION IN RUSSIA. THE
UPRISING OF 1848 REMAINS A PREMATURE BIRTH. THE GATE TO
THE EDENIC ISLAND IKARIA OF CABET REMAINS DOUBLY
LOCKED.
GEORGE SAND: A WOMAN IN MOTION, THE WOMAN OF POSI-
TION, PUTS DOWN HER GLOWING DAVIDOFF CIGAR. HER
GREAT HOUR HAS COME. SHE FIXES HER FEELINGS AND
THOUGHTS IN INK, AND NEVER LOOSES A WORD OR SPEAKS
IT INTO THE VOID.
MESDAMES MESSIEURS, THE END OF THE PERFORMANCE WEIGHS
HEAVILY, BECAUSE WHAT IS ALREADY POSSIBLE ON STAGE CAN-
NOT YET BE REAL IN REALITY. THE THEATER FLIES AHEAD:
FOLLOW IT FOLLOW IT FOLLOW IT.

* * *

MARIONETTE THEATRE ON THE AMATEUR STAGE
OF THE PALACE OF NOHANT

players: maurice and solange.
characters: BURATTINI, WORKER ANTS, leftist children of the revolution,
    workers and craftsmen of FAUBOURG SAINT ANTOINE who have or-
    ganized in guilds and corporations, MAURICE.
FANTOCCII, GUARD FOXES, right-wing children of those legions and
    horse-backed national guards faithful to the bourgeoisie in their military
    organizations, SOLANGE.
PROVINCIALS speaking dialect à la BLAISE BONNIN such as MAURICE
    DUDEVANT-SAND, mayor of VIC-NOHANT.
PARIGOTS, agitating for the cause of the upper middle-class reactionaries,
    such as the married MADAME CLESINGER, née DUDEVANT.

maurice as BURATTINO:
THE THEATER FLIES AHEAD. we must follow it.

solange as FANTOCCIA:
> we have flown. the theater has progressed from the marionette theater to the amateur stage.

maurice: hurrah. not a single spectator yet.

bends over the edge of the stage over the auditorium, holds his hands above his eyes in order to observe better.

solange: not a single watchful eye anywhere?

maurice: no watchful eye.

solange: not a single sniffing nose behind closed doors?

maurice: no sniffing nose.

solange inspects the set, walks around:
> not a single critical cur, payed nightly for his gossip column?

maurice: no cur in sight.

solange: don't they have to wear a muzzle?

maurice: i would call a cur with a muzzle a "cuzzle."

solange: i can't stand those damn kitchen smells.

maurice: wait until the invited and the uninvited have all had their dinner.

solange twiddles her thumbs: i am waiting.

maurice: in the glow of candles, they sit over their silver plates, maneuvering OYSTERS, BOYSTERS, MOYSTERS through the fences of their teeth, across the rug of their tongues embroidered with taste papillaries, under the heavenly hard palate, through the carefully guarded gullet, into the crevasses of the belly—

belches obscenely: down. in short: they dine and find the seven courses in NOHANT refreshing and entertaining in their way.

solange: all gourmands, those diners. fat bellies, coarse barrels, and punctured wine-skins. hospitality in my opinion is the poorest of all customs.

maurice: crow-headed scare-woman.

as maître echanson: dearest madame, may i offer you a glass of this ROMANEE-CONTI from the year 1801? GRAND PREMIER CRU: the choicest of choicest of wines! i presume you will soon think differently of our DINER.

toast each other.

solange: SANTE!

maurice: A LA VOTRE!

slurp and smack their lips.

exaggerate.

maurice: FLAUBERT, the amiable gentleman from the NORMANDIE with his maa—may—mee—moustache is slurping.

solange: TURGENEV, the sombre russian from the URAL, is smacking his lips.

maurice: DELACROIX sips. the melancholicus, to our great great regret has failed in picking a suitable side dish.

solange: the peasant LEROUX—maman says he is a philosopher—takes a piece of bread and dips it. how naughty—deplorable.

maurice: the clergyman LAMENNAIS is greedy. a good appetite is the mark of the clergy.

solange: CABET wolfs down his food. do you call this a utopian mood?

maurice: perhaps he thinks he has already arrived in his beloved IKARIA where everyone has what she desires and where no one is ever hungry.

solange: the BROTHERS GONCOURT converse.

maurice: CHOPIN sits facing them; he can hardly manage to guide the spoon into his mouth, he is coughing so hard.

solange: The fat barrel BERLIOZ is a great one for carving red partridges.

maurice: in comparison, BULOZ's big snout seems minute.

solange: typical. the NILE CROCODILE has plenty of style.

maurice: that is: neither too little nor too much.

solange in a good mood: CURTAIN, CURTAIN, MAURICE. the first spectators pour in. COUNTESS MARLIANI at the side of the GREAT COUNT, MARIE D'AGOULT on the arm of FRANZ LISZT.

maurice: CHOPIN and his sensitivity for queer notes are suddenly sorely missed at the table.

lowers the curtain.

BURATTINO and FANTOCCIA are completely hidden behind it.

music from the background.

silent play with the peep hole in the curtain.

now solange peeps, now maurice peers.

voices of amateur show spectators on the stage who could only sit in the auditorium.

INTERMEZZO accompanied by a CAVATINE by LISZT:

maurice as hanswurst under the curtain:

over here, honorable ladies and gentlemen, look at me over here. what we will present to you now is the so-called TOUR DE PROPRIETAIRE.

drum roll on a toy drum.

i myself have built the THEATER IN THE THEATER, incorporating many tricks invented by GARNIER.

sounds a cascade of bells.

lifts the curtain a little from the bottom:
  these brown wooden planks, to the PHALANSTERE OF FOURIER with
  them.
a little further:
  walls without decoration. Theatre stage fees.
and yet further:
  that gas lighting still needs work.
and yet further:
  the shop windows have to be isolated from a nordic draught.
by mistake, maurice lets the curtains drop completely. he pulls a recorder
  from his vest, plays, listens to his playing, cannot understand why it
  does not resonate, searches the curtain for the echo, does not find it.
  lifts the curtain: three doors. the RIGHT one and the LEFT one only
  functional, demonstrate the UBIQUITY, please repeat after me—
he is his own incapable student:
  UBIQUITY of the political conditions.
  the back stairs—
hand stand: leads via the back door—
head stand: into the MONARCHIST PAST—
does the splits: up into the ROYALIST FUTURE.
cartwheels. many.
NAPOLEON III., NAPPI 3, BOURGEOIS KING over WORKER ANTS,
  parades surrounded by GUARD FOXES,
aside: pant shitters and cowardly sissies.
throws his hand up to his face as if in accusation.
lets the curtain drop.
bends into a "bridge":
  in front of me and in themselves THE PROMISED LAND.
  affluence-pleasure. SABLEZ LE CHAMPAGNE. VIVE LA REVOLUTION.
  VIVE LA FRANCE. MA DOUCE CAMPAGNE.
as BLAISE BONNIN: citoyens, ts tss. vous avez été jusque la, ts tss—
  presque tous été privés des droits de citoyens, ts tss. c'est pur vous le
  faire assavour que je m'en vas vous le dire selon mes petits moyens afin
  que nous soyons tretous aussi savans les uns comme les autres, ts tss—
falls into lisping.
solange: how can you be so crude as to speak the crudely crude dialect of
  BERRY in front of MAMANS guests? you behave almost as if there were
  no ACADEMIE nor a COUPOLE.

maurice: LE FRONCAIS de TOUS LES FRONCAIS. and my dumb chick
of a sister is saying more than is good for her.
perform a kind of wrestling match in the curtain and in the wings. *(exit)*

REVOLUTIONARY ETUDE:
CHILDREN OF THE FATHERLAND, HARK TO THE SIGNALS,
THE DAY OF GLORY HAS FINALLY COME . . .

maurice at the peep hole: psst. quiet. it's coming closer, a sound like battle
drums, trumpets.
solange at the peep hole: the air is hissing. what's making it whistle is a
polit-aesthetic THRILLER.
maurice: beware of blood-shed in the heat of the battle.
solange: soldiers sing the MARSEILLAISE at the top of their lungs.
sings at the top of her lungs.
maurice: brigadiers intone the INTERNATIONAL.
intones.
solange's hand in the peep hole:
the times are rude.
maurice. psst. quiet.
the last bars of the REVOLUTIONARY ETUDE.

the curtain opens wide.

maurice enters as WORKER ANT:
curtain. open the curtain. IKARIA IN SIGHT. we are the workers of
the proletarian districts of the capital, organized in trade unions. the
future belongs to us. we won't be betrayed.
quick steps: from left to left.
always from left to left, lots of luck. all have come, all have come. old
and young. 30,000 bodies, poverty-stricken. comrades, colleagues,
friends, brothers, the union leadership has never succeeded at this. *(exit)*
solange enters as GUARD FOX, on horseback:
klalap. klalap. horses.
not a group but a herd. the utmost bliss in the world . . .
THE MORNING DAWNS,
THE MORNING YAWNS,
FOUR HOOVES—HOORAY,
IT'LL SOON BE . . . we are the national guard. 100,000 bodies. all on
horseback. comrades, advance. let's break a lance.

solange as GUARD FOX:

we come from the mansion district of the capital and attempt to protect the proprietors' class from the have-nots. with shiny uniforms, with bushy helmets. we form a lane. from right to right. with traditional might. those who disagree earn our slight. go, MILITIONARIES, into the heat of the battle. (*exits*)

maurice: from left to left. lots of luck.

can i help you, comrade? is your backpack too heavy? today's date is the 16th of april, '48, two P.M., the 16th BRUMAIRE. off to the HOTEL DE VILLE. come on, hurry up. i don't have that much. LAMARTINE has made a pact with the bourgeois. LEDRU-ROLLIN preaches to deaf ears. we must storm city hall. go to it, go to it. (exits)

solange: right is right. how the insurgent masses approach! we are too. horseshoes flash electric crocuses on cobblestones. it's money we're fighting for. charge ahead, soldiers of all ranks, grab your guns. the center of the battle ahead of us. that'll be a dance. long live the reactionaries. workers are the downfall of western civilization, upper, lower and middle middle classes.

REVOLUTIONARY ETUDE:
INTO THE FINAL BATTLE
AGAINST THE TYRANNY
INTERNATIONAL SOLDIERS ROAR SAVAGELY . . .

maurice: the PARISIAN people is the first people of the world. here, everything is proceeding as positively as possible. DREAM PEOPLE FOR A DREAM REPUBLIC. we are sovereign. we will not suffer domination of any kind. from left to left, brigades, workers and little craftsmen, as far as the eye can see, proletariat, let's go forward. No rest, no break. brothers, we will advance a mile each step, we, the historically ascending class. i swear.

solange: MERDE, the people is MERDE. our vanguard has told us the third estate has already reached the PONT DU CARROUSSEL.

exit.

maurice: comrades, close the gaps.

we now have the royal palace of the LOUVRE in our backs. here are our wives and daughters who are decorating the PONT DES ARTS with the TRICOLORE.

left, further to the left.

lots of luck (*exit*).

solange charges in:

COMMUNISM FROM HIGH PLACES INTO THE SEWER (*exit*).

maurice: si par communiste vous entendez une conspiration disposé à tenter un coup de main pour s'emparer de la dictature . . . nous ne sommes pas COMMUNISTES. mais si par communisme vous entendez le désir et la volonté que grâce à tous les moyens légitimes et avoués par la conscience publique L'INEGALITE REVOLTANTE DE L'EXTREME RICHESSE ET DE L'EXTREME PAUVRETE disparaisse dès aujourd'hui pour faire plâce à un commencement d'égalité véritable, oui, oui, oui, nous sommes COMMUNISTES (*exits*).

solange: I'D RATHER BE UNCHRISTIAN THAN SOCIAL. (*exits*)

maurice: THE SEINE, THE SEINE. this river carries the worker's movement across the stepping stone of the twentieth century. at the latest, the october of 1917 will bring the dawn, dawn, dawn. (*exit*)

solange: GUARD FOXES, surround the second bourgeois legion. there, there, there the insurgent WORKER ANTS are coming already. motto: WE'D RATHER BE DEAD THAN ALIVE. BY OUR OWN HANDS. (*exit*)

maurice: into the battle, valiantly, comrades, colleagues, friends, brothers. rip out cobble stones. we are fighting for SHORTER WORKING HOURS, THE NINE HOUR DAY, FOR PUBLIC HEALTH INSURANCE AND CHILD BENEFITS. and if we must die here, we will meet again on the other side. away with it. the exploitation of the people by their fellow people must be kicked out of history. (*exit*)

solange: CABET to the GALLOWS (*exit*)

maurice: head-on attack. flanks. no wavering no wondering. WORKER ANTS will put GUARD FOXES in their proper place. (*exit*)

solange: blood calls for revenge (*exit*)

maurice: blood shed. assassination. woe to me and my poor AMATEUR STAGE!

solange stomps him to a mush.

the curtain drops.

music in the background.

REVOLUTIONARY ETUDE:

AHEAD, AHEAD, COMRADES,

COLLEAGUES, FRIENDS, BROTHERS,
FORM BATALLIONS FOR HUMAN RIGHTS . . .

FILM MONTAGE SUPER 8
CABET'S IKARIA

a bataillion of WORKER ANTS eats itself through a mountain of mashed
potatoes covered with gravy and fried onions, into the utopian land
IKARIA, a lusty cockaigne.
the lusty cockaigne:
    mounds of ham, sausage hills, cutlet gardens, bread trees, roll shrubs,
    cake plants, fruit meadows, wine lakes, milk rivers, honey brooks, veg-
    etable roads.
original sound track:
    HUMANS ARE CONSUMPTION MACHINES WHO DESIRE TO DE-
    SIRE, ORAL GREEDINESS, NOTHING BUT LUST, BEAST.
the WORKER ANTS arrive at a settlement. clean houses with gardens and
    stables, an insolated island. family life: man works in the stable and in
    the fields, woman in the house and in the pantry. children experience
    freedom through child's play.
travelling salesmen carry goods from the small settlement to the larger one,
    and vice versa, give and take, the open and the closed hand. everyone
    is accountable and liable to everyone else.
life in the PRODUCTION collective resembles that in the CONSUMPTION
    collective. the wine grows, the grain spills over in the storehouse. no one
    makes a profit and no one lacks. no one is lazy, no one works themselves
    to death. no one sweats, no one freezes. persistent lack of class difference
    everywhere. affluence for the majority. enough, enough. enough is
    enough.
the WORKER ANTS are served delicacies. everyone has more than enough
    to spare to fulfill the other's needs whatever they are. that counts.
CABET: LA SOCIETE EQUITABLE ET DURABLE SERA CELLE OU
    LA PROPRIETE PUBLIQUE STREINDRA LA PROPRIETE PARTICU-
    LIERE . . .
close up:
HISTORY, a gracious virgin with flowing hair, enters vehemently. she walks
    in a zig-zag. those who want to follow her with their eyes do not know
    where she is heading. she takes one step forward and two steps back.
NAPOLEON III., NAPPI 3, THE CITIZEN KING in his royal ermine gown

with golden orb and scepter has her pull him to the crown of a hill in his golden carriage. there, he takes off his clothes.

everyone sees the ADAM's costume. (his nudity)

the stately dress he wears must come from the GRAND OPERA, and that means: from the PALAIS GARNIER, and that means: it is borrowed.

NAPPI 3 is in a hurry. he sets down his royal orb and scepter, and uses it to dig a grave for the REVOLUTION.

original sound-track:

THE THEATER HAS FLOWN AHEAD.

AS YET, THE YOUNG MISS HISTORY HAS MANAGED TO GET AROUND THE LIBERATOR OF THE PARISIAN COMMUNE.

Heidi von Plato

Worlds of Images: The First Women's Theater Troupe ANNA KONDA

Translated by Katrin Sieg

Performers: Beate Groß, Eva Hinze, Susanne Laki, Regina Rudnick, Christiane Rümenapf, Ulrike Sprenger, Agnes Wessels

The Strangling Snake

ANNA KONDA, the first women's troupe in the German off-theater scene, existed from 1980 to 1984. During this time, the group developed two productions, which were performed at various spaces in Berlin.

ANNA KONDA was founded at the School of Fine Arts, Berlin, in October 1980. I offered a course in women's theater as part of the theater education department's summer program. Six women from different disciplines signed up. They all had practical theater experience as well as the courage to engage in an experimental theater project. At the time I was working as an assistant director and dramaturg for different West German theaters.

Starting with one of my texts, the imagistic play *The Fugue,* we rehearsed for four weeks under my direction and first presented it at the School of Fine Arts. During the rehearsal period, we had already made plans to found a permanent women's theater group once the summer program was over—a group that was to financially support itself. We shared a pleasure in puns and word plays, which led to the name ANNA KONDA, a dangerous reptile transformed into a woman's name.

More performances in Berlin followed during the years 1981 and 1982. The first ones took place in Kreuzberg [a Berlin district famous for its alternative culture] in an old ballroom, where we had to build our own stage, get seating for the audience, and borrow stage lights. The performances were received with great interest, particularly on the part of the women's movement and women's media, so we decided to extend our run. Our next venue was the large theater in the School of Fine Arts, which had a professional lighting system, so we could make better use of the semiotic potential of stage light. After the artistic directors of the Freie Volksbühne Theater had seen a video recording of our piece, they offered us their space for further performances. We invested the incoming money into the group and bought costumes, makeup, and props. We also got an apartment in a squatter's house as a rehearsal space.

My next project with ANNA KONDA was *Wortmorde (Word Murders)*, a collage with texts by Unica Zürn, which we performed at the Berlin gallery Wewerka in 1983.

ANNA KONDA broke up when financial problems became too great for us to continue working as a theater company.

The Fugue

The text plays with images and symbols that address women's experiences, roles, and stereotypes. Not a plot play but a scenic collage condensing language, movement/dance, music, and sounds into images. Similar to dream logic, a number of motifs appear in different scenic settings and situations. I was influenced by Meredith Monk and Robert Wilson and tried to dissolve traditional narrative structures, attempting to create a stage world in which space, colors, costumes, and light would appear as scenic elements of equal value to language. Stage spaces and colors attained iconographic character. There were black and white spaces, red and white dresses. Words, liberated from their corsets of meaning, were used like bodies of sound, in word plays, as nonsense, in order to emphasize their musicality. Displacement and condensation often produced comic effects.

"Women have cried a lot in culture, but once their tears have dried up, what will be left is excessive laughter instead of tears, the eruption, the ebbing flow, a certain humor" (Hélène Cixous). We played with the motif of a woman whose hands are bandaged, who, as a young girl, lies in bed with a pig then dances with an older woman while wearing a pig's mask, and then, in a grotesque scene, writes her dissertation about "Woman as Pig." In between, the woman rids herself of her bandages by wrapping a doll like a mummy.

Bandages as a symbol of women's mutilation that is being passed on? Liberation? Shaking off shackles? The images were ambiguous, elusive signs

Scene from *The Fugue* by ANNA KONDA, directed by Heidi von Plato, Berlin, 1982. (Photo by Heidi von Plato.)

that could not be arrested in fixed meanings. In the dinner scene, the actors embodied various female stereotypes and tortured each other with their conventional patterns of behavior. Powerful women incessantly stuffed food down the throats of weaker ones, and one woman, who carried a nest with two birds on her head, unnerved everyone with her permanent, nonsensical admonitions: Stop whining with your feet, take the finger out of your head, keep your mouth together! A clown lugging brushes and brooms impersonated excessive cleanliness; a shell-woman called for collective memory but kept falling asleep. Finally, in a comic scene, the weak ones overcame their mighty opponents with pointed, wooden sticks. In a puppet scene, the women wrapped their own bandages around dolls, which they left behind in the leaves.

The men kept looking into the distance or speaking nonsensical military texts: "On hill #737, I spied two arithmetic errors, who were about to sneak off." In another scene, a man prohibited the women's laughter and dancing, but they were not intimidated by him. In the railway station scene, a fetishist father played with parts of a larger-than-life dummy, which he hid when his family entered the stage. The battle of the sexes took place in a boxing ring.

Word Murders

Our next project was *Word Murders,* a collage with texts by Unica Zürn. The play was organized around isolated fragments dealing with a woman's sadomasochistic fantasies. The action was performed in a large gallery space. It began in the dark with actresses whispering words from Unica Zürn's poems into the ears of audience members, while illuminating their mouths with flashlights: "word murders," "wound chamber," "heart eyes."

Unica Zürn, who killed herself in 1970, wrote anagrams, poems that are put together from the letters of a pregiven sentence. She wrote these anagrams obsessively in order to free herself from her severe depressions.

The stage space was marked by different objects, which became part of the action. Bloody beef hearts wrapped in transparent paper were hanging from meat hooks; two actresses cut them to pieces and ate them. In another scene, a woman was tied to black chairs, which she dragged after her. Women wrote an anagram onto a transparent foil: the art to play with words in a pregiven frame. Thus, the set replicated the action.

Through the reflection of light, another frame appeared, projected onto the back wall. The theme of imprisonment, which plays an important role in the texts of Unica Zürn, took up the bandage motif in *Fugue*. Wrapped into paper like a large parcel, one actress broke through the constrictive skin, first with one hand, then with her feet, finally with her entire body. Unica Zürn described writing as a magic act. The glass chimes, with which the performers played, produced musical sounds reminiscent of Zürn's melodic anagrams. She wrote about the prohibition of experiences, which produces and is produced by immobility and passivity: "One must not go into all rooms. Either they are too beautiful, and, upon leaving them, one has to long for them until the end of one's life, or they are too horrible, and their memory clings to a person like filth." We performed this text by fettering a woman with sticky tape, from which she continuously and in vain tried to disengage herself. The distant, inaccessible man who appears in Zürn's texts was played as a character devoid of all sensuality; he was driving a wheelchair.

The Game of Pool

The plays *The Fugue* and *Word Murders* were open enough to accommodate the performers' dreams and experiences and to allow their creative use during rehearsals. The following section discusses only a few aspects of the rehearsal process.

Inspired and "kicked" by the images' suggestive power, the performers rediscovered forgotten childhood memories, as in a game of pool. The "pig images" in *Fugue* activated memories of forbidden desires and fantasies, of playing doctor, and of pleasurable physical experiences. Again and again, the rehearsal process facilitated the mise-en-scène of the women's subjectivity by allowing them to slip into repressed roles. Each of them had a story to tell about dialogues with their stuffed animals, of mysterious metamorphoses and role switching. These childhood experiences served as foil and projection screen for the rehearsal process.

In *Word Murders*, the work with the women's imagination and with the objects took up much space. All women were to build a father dummy or man dummy in a wheelchair from various materials. In response to this assignment, one performer refused to collaborate and left the group to seek therapeutic help. The others stayed. The work with the anagrams led to fantastic word plays and a new feeling for language. ANNA KONDA designed and chose its own costumes—very imaginative affairs. Hats were used in a surreal manner, particularly in the dinner scene in *Fugue*. The shell-woman carried a large mussel shell on her head, the bird's-nest-woman wore a bird's nest, and the fat woman had a shrimp hat.

In the puppet scene in *Fugue*, the performers were largely responsible for developing imagery and choreography. All women had their own way of wrapping the bandages around the puppets, which they left in the leaves, each had her own mimic and gestural vocabulary. One kissed and slapped her doll in quick alternation; another held the doll at a distance from her own body; one pressed the doll so close as if to suffocate her; another seemed indifferent in her relation to the doll. Each woman developed her own choreography of leave-taking from her puppet.

We worked intensely on this scene and its psychodramatic content in order to stylize the women's actions, which carried a high emotional charge. Occasionally, the work process was blocked by our desire for therapeutic theater, by our wish to display ourselves within the group and turn our own problems into the center of attention. Since we were free from institutional constraints, we repeatedly had to define and redefine a common goal for our project. Once in a while, we would succeed in integrating personal problems into the theater work and make them fruitful for the production; sometimes private matters had to stay outside.

Group dynamic processes as they occur in any group—such as envy, hate, rivalry—but also strong positive feelings found an outlet in the staging of female subjectivity in both productions. The search for performance sites and the challenge this posed proved valuable for the collaborative work in this group.

Ursula Ahrens

FiT (Frauen im Theater): Women in Theater

Translated by Katrin Sieg

Actresses and female prompters are a matter of course in the theater, but what is the proportion of women in other positions in the hierarchically structured state and city theaters dominating the German theater scene? How many women occupy leadership positions; can women exert influence, even power, and develop their creativity? Why are there so few plays by women authors, and why are there so few women directors?

These were questions that women theater theorists and dramaturges began to pose in the early 1980s. While theater scholarship has been dominated by male scholars at the three universities offering degrees in theater theory and criticism, dramaturges traditionally have been subordinated to male directors. Following the lead of those women's organizations approaching film, the media, literature, and the fine arts from a feminist perspective, theater women perceived the need to examine history and the conditions and possibilities of feminist stage practices and to render women's issues visible in public discourse. In 1983 they founded the initiative "Women in Theater" (FiT), which since 1984 has constituted a forum within the Dramaturgische Gesellschaft [association of dramaturges], a non–trade union association of theater professionals.

The new women's movement in the Federal Republic had emerged about twelve years before, and since the late 1970s some theaters had worked on "women's productions." Actresses had left the institutional theater in order to explore women's concerns and performance strategies in one-woman shows. Still, the attempt to organize and to investigate feminist problematics, such as the issue of a "female aesthetic," were regarded as novel and exciting in the theater. Therefore, several public events sponsored by FiT met with considerable interest.

On one such occasion, Gerlind Reinshagen and Friederike Roth, two playwrights, met for the first time and were later joined by Andrea Breth and other directors. They discussed possibilities of approaching classical plays (a male domain!) and the images and roles of women they presented. Thus, one of FiT's initial goals was to counteract the isolation of women within the theatrical apparatus produced by the general competitiveness in this field and to articulate shared problems and interests.

We discovered that women generally have to work harder than men in order to be accepted and that women have to constantly struggle with and against male-defined criteria of professionalism and quality. Their failures are judged much more critically and harshly. The "other," female, point of view regarding characters and situations, a view unburdened by traditional perspectives, affords the opportunity to put women's predisposition for intense listening to a creative use and to empower them as directors, if directing is understood as the art of empathizing. But, in practice, women are confronted with the need to endure cynicism, develop and exercise authority, assert leadership, and openly deal with role conflicts instead of withdrawing out of a lack of confidence. We hold that these problems cannot be solved in women's groups alone and reject an uncritical assumption of women's solidarity.

Working with and analyzing texts written by women playwrights constitutes another area of activity. FiT sponsored staged readings and, if financially possible, productions of contemporary and "forgotten" women playwrights. Traditional theatrical praxis, as yet dominated by men, is often at a loss when it comes to women's drama. Those highly individual pieces have had few, and often unsuccessful, productions. (Reinshagen's *Clownin*, for instance, has been produced only once.) The theater should respond to reality and address social structures and relations. Women experience and reflect differently than men. Women playwrights account for this in many different ways, not only in the content of their text but also in a different dramatic form and language. "At present it is a fact that, if women's plays do not fit the canon, they are rejected as insufficient; they fall through the critical matrix," said Friederike Roth in 1986. Frequently the plays do not follow conventional dramaturgical rules; they appear unwieldy and strange and are often judged to be unfit for the stage. They demand imagination, curiosity, and the rethinking of critical categories in order to reveal their innovative potentials.

By now a number of very vocal younger authors and directors have entered the theatrical scene. A conspicuous number of women hold leading positions in private theaters, off-theaters, and in theater publishing. In contrast to that, nothing much has changed in the city and state theaters, whose budgets and personnel politics are run and approved by predominantly male politicians. Of two hundred of these theaters, only two employ a female producer [*Intendantin*]. The number of permanently employed female directors (a position guaranteeing economic security and continuous creative work) has increased over the last years, but its proportion relative to permanently employed male directors has remained the same number (at 15 percent). Moreover, they are not all committed to feminist politics.

FiT has been publishing the findings of its research in the form of papers and bibliographies. Its annual pamphlets also provide transcripts of discussions and interviews. These booklets document the growth, direction, and changing self-definition of the organization as well as record shifts within the profession and of women's position in it.

During recent years, sister organizations of FiT have sprung up in Switzerland and Austria. In the former German Democratic Republic (GDR), however, feminism and women's liberation are taboo terms, in spite—or because—of the decreed and formally practiced equality of the sexes. We know little about the concrete work of theater women there. Certainly, the reunification of the two German states will drastically aggravate the social position of women in the former GDR as well as the subsidization of all cultural institutions. Probably the number of theaters will decrease. FiT is now making an effort to establish a dialogue with these women artists, dramaturges, and critics (there are hardly any playwrights), to find out about their experiences and perspectives and provide women-specific impulses for their future work.

In 1991 we are sponsoring an international symposium in Berlin. That event, entitled "Women and the Languages of the Stage," will, we hope, reduce the gap between theater theory and practice which still exists in this country and set accents in gender politics and theatrical praxis.

1990

Translators

Wendy Arons received her Master of Fine Arts degree in dramaturgy from the University of California at San Diego in 1990. She is currently working as a freelance dramaturg and is completing her book *Castrating Bitches: Representations of Powerful Women in Contemporary Theater.* She performs under the name of Kitty Cannibal.

Beate Hein Bennett is the literary manager at the Third Step Theater in New York. She has also worked as a dramaturg, a professor of Comparative Literature, and a translator.

Angelika Czekay completed her master's studies at the Free University in Berlin and is presently a doctoral student in the Theater Department at the University of Wisconsin at Madison.

Jamie Owen Daniel is completing her dissertation in modern studies at the University of Wisconsin at Milwaukee. She has published translations of Peter Sloterdijk, Gertrud Koch, Ulrike Ottinger, Heidi Schlüpmann, and Oskar Negt.

Gitta Honegger is resident dramaturg at Yale Repertory Theater and associate professor at Yale School of Drama. She has published translations of the plays of Thomas Bernhard and Elias Canetti. Her translation of Kroetz's *Help Wanted* was produced by Mabou Mines and the Los Angeles Theatre Center, and her translation into German of *'Night, Mother* has been produced in Vienna, Dusseldorf, and Frankfurt.

Katrin Sieg recently completed her dissertation in the area of contemporary German women playwrights in the School of Drama at the University of Washington. She was the assistant to the editor for this book.

Arlene A. Teraoka is associate professor in the German department at the University of Minnesota. Her book is *The Silence of Entropy or Universal Discourse: The Postmodernist Poetics of Heiner Müller.* She has a forthcoming book on the Third World in postwar German Literature. She has published numerous articles on drama and minority literature in Germany in *New German Critique, The German Quarterly,* and *Cultural Critique.*

GUNTRAM H. WEBER is a professional translator living in Berlin. His many published translations include such authors as Heiner Müller, Robert Wilson, and Sylvère Lotringer. He has translated the subtitles for the films of Helga Reidemeister.

ANDRA WEDDINGTON is associate professor of theater and director of the acting program at Eckerd College in Florida. She has directed over sixty productions during her career and holds degrees in both theater and German.